T0083593

A Bibliography of Welsh Literature in English Translation

A Bibliography of Welsh Literature
in English Translation

edited by

S. Rhian Reynolds

UNIVERSITY OF WALES PRESS
CARDIFF
2005

British Library Cataloguing-in-Publication Data
A catalogue record for this book is available from the British Library.

ISBN 0-7083-1882-7

The publishers wish to acknowledge the financial support of the Higher Education Funding Council for Wales in the publication of this book.

Printed in Great Britain by Cambridge Printing, Cambridge

CONTENTS

ACKNOWLEDGEMENTS

BWLET began as a one-year AHRB-funded project with the ambitious aim of researching and creating a bibliography that could be accessed via an online database and launched at an international conference of translation studies, with a published print version to seal the project. The first two objectives were achieved within the projected timescale. The book has taken rather longer but develops greatly on the initial bibliography that can be found at *www.bwlet.net* and for this reason extensive revisions are planned for this site. The first phase of the project would not have been possible without the help of many individuals, too numerous to name here: our warmest thanks go to them all. As for those who primarily contributed to the project, Gethin Nichols and Mari Arthur are to be thanked for being so generous with their time and assistance in connection with the technical and creative elements of the initial phase. The set-up period was guided by a steering committee that included Dr Rhidian Griffiths, Mr Gwilym Huws and Dr Ian Glen and their support and advice was invaluable at this crucial stage. Ms Marleen Seegers gave us four months of her time to trawl nineteenth-century journals and her contribution is gratefully acknowledged. Professor Joseph Clancy, Tony Conran, Professor Sioned Davies, Dr Marged Haycock, Dr Wyn James, Professor Dafydd Johnston, Professor Meic Stephens and Professor Hywel Teifi Edwards were among those who shared their specialist knowledge with us and gave generously of their own expertise. Dr Claire Powell and Ms Alyce von Rothkirch provided us with support and practical help with the project. We should also like to thank the team at the University of Wales Press for their helpfulness and support: Duncan Campbell and Ceinwen Jones in the early stages and Nia Peris for our final leg.

Diolch i Gethin, Mari, Eurwen, Arwyn ac ambell i gyflogwr amyneddgar.

INTRODUCTION

A Bibliography of Welsh Literature in English Translation (BWLET) is intended to provide a map, for the first time, of materials that offer an insight into a national literature, ancient and rich, but inaccessible to many in its original language. Self-sufficient for cultural, political and economic reasons, Welsh-language literature has not traditionally courted an audience outside Wales and therefore remains relatively unexplored by international standards. One of the objectives of BWLET is to present this important part of the literary heritage of Wales both to a global scholarly community and to an anglophone reading culture worldwide.

The Welsh language belongs to the Brythonic branch of the Celtic family of languages (Goidelic – which gave rise to modern Irish – is another branch). Welsh established itself from the sixth to the late eighth century CE and was in part the product of a fusion of the original Brythonic with the Latinate culture that was the legacy of the collapse in Britain of the Roman Empire. The emergence of Early Welsh was more or less coterminous with the making of a new people in the west of Britain – the Welsh (*Cymry*), roughly translated as 'comrades'; tribes of aboriginal peoples bonded together in resistance to the 'foreign' threat from Saxon and Viking, who in turn regarded these native inhabitants as foreigners and styled them so, using a word (*wealas*) that was eventually to provide the root of the word 'Welsh'. The earliest Welsh-language literature (*c.* 600 CE) therefore bears some of the marks of a heroic 'nation building' literature (to use a modern anachronism), and it already evinces signs of that unique patterning of sounds that would eventually consolidate into the regulatory system known as *cynghanedd*. This in turn generated and governed the great, and still developing, tradition of strict-metre poetry that goes under the name of *barddas*, the chief glory of which remains the rich body of work produced during the later Middle Ages. The form is particularly untranslatable, not least because it is dependent on the mutation of initial consonants, a feature integral to the Welsh language.

Some of those sceptical of Welsh–English literary translation, usually motivated by the wish to preserve the integrity of the language, have used the difficulty of translating *barddas* – since

English lacks the means of reproducing its polyphonic effects – as a basis for argument against Welsh–English translation *per se*. They realize that a failure to address *barddas* involves not only a failure to convey the greatness of the Welsh literary tradition but also a failure to engage with the politics of cultural resistance inscribed in that tradition even at the level of form. Dominance of the *barddas* tradition means that in Welsh literature all other genres have existed in tension with it, and have had to resist marginalization by it. A strong body of metric verse, for instance, appeared in Welsh only in the nineteenth century; the sonnet was a twentieth-century innovation; free verse was very much an uneasy Johnny-come-lately that appeared at the beginning of the twentieth century; the novel, its appearance in Wales effectively delayed until the second half of the nineteenth century, had a hard time getting established (encountering strong religious as well as cultural resistance in the process). This leaves translators of twentieth-century Welsh literature facing the prospect that, re-situated in the foreign context of anglophone culture, much of the literature (though radical and liberating in its own context) can seem rather old-fashioned, suggestive of arrested literary development and a retarded culture. And yet, in context, this modern literature – ranging across every literary genre and encompassing a broad range of personal, social, religious and political experience – is an achievement every bit as resourcefully innovative as that of the poets of the Middle Ages whose remarkable corpus continues to be one of Europe's greatest (if least known) literary treasures. As for the centuries between the sixteenth and the nineteenth, they would seem primarily notable for the production of a wealth of devotional texts, few of which (with the exception of the prose classics of Morgan Llwyd and Ellis Wynne, the magisterially classical poetry of Goronwy Owen, and the explosively emotional hymns of William Williams Pantycelyn and Ann Griffiths) are likely to appeal to modern translators.

Welsh literature therefore spans some 1,500 years of Welsh cultural history, and BWLET aims to offer a valuable practical tool for locating specific translations of specific items from this body of work according to the categories of author/text/genre and literary movement. It thereby makes possible for the first time a comprehensive historical study of translation in a Welsh context, bringing Wales, albeit very belatedly, within the purview of modern Translation Studies. The translations recorded in this volume encompass virtually the whole of Welsh-language literature from the late sixth century to the present day, with the earliest recorded translations dating from the early 1700s. This bibliography has the potential to facilitate the tracking, down through the centuries, of some of the major trends in Welsh–English translation, and it throws light on subjects such as the choice of texts for translation and publication, as motivated by historical, cultural, religious and political factors; the question of who translated, commissioned and published which texts, and where translation activity took place; the influence of translation on the source and target cultures; the changing role of the translator; the influence of gender, race, sexuality and other factors on choice of text and translation practice; the critical reception of translations in both source and target cultures; the material conditions affecting textual production; and the style of presentation of translations; and the theory and practice of translation, including the problem of whether, and if so how, to translate material commonly regarded as 'untranslatable' (Welsh *barddas/* strict-metre poetry, for example). BWLET can facilitate scholarly study of such subjects, as well as alerting scholars to many other lines of research that might profitably be pursued in the context of Welsh–English literary translation.

There are extensive socio-political and cultural implications to any study of Welsh–English translation, but while the problematic aspects of the practice within a Welsh context will be discussed in greater detail below, there are several important reasons why the objectives of the BWLET project are very much in keeping with recent developments:

1. The creation of a National Assembly for Wales has made biculturalism a subject of urgent practical concern, as well as ideological interest. Textual acts of mediation between language communities are therefore recognized as contributing to the development of a bicultural Wales;
2. The continuing settlement in Wales, in very substantial numbers, of non-Welsh-speaking newcomers has again highlighted the urgent need for a wider variety of cross-cultural initiatives;
3. Several leading Welsh-language writers have come to acknowledge the ways in which translation of their work into English may be of service not only to them as creative artists but to the Welsh-language culture to which they remain committed;

4. There is a very active concern throughout the United Kingdom to recognize a new, multicultural society that celebrates and promotes cultural difference;

5. Anglophone culture worldwide has begun to show an interest in Welsh-language literature – witness the inclusion of materials in important recent anthologies edited by Seamus Heaney and Ted Hughes, and by Robert Crawford;

6. The interdisciplinary field of Translation Studies has gained enormous momentum in the last decades, and yet the absence of a 'map' of Welsh–English translation means that this, one of the richest fields in a British context, is never examined.

Welsh–English Literary Translation: Historical Background

The history of translation in Wales begins around the thirteenth century with the translation, mainly from the Latin (along with some French and English materials), of a variety of religious and secular texts. Scholars have even suggested that there may have been schools of translators active in Wales during the Middle Ages so that by the first Act of Union with England in 1536 the practice had reached a notable level of sophistication and had made a significant contribution to the native culture. Arguably, the most important work came in the wake of the intensification of English centralist rule when, motivated by the desire to consolidate the new Anglican dispensation, parliament was persuaded that the Bible and the Book of Common Prayer should be translated into Welsh. The complete version of the Bible, translated by Bishop William Morgan, was issued in 1588, and its rich idiomatic and literary Welsh was to be of inestimable value as a means of safeguarding literary and linguistic standards in a country without a government, a capital or institutions of its own. Imbued as it was with Morgan's knowledge of classical Welsh poetry and majestically evidencing his genius for language, this remarkable work (building as it did on the pioneering work of William Salesbury and Bishop Richard Davies) helped fashion Welsh literary output for centuries to come.

The humanist impulse driving the scriptural translation activity of great Tudor figures such as Morgan and Salesbury was to inspire later generations of Welsh scholars and intellectuals to similarly

Herculean achievements in the field of secular scholarship. Dr John Davies of Mallwyd (1567–1644) and Gruffydd Robert of Milan (pre-1532–post-1598) were the two outstanding figures of early studies in the Welsh language, and their work provided the beginnings of grammatical and lexicographic research. The period from the late sixteenth through to the late eighteenth century was one that uncovered, and recovered, the great literary wealth of Wales's ancient language and culture. Manuscripts were being copied and circulated all over the country, and Edward Lhuyd (1660?–1709) single-handedly exceeded the private endeavours of a handful of industrious men when in 1707 he took advantage of the available printing technology, as many had failed to do, to publish his pioneering study of the Celtic languages, *Archaeologia Britannica*. The work of this Oxford educated philologist inspired a new era of scholarship, which prepared the ground for the eventual appearance of Welsh–English literary translation.

Early Welsh–English translation owes a great debt to one family in particular; the Morris family of Anglesey, and specifically the three brothers Lewis, Richard and William. Their knowledge of Wales, its language and literature, was exceptional for their eighteenth-century period. They were highly literate, confidently bilingual and possessed a pragmatism which made them instrumental in several key cultural and scholarly developments of the time. Richard Morris used his position as an eminent London Welshman to found the Honourable Society of Cymmrodorion in 1751, an august society of the metropolitan centre that, in its several subsequent incarnations, was to play a significant role in the cultural life of the old country. However, it is Lewis Morris who warrants the closest attention in the present context. He shared with Edward Lhuyd both a scientific bent and an appreciation of the potential of print. Morris and his generation were growing increasingly aware of English influences on Welsh culture. There was no Welsh university, the bardic order had long since collapsed, and though Wales sustained a vibrant folk culture, the educated, and Anglicized, elite looked to England for instruction in all matters. Taking their lead, therefore, from contemporary English thinkers, the Welsh cognoscenti participated in what was a Europe-wide phenomenon – that 'search for origins' which became a key aspect of the modern process of nation building and which involved the attempt to define a nation as an ancient, established, historically rooted 'fact'. The ever closer relationship of Wales to England paradoxically resulted in a new consciousness of Wales's distinct identity at this time, fuelled by an increasing awareness amongst some individuals of the growing deracination of some sectors of Welsh society which were losing touch with the language and its associated culture.

Lewis Morris's most important protégé was the poet and antiquarian Evan Evans (Ieuan Fardd, Ieuan Brydydd Hir), whose *Some Specimens of the Poetry of the Ancient Welsh Bards* (1764) included the largest selection of early Welsh literature ever to be published, along with the most extensive early examples of Welsh–English literary translation. This volume was a seminal publication in that it attempted to define Wales as an ancient nation and the work of Evans (and others) in uncovering authentic, and authentically old, poetic manuscripts provided a culturally subordinated people with historical evidence of the genuine antiquity of their 'subaltern' culture. The dominant motive of Evans, and of most of the others active in Welsh–English translation during the eighteenth and nineteenth centuries, was to prove to even the most sceptical of the powerful English that Wales had a literary heritage and culture of great wealth and antiquity. They sought the approbation of the colonizer in an attempt to restore national self-respect and to assert an element of autonomy.[1]

Early translators like Evans understood the means by which translation could validate national identity. But Welsh–English translation was also fuelled, and marked, by an element of 'cultural cringe.' Eager translator-apologists, conditioned by the native inferiority complex, were painfully aware of the superiority assumed by the metropolitan and ethnocentric recipient culture, but lacked the intellectual tools to challenge it. This often led them, down to the end of the nineteenth century, to underline the distinction between

---

[1] Preface to 'De Bardis Dissertation': 'Certainly I would not be taking this task upon me, except for the tauntings of the English, that we have no poetry that it pays to show the world'; tr. Ffion Llywelyn Jenkins, 'Celticism and Pre-Romanticism: Evan Evans', in *A Guide to Welsh Literature c. 1700–1800*, ed. Branwen Jarvis (Cardiff: University of Wales Press, 2000), p. 120. See also Thomas Stephens's preface to *The Literature of the Kymry* and into the early twentieth century, H. Idris Bell, 'The Development of Welsh Poetry', in *Welsh Poems of the Twentieth Century in English Verse* (Wrexham: Hughes & Son, 1925), p. 83.

their own cultural nationalism and a political nationalism that would seem to threaten the integrity of the 'British' state. There was also – as prefaces from the period testify – an anxiety to represent translations as tributary offerings; that is, as evidence of the (laudable, but previously invisible) contribution Wales had made to what had become a gloriously world-dominating British culture.

This 'contributionist' attitude helped Welsh–English translation to play a pivotal role in the development of the eighteenth-century Celtic movement that became, to adopt a phrase later used by Lady Charlotte Guest, the cradle of English Romanticism. Despite expressing disdain for English ignorance of Welsh culture, Evan Evans was to benefit from the interest of several of his English contemporaries. For instance, Thomas Gray sought in the newly discovered (or accessible) Celtic literature qualities lacking in English poetry of the time. It was Gray who asked his friend Daines Barrington (then a judge in Wales) to commission, and ultimately to finance, Evans's *Specimens*. William Owen Pughe (1759–1835), scholar and suspect orthographer, was another (eccentric) Welshman who took advantage of contemporary English interest in all things Celtic when he published his translations from the saga cycles, Canu Llywarch Hen and Canu Heledd. Owen Pughe's *Heroic Elegies* (1792) enjoys the honour of being the first stand-alone collection of Welsh–English translations. But it is a dubious honour because, in the absence of the knowledge that only later scholarship was able to supply, Pughe was often left unable to grasp the meaning of the original texts. He was neither the first nor the last, however, to grossly embellish early Welsh poetry. This was perhaps most spectacularly accomplished by his friend and collaborator Edward Williams (better known today by his bardic name of Iolo Morganwg), who was one of the most erudite and fascinating of all the great exhibitors (and exhibitionists) of Welsh literary culture. More knowledgeable about the content of old Welsh manuscripts than anyone of the time, Iolo (1747–1826) became the first great creative 'translator' of Welsh literature, undertaking one of the most audacious, prolific and 'creative' acts of literary forgery in literary history; in the process he successfully fabricated a cultural tradition which, paradoxically, granted the Welsh access to their authentic, but occluded, cultural past. The beauty and paradoxical originality of some of his 'fraudulent' Welsh compositions is quite astounding, and these were later innocently represented, through the translations of his son Taliesin ab Iolo, as the genuine work of medieval bards. Such was the virtuosity of Iolo's inspired performance.

It was the nineteenth century, however, which saw the first sustained period of Welsh–English literary translation, so that Matthew Arnold was able to base all conjectures in his historic 'Lectures on Celtic Literature' (delivered in 1865; book form, 1867) on his reading of works in translation. William Barnes, the Dorset poet and philologist, mastered Welsh well enough not only to publish several articles on Welsh literature in the English press but also to translate several Welsh poems. But perhaps the most celebrated English *Cymrophile* of the day was George Borrow, whose literal and metaphorical journeys into Wales are recounted in his travelogue *Wild Wales* (1862). An enthusiastic translator from Welsh literature, Borrow offers, in his travels, a useful analogy for the very act of translation, since the word 'translate' derives from the Latin 'transferre': to move from one place to another. And interestingly enough, several later translators also make the link with travel, as they were engaged in crossing borders and entering new territories. Thus the much-travelled Gwyn Williams (1904–90), one of the most enterprising, influential and prolific of twentieth-century translators of Welsh literature, refers to one of his anthologies of translations as a 'guide book' to a foreign literary landscape, the idea being that his audience will be inspired 'to go to the country described'.[2] Similarly Joseph P. Clancy, a New Yorker who became one of the giants of Welsh–English literary translation of the post-war period, imagines his readers as being 'non-Welsh literary tourists'. He thus equates the process of translation with the discovery of new literary destinations, a discovery which had, for him personally, exerted a shaping influence on his life.[3] In Borrow's case, though, it was more a matter of exploring literary passions and capitalizing on English appetites for the 'picturesque', something that will be touched upon in greater detail below. But while he was an important popularizer of Welsh culture, equally significant were the developments in specialist scholarly translation that occurred around the same time. It was a Scotsman, William Forbes Skene, lawyer and civil servant, whose avid scholarly interest in Scottish and Celtic antiquity led to the publication, in 1868, of the groundbreaking

[2] Introduction, *To Look for a Word*, n.p.
[3] Introduction, *Twentieth Century Welsh Poems*, p. xiv.

The Four Ancient Books of Wales. Since they included both the original text and extensive translations by the Revd D. Silvan Evans and Revd Robert Williams, these two volumes represented the most complete and authoritative publication of the content of ancient manuscripts to date.

However, the most notable act of Welsh–English translation in the Victorian era was the translation of the medieval prose tales the *Mabinogi* by Lady Charlotte Guest. So influential was her English version that readers worldwide continue to know the tales by the (incorrect) title that she, following in the footsteps of William Owen Pughe, provided; *The Mabinogion* (3 vols, 1838–49). In producing one of the great, and enduring, achievements of Welsh–English literary translation, she may have had the assistance of Welsh poets like Tegid and Carnhuanawc; but whereas they could have supplied a helpful gloss or two it was she herself who concocted, in the heady spirit of Victorian medievalism, the captivatingly mannered and 'antique' prose style. One of the earliest of Welsh literature's female translators, Guest remains one of the most important. Felicia Hemans (1793–1835) and Elizabeth Sharp (followed by Grace Rhys) were other, less influential, translating voices of the period. Hemans produced some interesting readings of Welsh literature (though some might term them wild paraphrases) and, like many of her time, adopted archaisms and Romantic language as a deliberate strategy for replicating the antiquity and supposed mysticism of the original texts. Hemans, Elizabeth Sharp, and even Grace Rhys to a degree, can be accused of dehistoricizing and depoliticizing Welsh texts by representing them as primarily 'Celtic' (a highly problematic term), and only incidentally Welsh. There are many aspects to this practice, but it is obvious that in certain respects it can lead to the 'othering' of Welsh language culture along the same exoticizing lines as those identified by Edward Said in his famous discussion of Orientalism. *Lyra Celtica* (1896), edited by Elizabeth Sharp (wife of William Sharp ['Fiona Macleod']), limits 'Cymric' literature to texts from early and medieval poetry, while the editorial regrets that modern Wales has yet to produce 'contemporary' poetry in the English language. The implication is that works in Welsh belong to that 'vivid spell of the old Welsh bards' of the distant past and not to the modern imperial age.[4]

[4] Introduction, *Lyra Celtica: An Anthology of Representative Celtic Poetry*, ed. E. A. Sharp and J. Matthay (Edinburgh: John Grant, 1924), p. xxxvi.

The translations of J. Gwenogvryn Evans (1852–1930) at the close
of the nineteenth century were indicative of the advance of Celtic
studies, thanks in great part to the establishing of university depart-
ments, and the coming of age of a more specifically 'Welsh', and
impressively professional, scholarship. But as with the reductive
potential of anthologies of 'Celtic' literature, academic publications,
though valuable, were also in danger of appearing to mummify and
entomb the literature. Commenting on this trend, another important figure in Welsh–English translation history, Ernest Rhys
(1859–1946), decried the lack of engagement with Welsh poets
'solely for their own sake, for their literary qualities, their literary and
poetic and human interest'.[5] But the very end of the nineteenth
century and the beginning of the twentieth saw an attempt at exactly
such engagement, as A. P. Graves (1846–1931), Edmund O. Jones
(1858–1931), H. Idris Bell (1879–1967) and others began to translate
contemporary Welsh-language poetry. However, the new 'nativizing'
tendency common to some translators still frequently failed to ensure
that modern poets were presented on their own terms. Instead, such
leading figures as Islwyn and Ceiriog underwent a cultural as well as
linguistic translation, becoming known as 'the Welsh Wordsworth'
and the 'Welsh Burns' respectively as translators felt the need to
emphasize their worth in the kind of terms credible to an anglophone target culture otherwise disinclined to believe that a minor
culture could produce literary figures of any serious consequence.[6]
    Another new motive for Welsh–English translation had also
arisen at the end of the nineteenth century. The linguistic balance in
Wales was beginning to shift from the middle of the century, as the
influx of thousands of non-Welsh-speakers from all over the British
Isles and beyond into industrial south Wales turned the area into
one of the powerhouses of the British Empire. The 1847
Commissioners' *Report into the State of Education in Wales* (popu-
larly known as the *Blue Books*) documented the official English
government view of the Welsh language as the relic of a morally
backward, culturally inferior race – an attitude which helped
persuade generations of Welsh men and women to discard their

---

[5] Ernest Rhys, 'Welsh Bards and English Reviewers', *The Transactions of
the Honourable Society of Cymmrodorion* (1892–3), 29–45 [41].

[6] *A Celtic Psaltery* (1917), pp. 94–5. Dafydd ap Gwilym also succumbed to
such comparisons, being termed the 'Welsh Ovid' by one translator.

language and culture as objects of 'shame and guilt'.[7] O. M. Edwards (1858–1920) was among those whose national consciousness had been sharpened by the damning report of the Commission, and first as Oxford don and then as Chief Inspector of Schools in Wales he took it upon himself to do all that was necessary to rekindle in his compatriots (including recent immigrants and other monoglot English speakers) a love for the language and a respect for its culture. He made his intentions clear in the first editorial of *Wales* (1894–1917), the remarkable English-language periodical he founded to advance his cause:

> Another aim of *Wales* is to bring the influence of Welsh literature to act upon the thought of English Wales . . . My ambition is, before my working day is over, to give English Wales translations of the hundred best Welsh prose works . . .[8]

This kind of proselytizing rhetoric would become ever more important, as would the advocacy and practice of Welsh–English translation, in the coming years, since by 1900 only around half of the population were Welsh-speakers. English, of course, had a long history of use in Wales. No sooner had Middle English been developed in the thirteenth and fourteenth centuries out of a fusion of Old English (Anglo-Saxon), Old Norse and Norman French than it became the language first of the Anglo-Norman settlers and then of the Anglicized gentry and the professional and middle classes of Wales. But down to the mid-nineteenth-century, when the rate of Anglicization increased exponentially with the creation of the new cosmopolitan society of industrial south Wales, most of what was culturally distinctive about the country (from religion to literature), and much of what linked it to its past, had been preserved in and by the Welsh language.

But if the second half of the nineteenth century saw a dramatic change in this situation, it was the twentieth century, and specifically the period between the two World Wars, which saw the truly precipitous decline in the percentage of Welsh speakers that triggered a reactive politico-cultural nationalism symbolized by the uncompromising and brilliant figure of Saunders Lewis (1893–1985). With

---

[7] See Gwyneth Tyson Roberts, *The Language of the Blue Books: The Perfect Instrument of Empire* (Cardiff: University of Wales Press, 1998), p. 238.

[8] O. M. Edwards, *Wales*, 1 (1894), iv.

Tynged yr Iaith (The Fate of the Language), his lecture on the
hazardous future of Welsh which was broadcast in 1962, Lewis
galvanized a generation of young language activists into peaceful
protests which, for some, resulted in lawbreaking and imprisonment.
That, in the face of extinction, twentieth-century Welsh-language
culture nevertheless succeeded in producing a remarkable body of
literature unparalleled in quality and quantity since the 'golden age'
of late medieval culture is, perhaps, a paradox more apparent than
real. As historians have emphasized, the industrial revolution had
done at least as much to save as to destroy the Welsh language by
ensuring that the culture became thoroughly modern in its concerns
rather than merely the domain of a pre-industrial 'remnant'.
Moreover, a language, when intimately threatened, reactively takes
on a vividness and intensity of life upon which writers may capitalize.
What is certain is that twentieth-century Welsh-language literature,
in all its impressive variety, is the direct product of a language, and a
culture, in constant mortal peril – a language in very real and immi-
nent danger of being erased from history by English. It has been a
literature of brinkmanship. Nor is this situation merely an innocent
by-product of history; from the Acts of Union in the sixteenth
century no official legal recognition of the language's status in Wales
existed until the 1960s, when what had essentially been a colonial
policy was remedied. To realize this is to realize just how fraught, for
any contemporary Welsh-language speaker, must be the issue of
Welsh–English translation. Under these circumstances, translation
can sometimes seem suspiciously like trafficking – or even perhaps
sleeping – with the enemy.

But it can also be viewed, and treated, in diametrically opposite
terms; as an anti-colonial strategy, in the spirit of Saunders Lewis's
address, which assists in the creation of a cultural climate favourable
not only to the survival of Welsh but also to the creation of a nationalist consciousness. Thus, during the culturally and politically
turbulent 1960s, writers such as Harri Webb, instructed by the writings of post-colonial thinkers like Frantz Fanon, explicitly turned to
translation as a means of promoting an awareness in the English-
speaking population of the nationalist issues that had already been
addressed by many of the greatest of twentieth-century Welsh-language
writers. It is worth noting, at this point, that the two literatures
of Wales had been *politically* out of step for much of the twentieth
century, since some of the greatest Welsh-language literature was

written to a nationalist political agenda that was, at the time, anathema to anglophone Wales.[9] The 1960s saw a partial change in this politico-cultural alignment, as some anglophone writers worked to form a common front with Welsh-language writers. In 1967, only five years after Lewis's momentous lecture, the influential paper-back *The Penguin Book of Welsh Verse* was published, a volume that included an eclectic selection of translations from the earliest period to the present day, along with a superb introduction to the literature of Wales both ancient and modern. The translator, Tony Conran, had an explicitly ecumenical purpose, as he felt an 'urgent need to work for a united Wales'.[10] This was, perhaps, a less politicized and more conciliatory response to Lewis's warnings about the current state of affairs. For Conran and others, like the late R. Gerallt Jones (1934–99), translation could be used for cultural missionary work. English-speakers whose eyes had been opened by translation to the greatness of the indigenous Welsh-language literary tradition might thereby be made more sympathetic to the concept of a bilingual national culture.

Today, the whole process and practice of Welsh–English trans-lation continues to be a subject of tense controversy within a Welsh-language culture some members of which still tend to feel that an ability to speak Welsh is the *sine qua non* of Welsh national identity and that to practise, or condone, Welsh–English translation is im-plicitly to acknowledge that Welsh is replaceable by English. And, even when Welsh–English translation is countenanced other problems remain, such as whether only dual text editions should be permitted; and whether translation becomes acceptable only under certain conditions – is it culturally wise, for instance, to allow new Welsh-language works to be published from the outset with accompanying

---

[9] During the twentieth century several leading writers of what was then termed the Anglo-Welsh community became well-known translators of Welsh-language literature. One thinks of the excellent translation of the *Mabinogi* on which Gwyn Jones collaborated, or the groundbreaking translations of the *hen benillion* by Glyn Jones. Many other creative writers, including several of the most distinguished, have produced trans-lations which exist in a symbiotic relationship with their own original work (e.g. R. S. Thomas, Emyr Humphreys, Leslie Norris, John Ormond and Tony Conran).

[10] In Dafydd Johnston, 'An Interview with Tony Conran', *Modern Poetry in Translation*, 7 (1995), 184–97 [195].

translation? Arguments in favour of translation tend to range from the need to create a pluralist, multilingual Wales, to a pragmatic acceptance of Welsh–English translation because without such means of intercultural mediation the problems of contemporary Wales cannot hope to be addressed. There is also the recognition that, paradoxically, only by means of global English can Welsh-language culture reach out to non-anglophone cultures worldwide. During the last decades of the twentieth century, socio-political developments also seemed to many to have created a situation in which Welsh–English translation had become a culturally prudent necessity, as the Thatcher years saw a great influx into impoverished west Wales (then still a heartland of Welsh-language culture) of English speakers from the wealthier regions of England, as well as from anglophone south-east Wales. Faced with such a potentially overwhelming threat to their native culture, even writers such as the poet and language activist Menna Elfyn, who had originally been resistant to the translation of her work into English, eventually came to feel that translation might be an urgently necessary means of introducing newcomers to the indigenous culture and inducting them into it.

Welsh–English translation faces other challenges at the present time, such as those arising from the economics of production. It needs to be stressed that there is not, and has never been, a strong dependable market for Welsh–English translation. Therefore, very few initiatives have been market-led – and where they have been, that has usually been due to a market interest having briefly been created by *political* developments. So, for example, interest in Welsh Wales was stimulated during the 1960s by the political unrest in Wales at that time; and again, at the end of the twentieth century, devolution created a passing interest in things Welsh, as consequently did the brief popularity of a handful of Welsh pop bands and media personalities. Translation has therefore been either the result of personal initiative and commitment (hence unsystematic and not infrequently out of sync with publicly evident economic and political developments) or of cultural management (witness the role of educational institutions and the Arts Council of Wales in commissioning and fostering translation programmes).

Welsh–English Translation in Theory and Practice

Transplanting Welsh-language literature into 'English dress' (as early translators termed it) has, over the past few centuries, presented the would-be translator with a number of choices. The methods adopted have therefore varied almost as much as the original works selected for translation. As has been noted, translators have ranged from antiquarians, hobbyists, scholars, populists, cultural apologists and political activists to creative writers – some of whom have seen translation as a continuation of their original work by other means, while others have used it to signify solidarity with Wales's aboriginal culture. Each of these translators has had a particular objective in mind when approaching translation, with some translators, for instance, feeling compelled to modify source texts in order to make them more acceptable to the target audience. At the other extreme has been the frequently announced 'intention . . . above all . . . to keep as close as possible to the actual wording of the original'.[11] Questionable though the very concept of 'fidelity' to the 'original' may be when philosophically scrutinized (as has been repeatedly demonstrated in the context of Translation Studies), it may prove serviceable for some translation purposes, even though it is sure to prompt many to protest that the music of what matters has been entirely lost in the process. In general, styles of translation have been as diverse as the aims of translators and publishers and have thus been variously academic, literal, creative or loosely approximate. One example of the latter are the 'translations' of Dafydd ap Gwilym's work by the distinguished American poet Rolfe Humphries, which, whilst certainly not faithful line-by-line representations, are successful in capturing the energy and playfulness of the original poems. The Dafydd ap Gwilym corpus also supplies the most striking example of another feature of Welsh–English translation – the reluctance there has been, until very recently, to translate material regarded as to any degree risqué. Although the poems of Dafydd ap Gwilym were, naturally, among the very first to be translated into English, the poet's more ribald repertoire was to remain untranslated until the later twentieth century.

Some of the decisions with which translators are faced when translating may be illuminatingly explored by comparing the terms in which Joseph P. Clancy and Tony Conran, two of Welsh

[11] Kenneth Hurlstone Jackson, introduction to *A Celtic Miscellany* (1971), p. 16.

literature's greatest twentieth-century translators, have recorded
their experience of translating Waldo Williams's remarkable lyric
'Eirlysiau' (Snowdrops). Clancy has described how the poem seemed
beyond his capacity to translate, how it haunted him, and how,
returning to it time and again, he eventually felt compelled, as much
as emboldened, to venture a translation.[12] Conran is even more
deliberate in his reservations: 'It is probably the hardest to put into
English verse of any poem I've ever done – it's taken me thirty years,
off and on, even to get as far as I have.' To understand why both
translators found the poem so difficult to translate is, first, to realize
anew that every language is a unique, self-enclosed, self-referential
and self-sufficient phonic system. It is also to appreciate that a poem
by Waldo Williams emanates from his personal symbolic universe,
suspended, as it is, in an intertextual web extending through a range
of religious and literary associations specific to Wales as a whole
and to Waldo's beloved Preseli in particular. Two such sensitive,
experienced and culturally knowledgeable writers as Clancy and
Conran cannot fail to be aware of this problem, to a degree that
threatens to disempower them as much as to empower their translations. The poet's 'intricate verse pattern' (Clancy) and 'verbal music'
(Conran) make it virtually impossible fully to 'realize' it in a
different language, to capture 'the chief qualities in thought, feeling
and style of the original'.[13]

Since a comparative approach, where the processes and strategies
of individual translators are analysed and contrasted, can offer valuable insight into the intellectual and creative choices facing the
translator, it is worth examining brief examples of the English translations of 'Eirlysiau' produced by Clancy and Conran respectively.
This is how they choose to render the notoriously difficult final
stanza:

> Chaste, chaste,
> With the first whiteness their song is graced.
> When the spectrum separates
> The land will blaze, its hues unfurled.
> But pureness, pureness blossoms now
> From the mouth of the Bard who forms the world.
>   (Clancy, *Twentieth Century Welsh Poems*)

[12] Joseph P. Clancy, *Other Words*, pp. 6–9.
[13] Joseph P. Clancy, introduction, *Twentieth Century Welsh Poems*, p. xlii.

Pure, pure
In their song, the primal white.
When the shards of it scatter
Like a myriad fires they'll colour the fields.
But here it is purity, purity springs
From the Poet's lips who fashions the world.

(Conran, *Peacemakers*)

In roughly capturing the recurrent end and internal rhymes of the original, Clancy may be said to have managed to delineate not only the form but the visionary armature of the original poem, since Waldo, Quaker mystic that he was, is intent on hymning the creation through a ritual incantation that constitutes a kind of *Gloria*. It could fairly be said that repetition, in various forms and at various discursive levels, is of the very essence of the spiritual vision of his poem. But Clancy has to pay a price for this success, in the form of a rather stilted, poeticized vocabulary, a world removed from the simple swift directness of Waldo's otherwise complex utterance. In this respect, Conran's verbally unadorned version is closer to the original – and truer to the sophisticated 'primitivism' of Waldo's Quaker faith. But then Conran fails to convey the ritualistic aspect of the discourse, and is also unable to reproduce the haunting recurrent rhythms of the Welsh text, revolving as it does, by means of the 'returns' in its verbal and syntactical structure, around the mystery of the many in one and the one in the many.

Conclusion

Spanning the best part of three centuries, Welsh–English translation has grown to encompass virtually the whole of Welsh literature, from the earliest poetry (sixth century), through the literature of the classical period (*Cynfeirdd, Gogynfeirdd, Beirdd yr Uchelwyr*), on to the rich religious and pietistic literature of the eighteenth century (with its culturally transformative Methodist Revival), and down, through the popular poetry and pioneering fiction of the nineteenth century, to the great Welsh literary renaissance of the twentieth century of which present-day writers (well represented in translation) are heirs. Among the works translated have been acknowledged classics of European culture – the *Mabinogi*, the work of Dafydd ap Gwilym, the hymns of William Williams,

Pantycelyn and Ann Griffiths, the short stories of Kate Roberts and the plays, poetry, fiction and political writings of Saunders Lewis. And ever since it was first instigated in the eighteenth century, Welsh–English literary translation has provided an invaluable interface between Wales and the wider world. The adoption of English as a *lingua franca* has, paradoxically, enabled Welsh-language culture to use translation as a way of connecting worldwide with other cultures which are struggling against the hegemonic power of anglophone culture. Additionally, Welsh–English translation has assisted Welsh literature to reconnect with the European culture of which it considers itself a part. But translation has also played a significant role in fostering links between Wales and the other countries of the British Isles; and, most importantly of all, perhaps, it has contributed to the dialogue between the two cultures of Wales itself. In all these connections, Welsh-language culture has operated from a basis both of strength and of weakness – weakness, in that it continues to be a culture surviving under conditions of threat; but strength, in that it continues to form a major component of Welsh national identity and is fortunate enough to benefit from a critical mass of population sufficient to sustain not only every form of literary and scholarly production but also a flourishing media culture, including a modest 'film industry'.[14] Thus, Welsh is simultaneously 'ancient' and modern, 'worn new' (as Edward Thomas, a poet of Welsh descent put it) by the abrasive processes of recent historical changes, those very processes which also threaten to erode it. Under these conditions, cultural anxiety inevitably finds expression in an ambivalent response to the translation of Welsh-language materials into the powerful, and potentially overwhelming, rival language of English. Welsh–English translation thus offers a particularly fraught example of the inherently ambiguous character of all literary translation when regarded as a significant form of intercultural transaction. Its potential for both negative and positive results, its capacity to act either as cultural broker or cultural breaker, may most conveniently be highlighted through the juxtaposition of three contrasting comments, made in the context of what has come to be known as Translation Studies:

---

[14] Which in recent years has produced such internationally acclaimed films as *Hedd Wyn, Solomon and Gaenor* and *Eldra*.

There is in every act of translation – especially where it succeeds – a touch of treason. Hoarded dreams, patterns of life, are being taken across the frontier.

(George Steiner)

At the heart of every imperial fiction (the heart of darkness) there is a fiction of translation. The colonial Other is translated into terms of the imperial self, with the end result of alienation for the colonized and a fiction of understanding for the colonizer.

(Eric Cheyfitz)

Co-existence implies translating the cultural, political, religious, emotional language of the other into a language and culture that is strengthened by the presence of the other. The alternative to translation is the muteness of fear.

(Michael Cronin)

BWLET has been constructed in the full recognition of such ambivalences and is in no way intended to undermine the original, irreplaceable, Welsh-language literature or to shift attention away from it. Rather, it is intended, in part, to encourage the kind of sophisticated and complex reflection on the cultures of Wales at the heart of which must be the 'matter' of the country's two dominant languages – an issue that matters in a much wider context, as languages worldwide struggle to establish a *modus vivendi* with globalized English. It is therefore hoped that BWLET will encourage the asking, and facilitate the answering, of questions such as why, where, and when translation has been employed in a Welsh–English context, and will thus help throw light on the complex intercultural negotiations that are conducted by transposing literary texts from one language to another.

No claims are made for the completeness, comprehensiveness or definitiveness of this bibliography, as these are standards beyond the reach of what was planned as a one-year funded project but has actually taken three years to 'complete'. It can be no more than an interim report – a 'bwletin' on work in progress – as there is undoubtedly a wealth of further material that awaits discovery; but it is hoped that this indicative resource will lead to more sophisticated understanding in a Welsh context of the socio-cultural aspects of translation and will thus promote new insights into the very infrastructure of Welsh culture. In compiling BWLET, there has been no attempt to make value judgements about the translators or translations themselves and nothing has been knowingly included or excluded on these terms. To have done so would have been contrary to the modern approach to translation as an exchange which is of scholarly interest because it signifies the cultural and linguistic negotiations that are involved in the act of translating texts. Terms such as 'version' and 'adaptation' have also been avoided in this bibliography for the same reasons. Individual scholars, students and readers are left to make up their own minds as to the success or significance of the translated texts that are here recorded.

Rhian Reynolds and M. Wynn Thomas
CREW (Centre for Research into the English Literature and Language of Wales)
University of Wales Swansea

EDITORIAL METHOD

This bibliography is set out chronologically with each period of Welsh literary history forming a separate section. The first section contains references to the earliest Welsh poetry recorded according to the contents of ancient manuscripts, and the final section notes the work of contemporary writers. Medieval prose and poetry have been dealt with separately because of the volume and importance of both in terms of Welsh literature and Welsh–English translation history. Categorization of this nature is rarely without complication, with certain authors overlapping historical periods, and this is nowhere more problematic than in the final two sections: twentieth-century writing and contemporary writing. Writers who contributed greatly to the literature of the twentieth century but continue to publish today have invariably been included in the final section on contemporary writing.

There is a general bibliography at the beginning of this book listing publications that include translations from Welsh literature through the ages. Full publication details are printed here though abbreviated titles are adopted thereafter. Wide-ranging publications specific to literary periods are listed in the relevant sections only. Usually only the first edition of a publication has been listed – however, in some cases where later editions include extensive revisions, additional translations or are more accessible this has been taken into account. The page numbers of the later edition will either be noted alongside the first (with full publication details listed at the beginning of the section or in the general list at the start of the book) or, in some exceptional cases, there will be a note that page numbers will be quoted from the later edition only.

Within each section the bibliography is structured alphabetically according to author. The only exception to this layout occurs in the first section on early Welsh poetry, where the content has been recorded according to the medieval books in which the original texts are found in order to avoid putative dating and academic debate over authorship. Surnames were not commonplace in Wales until the sixteenth century, but the practice of adopting bardic names continues to the present day, making the work of the Welsh bibliographer somewhat problematic at times. As a rule we have followed

The New Companion to the Literature of Wales,[1] although we have avoided printing names in full when authors use initials only. And there have been other exceptions: for example, we have listed Bobi Jones (the poet) rather than his academic alter ego R. M. Jones which is given precedence in the *Companion*. The names of contemporary writers, yet to appear in the *Companion*, have been recorded as they appear in publications or library catalogues. Translators' names have generally been published as they appear in print. However, there are some special cases. Tony Conran published translations under his full name Anthony Conran for some years, but for the last few decades has been known to all as Tony, the form adopted throughout this bibliography.

Individual Author Entries

Each record for an individual author contains his/her full name, bardic name if relevant and dates if known. The bibliographical information opens with a listing of any collections of translations, books (e.g. novels, autobiographies) and any miscellaneous publications (pamphlets or booklets of translations perhaps). It is important to note that the contents of these publications are *not* separately recorded. This is then followed by a list of individual translations, those published in books, anthologies, periodicals, manuscripts, websites, broadcasts and so on. The subheading entitled 'Individual Translations' is also ordered alphabetically according to the original source title. The Welsh title is followed by an English-language title (usually selected from the translations).[2]

Welsh-speaking readers will note that the bibliography follows the English alphabet rather than the Welsh alphabet.[3] When there is no original Welsh title, the first lines of the Welsh original are noted within square brackets. Titles for much of the earliest literature have been allotted by academics and are accepted in general discussions

---

[1] Ed. Meic Stephens (Cardiff: University of Wales Press, 1998).
[2] In the case of some early poetry or Welsh hymns the English title is often taken from the first line of the translation and this is indicated by the inverted commas within brackets.
[3] This is most significant when considering the placing of the definite article under 'y' rather than the first letter of the source title.

of the work; these are adopted, where possible, in this bibliography. Where a source title is not suitably descriptive (e.g. 'Cân' [song]) or an author has composed several pieces with the same title, the first lines of the Welsh original appear in square brackets after the title. If an English title does not appear after the original title this indicates that the original is a place name or a personal name.

Poetry and prose are listed separately under each author. This distinction is necessary from the sixteenth century onwards. The first three sections record poetic output only and medieval prose has a section of its own. Poetry is almost invariably listed before prose. Exceptions include authors who are primarily prose writers or writers who have published novels that have subsequently been translated (and therefore appear before the individual entries). A list of prose translations would follow first for sense in that case, even if the author were recognized primarily as a poet. The categories for an individual author therefore generally look something like this:

Name (Dates)
Collections
Individual Translations *Po.* [Poetry]
Individual Translations *Pr.* [Prose]

A very few authors have one additional category: 'Selections'. It has not been possible within the confines of this volume to record every single translation published within each collection of translations from the work of individual authors. Readers are strongly advised to refer to collections of translations at every opportunity rather than relying solely on information recorded under 'Individual Translations'. Working exclusively from this category would lead to a very misleading representation as many collections contain the only translations of particular texts, or by specific translators. We have made a few exceptions and have published a selection of the most prolifically translated texts, for example from the work of Dafydd ap Gwilym (with more than a dozen collections of translations). The selection records translations from across the collections as well as from individual sources (which would normally be listed as individual translations), thus giving a comprehensive view of the translation history of particular texts.

Some Difficulties

Some recurring difficulties have hampered the research and prepara-
tion of this bibliography. The editor takes full responsibility for
errors and omissions that stem from lack of expertise in specialist
fields, time constraints and the sheer volume of material to be
recorded. There are certain external factors that have exacerbated
matters. Translators rarely acknowledge the original titles of source
texts or their location – their audience has little use for them. For
translations of well-known authors or works this has not been a
problem, but in the case of a translation of a poem published only
in a Welsh-language journal (once) or a lesser-known hymn verse or
a rare extract and so on the search for the source may assume myth-
ical proportions. It is a task often hindered by the exigencies of the
Welsh publishing context since many writers from the nineteenth
century to the present day have published (some almost exclusively)
in periodicals and magazines rather than collections or books. The
Welsh periodical press, as specialists know, is exceptional in its size
and quality, making it very difficult for the would-be bibliographer
to locate specific original poems from one English-language translation. In the case of BWLET the challenge to find that one elusive
title has rarely ended in failure but where this has been the case it has
been noted in a footnote to accompany the relevant entry. No doubt
specialist scholars will solve several of these mysteries in the very
near future.

In compiling this bibliography several specialists were consulted
for advice in their respective fields, but any inaccuracies or inconsist-
encies that remain are the editor's responsibility. The first section
on early Welsh poetry is as comprehensive as could reasonably
be expected within the confines of this volume. However it should
be noted that many of the first translators, without the benefits of
modern scholarship, attributed later work to this early period.
Where possible, the translations have been included but at times,
lacking an academic context, it proved too misleading to include a
small number of them. As these translations are generally found
in the works listed in the section bibliography, readers can turn to
these texts to see for themselves where omissions have been made
and why. Another area of concern related to the words of Welsh
hymns which are a unique contribution to Welsh literary history, and
due attention has been paid to them by the most accomplished of

translators. But translators and publishers alike are disconcertingly indiscriminatory when it comes to printing verses and whole hymns. Sometimes they appear as single verses, often with one or two verses missing, while an added verse by another writer altogether is also not uncommon. Of course these anomalies only reflect the movements of Welsh religious history when individual verses were extracted for use during periods of spiritual fervour. Translations have been recorded as clearly as possible despite these complications.[4]

This bibliography does not claim to record the specifics of the original or target text but merely to act as a signpost to what can be found in the original Welsh-language literature and in English-language translations. It is our hope that it will provide a useful starting point from a variety of different directions.

S. Rhian Reynolds

---

[4] There are several anonymous hymns recorded in H. Elvet Lewis's *Sweet Singers of Wales*. These hymns were published (anonymously) in the seminal Samuel Roberts collection (1841). Roberts included over two thousand hymns and excluded original authors. The colossal task of attribution has not been attempted for this particular bibliography.

GENERAL BIBLIOGRAPHY[1]

Revd Evan Evans (Ieuan Fardd, Ieuan Brydydd Hir), *Some Specimens of the Poetry of the Ancient Welsh Bards* (London: R. and J. Dodsley, 1764). Reprinted (Llanidloes: John Pryse, 1862). [*Some Specimens of the Poetry of the Ancient Welsh Bards*]

John Walters, *Translated Specimens of Welsh Poetry in English Verse, with some original pieces and notes* (London: by J. Dodsley [&c.], 1782). [*Translated Specimens of Welsh Poetry*]

Edward Jones (Bardd y Brenin), *The Musical, poetical, and historical relicks of the Welsh bards and druids . . . containing, the bardic triads, historic odes, eulogies, songs, elegies, memorials of the tombs of the warriors, of King Arthur and his knights, regalias, the wonders of Wales, et cætera: with English translations and historic illustrations* (London: Printed for author, 1784). [*The Musical, Poetical, and Historical Relicks*]

Richard Llwyd, *Poems, Tales, Odes, Sonnets, Translations from the British* (Chester: Printed by J. Fletcher and sold in London by E. Williams, 1804). [*Poems, Tales, Odes, Sonnets, Translations from the British*]

Owen Jones et al., *The Myvyrian Archaiology of Wales, Collected out of Ancient Manuscripts* (London: S. Rousseau, 1801–7). Reprinted (Denbigh: Thomas Gee, 1870). [*The Myvyrian Archaiology*]

Edward Jones (Bardd y Brenin), *The Bardic Museum, of Primitive British Literature; and other Admirable Rarities; Forming the second volume to the Musical, Poetical, and Historical Relicks of the Welsh Bards and Druids . . .* (London: Printed for the author by A. Strahan, 1802). [*The Bardic Museum*]

---

[1] The abbreviations adopted here will be used throughout the bibliography.

T. J. Llewelyn Prichard (ed.), *The Cambrian Wreath: a selection of English poems on Welsh subjects, original and translated from the Cambro-British, historic and legendary, including Welsh melodies, by various authors of celebrity, living and departed* (Aberystwyth: J. Cox, 1828).
[*Cambrian Wreath*]

Taliesin Williams (ab Iolo), *Iolo Manuscripts: a selection of ancient Welsh manuscripts, in prose and verse, from the Collection made by the late Edward Williams, Iolo Morganwg, for the purpose of forming a continuation of the Myfyrian Archaiology; and subsequently proposed as materials for a new history of Wales* (Llandovery: William Rees, 1848).
[*Iolo Manuscripts*]

Thomas Stephens, *The Literature of the Kymry: Being a Critical Essay on the History of the Language and Literature of Wales during the Twelfth and Two Succeeding Centuries* (Llandovery: William Rees; London: Longman & Co., 1849).
Second edition (London: Longmans, Green & Co., 1876; ed. Revd D. Silvan Evans).[2]
[*The Literature of the Kymry* (1876)]

John Jenkins (ed.), *The Poetry of Wales* (London: Houlston & Sons, 1873).
[*The Poetry of Wales* (1873)]

Charles Wilkins, *The History of the Literature of Wales from the year 1300 to the year 1650* (Cardiff: Daniel Owen & Company, 1884).
[*The History of the Literature of Wales*]

Edmund O. Jones (ed.), *Welsh Poets of To-day and Yesterday* (Llanidloes: John Ellis, 1901).
[*Welsh Poets of To-day and Yesterday*]

---

[2] Page numbers for the second edition follow those for the first throughout the bibliography.

R. L. Davies (ed. & tr.), *Cambrian Lyrics* (Merthyr Tydfil: The Welsh Educational Publishing Co., 1905).
[*Cambrian Lyrics*]

Emlyn D. Evans (ed.), *Treasury of Welsh Songs* (Wrexham, Cardiff: Hughes & Son and The Educational Publishing Co., 1909).
[*Treasury of Welsh Songs*]

A. P. Graves (ed. & tr.), *Welsh Poetry Old and New in English Verse* (London: Longmans, Green and Co., 1912).
[*Welsh Poetry Old and New*]

Francis Edwards (ed. & tr.), *Translations from the Welsh* (privately printed: Chiswick Press, 1913).
[*Translations from the Welsh*]

H. Idris Bell (ed. & tr.) (with some additional renderings by C. C. Bell), *Poems from the Welsh* (Caernarvon: Welsh Publishing Co. Ltd, 1913).
[*Poems from the Welsh*]

George Borrow, *Welsh Poems and Ballads* (London: Jarrold & Sons, 1915).
[*Welsh Poems and Ballads*]

W. Lewis Jones (ed.), *The Land of my Fathers: A Welsh Gift Book* (London: Hodder & Stoughton, 1915).
[*Land of My Fathers*]

A. P. Graves (ed. & tr.), *A Celtic Psaltery: being mainly renderings in English verse from Irish & Welsh Poetry*, ed. & tr. A. P. Graves (London: Society for Promoting Christian Knowledge, 1917).
[*A Celtic Psaltery*]

Grace Rhys (ed.), *A Celtic Anthology* (London: George G. Harrap & Co., 1927).
[*A Celtic Anthology*]

Gwyn Williams (ed. & tr.), *The Rent that's Due to Love* (London: Editions Poetry, 1950).
[*The Rent that's Due to Love*]

Kenneth Hurlstone Jackson (ed. & tr.), *A Celtic Miscellany: translations from the Celtic Literatures* (London: Routledge & Kegan Paul, 1951). Reprinted (Harmondsworth: Penguin Books, 1971).[3]
[*A Celtic Miscellany* (1951) [1971]]

Gwyn Williams (ed. & tr.), *An Introduction to Welsh Poetry* (London: Faber & Faber, 1953).
[*Introduction to Welsh Poetry*]

D. M. Lloyd and E. M. Lloyd (eds), *A Book of Wales* (London & Glasgow: Collins, 1953).
[*A Book of Wales* (1953)]

Thomas Parry, *A History of Welsh Literature*, tr. H. Idris Bell (Oxford: Clarendon Press, 1955).
[*A History of Welsh Literature*]

Gwyn Williams (ed. & tr.), *The Burning Tree* (London: Faber & Faber, 1956).
[*The Burning Tree*]

Gwyn Williams (ed. & tr.), *Presenting Welsh Poetry: An Anthology of Welsh Verse in Translation and of English Verse by Welsh Poets* (London: Faber & Faber, 1959).
[*Presenting Welsh Poetry*]

Anthony Conran (ed. & tr.), *The Penguin Book of Welsh Verse* (London: Penguin, 1967).[4]
[*The Penguin Book of Welsh Verse*]

Robert Gurney (tr.), *Bardic Heritage* (London: Chatto & Windus, 1969).
[*Bardic Heritage*]

Gwyn Williams (ed. & tr.), *Welsh Poems: Sixth Century to 1600* (London: Faber & Faber, 1973).
[*Welsh Poems: Sixth Century to 1600*]

---

[3] Page numbers for the later paperback edition are noted alongside entries for the 1951 edition.

[4] This is how the translator's name appears on this publication. However he has been known as Tony Conran for the past two decades and in order to ensure consistency throughout the bibliography it is in this shortened form that his name will appear.

Gwyn Williams (ed. & tr.), *To Look for a Word: Collected Translations from Welsh Poetry* (Llandysul: Gwasg Gomer, 1976). [*To Look for a Word*]

Bryan Walters (tr.), *From the Welsh* (Aberystwyth: Celtion Publishing Company, 1977). [*From the Welsh*]

Gwyn Jones (ed.), *The Oxford Book of Welsh Verse in English* (Oxford: Oxford University Press, 1983). [*Oxford Book*]

Tony Conran (ed. & tr.), *Welsh Verse* (Bridgend: Poetry Wales Press, 1986). [*Welsh Verse*][5]

Meic Stephens (ed.), *A Book of Wales* (London: J. M. Dent & Sons Ltd, 1987). [*A Book of Wales* (1987)]

John Matthews (ed.), *The Bardic Source Book* (London: Blandford, 1998). [*The Bardic Source Book*]

Joseph P. Clancy, *Other Words: Essays on Poetry and Translation* (Cardiff: University of Wales Press, 1999). [*Other Words*]

Collected Translations of Welsh Hymns[6]

Favourite Welsh Hymns Translated into English (Carmarthen: W. Spurrell, 1854). [*Favourite Welsh Hymns*]

---

[5] This is a revised edition of *The Penguin Book of Welsh Verse* and includes many additional translations along with much revised earlier translations. The page numbers for the third edition (2003) are the same as those for the second edition except for some new translations from early Welsh poetry. The additional translations are indicated by noting the volume as *Welsh Verse* (2003).

[6] These are for use in conjunction with the sections on eighteenth- and nineteenth-century literature.

Mrs Penderel Llewelyn, *Hymns Translated from the Welsh* (London: Chiswick printed, 1850). Second Edition (London: James Toovey, 1857).
[*Hymns Translated from the Welsh*]

H. Elvet Lewis, *Sweet Singers of Wales: A Story of Welsh Hymns and their Authors with Original Translations* (London: The Religious Tract Society, 1889?). Reprinted (Stoke-On-Trent: Tentmaker, 1994).
[*Sweet Singers of Wales*]

Revd R. Parry, *Hymns of the Welsh Revival, and Others* (Wrexham: Hughes & Son, 1907).
[*Hymns of the Welsh Revival*]

Revd Lemuel John Hopkin James (Hopcyn), *Welsh Melodies in the Old Notation for Hymns in English Translated and Original* (Cardiff: Evans & Williams Ltd, 1911).
[*Welsh Melodies in the Old Notation for Hymns in English Translated and Original*]

Revd Lemuel John Hopkin James (Hopcyn), *Welsh National Supplement of Hymns: Chiefly Translated from the Welsh* (Cardiff: Evans & Williams Ltd, 1912).
[*Welsh National Supplement*][7]

Alan Luff (ed.), *Welsh Hymns and their Tunes* (London: Staines & Bell, 1990).
[*Welsh Hymns and their Tunes*]

---

[7] This is a revised edition of the 1911 publication. However there are several additional translations not included in the earlier edition. If the translation occurs in both publications the latter is recorded as (1912: p. __) however if the translation only appears in the later version the abbreviated title is used.

YR HENGERDD:
EARLY WELSH POETRY

Nineteenth-century Publications and Scholarship

Sharon Turner, *A Vindication of the Genuiness of the Ancient British Poems of Aneurin, Taliesin, Llywarch Hen and Merdhin, with Specimens of the Poems* (London: Printed for E. Williams, 1803).
[*A Vindication of the Genuiness of the Ancient British Poems*]

Edward Davies, *The Mythology and Rites of the British Druids, ascertained by National Documents; and compared with the General Traditions and Customs of Heathenism, as illustrated by the most eminent antiquaries of our age. With an appendix, containing ancient poems and extracts, with some remarks on ancient British coins* (London: Printed for J. Booth, 1809).
[*The Mythology and Rites of the British Druids*]

D. W. Nash, *Taliesin; or, the Bards and Druids of Britain. A Translation of the Remains of the Earliest Welsh Bards, and an Examination of the Bardic Mysteries* (London: John Russel Smith, 1858).
[*Taliesin; or, the Bards and Druids of Britain*]

The Four Ancient Books of Wales: Containing the Cymric Poems attributed to the Bards of the Sixth Century, ed. William Forbes Skene (Edinburgh: Edmonston, 1868).
[*The Four Ancient Books of Wales*]

Thomas Stephens, *The Literature of the Kymry: Being a Critical Essay on the History of the Language and Literature of Wales during the Twelfth and Two Succeeding Centuries* (Llandovery: William Rees; London: Longmans & Co., 1849). Second edition (ed. Revd D. Silvan Evans; London: Longmans, Green & Co., 1876).
[*The Literature of the Kymry*][1]

---

[1] The page numbers for the second edition are noted in brackets alongside the reference for the first edition.

Critical Editions

Kenneth Hurlstone Jackson, *Studies in Early Celtic Nature Poetry* (Cambridge: Cambridge University Press, 1935).
[*Early Celtic Nature Poetry*]

Ifor Williams, *Lectures on Early Welsh Poetry* (Dublin Institute for Advanced Studies, 1944).
[*Lectures on Early Welsh Poetry*]

A Guide to Welsh Literature, Vol. 1, ed. A. O. H. Jarman and Gwilym Rees Hughes (Swansea: Christopher Davies, 1976).
[*A Guide to Welsh Literature*, Vol. 1]

The Beginnings of Welsh Poetry: Studies by Sir Ifor Williams, ed. Rachel Bromwich (Cardiff: University of Wales Press, 1980).
[*The Beginnings of Welsh Poetry*]

A. O. H. Jarman, *The Cynfeirdd: Early Welsh Poets and Poetry*, Writers of Wales Series (Cardiff: University of Wales Press, 1981).
[*The Cynfeirdd: Early Welsh Poets and Poetry*]

Jenny Rowland, *Early Welsh Saga Poetry: A Study and Edition of the Englynion (with translations)* (Cambridge: D. S. Brewer, 1990).
[*Early Welsh Saga Poetry*]

John T. Koch, *The Celtic Heroic Age* (Malden, Massachusetts: Celtic Studies Publications, 1995).
[*The Celtic Heroic Age* (1995)]

Patrick K. Ford, *The Celtic Poets: Songs and Tales from Early Ireland and Wales* (Belmont, Massachusetts: Ford & Bailie, 1999).
[*The Celtic Poets*]

The Celtic Heroic Age: Literary Sources for Ancient Celtic Europe and Early Ireland and Wales, ed. John T. Koch in collaboration with John Carey (Andover, Massachusetts, and Aberystwyth: Celtic Studies Publications, Inc., 2000).
[*The Celtic Heroic Age* (2000)]

Anthologies

Joseph P. Clancy, *The Earliest Welsh Poetry* (London: Macmillan, St. Martin's Press, 1970).
[*The Earliest Welsh Poetry*]

Carl Lofmark, *Bards and Heroes: an Introduction to Old Welsh Poetry* (Llanerch: Felinfach, 1989).
[*Bards and Heroes*]

Joseph P. Clancy, *Medieval Welsh Poems* (Dublin: Four Courts Press, 2003).
[*Medieval Welsh Poems* (2003)]

Miscellaneous

H. Idris Bell, *Caseg Broadsheet no. 2: Rhyfel a Chymru/War and Wales* (Caseg Press, 1942).

THE BOOK OF ANEIRIN

Collections

Y Gododdin (The Gododdin)

William Probert, *The Gododin, and the odes of the months* (Alnwick: W. Davison, 1820).

John Williams ab Ithel, *Y Gododin: a Poem on the Battle of Cattraeth; by Aneurin, a Welsh Bard of the Sixth Century; with an English Translation, and Numerous Historical and Critical Annotations* (Llandovery: William Rees, 1852).

Thomas Stephens, *The Gododin of Aneurin Gwawdrydd: an English translation, with copious explanatory notes; A life of Aneurin; and several lengthy dissertations illustrative of the 'Gododin' and the Battle of Cattraeth*, ed. Thomas Powell (London: Honourable Society of Cymmrodorion, 1888).

Kenneth Hurlstone Jackson, *The Gododdin: The Oldest Scottish Poem* (Edinburgh: Edinburgh University Press, 1969).

Desmond O'Grady, *Y Gododdin: A Version* (Dublin: Dolmen Press, 1977).

A. O. H. Jarman, *Aneirin: Y Gododdin: Britain's Oldest Heroic Poem* (Llandysul, Dyfed: Gomer, 1988).

Steve Short, *Aneirin: The Gododdin* (Felinfach: Llanerch, 1994).

John T. Koch, *The Gododdin of Aneirin: Text and Context from Dark-Age North Britain* (Cardiff: University of Wales Press, 1997).

Individual Translations

from Y Gododdin, tr. Meirion, *The Cambrian Register*, 1 (1795), 402–3; tr. Edward Davies, *The Mythology and Rites of the British Druids*, pp. 326–80; tr. Thomas Stephens, *Archaeologia Cambrensis*, 3 (New Series, 1852), 113–14; tr. Revd D. Silvan Evans, *The Four Ancient Books of Wales*, pp. 374–409; tr. E. J. Newell, *The Red Dragon*, 11 (1887), 115–18, 414–17; tr. Edward Anwyl, *Transactions of the Honourable Society of Cymmrodorion* (1909/1910), 120–36; tr. A. P. Graves, *Welsh Poetry Old and New*, pp. 1–2; tr. T. Gwynn Jones, *Y Cymmrodor*, 32 (1922), 13–47; tr. H. Idris Bell, *A Celtic Anthology*, p. 257; tr. Gwyn Williams, *Introduction to Welsh Poetry*, pp. 21–3; tr. Gwyn Williams, *The Burning Tree*, pp. 23–7; tr. D. M. Lloyd, *A Book of Wales* (1953), p. 184; tr. Tony Conran, *The Penguin Book of Welsh Verse*, pp. 75–8; tr. Joseph P. Clancy, *The Earliest Welsh Poetry*, pp. 33–64; tr. Gwyn Williams, *Welsh Poems: Sixth Century to 1600*, pp. 17–19; tr. Gwyn Williams, *To Look for a Word*, pp. 1–4; tr. Thomas Gray, *Presenting Welsh Poetry*, p. 17; tr. Bryan Walters, *From the Welsh*, p. 7; tr. Ifor Williams, *The Beginnings of Welsh Poetry*, pp. 65–6; tr. Joseph P. Clancy, *Oxford Book*, pp. 3–6; tr. Carl Lofmark, *Bards and Heroes*, pp. 45–9; tr. Steve Short, *Materion Dwyieithog: Bilingual Matters*, 2 (1990), 15–17; tr. Joseph P. Clancy, *The Triumph Tree: Scotland's Earliest Poetry AD 550–1350*, ed. Thomas Owen Clancy (Edinburgh: Canongate Classics, 1998), pp. 47–78; tr. Patrick K. Ford, *The Celtic Poets*, pp. 169–76; tr. Joseph P. Clancy, *Medieval Welsh Poems* (2003), pp. 45–76; '**Pais Dinogad**'

(Dinogad's Petticoat),[2] tr. Edward Davies, *The Mythology and Rites of the British Druids*, p. 318; tr. Revd D. Silvan Evans, *The Four Ancient Books of Wales*, p. 406; tr. Gwyn Williams, *The Welsh Review*, 5.4 (1946), 255; tr. D. M. Lloyd, *A Book of Wales* (1953), p. 308; tr. H. Idris Bell, *A History of Welsh Literature*, p. 22; tr. Gwyn Williams, *The Rent that's Due to Love*, p. 27; tr. Gwyn Williams, *Introduction to Welsh Poetry*, p. 48; tr. Gwyn Williams, *Presenting Welsh Poetry*, p. 19; tr. Leonard Owen, *The London Welshman*, 19.4 (1964), 18; tr. Tony Conran, *The Penguin Book of Welsh Verse*, p. 79; tr. Joseph P. Clancy, *The Earliest Welsh Poetry*, p. 87; tr. Gwyn Williams, *To Look for a Word*, p. 7; tr. Ifor Williams, *The Beginnings of Welsh Poetry*, p. 63; tr. Gwyn Williams, *Oxford Book*, p. 7; tr. Tony Conran, *Welsh Verse*, p. 117; tr. Joseph P. Clancy, *The Triumph Tree: Scotland's Earliest Poetry AD 550–1350*, ed. Thomas Owen Clancy (Edinburgh: Canongate Classics, 1998), p. 94; tr. Revd D. Silvan Evans, *The Bardic Source Book*, pp. 43–67, 191–2; tr. Joseph P. Clancy, *Medieval Welsh Poems* (2003), p. 97.

THE BOOK OF TALIESIN

Collections

J. Gwenogvryn Evans, *Poems from the Book of Taliesin* (Tremvan, Llanbedrog, 1915).

Meirion Pennar, *Taliesin Poems* (Llanerch Enterprises, 1988).

Meirion Pennar, *The Poems of Taliesin* (with prints by Nicholas Parry) (Tern Press: 1989).

Individual Translations
'**Angar Cyvyndawd**' (Hostile Confederacy), tr. Edward Davies, *The Mythology and Rites of the British Druids*, pp. 573–4; tr. D. W. Nash, *Taliesin; or, the Bards and Druids of Britain*, pp. 285–92; tr. Revd Robert Williams, *The Four Ancient Books of Wales*, pp. 525–33; tr. Ifor Williams, *Lectures on Early Welsh Poetry*, pp. 58–9; tr. Gwyn

---

[2] Ifor Williams explained that this poem, found in the text of the *Gododdin*, is in fact a lullaby that is not related to the body of that text. For this reason scholars and translators have usually treated it as a distinct poem.

Williams, *Introduction to Welsh Poetry*, pp. 29–30; tr. Ifor Williams, *The Poems of Taliesin*, ed. Ifor Williams with English version by J. E. Caerwyn Williams (Dublin: The Dublin Institute of Advanced Studies, 1968), pp. xv–xvi; tr. Ifor Williams, *Oxford Book*, pp. 19–20; tr. Ifor Williams, *The Streets and the Stars*, ed. John Davies and Melvyn Jones (Bridgend: Seren, 1992), p. 128; tr. Sarah Lynn Higley, *Between Languages: The Uncooperative Text in Early Welsh and Old English Nature Poetry* (University Park, Pa: Pennsylvania State University Press, 1993), pp. 284–92; '**Anrec Urien**' (A Gift to Urien), tr. Thomas Stephens, *Archaeologia Cambrensis*, 2 (New Series, 1851), 208–9; tr. D. W. Nash, *Taliesin; or, the Bards and Druids of Britain*, pp. 116–17; '**Arddwyre Reged**' (Rheged Arise), tr. Revd Robert Williams, *The Four Ancient Books of Wales*, pp. 350–1; tr. D. W. Nash, *Taliesin; or, the Bards and Druids of Britain*, pp. 111–12; tr. Joseph P. Clancy, *The Triumph Tree: Scotland's Earliest Poetry AD 550–1350*, ed. Thomas Owen Clancy (Edinburgh: Canongate Classics, 1998), pp. 85–6; '**Armes Prydain Fawr**' (The Prophecy of Britain), tr. unsigned, *The Cambrian Register*, 2 (1796), 554–63; tr. Thomas Stephens, *The Literature of the Kymry*, pp. 286–7 (1876: pp. 275–7); tr. Revd Robert Williams, *The Four Ancient Books of Wales*, pp. 436–42; tr. Joseph P. Clancy, *The Earliest Welsh Poetry*, pp. 107–12; tr. Rachel Bromwich, *Armes Prydain: The Prophecy of Britain*, ed. Sir Ifor Williams (Dublin: The Dublin Institute for Advanced Studies, 1972), pp. 3–15; tr. Joseph P. Clancy, *A Guide to Welsh Literature*, Vol. 1, pp. 116–17; tr. Joseph P. Clancy, *Medieval Welsh Poems* (2003), pp. 115–20; '**Cân i Wallawg ap Lleenawg**' ['En enw gwledic nef goludawc. ydrefynt'] (In Praise of Gwallawg), tr. D. W. Nash, *Taliesin; or, the Bards and Druids of Britain*, pp. 91–3; tr. Revd Robert Williams, *The Four Ancient Books of Wales*, pp. 337–8; tr. Edward Jones, *The Bardic Museum*, pp. 53–4; tr. Thomas Stephens, *Archaeologia Cambrensis*, 3 (New Series, 1852), 245–9; tr. Joseph P. Clancy, *The Triumph Tree: Scotland's Earliest Poetry AD 550–1350*, ed. Thomas Owen Clancy (Edinburgh: Canongate Classics, 1998), pp. 91–2; '**Cân i Wallawg ap Lleenawg**' ['En enw gwledic nef gorchordyon. rychanant'] (Elegy for Gwallawg), tr. D. W. Nash, *Taliesin; or, the Bards and Druids of Britain*, pp. 94–5; tr. Thomas Stephens, *Archaeologia Cambrensis*, 4 (New Series, 1853), 52–4; tr. Revd Robert Williams, *The Four Ancient Books of Wales*, pp. 338–40; tr. Joseph P. Clancy, *The Triumph Tree: Scotland's Earliest Poetry AD 550–1350*, ed. Thomas Owen Clancy

(Edinburgh: Canongate Classics, 1998), pp. 92–3; '**Canu i Urien Reged**' ['Urien yr Echwydd/Haelaf Dyn bedydd'] (Song to Urien Reged), tr. Revd Robert Williams, *The Four Ancient Books of Wales*, pp. 344–6; tr. John Morris-Jones, *Y Cymmrodor*, 28 (1918), 172–3; tr. Gwyn Williams, *Introduction to Welsh Poetry*, p. 28; tr. Saunders Lewis, *Transactions of the Honourable Society of Cymmrodorion* (1968), 294; tr. Joseph P. Clancy, *The Earliest Welsh Poetry*, pp. 25–7; tr. Gwyn Williams, *To Look for a Word*, p. 5; tr. Saunders Lewis, *A Guide to Welsh Literature*, Vol. 1, p. 58; tr. Saunders Lewis, *Presenting Saunders Lewis*, ed. Alun R. Jones and Gwyn Thomas (Cardiff: University of Wales Press, 1983), pp. 146–7; tr. John T. Koch, *The Celtic Heroic Age* (1995), pp. 339–41; tr. Joseph P. Clancy, *The Triumph Tree: Scotland's Earliest Poetry AD 550–1350*, ed. Thomas Owen Clancy (Edinburgh: Canongate Classics, 1998), pp. 80–1; tr. Joseph P. Clancy, *Medieval Welsh Poems* (2003), p. 40; '**Canu y Byd Bychan**' (The Lesser Song of the World), tr. Edward Davies, *The Mythology and Rites of the British Druids*, pp. 54–5; tr. D. W. Nash, *Taliesin; or, the Bards and Druids of Britain*, p. 279; tr. Revd Robert Williams, *The Four Ancient Books of Wales*, pp. 541–2; tr. Robert Gurney, *Bardic Heritage*, p. 3; tr. Marged Haycock, in *Ysgrifau a cherddi cyflwynedig i/Essays and Poems presented to Daniel Huws*, ed. Tegwyn Jones and E. B. Fryde (Aberystwyth: National Library of Wales, 1994), pp. 246–7; '**Canu y Byd Mawr**' (Song to the Great World), tr. D. W. Nash, *Taliesin; or, the Bards and Druids of Britain*, p. 281; tr. Revd Robert Williams, *The Four Ancient Books of Wales*, pp. 539–41; '**Canu y Medd**' (The Mead Song), tr. Sharon Turner, *A Vindication of the Genuiness of the Ancient British Poems*, pp. 59–61; tr. D. W. Nash, *Taliesin; or, the Bards and Druids of Britain*, p. 174; tr. Revd Robert Williams, *The Four Ancient Books of Wales*, pp. 538–9; tr. Thomas Stephens, *The Literature of the Kymry*, pp. 190–1 (1876: pp. 181–2); '**Cân y Gwynt**' (To the Wind), tr. D. W. Nash, *Taliesin; or, the Bards and Druids of Britain*, pp. 171–2; tr. Revd Robert Williams, *The Four Ancient Books of Wales*, pp. 535–8; tr. Ernest Rhys, *Transactions of the Honourable Society of Cymmrodorion* (1892–3), 39; tr. A. P. Graves, *Welsh Poetry Old and New*, pp. 6–9; tr. Ernest Rhys, *Land of My Fathers*, pp. 27–8; tr. Revd Robert Williams [but printed as W. F. Skene], *Lyra Celtica: An Anthology of Representative Celtic Poetry*, ed. E. A. Sharp and J. Matthay (Edinburgh: John Grant, 1924), pp. 73–4; tr. Ernest Rhys, *A Celtic Anthology*, pp. 256–7; tr. Joseph P. Clancy, *The Earliest*

Welsh Poetry, pp. 105–7; tr. Joseph P. Clancy, *A Guide to Welsh Literature*, Vol. 1, p. 120; tr. Joseph P. Clancy, *Medieval Welsh Poems* (2003), pp. 114–15; '**Dadolwch Urien**' (The Reconciliation with Urien), tr. Sharon Turner, *A Vindication of the Genuiness of the Ancient British Poems*, pp. 244–6; tr. D. W. Nash, *Taliesin; or, the Bards and Druids of Britain*, pp. 107–8; tr. Revd Robert Williams, *The Four Ancient Books of Wales*, pp. 352–3; tr. John Morris-Jones, *Y Cymmrodor*, 28 (1918), 181–2; tr. Joseph P. Clancy, *The Earliest Welsh Poetry*, pp. 29–30; tr. Joseph P. Clancy, *A Guide to Welsh Literature*, Vol. 1, pp. 65–6; tr. Joseph P. Clancy, *The Triumph Tree: Scotland's Earliest Poetry AD 550–1350*, ed. Thomas Owen Clancy (Edinburgh: Canongate Classics, 1998), pp. 88–9; tr. Tony Conran, *Welsh Verse* (2003), pp. 110–11; tr. Joseph P. Clancy, *Medieval Welsh Poems* (2003), pp. 43–4; '**Gwaith Argoed Llwyfain**' (The Battle of Argoed Llwyfain), tr. unsigned, in John Lewis, *The History of Great-Britain, from the first inhabitants thereof, 'till the death of Cadwalader, last king of the Britains* (London: Printed for F. Gyles, Mess. Woodman and Lyon, and C. Davis, 1729), p. 202; tr. Edward Jones, *The Musical, Poetical, and Historical Relicks*, pp. 5–6; tr. Lewis Morris, *The Myvyrian Archaiology*, p. 54; tr. Sharon Turner, *A Vindication of the Genuiness of the Ancient British Poems*, pp. 248–9; tr. D. W. Nash, *Taliesin; or, the Bards and Druids of Britain*, p. 100; tr. William Whitehead, *The Cambrian Journal* (1861), 145; tr. Revd Robert Williams, *The Four Ancient Books of Wales*, pp. 365–6; tr. John Morris-Jones, *Y Cymmrodor*, 28 (1918), 156–7; tr. Ifor Williams, *Lectures on Early Welsh Poetry*, pp. 63–4; tr. Gwyn Williams, *The Burning Tree*, p. 29; tr. Gwyn Williams, *Presenting Welsh Poetry*, p. 18; tr. Tony Conran, *The Penguin Book of Welsh Verse*, p. 73; tr. Joseph P. Clancy, *The Earliest Welsh Poetry*, pp. 30–1; tr. Gwyn Williams, *Welsh Poems: Sixth Century to 1600*, p. 20; tr. Gwyn Williams, *To Look for a Word*, p. 6; tr. Tony Conran, *Oxford Book*, p. 1; tr. Tony Conran (with slight variations by Saunders Lewis), *A Guide to Welsh Literature*, Vol. 1, p. 60; tr. Tony Conran (with slight variations by Saunders Lewis), *Presenting Saunders Lewis*, ed. Alun R. Jones and Gwyn Thomas (Cardiff: University of Wales, 1983), p. 149; tr. Tony Conran, *Welsh Verse*, p. 111; tr. Carl Lofmark, *Bards and Heroes*, pp. 40–1; tr. John T. Koch, *The Celtic Heroic Age* (1995), pp. 343–4; tr. Evan Evans (Ieuan Fardd, Ieuan Brydydd Hir), *The Bardic Source Book*, pp. 192–3; tr. Joseph P. Clancy, *The Triumph Tree: Scotland's Earliest Poetry AD*

550–1350, ed. Thomas Owen Clancy (Edinburgh: Canongate Classics, 1998), p. 85; tr. Joseph P. Clancy, *Medieval Welsh Poems* (2003), pp. 42–3; '**Gwawd Lluydd Mawr**' (The Praise of Lludd the Great), tr. William Owen Pughe and adapted by Mr Herbert, *Taliesin; or, the Bards and Druids of Britain*, pp. 257–61; tr. Revd Robert Williams, *The Four Ancient Books of Wales*, pp. 271–4; '**Gweith Gwen Ystrat**' (The Battle of Gwenystrad), tr. Evan Evans (Ieuan Fardd, Ieuan Brydydd Hir), *The Myvyrian Archaiology*, pp. 52–3; tr. Evan Evans (Ieuan Fardd, Ieuan Brydydd Hir), *Gwaith y Parchedig Evan Evans (Ieuan Brydydd Hir)*, ed. D. Silvan Evans (Caernarfon: H. Humphreys, 1876), p. 12; tr. unsigned, *The Cambrian Wreath*, pp. 88–91; tr. D. W. Nash, *Taliesin; or, the Bards and Druids of Britain*, p. 98; tr. Revd Robert Williams, *The Four Ancient Books of Wales*, pp. 343–4; tr. William Morris, *Transactions of the Honourable Society of Cymmrodorion* (1892–3), 40; tr. unsigned, *The Poetry of Wales* (1873), pp. 84–6; tr. John Morris-Jones, *Y Cymmrodor*, 28 (1918), 162; tr. Joseph P. Clancy, *The Earliest Welsh Poetry*, pp. 24–5; tr. Joseph P. Clancy, *A Guide to Welsh Literature*, Vol. 1, p. 59; tr. John T. Koch, *The Celtic Heroic Age* (1995), pp. 338–9; tr. G. R. Isaac, *Cambrian Medieval Celtic Studies*, 36 (1998), 63; tr. Joseph P. Clancy, *The Triumph Tree: Scotland's Earliest Poetry AD 550–1350*, ed. Thomas Owen Clancy (Edinburgh: Canongate Classics, 1998), pp. 79–80; tr. Patrick K. Ford, *The Celtic Poets*, pp. 164–5; tr. Tony Conran, *Welsh Verse* (2003), pp. 109–10; tr. Joseph P. Clancy, *Medieval Welsh Poems* (2003), pp. 39–40; '**Kadeir Teyrnon**' (The Chair of the Sovereign), tr. Edward Davies, *The Mythology and Rites of the British Druids*, pp. 528–32; tr. D. W. Nash, *Taliesin; or, the Bards and Druids of Britain*, pp. 209–10; tr. Revd Robert Williams, *The Four Ancient Books of Wales*, pp. 259–61; tr. unsigned, in Jon B. Coe and Simon Young, *The Celtic Sources for the Arthurian Legend* (Felinfach: Llanerch Publishers, 1995), p. 149; '**Kat Godeu**' (The Battle of the Trees), tr. Edward Davies, *The Mythology and Rites of the British Druids*, pp. 538–46; tr. D. W. Nash, *Taliesin; or, the Bards and Druids of Britain*, pp. 227–34; tr. Revd Robert Williams, *The Four Ancient Books of Wales*, pp. 276–84; tr. Gwyn Williams, *The Rent that's Due to Love*, p. 11; tr. unsigned, in Jon B. Coe and Simon Young, *The Celtic Sources for the Arthurian Legend* (Felinfach: Llanerch Publishers, 1995), pp. 145–7; tr. Marged Haycock, *Cambrian Medieval Celtic Studies*, 33 (1997), 66; '**Kerdd am Veib Llyr ab Brychwel Powys**'

(Song Concerning the Sons of Llyr ab Brochwel Powys), tr. Edward Davies, *The Mythology and Rites of the British Druids*, pp. 502–6; tr. D. W. Nash, *Taliesin; or, the Bards and Druids of Britain*, pp. 193–4; tr. Revd Robert Williams, *The Four Ancient Books of Wales*, pp. 274–6; '**Mabgyfrau Taliesin**' (Taliesin's Juvenilia), tr. Edward Davies, *The Mythology and Rites of the British Druids*, pp. 50–2; tr. Revd Robert Williams, *The Four Ancient Books of Wales*, pp. 542–4; '**Marwnad Corroy ab Dairy**' (Elegy on Corroy the Son of Dairy), tr. Thomas Stephens, *Archaeologia Cambrensis*, 2 (New Series, 1851), 151–2; tr. Revd Robert Williams, *The Four Ancient Books of Wales*, pp. 254–5; tr. Patrick Sims-Williams, in *Ireland in Early Medieval Europe*, ed. D. Whitelock et al. (Woodbridge: 1982), pp. 235–57; '**Marwnad Cunedda**' (The Elegy of Cunedda), tr. Thomas Stephens, *Archaeologia Cambrensis*, 3 (New Series, 1852), 52–3; tr. D. W. Nash, *Taliesin; or, the Bards and Druids of Britain*, pp. 83–4; tr. Revd Robert Williams, *The Four Ancient Books of Wales*, pp. 257–8; tr. John T. Koch, *The Celtic Heroic Age* (1995), pp. 285–7; '**Marwnad Cynaethwy**' *or* '**Echrys Ynys**' (Eulogy of Aeddon of Mona *or* Desolate is the Island), tr. Edward Davies, *The Mythology and Rites of the British Druids*, pp. 553–7; tr. Thomas Stephens, *Archaeologia Cambrensis*, 2 (New Series, 1851), 267–8; tr. D. W. Nash, *Taliesin; or, the Bards and Druids of Britain*, pp. 130–1; tr. Revd Robert Williams, *The Four Ancient Books of Wales*, pp. 299–300; tr. Ifor Williams, *The Beginnings of Welsh Poetry*, pp. 177–8; tr. R. Geraint Gruffydd, *Ildanach Ildirech: A Festschrift for Proinsias Mac Cana*, ed. John Carey, John T. Koch and Pierre-Yves Lambert (Andover & Aberystwyth: Celtic Studies Publications, Inc., 1999), p. 45; '**Marwnad Owain ab Urien**' (Lament for Owain ab Urien), tr. D. W. Nash, *Taliesin; or, the Bards and Druids of Britain*, pp. 108–9; tr. Revd Robert Williams, *The Four Ancient Books of Wales*, pp. 366–7; tr. John Morris-Jones, *Y Cymmrodor*, 28 (1918), 187–8; tr. Ifor Williams, *Lectures on Early Welsh Poetry*, pp. 64–5; tr. H. Idris Bell, *A History of Welsh Literature*, p. 3; tr. Padraig O' Broin, *The Anglo-Welsh Review*, 15.36 (1965), 14; tr. Tony Conran, *The Penguin Book of Welsh Verse*, p. 74; tr. Joseph P. Clancy, *The Earliest Welsh Poetry*, pp. 31–2; tr. Tony Conran, *Oxford Book*, p. 2; tr. Tony Conran (with slight variations by Saunders Lewis), *A Guide to Welsh Literature*, Vol. 1, p. 62; tr. Tony Conran (with slight variations by Saunders Lewis), *Presenting Saunders Lewis*, ed. Alun R. Jones and Gwyn Thomas (Cardiff: University of Wales Press, 1983), p. 151; tr.

Saunders Lewis, *Presenting Saunders Lewis*, ed. Alun R. Jones and Gwyn Thomas (Cardiff: University of Wales Press, 1983), p. 153; tr. Tony Conran, *Welsh Verse*, p. 112; tr. Carl Lofmark, *Bards and Heroes*, p. 42; tr. John T. Koch, *The Celtic Heroic Age* (1995), pp. 346–7; tr. Joseph P. Clancy, *The Triumph Tree: Scotland's Earliest Poetry AD 550–1350*, ed. Thomas Owen Clancy (Edinburgh: Canongate Classics, 1998), pp. 89–90; tr. Joseph P. Clancy, *Medieval Welsh Poems* (2003), p. 44; '**Moliant Dinbych Penfro**' [Mic Dinbych] (In Praise of Tenby), tr. Edward Davies, *The Mythology and Rites of the British Druids*, pp. 507–13; tr. Thomas Stephens, *The Cambrian Journal*, 4 (1857), 86–9; tr. D. W. Nash, *Taliesin; or, the Bards and Druids of Britain*, pp. 219–21; tr. Revd Robert Williams, *The Four Ancient Books of Wales*, pp. 303–6; tr. Ifor Williams, *Transactions of the Honourable Society of Cymmrodorion* (1940), 75–7; tr. Gwyn Williams, *Introduction to Welsh Poetry*, p. 59; tr. Tony Conran, *The Penguin Book of Welsh Verse*, pp. 80–2; tr. Joseph P. Clancy, *The Earliest Welsh Poetry*, pp. 89–91; tr. Ifor Williams, *The Beginnings of Welsh Poetry*, pp. 163–6; tr. Joseph P. Clancy, *Oxford Book*, pp. 7–9; tr. Tony Conran, *Welsh Verse*, pp. 117–19; tr. Joseph P. Clancy, *Medieval Welsh Poems* (2003), pp. 99–101; '**Preiddeu Annwfn**' (The Spoils of Annwn), tr. Sharon Turner, *A Vindication of the Genuiness of the Ancient British Poems*, pp. 239–43; tr. Edward Davies, *The Mythology and Rites of the British Druids*, pp. 515–26; tr. D. W. Nash, *Taliesin; or, the Bards and Druids of Britain*, pp. 212–14; tr. Thomas Stephens, *The Literature of the Kymry*, pp. 192–4 (1876: pp. 183–7); tr. Roger Sherman Loomis, *Wales and the Arthurian Tradition* (Cardiff: University of Wales Press, 1956), pp. 131–78; tr. Tony Conran, *Welsh Verse*, p. 133; tr. Marged Haycock, *Studia Celtica*, 18/19 (1983–4), 52–78; tr. John T. Koch, *Bulletin for the Board of Celtic Studies*, 31 (1984), 87–92; tr. unsigned, in Jon B. Coe and Simon Young, *The Celtic Sources for the Arthurian Legend* (Felinfach: Llanerch Publishers, 1995), pp. 137–9; tr. Tony Conran, *World Poetry: An Anthology of Verse from Antiquity to our Time*, ed. Katharine Washburn and John S. Major (New York; London: Norton, 1998), pp. 334–5; tr. John T. Koch, *The Celtic Heroic Age* (2000), pp. 290–2; tr. Sarah Higley, http://www.lib.rochester.edu/camelot/preideu.html; '**Trawsganu Cynan Garwyn**' (The Panegyric of Cynan Garwyn), tr. Revd Robert Williams, *The Four Ancient Books of Wales*, pp. 447–8; tr. Thomas Stephens, *Archaeologia Cambrensis*, 3 (New Series, 1852), 108–9; tr. Idris Foster, in

Prehistoric and Early Wales, ed. I. Ll. Foster and Glyn Daniel (London: Routledge and Kegan Paul, 1965), pp. 229–30; tr. Joseph P. Clancy, *The Earliest Welsh Poetry*, pp. 23–4; tr. John T. Koch, *The Celtic Heroic Age* (1995), pp. 295–6; tr. Patrick K. Ford, *The Celtic Poets*, pp. 162–3; '**Urien Yng Ngorffowys**' (Urien at Home), tr. D. W. Nash, *Taliesin; or, the Bards and Druids of Britain*, pp. 113–14; tr. Revd Robert Williams, *The Four Ancient Books of Wales*, pp. 346–8; tr. John Morris-Jones, *Y Cymmrodor*, 28 (1918), 176; tr. Joseph P. Clancy, *The Triumph Tree: Scotland's Earliest Poetry AD 550–1350*, ed. Thomas Owen Clancy (Edinburgh: Canongate Classics, 1998), pp. 82–3; tr. Patrick K. Ford, *The Celtic Poets*, pp. 166–7; tr. Joseph P. Clancy, *Medieval Welsh Poems* (2003), pp. 40–1; '**Urien Yrechwydd**' (Uryen of Yrechwydd), tr. D. W. Nash, *Taliesin; or, the Bards and Druids of Britain*, pp. 104–5; tr. Revd Robert Williams, *The Four Ancient Books of Wales*, pp. 348–9; tr. Joseph P. Clancy, *The Earliest Welsh Poetry*, pp. 27–9; tr. Carl Lofmark, *Bards and Heroes*, pp. 39–40; tr. Joseph P. Clancy, *A Guide to Welsh Literature*, Vol. 1, pp. 63–4; tr. Joseph P. Clancy, *The Triumph Tree: Scotland's Earliest Poetry AD 550–1350*, ed. Thomas Owen Clancy (Edinburgh: Canongate Classics, 1998), pp. 83–4; tr. Joseph P. Clancy, *Medieval Welsh Poems* (2003), pp. 41–2; '**Ymarwar Lludd Bychan**' (The Reconciliation of Lludd), tr. Edward Davies, *The Mythology and Rites of the British Druids*, pp. xii-xiii; tr. D. W. Nash, *Taliesin; or, the Bards and Druids of Britain*, pp. 118–19; tr. Revd Robert Williams, *The Four Ancient Books of Wales*, pp. 253–4; '**Yspeil Taliesin**' (The Spoils of Taliesin), tr. D. W. Nash, *Taliesin; or, the Bards and Druids of Britain*, pp. 102–3; tr. Revd Robert Williams, *The Four Ancient Books of Wales*, pp. 353–5; tr. Joseph P. Clancy, *The Triumph Tree: Scotland's Earliest Poetry AD 550–1350*, ed. Thomas Owen Clancy (Edinburgh: Canongate Classics, 1998), pp. 87–8.

THE BLACK BOOK OF CARMARTHEN

Collections

Meirion Pennar, *The Black Book of Carmarthen* (Felinfach: Llanerch, 1989).

Individual Translations
'**Afallennau Myrddin**' (The Apple Tree Stanzas), tr. Edward Jones, *The Musical, Poetical, and Historical Relicks*, pp. 8–10; tr. unsigned, *Cambrian Quarterly Magazine*, 1 (1829), 3–4; tr. Revd D. Silvan Evans, *The Four Ancient Books of Wales*, pp. 370–3; tr. Thomas Stephens, *The Literature of the Kymry*, pp. 222–31 (1876: pp. 212–22); tr. Thomas Love Peacock, *Land of my Fathers*, p. 83; tr. H. Idris Bell, *History of Welsh Literature*, p. 29; tr. A. O. H. Jarman, in *Life of Merlin: Geoffrey of Monmouth, vita Merlini*, ed. Basil Clarke (Cardiff: University of Wales Press, 1973), p. 235; tr. Gwyn Williams, *To Look for a Word*, p. 26; tr. A. O. H. Jarman, *The Cynfeirdd: Early Welsh Poets and Poetry*, p. 109; tr. John K. Bollard, *The Romance of Merlin: An Anthology*, ed. Peter Goodrich (New York & London: Garland Publishing, Inc., 1990), pp. 22–4; '**Boddi Maes Gwyddnau**' (The Inundation of Cantref Gwaelod), tr. Edward Jones, *The Bardic Museum*, pp. 17–18; tr. Revd D. Silvan Evans, *The Four Ancient Books of Wales*, p. 302; tr. Anthony Todd Thomson, *The Cambrian Wreath*, pp. 71–2; tr. Jenny Rowland, *Early Welsh Saga Poetry*, pp. 508–9; '**Englynion y Beddau**' (The Stanzas of the Graves), tr. Edward Jones, *The Bardic Museum*, pp. 10–12, 18; tr. Revd D. Silvan Evans, *The Four Ancient Books of Wales*, pp. 309–18; tr. Ernest Rhys, *A Celtic Anthology*, pp. 258–9; tr. Ernest Rhys, *Oxford Book of Modern Verse 1892–1935*, ed. W. B. Yeats (Oxford: Clarendon Press, 1936), pp. 50–2; tr. D. M. Lloyd, *A Book of Wales* (1953), pp. 308–10; tr. H. Idris Bell, *A History of Welsh Literature*, pp. 41–2; tr. Thomas Jones, in 'The Black Book of Carmarthen "Stanzas of the Graves"' (Sir John Rhŷs Memorial Lecture), *Proceedings of the British Academy*, 53 (1967), pp. 97–137; tr. Gwyn Williams, *Introduction to Welsh Poetry*, p. 55; tr. Gwyn Williams, *The Burning Tree*, pp. 39–41; tr. Gwyn Williams, *Welsh Poems: Sixth Century to 1600*, pp. 25–6; tr. Gwyn Williams, *To Look for a Word*, pp. 17–19; tr. Thomas Jones, *The Cynfeirdd: Early Welsh Poets and Poetry*, p. 114; tr. Gwyn Jones, *Oxford Book*, pp. 13–14; tr. Carl Lofmark, *Bards and Heroes*, p. 64; tr. unsigned, in Jon B. Coe and Simon Young, *The Celtic Sources for the Arthurian Legend* (Felinfach: Llanerch Publishers, 1995), p. 101; '**Gereint Fil Erbin**' (Geraint, Son of Erbin), tr. William Owen Pughe, *The Heroic Elegies*, pp. 3–11; tr. Revd D. Silvan Evans, *The Four Ancient Books of Wales*, pp. 266–8; tr. unsigned, in David James (Defynnog), *A Primer of Kymric Literature* (Cardiff: The Educational Publishing

Co. Ltd, [1913]), pp. 23–5; tr. Gwyn Williams, *The Burning Tree*, pp. 43–5; tr. Joseph P. Clancy, *The Earliest Welsh Poetry*, pp. 103–5; tr. Gwyn Williams, *Welsh Poems: Sixth Century to 1600*, pp. 27–8; tr. Gwyn Williams, *To Look for a Word*, pp. 20–2; tr. Joseph P. Clancy, *Oxford Book*, pp. 14–16; tr. Carl Lofmark, *Bards and Heroes*, pp. 66–8; tr. Jenny Rowland, *Early Welsh Saga Poetry*, pp. 504–5; tr. John T. Koch, *The Celtic Heroic Age* (1995), pp. 288–90; tr. unsigned, in Jon B. Coe and Simon Young, *The Celtic Sources for the Arthurian Legend* (Felinfach: Llanerch Publishers, 1995), pp. 119–21; tr. Joseph P. Clancy, *Medieval Welsh Poems* (2003), pp. 107–8; '**Gogonedauc argluit hanpich Guell**' (Hail Glorious Lord), tr. Revd D. Silvan Evans, *The Four Ancient Books of Wales*, p. 510; tr. A. P. Graves, *Welsh Poetry Old and New*, pp. 116–17; tr. A. P. Graves, *A Celtic Psaltery*, p. 75; tr. H. Idris Bell, *A History of Welsh Literature*, pp. 40–1; tr. Gwyn Williams, *Introduction to Welsh Poetry*, p. 63; tr. Joseph P. Clancy, *The Earliest Welsh Poetry*, p. 113; tr. Gwyn Williams, *To Look for a Word*, p. 63; tr. Joseph P. Clancy, *Medieval Welsh Poems* (2003), p. 120; '**Kyntaw geir**' ('The first word that I will utter'), tr. Revd D. Silvan Evans, *The Four Ancient Books of Wales*, pp. 519–21; tr. unsigned, in P. L. Henry, *The Early English and Celtic Lyric* (London: George Allen and Unwin, 1966), pp. 86–8; tr. Jenny Rowland, *Early Welsh Saga Poetry*, pp. 499–500; '**Tristwch yn y Gwanwyn**' ['Cyntefin Ceinaf Amser'] (Sadness in Springtime), tr. Kenneth Hurlstone Jackson, *Studies in Early Celtic Nature Poetry*, p. 50; tr. H. Idris Bell, *Caseg Broadsheet no. 6: Spring/Gwanwyn* (Caseg Press, 1942); tr. Ifor Williams, *Lectures on Early Welsh Poetry*, p. 12; tr. Gwyn Jones, *Oxford Book*, p. 18; tr. Tony Conran, *The Penguin Book of Welsh Verse*, p. 101; tr. Joseph P. Clancy, *The Earliest Welsh Poetry*, pp. 98–9; tr. Tony Conran, *Welsh Verse*, p. 139; tr. Patrick K. Ford, *The Celtic Poets*, p. 160; '**Y Gaeaf**' ['Llym awel'] (Winter), tr. Revd D. Silvan Evans, *The Four Ancient Books of Wales*, pp. 321–5; tr. Ernest Rhys, *A Celtic Anthology*, p. 255; tr. Kenneth Hurlstone Jackson, *Studies in Early Celtic Nature Poetry*, pp. 50–3; tr. Kenneth Hurlstone Jackson, *A Celtic Miscellany* (1951), p. 68 (1971: pp. 65–6); tr. H. Idris Bell, *A History of Welsh Literature*, p. 36; tr. Kenneth Hurlstone Jackson, *Presenting Welsh Poetry*, p. 21; tr. Tony Conran, *The Penguin Book of Welsh Verse*, pp. 96–7; tr. Joseph P. Clancy, *The Earliest Welsh Poetry*, pp. 95–8; tr. Patrick K. Ford, *The Poetry of Llywarch Hen* (Los Angeles: University of California Press, 1974), pp. 120–31; tr. Joseph P.

Clancy, *Oxford Book*, pp. 16–17; tr. Tony Conran, *Welsh Verse*, pp. 134–5; tr. Jenny Rowland, *Early Welsh Saga Poetry*, pp. 501–3; tr. Sarah Lynn Higley, *Between Languages: The Uncooperative Text in Early Welsh and Old English Nature Poetry* (University Park, Pa: Pennsylvania State University Press, 1993), pp. 279–82; tr. Patrick K. Ford, *The Celtic Heroic Age* (2000), pp. 378–80; tr. Joseph P. Clancy, *Medieval Welsh Poems* (2003), pp. 104–6; '**Yr Oianau**' (Greetings), tr. Thomas Stephens, *The Literature of the Kymry*, pp. 247–50, 252–5, 257–62, 264–6 (1876: pp. 236–7, 239–44, 249–55, 257–64); tr. Revd D. Silvan Evans, *The Four Ancient Books of Wales*, pp. 482–90; tr. Gwyn Williams, *Introduction to Welsh Poetry*, p. 69; tr. H. Idris Bell, *A History of Welsh Literature*, pp. 29–30; tr. Gwyn Williams, *To Look for a Word*, pp. 26–7; tr. John K. Bollard, *The Romance of Merlin: An Anthology*, ed. Peter Goodrich (New York & London: Garland Publishing, Inc., 1990), pp. 24–30; '**Ysgolan**', tr. Revd D. Silvan Evans, *The Four Ancient Books of Wales*, p. 518; tr. Gwyn Williams, *Introduction to Welsh Poetry*, pp. 40–1; tr. Jenny Rowland, *Early Welsh Saga Poetry*, p. 510; tr. W. S. Merwin, *World Poetry: An Anthology of Verse from Antiquity to our Time*, ed. Katharine Washburn and John S. Major (New York; London: Norton, 1998), p. 328.

THE RED BOOK OF HERGEST

Individual Translations

'**Baglawg Byddin**' ('Entangling is the snare, clustered is the ash'), tr. Revd D. Silvan Evans, *The Four Ancient Books of Wales*, pp. 574–5; tr. Revd D. Silvan Evans [but printed as W. F. Skene], *Lyra Celtica: An Anthology of Representative Celtic Poetry*, ed. E. A. Sharp and J. Matthay (Edinburgh: John Grant, 1924), p. 72; tr. A. P. Graves, *A Celtic Psaltery*, p. 74; tr. Joseph P. Clancy, *The Earliest Welsh Poetry*, p. 99; tr. Gwyn Williams, *Planet*, 10 (1972), 12–15; tr. Gwyn Williams, *To Look for a Word*, pp. 23–4; '**Bidiau I**' ['Bit goch crib Keilyawc'] ('Let the Cock's Comb be Red'), tr. William Owen Pughe, *The Heroic Elegies and Other Pieces of Llywarç Hen, Prince of the Cumbrian Britons* (London: J. Owen, 1792), p. 51; tr. Revd D. Silvan Evans, *The Four Ancient Books of Wales*, pp. 569–71; tr. Kenneth Hurlstone Jackson, *Early Celtic Nature Poetry*, pp. 69–70; tr. Jenny Rowland, *Journal of Celtic Studies*, 3 (1981), 59–87; tr. Patrick K.

Ford, *Sources and Analogues of Old English Poetry II*, ed. Daniel G. Calder, Robert E. Bjork, Patrick K. Ford and Daniel F. Melia (Cambridge: Boydell & Brewer, 1983), p. 95; tr. Sarah Lynn Higley, *Between Languages: The Uncooperative Text in Early Welsh and Old English Nature Poetry* (University Park, Pa: Pennsylvania State University Press, 1993), pp. 276–8; '**Calan Gaeaf**' (Winter), tr. William Owen Pughe, *The Heroic Elegies and Other Pieces of Llywarç Hen, Prince of the Cumbrian Britons* (London: J. Owen, 1792), p. 45; tr. Revd D. Silvan Evans, *The Four Ancient Books of Wales*, pp. 573–4; tr. Kenneth Hurlstone Jackson, *Studies in Early Celtic Nature Poetry*, pp. 63–4; '**Claf Abercuawg**' (The Sick Man of Aber Cuawg),[3] tr. Edward Jones, *The Musical, Poetical, and Historical Relicks*, p. 7; tr. Revd D. Silvan Evans, *The Four Ancient Books of Wales*, pp. 580–4; tr. unsigned, in Edward Thomas, *Wales* (London: A & C Black Ltd [1924]), p. 39; tr. Kenneth Hurlstone Jackson, *Early Celtic Nature Poetry*, pp. 53–6; tr. Gwyn Williams, *The Burning Tree*, pp. 35–7; tr. unsigned, in P. L. Henry, *The Early English and Celtic Lyric* (London: George Allen and Unwin, 1966), pp. 75–7; tr. Joseph P. Clancy, *The Earliest Welsh Poetry*, pp. 91–5; tr. Gwyn Williams, *Welsh Poems: Sixth Century to 1600*, pp. 23–4; tr. Patrick K. Ford, *The Poetry of Llywarch Hen* (Los Angeles: University of California Press, 1974), pp. 67–75; tr. Gwyn Williams, *To Look for a Word*, pp. 28–9; tr. Jenny Rowland, *Early Welsh Saga Poetry*, pp. 497–9; tr. Sarah Lynn Higley, *Between Languages: The Uncooperative Text in Early Welsh and Old English Nature Poetry* (University Park, Pa: Pennsylvania State University Press, 1993), pp. 263–8; tr. Edward Jones, *The Bardic Source Book*, p. 194; tr. Patrick K. Ford, *The Celtic Poets*, pp. 179–82; tr. Patrick K. Ford, *The Celtic Heroic Age* (2000), pp. 363–6; tr. Joseph P. Clancy, *Medieval Welsh Poems* (2003), pp. 101–4; '**Eiry Mynydd**' (Mountain Snow), tr. Revd D. Silvan Evans, *The Four Ancient Books of Wales*, pp. 586–94; tr. Kenneth Hurlstone Jackson, *Studies in Early Celtic Nature Poetry*, pp. 58–61; tr. Joseph P. Clancy, *The Earliest Welsh Poetry*, pp. 99–103; tr. Joseph P. Clancy, *Medieval Welsh Poems* (2003), pp. 111–14; '**Gorwynion**' ('Bright are the Ash tops'), tr. William Owen Pughe, *The Heroic Elegies and Other Pieces of Llywarç Hen, Prince of the Cumbrian Britons* (London: J. Owen, 1792), pp. 13–21; tr. Revd

---

[3] This poem appears before the Llywarch Hen poems in the Red Book of Hergest but has been associated with them.

D. Silvan Evans, *The Four Ancient Books of Wales*, pp. 576–80; tr. Revd D. Silvan Evans, *Lyra Celtica: An Anthology of Representative Celtic Poetry*, ed. E. A. Sharp and J. Matthay (Edinburgh: John Grant, 1924), pp. 68–71; tr. Thomas Love Peacock, *Land of my Fathers*, p. 82; tr. Kenneth Hurlstone Jackson, *Early Celtic Nature Poetry*, pp. 64–8.

EARLY SAGA POETRY

Scholarly Edition

Jenny Rowland, *Early Welsh Saga Poetry: A Study and Edition of the Englynion* (Cambridge: D. S. Brewer, 1990).

Canu Llywarch

Collections

William Owen [Pughe], *The Heroic Elegies and Other Pieces of Llywarç Hen, Prince of the Cumbrian Britons* (London: J. Owen, 1792).

Glyn Jones and T. J. Morgan, *The Saga of Llywarch the Old* (London: Cockerel Press, 1955).

Patrick K Ford, *The Poetry of Llywarch Hen* (Los Angeles: University of California Press, 1974).

Individual Translations

'Cân yr Henwr' ['Kynn bum kein vaglawc'] (The Song of the Old Man), tr. Edward Jones, *The Musical, Poetical, and Historical Relicks*, pp. 7–8; tr. Revd D. Silvan Evans, *The Four Ancient Books of Wales*, pp. 326–35; tr. Felicia Hemans, *The Poetry of Wales* (1873), p. 93; tr. Ernest Rhys, *Land of My Fathers*, pp. 51–2; tr. Ernest Rhys, *A Celtic Anthology*, pp. 260–1; tr. Philip P. Graves, *The Welsh Review*, 2.2 (1939), 78–9; tr. Ifor Williams, *Lectures on Early Welsh Poetry*, pp. 41–2; tr. D. M. Lloyd, *A Book of Wales* (1953), p. 272; tr. Gwyn Williams, *The Rent that's Due to Love*, pp. 21–5; tr. Kenneth Hurlstone Jackson, *A Celtic Miscellany* (1951), pp. 282–3

(1971: pp. 257–8); tr. Gwyn Williams, *Introduction to Welsh Poetry*, pp. 34–5; tr. Tony Conran, *The Penguin Book of Welsh Verse*, pp. 87–9; tr. Joseph P. Clancy, *The Earliest Welsh Poetry*, pp. 76–8; tr. Gwyn Williams, *To Look for a Word*, pp. 11–13; tr. Ifor Williams, *The Beginnings of Welsh Poetry*, pp. 133–5; tr. Carl Lofmark, *Bards and Heroes*, pp. 56–8; tr. Gwyn Jones, *Oxford Book*, pp. 9–10; tr. Sarah Lynn Higley, *Between Languages: The Uncooperative Text in Early Welsh and Old English Nature Poetry* (University Park, Pa: Pennsylvania State University Press, 1993), pp. 268–71; tr. Leslie Norris, *Leslie Norris: Collected Poems* (Bridgend: Seren, 1996), pp. 14–15; tr. Edward Jones, *The Bardic Source Book*, pp. 194–5; tr. Emyr Humphreys, *Emyr Humphreys: Collected Poems* (Cardiff: University of Wales Press, 1999), pp. 125–7; tr. Jenny Rowland, *Early Welsh Saga Poetry*, pp. 474–6; tr. Patrick K. Ford, *The Celtic Poets*, pp. 182–4; tr. Patrick K. Ford, *The Celtic Heroic Age* (2000), pp. 366–8; tr. Joseph P. Clancy, *Medieval Welsh Poems* (2003), pp. 87–9; '**Llywarch a Gwên**' (Llywarch and Gwên), tr. Ifor Williams, *Lectures on Early Welsh Poetry*, p. 39; tr. Joseph P. Clancy, *The Earliest Welsh Poetry*, pp. 73–4; tr. Carl Lofmark, *Bards and Heroes*, pp. 51–3; tr. Jenny Rowland, *Early Welsh Saga Poetry*, pp. 468–9; tr. Joseph P. Clancy, *Medieval Welsh Poems* (2003), pp. 84–6; '**Marwnad Gwên**' (Lament for Gwên), tr. Ifor Williams, *Lectures on Early Welsh Poetry*, pp. 40–1; tr. Joseph P. Clancy, *The Earliest Welsh Poetry*, pp. 74–6; tr. Ifor Williams, *The Beginnings of Welsh Poetry*, pp. 136–9; tr. Carl Lofmark, *Bards and Heroes*, pp. 54–5; tr. Jenny Rowland, *Early Welsh Saga Poetry*, pp. 469–70; tr. Joseph P. Clancy, *Medieval Welsh Poems* (2003), pp. 86–7; (**Llywarch and his Sons**: various stanzas), tr. Revd D. Silvan Evans, *The Four Ancient Books of Wales*, pp. 319–20, 584–5; tr. Joseph P. Clancy, *The Earliest Welsh Poetry*, pp. 71–3; tr. Carl Lofmark, *Bards and Heroes*, pp. 50–1; tr. Jenny Rowland, *Early Welsh Saga Poetry*, pp. 470–3; tr. Patrick K. Ford, *The Celtic Heroic Age* (2000), pp. 363–73, 377, 380–4; tr. Joseph P. Clancy, *Medieval Welsh Poems* (2003), pp. 83–4.

Canu Urien

'**Celain Urien Rheged**' (The Corpse of Urien), tr. William Owen Pughe, *The Heroic Elegies and Other Pieces of Llywarç Hen, Prince of the Cumbrian Britons* (London: J. Owen, 1792), pp. 23–43; tr.

Ernest Rhys, *Oxford Book of Modern Verse 1892–1935*, ed. W. B. Yeats (Oxford: Clarendon Press, 1936), p. 53; tr. Joseph P. Clancy, *The Earliest Welsh Poetry*, pp. 67–8; tr. Gwyn Williams, *To Look for a Word*, p. 10; tr. Jenny Rowland, *Early Welsh Saga Poetry*, pp. 478–9; tr. John T. Koch, *The Celtic Heroic Age* (1995), pp. 345–6; '**Diffaith Aelwyd Rheged**' (The Ruined Hearth of Rheged), tr. Tony Conran, *The Penguin Book of Welsh Verse*, pp. 93–5; tr. Joseph P. Clancy, *The Earliest Welsh Poetry*, pp. 68–70; tr. Tony Conran, *Welsh Verse*, pp. 130–2; tr. Jenny Rowland, *Early Welsh Saga Poetry*, pp. 481–2; tr. Patrick K. Ford, *The Celtic Poets*, pp. 187–9; '**Pen Urien**' (The Head of Urien), tr. Ernest Rhys, *Oxford Book of Modern Verse 1892–1935*, ed. W. B. Yeats (Oxford: Clarendon Press, 1936), pp. 52–3; tr. Joseph P. Clancy, *The Earliest Welsh Poetry*, pp. 66–7; tr. Gwyn Williams, *Planet*, 3 (1970–1), 28–31; tr. Gwyn Williams, *To Look for a Word*, p. 9; tr. Jenny Rowland, *Early Welsh Saga Poetry*, pp. 477–8; tr. John T. Koch, *The Celtic Heroic Age* (1995), pp. 344–5.

Canu Heledd

Collections

William Owen [Pughe], *The Heroic Elegies and Other Pieces of Llywarç Hen, Prince of the Cumbrian Britons* (London: J. Owen, 1792).

Glyn Jones and T. J. Morgan, *The Story of Heledd* (Newtown: Gwasg Gregynog, 1994).

Individual Translations

'**Eglwysseu Bassa**' (The Churches of Bassa), tr. Jenny Rowland, *Early Welsh Saga Poetry*, p. 487; tr. John T. Koch, *The Celtic Heroic Age* (1995), p. 359; tr. Joseph P. Clancy, *Medieval Welsh Poems* (2003), pp. 91–2; '**Englynion Cadwallon**', tr. Rachel Bromwich, in Richard Barber, *The Figure of Arthur* (London: 1972), pp. 98–9; tr. Jenny Rowland, *Early Welsh Saga Poetry*, pp. 98–9; '**Eryr Eli**' (The Eagle of Eli), tr. Ernest Rhys, *A Celtic Anthology*, p. 261; tr. Tony Conran, *The Penguin Book of Welsh Verse*, pp. 92–3; tr. Tony Conran, *Welsh Verse*, p. 129; tr. Jenny Rowland, *Early Welsh Saga*

Poetry, p. 486; tr. John T. Koch, *The Celtic Heroic Age* (1995), p. 358; 'Eryr Pengwern' (The Eagle of Pengwern), tr. Gwyn Williams, *The Burning Tree*, p. 31; tr. Joseph P. Clancy, *The Earliest Welsh Poetry*, pp. 81–2; tr. Gwyn Williams, *Welsh Poems: Sixth Century to 1600*, p. 21; tr. Gwyn Williams, *To Look for a Word*, p. 16; tr. Tony Conran, *Welsh Verse*, p. 130; tr. Jenny Rowland, *Early Welsh Saga Poetry*, p. 486; tr. John T. Koch, *The Celtic Heroic Age* (1995), p. 358; tr. Joseph P. Clancy, *Medieval Welsh Poems* (2003), p. 91; 'Marwnad Cynddylan' (Lament for Cynddylan), tr. Revd D. Silvan Evans, *The Four Ancient Books of Wales*, pp. 449–50; tr. unsigned, in David James (Defynnog), *A Primer of Kymric Literature* (Cardiff: The Educational Publishing Co. Ltd [1913]), p. 25; tr. Joseph P. Clancy, *The Earliest Welsh Poetry*, pp. 87–9; tr. Jenny Rowland, *Early Welsh Saga Poetry*, pp. 483–4; tr. John T. Koch, *The Celtic Heroic Age* (1995), p. 356; tr. Joseph P. Clancy, *Medieval Welsh Poems* (2003), pp. 89–91; 'Stafell Cynddylan' (The Hall of Cynddylan), tr. Arthur James Johnes (Maelog), *Cambrian Quarterly Magazine*, 1 (1829), 180; tr. Revd D. Silvan Evans, *The Four Ancient Books of Wales*, pp. 450–2; tr. Felicia Hemans, *The Poetry of Wales* (1873), pp. 93–4; tr. Ernest Rhys, *Land of My Fathers*, pp. 28–9; tr. Ernest Rhys, *A Celtic Anthology*, pp. 259–60; tr. Gwyn Williams, *The Rent that's Due to Love*, pp. 15–19; tr. William Barnes, *Presenting Welsh Poetry*, p. 20; tr. Tony Conran, *The Penguin Book of Welsh Verse*, pp. 90–1; tr. Joseph P. Clancy, *The Earliest Welsh Poetry*, pp. 82–4; tr. Gwyn Williams, *To Look for a Word*, pp. 14–15; tr. Ifor Williams, *The Beginnings of Welsh Poetry*, p. 147; tr. Joseph P. Clancy, *A Book of Wales* (1987), pp. 297–8; tr. John T. Koch, *The Celtic Heroic Age* (1995), p. 357; tr. Dannie Abse, *A Welsh Retrospective* (Bridgend: Seren, 1997), pp. 26–7; tr. Joseph P. Clancy, *Medieval Welsh Poems* (2003), pp. 92–4; 'Chwiorydd Heledd' (Heledd's Sisters), tr. Gwyn Williams, *Planet*, 51 (1985), 66–7; tr. Jenny Rowland, *Early Welsh Saga Poetry*, pp. 484–5; tr. Joseph P. Clancy, *Medieval Welsh Poems* (2003), p. 94; 'Y Dref Wen' (The White Town), tr. Gwyn Williams, *The Rent that's Due to Love*, p. 13; tr. Gwyn Williams, *Introduction to Welsh Poetry*, p. 37; tr. Joseph P. Clancy, *The Earliest Welsh Poetry*, p. 82; tr. Gwyn Williams, *To Look for a Word*, p. 13; tr. Jenny Rowland, *Early Welsh Saga Poetry*, p. 487; tr. Joseph P. Clancy, *Medieval Welsh Poems* (2003), pp. 95–6.

THE JUVENCUS MANUSCRIPT[4] (ninth-century MS.)

from 'The Juvencus Englyns', tr. John Rhŷs, *Y Cymmrodor*, 18 (1905), 103–4; tr. Ifor Williams, *Lectures on Early Welsh Poetry*, p. 29; tr. H. Idris Bell, *A History of Welsh Literature*, p. 21; tr. Ifor Williams, *The Beginnings of Welsh Poetry*, pp. 90, 102; tr. A. O. H. Jarman, *The Cynfeirdd: Early Welsh Poets and Poetry*, p. 100; tr. Gwyn Williams, *To Look for a Word*, p. 8; tr. Jenny Rowland, *Early Welsh Saga Poetry*; pp. 510–11.

[4] This manuscript includes two important series of *englynion* from Old Welsh written in its margins: three narrative verses that have been connected to the early saga poetry and nine religious verses pertaining to the Trinity. These verses are sometimes translated together and sometimes separately as the nine or as the three.

Y GOGYNFEIRDD:
THE POETS OF THE PRINCES

Early Publications and Scholarship

Revd Evan Evans (Ieuan Fardd, Ieuan Brydydd Hir), *Some Specimens of the Poetry of the Ancient Welsh Bards* (London: R. and J. Dodsley, 1764). Reprinted (Llanidloes: John Pryse, 1862).
[*Some Specimens of the Poetry of the Ancient Welsh Bards*]

Thomas Stephens, *The Literature of the Kymry: Being a Critical Essay on the History of the Language and Literature of Wales during the Twelfth and Two Succeeding Centuries* (Llandovery: William Rees; London: Longman & Co., 1849). Second edition (ed. Revd D. Silvan Evans; London: Longmans, Green & Co., 1876).
[*The Literature of the Kymry*][1]

Critical Editions

J. Lloyd-Jones, *The Court Poets of the Welsh Princes*, from *The Proceedings of the British Academy*, 34 (London: Geoffrey Cumberlege, 1948).

Catherine A. McKenna, *The Medieval Welsh Religious Lyric* (Belmont, Massachusetts: Ford & Bailie, 1991).
[*The Medieval Welsh Religious Lyric*]

J. E. Caerwyn Williams, *The Poets of the Welsh Princes* (Cardiff: University of Wales Press for Welsh Arts Council, 1978). Second Edition (Cardiff: University of Wales Press, 1994).
[*The Poets of the Welsh Princes*][2]

---

[1] The page numbers for the second edition are noted in brackets beside the reference for the first edition.

[2] The second edition is much revised and expanded and includes many more translations. Page numbers for the first edition are noted in brackets when there are corresponding translations.

John T. Koch, *The Celtic Heroic Age* (Malden, Massachusetts: Celtic Studies Publications, 1995).
[*The Celtic Heroic Age* (1995)]

Patrick K. Ford, *The Celtic Poets: Songs and Tales from Early Ireland and Wales* (Belmont, Massachusetts: Ford & Bailie, 1999).
[*The Celtic Poets*]

Anthologies

Joseph P. Clancy, *The Earliest Welsh Poetry* (London: Macmillan, St. Martin's Press, 1970).
[*The Earliest Welsh Poetry*]

Carl Lofmark, *Bards and Heroes: an Introduction to Old Welsh Poetry* (Llanerch: Felinfach, 1989).
[*Bards and Heroes*]

Joseph P. Clancy, *Medieval Welsh Poems* (Dublin: Four Courts Press, 2003).
[*Medieval Welsh Poems* (2003)]

ANON.

Individual Translations
'**Mawl Cuhelyn Fardd**' (A Poem in Praise of Cuhelyn Fardd), tr. Revd D. Silvan Evans, *The Four Ancient Books of Wales*, pp. 498–500; tr. R. Geraint Gruffydd, *Studia Celtica*, 10/11 (1975–6), 203–6.

BLEDDYN FARDD (*fl.* 1258–84)

Individual Translations
'**Awdl Farwnad Llywelyn ap Gruffudd**' (Elegy for Llywelyn ap Gruffydd), tr. Thomas Stephens, *The Literature of the Kymry*, pp. 381–3 (1876: pp. 365–6); tr. D. M. Lloyd, *A Book of Wales* (1953), pp. 123–4; tr. Tony Conran, *The Penguin Book of Welsh Verse*, pp.

132–3; tr. Joseph P. Clancy, *The Earliest Welsh Poetry*, pp. 168–9; tr. Tony Conran, *Welsh Verse*, pp. 165–6; tr. Patrick K. Ford, *The Celtic Poets*, pp. 200–2; tr. Joseph P. Clancy, *Medieval Welsh Poems* (2003), pp. 168–70; '**Marwnad y tri meib Gruffudd ap Llywelyn**' (Lament for Gruffudd's Three Sons), tr. William Owen Pughe, *The Cambrian Journal*, 5 (1858), 39; tr. J. Lloyd-Jones, *A Book of Wales* (1953), p. 315; tr. Joseph P. Clancy, *The Earliest Welsh Poetry*, pp. 169–70; tr. Joseph P. Clancy, *Medieval Welsh Poems* (2003), pp. 170–1; '**Marwysgafn Bleddyn Fardd. Ef ei Hun a'i Cant**' (The Deathbed Song of Bleddyn Fardd. He Himself Sang it), tr. Tony Conran, *The Penguin Book of Welsh Verse*, pp. 133–4; tr. Tony Conran, *Welsh Verse*, pp. 166–7; tr. Catherine A. McKenna, *The Medieval Welsh Religious Lyric*, p. 205.

CYNDDELW BRYDYDD MAWR (*fl.* 1155–1195)

Individual Translations

'**Arwyrain Owain Gwynedd**' (In Praise of Owain Gwynedd), tr. Joseph P. Clancy, *The Earliest Welsh Poetry*, pp. 145–6; tr. Joseph P. Clancy, *Oxford Book*, pp. 25–7; tr. Joseph P. Clancy, *Medieval Welsh Poems* (2003), pp. 147–9; '**Arwyrain Madawg fab Maredudd**' (In Praise of Madawg ap Maredudd), tr. William Owen Pughe, *The Cambrian Journal*, 5 (1858), 29–30; tr. Joseph P. Clancy, *The Earliest Welsh Poetry*, pp. 136–7; tr. Joseph P. Clancy, *The Poets of the Welsh Princes*, pp. 25–6; tr. Joseph P. Clancy, *Medieval Welsh Poems* (2003), pp. 140–1; '**Awdl Ddadolwch yr Arglwydd Rhys**' (A Conciliatory Address to Rhys ab Gruffydd), tr. Thomas Stephens, *The Literature of the Kymry*, p. 118 (1876: p. 108); '**Dau Englyn i Lywelyn ap Madog i ddiolch am gorn hela**' (Two Verses, Sung by Cynddelw, the Bard, to the Huntsmen of Llywelyn, the son of Madog ab Maredudd, Prince of Powys, and to their horns; on the occasion of their presenting him the stag, which they had chased, and killed near his house), tr. Edward Jones, *The Bardic Museum*, p. 40; tr. Gwyn Williams, *The Burning Tree*, p. 51; tr. Gwyn Williams, *Welsh Poems: Sixth Century to 1600*, p. 31; tr. Gwyn Williams, *To Look for a Word*, p. 43; tr. Carl Lofmark, *Bards and Heroes*, p. 82; '**Englyn i Fynach o Ystrad Marchell**' (Englyn to the Monk of Ystrad Marchell), tr. Thomas Stephens, *The Literature of the Kymry*, p. 130 (1876: p. 119); '**Englynion Dadolwch yr Arglwydd Rhys**' (Stanzas to the Lord Rhys), tr. William Owen Pughe, *The Literature of the Kymry*, pp. 135–6 (1876: pp. 124–5); tr. Tony Conran, *The Penguin Book of Welsh Verse*, pp. 120–1; tr. Joseph P. Clancy, *The Earliest Welsh Poetry*, pp. 147–8; tr. Joseph P. Clancy, *Oxford Book*, pp. 24–5; tr. Tony Conran, *Welsh Verse*, pp. 154–5; tr. Joseph P. Clancy, *Medieval Welsh Poems* (2003), pp. 150–1; '**I Dduw**' (To God), tr. Thomas Stephens, *The Literature of the Kymry*, pp. 130–1 (1876: pp. 119–20); '**I Ferch**' (To a Girl), tr. Tony Conran, *The Penguin Book of Welsh Verse*, p. 118; tr. Joseph P. Clancy, *The Earliest Welsh Poetry*, p. 136; tr. Gwyn Williams, *To Look for a Word*, p. 43; tr. Tony Conran, *Welsh Verse*, pp. 152–3; tr. Carl Lofmark, *Bards and Heroes*, p. 82; tr. Tony Conran, *The Poets of the Welsh Princes*, p. 47; tr. Joseph P. Clancy, *Medieval Welsh Poems* (2003), p. 140; '**I Ririd Flaidd i ddiolch am Gleddyf**' (The Three Englynion by Cynddelw in Praise of Rhirid), tr. C. A. Ralegh Radford and W. J. Hemp, *Archaeologia Cambrensis*, 108 (1959), 113; '**Marwnad Dygynnelw**' (Elegy for Dygynnelw), tr. Joseph P. Clancy, *The Earliest Welsh Poetry*, p. 147; tr. Dafydd Johnston, *Galar y Beirdd: Marwnadau Plant/Poets' Grief: Medieval Welsh Elegies for Children* (Cardiff: Tafol, 1993), p. 41; tr. Carl Lofmark, *Bards and Heroes*, p. 83; tr. Joseph P. Clancy, *The Poets of the Welsh Princes*, p. 53; tr. Joseph P. Clancy, *Medieval Welsh Poems* (2003), p. 149; '**Marwnad Madog ap Maredudd**' (Lament for Madawg ap Maredudd), tr. Tony Conran, *The Penguin Book of Welsh Verse*, pp. 118–19; tr. Joseph P. Clancy, *The Earliest Welsh Poetry*, pp. 141–2; tr. Tony Conran, *Welsh Verse*, pp. 153–4, tr. Joseph P. Clancy, *Medieval Welsh Poems* (2003), 144–5; '**Marwnad Madog ap Maredudd, Llywelyn ei fab a theulu Powys**' (The Fall of Powys), tr. D. M. Lloyd, *A Book of Wales* (1953), pp. 117–20; tr. Joseph P. Clancy, *The Earliest Welsh Poetry*, pp. 142–3; tr. Joseph P. Clancy, *Medieval Welsh Poems* (2003), pp. 145–7; '**Mawl Owain Cyfeiliog**' (In Praise of Owain Cyfeiliog), tr. Meirion, *The Cambrian Register*, 1 (1795), 411–12; tr. unsigned, *The Cambro-Briton*, 2 (1820/21), 281–2; tr. William Owen Pughe (with some alterations by Thomas Stephens), *The Literature of the Kymry*, pp. 136–8 (1876: pp. 126–7); tr. Robert Gurney, *Bardic Heritage*, pp. 59–60; '**Rhieingerdd Efa ferch Madog ap Maredudd**' (Maiden Song for Efa, daughter of Madog ap Maredudd), tr. Edward Jones, *The Bardic Museum*, p. 40; tr. A. P. Graves, *Welsh Poetry Old and New*, p. 15; tr. Tony Conran, *The Penguin Book of Welsh Verse*, p. 117; tr. Joseph P. Clancy, *The Earliest Welsh Poetry*, pp. 137–41; tr. Tony

Conran, *Welsh Verse*, p. 152; tr. Joseph P. Clancy, *Medieval Welsh Poems* (2003), pp. 141–4; *from* '**Marwnad Owain Gwynedd**' (Elegy on Owain Gwynedd), tr. Sharon Turner, *A Vindication of the Genuiness of the Ancient British Poems of Aneurin, Taliesin, Llywarch Hen and Merdhin, with Specimens of the Poems* (London: Printed for E. Williams, 1803), pp. 46–9; tr. Thomas Stephens, *The Literature of the Kymry*, pp. 132–3 (1876: pp. 121–2); '**Marwysgafn Cynddelw y Gelwir y Pumawdl Hyn**' (These Five Stanzas are called the Deathbed song of Cynddelw), tr. Joseph P. Clancy, *The Earliest Welsh Poetry*, pp. 149–51; tr. Joseph P. Clancy, *Oxford Book*, pp. 27–30; tr. Joseph P. Clancy, *A Book of Wales* (1987), pp. 23–4; tr. Catherine A. McKenna, *The Medieval Welsh Religious Lyric*, pp. 165–9; tr. Joseph P. Clancy, *Medieval Welsh Poems* (2003), pp. 151–3.

DAFYDD BENFRAS (*fl. c.* 1220–58)

Individual Translations
'**Englynion ar fyrder oes dyn**' (The Grave), tr. Thomas Stephens, *The Literature of the Kymry*, p. 160 (1876: p. 150); tr. Joseph P. Clancy, *The Earliest Welsh Poetry*, p. 162; '**I Lywelyn ab Iorwerth**' (To Llywelyn ab Iorwerth), tr. Revd Evan Evans (Ieuan Fardd, Ieuan Brydydd Hir), *Some Specimens of the Poetry of the Ancient Welsh Bards*, pp. 17–19; tr. Revd Rd Williams of Vron, *The Bardic Museum*, pp. 40–1; tr. unsigned, *The Cambro-Briton*, 1 (1820), 470–2; tr. Maurice Roberts, *The Literature of the Kymry*, pp. 157–9 (1876: pp. 147–9); tr. William Owen Pughe, *The Cambrian Journal*, 5 (1858), 36; tr. George Borrow, *Welsh Poems & Ballads*, pp. 133–4; *from* '**Marwnad Llywelyn ab Iorwerth**' (Lament for Llywelyn ab Iorwerth), tr. William Owen Pughe, *The Cambrian Journal*, 5 (1858), 36; *from* '**Marwnad Llywelyn ab Iorwerth a'i Feibion**' (Lament for Llywelyn ab Iorwerth and his Sons), tr. William Owen Pughe, *The Cambrian Journal*, 5 (1858), 37; tr. J. Lloyd-Jones, *A Book of Wales* (1953), p. 315; '**Mawl Dafydd ap Llywelyn**' (From Exile), tr. Tony Conran, *The Penguin Book of Welsh Verse*, p. 127; tr. Tony Conran, *Oxford Book*, p. 30; tr. Tony Conran, *Welsh Verse*, pp. 160–1.

DAFYDD Y COED (*fl.* late fourteenth century)

Individual Translations

'Dafydd y Coed i Hopcyn ap Thomas' (In Praise of Hopkin ap Thomas), tr. Lowri Lloyd, *A Swansea Anthology, ed. James A.* Davies (Bridgend: Seren, 1996), p. 16; 'Rhaeadr Gwy' (The Waterfall), tr. Joseph P. Clancy, *The Earliest Welsh Poetry*, p. 182; tr. Gwyn Williams, *To Look for a Word*, p. 78.

EINION AP GWALCHMAI (*fl.* 1203–23)

Individual Translations

'Awdl a Gant Einion ap Gwalchmai i Dduw' ['Addef nef neirthiad'] (A Poem that Einion ap Gwalchmai Sang to God), tr. Catherine A. McKenna, *The Medieval Welsh Religious Lyric*, pp. 185–7; 'Awdl a Gant Einion ap Gwalchmai i Dduw' ['Peryf nef, pura fy ngheudawd'] (A Poem that Einion ap Gwalchmai Sang to God), tr. Catherine A. McKenna, *The Medieval Welsh Religious Lyric*, pp. 189–91; 'Awdl a Gant Einion ap Gwalchmai i Dduw' ['Duw dewin'] (A Poem that Einion ap Gwalchmai Sang to God), tr. Joseph P. Clancy, *The Earliest Welsh Poetry*, pp. 158–61; tr. Catherine A. McKenna, *The Medieval Welsh Religious Lyric*, pp. 191–7; tr. Joseph P. Clancy, *The Poets of the Welsh Princes*, pp. 50–1; tr. Joseph P. Clancy, *Medieval Welsh Poems* (2003), pp. 162–5; 'Mawl Llywelyn ab Iorwerth' (In Praise of Llewelyn the Great), tr. Robert Gurney, *Bardic Heritage*, pp. 63–4; 'Marwnad Nest ferch Hywel' (Elegy for Nest, daughter of Hywel), tr. Revd Evan Evans (Ieuan Fardd; Ieuan Brydydd Hir), *Some Specimens of the Poetry of the Ancient Welsh Bards*, pp. 27–9; tr. John Walters, *Translated Specimens of Welsh Poetry*, pp. 14–16; tr. Revd Rd Williams, *The Bardic Museum*, pp. 41–2; tr. John Walters, *The Cambrian Wreath*, pp. 96–7; tr. William Owen Pughe, *The Cambrian Journal*, 5 (1858), 37–8; tr. Revd Evan Evans (Ieuan Fardd, Ieuan Brydydd Hir), *The Literature of the Kymry*, pp. 57–9 (1876: pp. 48–51); tr. Tony Conran, *The Penguin Book of Welsh Verse*, pp. 122–5; tr. Robert Gurney, *Bardic Heritage*, pp. 61–2; tr. Joseph P. Clancy, *The Earliest Welsh Poetry*, pp. 157–8; tr. Tony Conran, *Welsh Verse*, pp. 156–7; tr. Joseph P. Clancy, *Medieval Welsh Poems* (2003), pp. 161–2.

EINION AP GWGON (*fl.* 1215)

Individual Translations
'**Mawl Llywelyn ab Iorwerth**' (Address to Llewelyn ab Iorwerth), tr. Revd Evan Evans (Ieuan Fardd; Ieuan Brydydd Hir), *Some Specimens of the Poetry of the Ancient Welsh Bards*, pp. 20–4; tr. Thomas Stephens, *The Literature of the Kymry*, pp. 155–7 (1876: pp. 145–7); tr. Thomas Stephens, *The History of the Literature of Wales*, p. 4.

EINION AP MADOG AP RHAHAWD (*fl.* 1237)

Individual Translations
'**Mawl Gruffudd ap Llywelyn**' (In Praise of Gruffudd ap Llywelyn), tr. Thomas Stephens, *The Literature of the Kymry*, pp. 371–2 (1876: pp. 355–6).

EINION WAN (*fl.* 1200–45)

Individual Translations
'**Marwnad Madog ap Gruffudd**' (Elegy for Madog ap Gruffudd), tr. Thomas Stephens, *The Literature of the Kymry*, pp. 170–2 (1876: pp. 161–3).

ELIDIR SAIS (*fl.* 1195–1246)

Individual Translations
'**Dadolwch Llywelyn ab Iorwerth**' (An Atonement to Llywelyn ab Iorwerth), tr. Sharon Turner, *A Vindication of the Genuiness of the Ancient British Poems of Aneurin, Taliesin, Llywarch Hen and Merdhin, with Specimens of the Poems* (London: Printed for E. Williams, 1803), pp. 69–72; tr. Thomas Stephens, *The Literature of the Kymry*, pp. 160–4 (1876: pp. 150–4).

[Elidir Sais?] ['**Brenhin Gogonhet . . .**'] (It Must Someday be Answered), tr. Thomas Stephens, *The Literature of the Kymry*, pp.

393–5 (1876: pp. 377–9); tr. Tony Conran, *The Penguin Book of Welsh Verse*, pp. 124–5; tr. Tony Conran, *Welsh Verse*, pp. 158–9.[3]

GRUFFUDD AP GWRGENAU (*fl.* end of the twelfth century)

Individual Translations
'Gruffudd ab Gwrgenau a gant yr Englynion hyn i'w gymdeithion' (Lament for his Comrades), tr. Thomas Stephens, *The Literature of the Kymry*, pp. 173–4 (1876: pp. 164–5); tr. Joseph P. Clancy, *Medieval Welsh Poems* (2003), p. 155; '**Marwnad Gruffudd ap Cynan**' (Lament for Gruffudd ap Cynan), tr. Joseph P. Clancy, *Medieval Welsh Poems* (2003), pp. 153–5.

GRUFFUDD AB YR YNAD COCH (*fl.* 1277–82)

Individual Translations
'**Awdl i Dduw**' ['Nawdd y Tad a'r Mab rhad rhof a'm gallon'] ('The protection of the Father and the Son of grace between me and my enemies'), tr. Thomas Stephens, *The Literature of the Kymry*, pp. 402–5 (1876: pp. 386–9); tr. Catherine A. McKenna, *The Medieval Welsh Religious Lyric*, pp. 213–15; '**Awdl i Dduw**' ['Och hyd ar Frenin'] ('Alas to the king of high silent privelege'), tr. Thomas Stephens, *The Literature of the Kymry*, pp. 401–2 (1876: pp. 385–6); tr. Catherine A. McKenna, *The Medieval Welsh Religious Lyric*, pp. 207–9; '**Awdl i Dduw**' ['Ponid gwan truan trymder pechadur'] ('Is not foolish and wretched the sinner's burden'), tr. Catherine A. McKenna, *The Medieval Welsh Religious Lyric*, pp. 209–11; '**Awdl i Dduw**' ['Y Gŵr a'n rhoddes rhiniau ar dafawd'] ('May the hero who gave us spoken mysteries'), tr. Catherine A. McKenna, *The Medieval Welsh Religious Lyric*, pp. 215–19; '**Marwnad Llywelyn ap Gruffudd**' (Elegy on Llywelyn ap Gruffudd), tr. Revd Rd. Williams, *The Bardic Museum*, p. 42; tr. William Owen Pughe, *The Cambrian Journal*, 5

---

[3] Recent scholarship points to this poem having been mistakenly attributed to Elidir Sais by the editors of the *Myvyrian Archaiology*, and subsequently by various translators. Closer inspection of the Red Book of Hergest would seem to suggest Gruffudd ab yr Ynad Goch as the most likely author. See *Gwaith Meilyr Brydydd a'i Ddisgynyddion*, ed. J. E. Caerwyn Williams (Cardiff: University of Wales Press, 1994), pp. 318–19.

(1858), 40; tr. Thomas Stephens and Jones, *The Literature of the Kymry*, pp. 386–91 (1876: pp. 370–5); tr. Revd K. Williams, *The History of the Literature of Wales*, pp. 9–10; tr. Kenneth Hurlstone Jackson, *A Celtic Miscellany* (1951), pp. 251–3 (1971: pp. 229–31); tr. Gwyn Williams, *Introduction to Welsh Poetry*, p. 93; tr. Gwyn Williams, *The Burning Tree*, pp. 81–5; tr. H. Idris Bell, *A History of Welsh Literature*, p. 54; tr. Tony Conran, *The Penguin Book of Welsh Verse*, pp. 128–31; tr. Joseph P. Clancy, *The Earliest Welsh Poetry*, pp. 174–5; tr. Gwyn Williams, *Welsh Poems: Sixth Century to 1600*, pp. 46–8; tr. Gwyn Williams, *To Look for a Word*, pp. 44–6; tr. Joseph P. Clancy, *Llywelyn 1282* (Newtown: Gwasg Gregynog, 1982); tr. Joseph P. Clancy, *Oxford Book*, pp. 31–3; tr. Tony Conran, *Welsh Verse*, pp. 161–4; tr. Joseph P. Clancy, *A Book of Wales* (1987), pp. 89–91; tr. Gwyn Williams, *Materion Dwyieithog: Bilingual Matters*, 1 (1989), 7–9; tr. Tony Conran, *Materion Dwyieithog: Bilingual Matters*, 1 (1989), 10–11; tr. Greg Hill, *Materion Dwyieithog: Bilingual Matters*, 1 (1989), 12–13; tr. Carl Lofmark, *Bards and Heroes*, pp. 85–7; tr. Tony Conran, *The Poets of the Welsh Princes*, pp. 36–9; tr. Greg Hill, *Agenda*, 36.3 (1998), 13–15; tr. Patrick K. Ford, *The Celtic Poets*, pp. 204–7; tr. Joseph P. Clancy, *Medieval Welsh Poems* (2003), pp. 171–4.

GRUFFUDD AP DAFYDD AP TUDUR (*fl.* 1300)

Individual Translations
'I Ferch' (The Wordless Girl), tr. Joseph P. Clancy, *The Earliest Welsh Poetry*, pp. 176–9; tr. Joseph P. Clancy, *Medieval Welsh Poems* (2003), pp. 180–3.

GRUFFUDD AP MAREDUDD AP DAFYDD (*fl.* 1346–82)

Individual Translations
'Marwnad Gwenhwyfar' (Lament for Gwenhwyfar), tr. H. Idris Bell, *A Celtic Anthology*, p. 272; tr. Gwyn Williams, *To Look for a Word*, p. 77; tr. Tony Conran, *The Penguin Book of Welsh Verse*, pp. 135–6; tr. Joseph P. Clancy, *The Earliest Welsh Poetry*, 183–8; tr. Tony Conran, *Welsh Verse*, pp. 167–9; tr. H. Idris Bell, *The Bardic Source Book*, p. 245; tr. Joseph P. Clancy, *Medieval Welsh Poems* (2003), pp. 256–61.

GWALCHMAI AP MEILYR (*fl.* 1130–80)

Individual Translations
'**Arwyrain Madog ap Maredudd**' (In Praise of Madawg), tr.
unsigned, *The Cambro-Briton*, 2 (1820/21), 460–1; '**Arwyrain Owain
Gwynedd**' ['Arddwyreaf-i hael o hil Gruffudd'] (In Praise of King
Owain Gwynedd), tr. unsigned, *The Cambro-Briton*, 2 (1820/21),
184–5; tr. Robert Gurney, *Bardic Heritage*, pp. 33–4; '**Arwyrain
Owain Gwynedd**' ['Arddwyreaf hael o hil Iago'] (In Praise of King
Owain Gwynedd), tr. Robert Gurney, *Bardic Heritage*, p. 32;
'**Arwyrain Owain Gwynedd**' ['Arddwyreaf hael o hil Rhodri'] (The
Battle of Tal Moelfre), tr. Meirion, *Cambrian Register*, 1 (1795),
409–10; tr. Revd Evan Evans (Ieuan Fardd; Ieuan Brydydd Hir),
Some Specimens of the Poetry of the Ancient Welsh Bards, pp. 25–6;
tr. Edward Jones, *The Bardic Museum*, p. 36; tr. J. Humphreys Parry, *The
Cambro-Briton*, 1 (1820), 231–3; tr. J. Humphreys Parry, *Archaeologia
Cambrensis*, 3 (1848), 75; tr. J. Humphreys Parry (revised by Thomas
Stephens), *The Literature of the Kymry*, pp. 26–8 (1876: pp. 18–19);
tr. Thomas Gray, *Land of My Fathers*, pp. 34–5; tr. Kenneth
Hurlstone Jackson, *A Celtic Miscellany* (1951), p. 254 (1971: pp.
231–2); tr. Thomas Gray, *Presenting Welsh Poetry*, pp. 25–6; tr. Tony
Conran, *The Penguin Book of Welsh Verse*, pp. 105–6; tr. Joseph P.
Clancy, *The Earliest Welsh Poetry*, p. 119; tr. Tony Conran, *Welsh
Verse*, pp. 142–3; tr. Tony Conran, *The Poets of the Welsh Princes*,
pp. 24–5 (1978: 25–6); tr. Carl Lofmark, *Bards and Heroes*, pp. 74–5;
tr. Tony Conran, *The Poets of the Welsh Princes*, pp. 24–5 (1978:
pp. 25–6); tr. Thomas Gray, *An Anglesey Anthology*, ed. Dewi
Roberts (Gwasg Carreg Gwalch, 1999), pp. 60–1; tr. Joseph P.
Clancy, *Medieval Welsh Poems* (2003), pp. 127–8; '**Arwyrain Owain
Gwynedd**' ['Arddwyreaf hael o hil Eneas'] (Plea for Reconciliation),
tr. Tony Conran, *The Penguin Book of Welsh Verse*, pp. 106–7; tr.
Tony Conran, *Welsh Verse*, pp. 143–4; tr. Joseph P. Clancy, *Medieval
Welsh Poems* (2003), pp. 128–9; '**Breuddwyd Gwalchmai**'
(Gwalchmai's Dream), tr. Robert Gurney, *Bardic Heritage*, pp. 36–7;
tr. Joseph P. Clancy, *Medieval Welsh Poems* (2003), pp. 129–30;
'**Canu a Gant Gwalchmai ap Meilyr i Dduw**' (A Poem that
Gwalchmai ap Meilyr Sang to God), tr. Catherine A. McKenna,
The Medieval Welsh Religious Lyric, pp. 157–63; *from* '**Gorhoffedd**'
(Gwalchmai's Boast), tr. R. W., in Thomas Pennant, *A Tour in
Wales Vol. II* (London: Benjamin White, 1784), p. 399; tr. Thomas

Stephens, *The Literature of the Kymry*, pp. 24–5 (1876: pp. 16–17); tr. A. P. Graves, *Welsh Poetry Old and New*, pp. 16–17; tr. H. Idris Bell, *A Celtic Anthology*, pp. 261–2; tr. J. Lloyd-Jones, *The Court Poets of the Welsh Princes*, pp. 23–4; tr. D. M. Lloyd, *A Book of Wales* (1953), pp. 310–11; tr. Gwyn Williams, *The Burning Tree*, pp. 53–9; tr. Robert Gurney, *Bardic Heritage*, pp. 24–9; tr. Tony Conran, *The Penguin Book of Welsh Verse*, pp. 104–5; tr. Joseph P. Clancy, *The Earliest Welsh Poetry*, pp. 119–23; tr. Gwyn Williams, *Welsh Poems: Sixth Century to 1600*, pp. 32–5; tr. Gwyn Williams, *To Look for a Word*, pp. 39–42; tr. Tony Conran, *Welsh Verse*, pp. 141–2; tr. Carl Lofmark, *Bards and Heroes*, pp. 74–5; tr. Tony Conran, *Love from Wales: An Anthology*, ed. Tony Curtis and Siân James (Bridgend: Seren Books, 1991), p. 25; tr. H. Idris Bell, *The Bardic Source Book*, p. 240; tr. Patrick K. Ford, *The Celtic Poets*, pp. 212–17; tr. Joseph P. Clancy, *Medieval Welsh Poems* (2003), pp. 124–7; *from* '**Marwnad Madog ap Maredudd**' (Elegy for Madawg ap Maredudd Prince of Powys), tr. Robert Gurney, *Bardic Heritage*, p. 36; '**Mawl Dafydd ab Owain**' (Ode to Davydd ab Owain), tr. unsigned, *The Cambro-Briton*, 3 (1821/22), 182–5; tr. Robert Gurney, *Bardic Heritage*, p. 35.

GWILYM DDU O ARFON (*fl.* 1280–1320)

Individual Translations

'**Awdl y Misoedd**' (The Ode of the Months), tr. Revd Evan Evans (Ieuan Fardd, Ieuan Brydydd Hir), *Some Specimens of the Poetry of the Ancient Welsh Bards*, pp. 47–50; tr. John Walters, *Translated Specimens of Welsh Poetry*, pp. 21–4; tr. Richard Llwyd, *Poems, Tales, Odes, Sonnets, Translations from the British*, pp. 53–64; tr. Thomas Stephens, *The Literature of the Kymry*, pp. 465–7 (1876: pp. 445–8); '**I Syr Gruffudd Llwyd pan oedd yng ngharchar yng Nghastell Rhuddlan**' (To Sir Gruffudd Lloyd), tr. Richard Llwyd, *The Cambrian Wreath*, pp. 119–24; tr. William Owen Pughe, *The Cambrian Journal*, 5 (1858), 105; '**Marwnad Trahaearn Brydydd Mawr**' (An Elegy on Trahaiarn the Poet, the Son of Gronwy), tr. Thomas Stephens, *The Literature of the Kymry*, pp. 469–71 (1876: pp. 449–51).

GWYNFARDD BRYCHEINIOG (*fl.* 1170)

Individual Translations
'**Canu i Ddewi Sant**' (Ode to Saint David), tr. Edward Davies, *The Mythology and Rites of the British Druids*, p. 141; tr. Thomas Stephens, *The Literature of the Kymry*, pp. 164–5 (1876: pp. 154–5).

HYWEL AB EINION LYGLIW (*fl.* 1330–70)

Individual Translations
'**Myfanwy Fechan**' (A Love Song for Myfanwy Fechan), tr. Revd Evan Evans (Ieuan Fardd, Ieuan Brydydd Hir), *Some Specimens of the Poetry of the Ancient Welsh Bards*, pp. 14–16; tr. R. W., *The Cambrian Wreath*, p. 101; tr. A. P. Graves, *Welsh Poetry Old and New*, pp. 18–21; tr. Joseph P. Clancy, *The Earliest Welsh Poetry*, pp. 180–1.

HYWEL AB OWAIN GWYNEDD (*fl.* 1140–70)

Individual Translations
'**Awdl i Ferch**' ['Caraf-i amser haf . . .'] (In Summer), tr. Edward Davies, *The Mythology and Rites of the British Druids*, pp. 284–5; tr. J. Humphreys Parry, *The Cambro-Briton*, 2 (1820/21), 136–7; tr. M. C. Ll., *Archaeologia Cambrensis*, 1 (1846), 440–1; tr. Thomas Stephens, *The Literature of the Kymry*, pp. 121–2 (1876: pp. 111–12); tr. Gwyn Williams, *The Burning Tree*, p. 67; tr. Joseph P. Clancy, *The Earliest Welsh Poetry*, p. 129; tr. Gwyn Williams, *Welsh Poems: Sixth Century to 1600*, p. 39; tr. Gwyn Williams, *To Look for a Word*, p. 35; tr. Joseph P. Clancy, *Medieval Welsh Poems* (2003), p. 134; '**Awdl i Ferch**' ['Caraf-i gaer falchwaith . . .'] (Desire), tr. Edward Davies, *The Mythology and Rites of the British Druids*, p. 286; tr. M. C. Ll., *Archaeologia Cambrensis*, 1 (1846), 440; tr. William Owen Pughe, *The Literature of the Kymry*, pp. 120–1 (1876: pp. 110–11); tr. William Owen Pughe, *The Cambrian Journal*, 5 (1858), 32; tr. Gwyn Williams, *The Burning Tree*, p. 69; tr. Joseph P. Clancy, *The Earliest Welsh Poetry*, p. 130; tr. Gwyn Williams, *Welsh Poems: Sixth Century to 1600*, p. 40; tr. Gwyn Williams, *To Look for a Word*, p. 36; tr. Carl Lofmark, *Bards and Heroes*, pp. 77–8; tr. Joseph P. Clancy, *Medieval Welsh Poems* (2003), p. 135; '**Awdl i Ferch**' ['As unaswn i

heddiw . . .'] (Rejection), tr. M. C. Ll., *Archaeologia Cambrensis*, 1 (1846), 440; tr. Gwyn Williams, *The Burning Tree*, p. 71; tr. Gwyn Williams, *Welsh Poems: Sixth Century to 1600*, p. 41; tr. Gwyn Williams, *To Look for a Word*, p. 36; tr. Joseph P. Clancy, *Medieval Welsh Poems* (2003), p. 135–6; '**Awdl i Ferch**' ['Fy newis i'] (Hywel's Choice), tr. Meirion, *The Cambrian Register*, 1 (1795), 412–13; tr. Edward Jones, *The Bardic Museum*, p. 38; tr. J. Humphreys Parry, *The Cambro-Briton*, 1 (1820), 312; tr. J. Humphreys Parry, *The Cambrian Wreath*, pp. 117–18; tr. M. C. Ll., *Archaeologia Cambrensis*, 1 (1846), 275–6; tr. Mrs Llewelyn, *The Literature of the Kymry*, pp. 55–6 (1876: p. 47); tr. A. P. Graves, *Welsh Poetry Old and New*, p. 14; tr. H. Idris Bell, *A Celtic Anthology*, pp. 262–3; tr. J. Lloyd-Jones, *The Court Poets of the Welsh Princes*, p. 26; tr. Gwyn Williams, *Introduction to Welsh Poetry*, pp. 80–1; tr. J. Lloyd-Jones, *A Book of Wales* (1953), p. 311; tr. H. Idris Bell, *A History of Welsh Literature*, pp. 59–60; tr. Gwyn Williams, *The Burning Tree*, p. 73; tr. Gwyn Williams, *Presenting Welsh Poetry*, p. 27; tr. Tony Conran, *The Penguin Book of Welsh Verse*, pp. 110–11; tr. Robert Gurney, *Bardic Heritage*, p. 43; tr. Joseph P. Clancy, *The Earliest Welsh Poetry*, pp. 130–1; tr. Gwyn Williams, *Welsh Poems: Sixth Century to 1600*, p. 42; tr. Gwyn Williams, *To Look for a Word*, p. 37; tr. Tony Conran, *Welsh Verse*, pp. 147–8; tr. Carl Lofmark, *Bards and Heroes*, p. 78; tr. J. Lloyd-Jones, *The Poets of the Welsh Princes*, p. 48 (1978: p. 41); tr. H. Idris Bell, *The Bardic Source Book*, p. 241; tr. Joseph P. Clancy, *Medieval Welsh Poems* (2003), p. 134; '**Awdl i Ferch**' ['Caraf-i gaer wenglaer . . .'] (Complaint), tr. M. C. Ll., *Archaeologia Cambrensis*, 1 (1846), 439; tr. William Owen Pughe, *The Cambrian Journal*, 5 (1858), 31; tr. William Owen Pughe, *The Literature of the Kymry*, pp. 119–20 (1876: pp. 109–10); tr. Gwyn Williams, *The Burning Tree*, p. 75; tr. Joseph P. Clancy, *The Earliest Welsh Poetry*, pp. 129–30; tr. Gwyn Williams, *To Look for a Word*, p. 37; tr. Joseph P. Clancy, *Medieval Welsh Poems* (2003), 135; '**Dathlu Buddugoliaeth Gwynedd**' ['Pan fyddai brain yn llawen . . .'] (The Battle of Tal Moelfre), tr. Edward Jones, *The Bardic Museum*, p. 36; tr. Thomas Stephens, *The Literature of the Kymry*, p. 47 (1876: p. 38); tr. Gwyn Williams, *The Burning Tree*, p. 77; tr. Joseph P. Clancy, *The Earliest Welsh Poetry*, p. 131; tr. Gwyn Williams, *Welsh Poems: Sixth Century to 1600*, p. 44; tr. Gwyn Williams, *To Look for a Word*, p. 38; tr. Carl Lofmark, *Bards and Heroes*, p. 77; tr. Joseph P. Clancy, *Medieval Welsh Poems* (2003), p. 136; '**Dathlu Buddugoliaeth**

Gwynedd' ['Pan uchel uched, pan achubed-Ffrainc . . .'], tr. Gwyn Williams, *Welsh Poems: Sixth Century to 1600*, p. 45; tr. Gwyn Williams, *To Look for a Word*, p. 38; *from* '**Gorhoffedd**' ['Ton wen orewyn a orwlych bedd'] (Hywel's Boast of his Country),[4] tr. Edward Jones, *The Bardic Museum*, p. 37; tr. Thomas Stephens, *The Literature of the Kymry*, pp. 51–3 (1876: pp. 42–4); tr. Ernest Rhys, *Transactions of the Honourable Society of Cymmrodorion* (1892–3), 43; tr. A. P. Graves, *Land of my Fathers*, p. 40; tr. unsigned, in Edward Thomas, *Wales* (London: A & C Black Ltd [1924]), pp. 174–5; tr. unsigned, *A Celtic Anthology*, p. 262; tr. J. Lloyd-Jones, *The Court Poets of the Welsh Princes*, pp. 22–3; tr. Gwyn Williams, *Introduction to Welsh Poetry*, p. 82; tr. D. M. Lloyd, *A Book of Wales* (1953) pp. 72–3; tr. Tony Conran, *The Penguin Book of Welsh Verse*, pp. 108–10; tr. Gwyn Williams, *The Burning Tree*, pp. 61–3; tr. Edward Thomas [?], *Transactions of the Honourable Society of Cymmrodorion* (1968), 59–60; tr. Joseph P. Clancy, *The Earliest Welsh Poetry*, pp. 131–2; tr. Gwyn Williams, *Welsh Poems: Sixth Century to 1600*, pp. 36–7; tr. Gwyn Williams, *To Look for a Word*, pp. 32–3; tr. Gwyn Williams, *Oxford Book*, pp. 21–2; tr. Tony Conran, *Welsh Verse*, pp. 145–6; tr. Gwyn Williams, *A Book of Wales* (1987), pp. 117–18; tr. unsigned, *The Bardic Source Book*, p. 240; tr. Patrick K. Ford, *The Celtic Poets*, pp. 209–10; tr. Joseph P. Clancy, *Medieval Welsh Poems* (2003), pp. 136–7; '**Gorhoffedd**' ['Cyfarchaf ddewin gwerthefin'] (In Praise of Fair Women), tr. Thomas Stephens, *The Literature of the Kymry*, pp. 54–5 (1876: pp. 45–6); tr. Gwyn Williams, *Introduction to Welsh Poetry*, p. 83; tr. Tony Conran, *The Penguin Book of Welsh Verse*, p. 110; tr. Gwyn Williams, *The Burning Tree*, pp. 63–5; tr. Joseph P. Clancy, *The Earliest Welsh Poetry*, pp. 133–4; tr. Gwyn Williams, *Welsh Poems: Sixth Century to 1600*, pp. 37–8; tr. Gwyn Williams, *To Look for a Word*, pp. 33–4; tr. Gwyn Williams, *Oxford Book*, pp. 23–4; tr. Tony Conran, *Welsh Verse*, pp. 146–7; tr. Carl Lofmark, *Bards and Heroes*, p. 79; tr. Dannie Abse, *A Welsh Retrospective* (Bridgend: Seren, 1997), p. 28; tr. Patrick K. Ford, *The Celtic Poets*, pp. 210–11; tr. Joseph P. Clancy, *Medieval Welsh Poems* (2003), pp. 137–8.

---

[4] Some translators and academics treat the two elements of Hywel's 'Gorhoffedd' as separate poems, one about his country and the other about women. However some translate the two subjects as one poem and separate page numbers have been recorded when this has been the case.

HYWEL FOEL AP GRIFFRI AP PWYLL WYDDEL (*c.* 1240–1300)

Individual Translations
'Gofyn am ryddid i Owain ap Gruffudd' ['Gwr yssyt yn twr yn hir westi'] (The Imprisonment of Owain), tr. unsigned, in G. N. Wright, *Scenes in North Wales* (London: Printed for T. T. and J. Tegg, Cheapside, 1833), pp. 56–7; tr. Thomas Stephens, *The Literature of the Kymry*, pp. 379–81 (1876: pp. 362–5).

IORWERTH FYCHAN (*fl.* 1290)

Individual Translations
'I Weirfyl' (A Love Poem for Gweirfyl), tr. Joseph P. Clancy, *The Earliest Welsh Poetry*, pp. 174–5; tr. Joseph P. Clancy, *Medieval Welsh Poems* (2003), pp. 179–80.

LLYGAD GŴR (*fl.* 1258–92/3)

Individual Translations
'Mawl Llywelyn ap Gruffudd' (In Praise of Llywelyn ap Gruffudd), tr. Revd Evan Evans (Ieuan Fardd, Ieuan Brydydd Hir), *Some Specimens of the Poetry of the Ancient Welsh Bards*, pp. 38–44; tr. Richard Llwyd, *Poems, Tales, Odes, Sonnets, Translations from the British*, pp. 177–83; tr. unsigned, *The Cambrian Register*, 3 (1818), 506–12; tr. Richard Llwyd, *The Cambrian Wreath*, pp. 104–7; tr. John Thomas (Ieuan Ddu), *The Literature of the Kymry*, pp. 362–70 (1876: pp. 346–54); tr. Revd Evan Evans (Ieuan Fardd, Ieuan Brydydd Hir), *The Red Dragon*, 2 (1882), 256; tr. Charles Wilkins, *The History of the Literature of Wales*, pp. 2–3; tr. Joseph P. Clancy, *The Earliest Welsh Poetry*, p. 167.

LLYWARCH AP LLYWELYN (Prydydd y Moch; *fl.* 1174/5–1200)

Individual Translations

'**Awdl yr Haearn Twym**' (Ordeal by Hot Iron), tr. unsigned, *The Cambrian Journal*, 6 (1858), 94; tr. Thomas Stephens, *The Literature of the Kymry*, p. 142 (1876: pp. 131–2); tr. Patrick K. Ford, *The Celtic Poets*, pp. 244–5; tr. Joseph P. Clancy, *Medieval Welsh Poems* (2003), p. 157; '**Bwgwth Dafydd ab Owain o Wynedd**' (The Threat of Dafydd ab Owain Gwynedd), tr. Gwyn Williams, *Introduction to Welsh Poetry*, p. 88; tr. Joseph P. Clancy, *The Earliest Welsh Poetry*, pp. 153–5; tr. Patrick K. Ford, *The Celtic Poets*, pp. 229–30; tr. Joseph P. Clancy, *Medieval Welsh Poems* (2003), pp. 157–9; '**Bygwth Gruffudd ap Cynan**' (A Threat to Gruffudd ap Cynan), tr. Patrick K. Ford, *The Celtic Poets*, pp. 231–2; '**Gofyn am iachâd i Fadog ap Gruffudd Maelor**' (A Prayer for the Health of Madog ap Gruffudd), tr. Patrick K. Ford, *The Celtic Poets*, pp. 242–3; '**Marwnad Gruffudd ap Cynan**' (An Elegy for Gruffudd ap Cynan), tr. Patrick K. Ford, *The Celtic Poets*, pp. 235–7; '**Mawl Gruffudd ap Cynan**' (In Praise of Gruffudd ap Cynan), tr. Patrick K. Ford, *The Celtic Poets*, pp. 233–4; '**Mawl Gwenllïan ferch Hywel**' (A Love Song for Gwenllian), tr. A. P. Graves, *Welsh Poetry Old and New*, p. 18; tr. Joseph P. Clancy, *The Earliest Welsh Poetry*, pp. 152–3; tr. Patrick K. Ford, *The Celtic Poets*, pp. 225–7; tr. Joseph P. Clancy, *Medieval Welsh Poems* (2003), pp. 156–7; '**Mawl Llywelyn ab Iorwerth o Wynedd**' ['Crist Creawdwr . . .'] (Address to Llewelyn ab Iorwerth), tr. Sharon Turner, *A Vindication of the Genuiness of the Ancient British Poems*, pp. 66–7; tr. Revd Evan Evans (Ieuan Fardd, Ieuan Brydydd Hir), *Some Specimens of the Poetry of the Ancient Welsh Bards*, pp. 30–7; tr. Thomas Stephens, *The Literature of the Kymry*, pp. 139–40 (1876: pp. 128–30); '**Mawl Llywelyn ab Iorwerth o Wynedd**' ['Nad dig trist i'r rhai . . .'] (In Praise of Llywelyn ab Iorwerth), tr. Joseph P. Clancy, *The Earliest Welsh Poetry*, pp. 155–6; tr. Joseph P. Clancy, *Medieval Welsh Poems* (2003), pp. 159–60; '**Mawl Llywelyn ab Iorwerth o Wynedd**' ['A'th fendicwy Dwy Dëyrn . . .'] (In Praise of Llywelyn ap Iorwerth: 1), tr. Patrick K. Ford, *The Celtic Poets*, pp. 238–9; '**Mawl Llywelyn ab Iorwerth o Wynedd**' ['Neu'm dydd cer elfydd Elwy . . .'] (In Praise of Llywelyn ap Iorwerth: 2), tr. Patrick K. Ford, *The Celtic Poets*, pp. 240–1; '**Mawl Llywelyn ab Iorwerth o Wynedd**' ['Dybryd in' veirdd byd . . .'], tr. William Owen Pughe, *The Cambrian*

Journal, 5 (1858), 35; *from* '**Mawl Rhodri ab Owain**' (Ode to Rhodri ap Owain), tr. Gwyn Williams, *An Introduction to Welsh Poetry*, p. 91; '**Mawl Rhys Grug**' (To Rhys Gryg, Prince of South Wales), tr. Thomas Stephens, *The Literature of the Kymry*, pp. 148–55 (1876: pp. 138–44).

LLYWELYN FARDD (*fl.* 1125–1200)

Individual Translations
'**Arwyddion cyn dydd Brawd**' (The signs before Judgement Day), tr. Thomas Stephens, *The Literature of the Kymry*, pp. 396–8 (1876: pp. 380–2).

MADOG AP GWALLTER (*fl.* second half of the thirteenth century)

Individual Translations
'**I Dduw**' (Ode to God), tr. Thomas Stephens, *The Literature of the Kymry*, pp. 408–10 (1876: pp. 392–5); tr. Charles Wilkins, *The History of the Literature of Wales*, pp. 15–17; tr. Catherine A. McKenna, *The Medieval Welsh Religious Lyric*, pp. 199–203; '**Geni Iesu**' (The Nativity), tr. Thomas Stephens, *The Literature of the Kymry*, pp. 406–8 (1876: pp. 390–2); tr. Charles Wilkins, *The History of the Literature of Wales*, pp. 15–17; tr. H. Idris Bell, *A History of Welsh Literature*, pp. 56–7; tr. Joseph P. Clancy, *The Earliest Welsh Poetry*, pp. 163–6; tr. Joseph P. Clancy, *Medieval Welsh Poems* (2003), pp. 165–8.

MADOG DWYGRAIG (*fl.* 1370–80)

Individual Translations
['Gwrach gallawdyr . . .'] (Old Hag), tr. Gwyn Williams, *Introduction to Welsh Poetry*, p. 129; tr. Gwyn Williams, *To Look for a Word*, p. 77.[5]

---

[5] In the *Red Book of Hergest* there are seven untitled *englynion* that begin with the word 'gwrach'. Williams here translates one of these.

MEILYR BRYDYDD (*fl.* 1100–57)

Individual Translations

'Cerdd Ddarogan Meilyr', tr. Thomas Stephens, *The Literature of the Kymry*, p. 20 (1876: p. 11); '**Marwnad Gruffudd ap Cynan**' (Elegy for Gruffudd ap Cynan), tr. Robert Gurney, *Bardic Heritage*, pp. 12–14; tr. Patrick K. Ford, *The Celtic Poets*, pp. 195–9; '**Marwysgafn Feilyr Brydydd**' (The Deathbed Song of Meilyr Brydydd), tr. Meirion, *The Cambrian Register*, 1 (1795), 406–7; tr. Thomas Stephens, *The Literature of the Kymry*, pp. 21–3 (1876: pp. 13–15); tr. A. P. Graves, *Welsh Poetry Old and New*, p. 15; tr. J. Lloyd-Jones, *The Court Poets of the Welsh Princes*, p. 17; tr. Gwyn Williams, *Introduction to Welsh Poetry*, p. 73; tr. J. Lloyd-Jones, *A Book of Wales* (1953), pp. 86–7; tr. Gwyn Williams, *The Burning Tree*, pp. 47–9; tr. Tony Conran, *The Penguin Book of Welsh Verse*, pp. 102–3; tr. Robert Gurney, *Bardic Heritage*, p. 17; tr. Joseph P. Clancy, *The Earliest Welsh Poetry*, pp. 117–18; tr. Gwyn Williams, *Welsh Poems: Sixth Century to 1600*, pp. 29–30; tr. Gwyn Williams, *To Look for a Word*, pp. 30–1; tr. Joseph P. Clancy, *Oxford Book*, pp. 20–1; tr. Tony Conran, *Welsh Verse*, pp. 139–41; tr. J. Lloyd-Jones, *The Poets of the Welsh Princes*, pp. 51–2 (1978: p. 43); tr. Catherine A. McKenna, *The Medieval Welsh Religious Lyric*, pp. 155–7; tr. Joseph P. Clancy, *Medieval Welsh Poems* (2003), p. 123.

MEILYR AP GWALCHMAI (*fl.* 1170–1220)

Individual Translations

'**Awdl i Dduw**' ['A'm bo i gan Dduw'] ('May I have from God, may I have mercy'), tr. Catherine A. McKenna, *The Medieval Welsh Religious Lyric*, pp. 171–3; '**Awdl i Dduw**' ['Duw Arglwydd, erglyw Dy foliant'] ('Lord God, hear Your praise'), tr. Catherine A. McKenna, *The Medieval Welsh Religious Lyric*, pp. 177–9; '**Awdl i Dduw**' ['Rhëen rhieddawg rhwysg rhyferthi'] ('Royal lord, ruler of tempests'), tr. Robert Gurney, *Bardic Heritage*, p. 65 (only 10 lines); tr. Catherine A. McKenna, *The Medieval Welsh Religious Lyric*, pp. 179–85; '**Awdl i Dduw**' ['Rheitiaf oedd imi, rheitaf i'm bywyd'] ('It was most needful to me, most needful to my life'), tr. Catherine A. McKenna, *The Medieval Welsh Religious Lyric*, pp. 173–5.

OWAIN AP GRUFFUDD AP MAREDUDD (Owain Cyfeiliog; *c.* 1128–97)[6]

Individual Translations
'**Englynion Cylchu**' (The Circuit Through Powys), tr. R. Fenton, *The Literature of the Kymry*, pp. 41–5 (1876: pp. 32–6); tr. Robert Gurney, *Bardic Heritage*, pp. 49–50; '**Hirlas Owain**' (The Drinking-Horn), tr. Revd Evan Evans (Ieuan Fardd, Ieuan Brydydd Hir), *Some Specimens of the Poetry of the Ancient Welsh Bards*, pp. 7–13; tr. R. W., in Thomas Pennant, *A Tour in Wales Vol. II* (London: Benjamin White, 1784), pp. 301–7; tr. R. W. [but printed as Thomas Pennant], *The Musical, Poetical, and Historical Relicks*, pp. 43–4; tr. Sharon Turner, *A Vindication of the Genuiness of the Ancient British Poems*, p. 57; tr. R. W., *The Cambrian Wreath*, pp. 107–13; tr. Sharon Turner (with alterations by Thomas Stephens), *The Literature of the Kymry*, pp. 38–41 (1876: pp. 29–32); tr. T. Gwynn Jones, *Y Cymmrodor*, 32 (1922), 47–57; tr. T. Gwynn Jones, *A Book of Wales* (1953), pp. 312–14; tr. Tony Conran, *The Penguin Book of Welsh Verse*, pp. 114–16; tr. Robert Gurney, *Bardic Heritage*, pp. 51–6; tr. Joseph P. Clancy, *The Earliest Welsh Poetry*, pp. 124–8; tr. Tony Conran, *Welsh Verse*, pp. 149–51; tr. Joseph P. Clancy, *Medieval Welsh Poems* (2003), pp. 130–3.

PERYF AP CEDIFOR WYDDEL (*fl.* 1170)

Individual Translations
'**Lladd Brodyr Maeth Hywel ab Owain**' (The Killing of Hywel ab Owain and his Foster-Brothers),[7] [with 'Caradawg fab Cedifor'] tr.

---

[6] Recent scholarship has raised grave doubts over the validity of attributing these poems to Owain Cyfeiliog. See Gruffydd Aled Williams, 'Owain Cyfeiliog: Bardd-dywysog?', in *Beirdd a Thywysogion: Barddoniaeth Llys yng Nghymru, Iwerddon a'r Alban*, ed. Morfydd E. Owen and Brynley F. Roberts (Cardiff: University of Wales Press, 1996), pp. 180–201.

[7] There are six stanzas in this elegy which describe the killing of Hywel and his brothers, but there is an additional stanza naming Caradawg which appears in a different metre. Many scholars and translators view this as a misplaced stanza and therefore do not include it with the other six. Some translators have translated the six followed by the Caradawg verse and this is indicated above.

Thomas Stephens, *The Literature of the Kymry*, pp. 49–50 (1876: pp. 40–1); [with 'Caradawg fab Cedifor'] tr. Ifor Williams, *Anglesey Antiquarian Society and Field Club Transactions* (1923), 56; tr. Kenneth H. Jackson, *A Celtic Miscellany*, (1951) pp. 254–5 (1971: p. 232); tr. Tony Conran, *The Penguin Book of Welsh Verse*, pp. 112–13; tr. Carl Lofmark, *Bards and Heroes*, pp. 80–1; tr. Joseph P. Clancy, *The Earliest Welsh Poetry*, p. 135; tr. Tony Conran, *Welsh Verse*, pp. 148–9; tr. Tony Conran, *The Poets of the Welsh Princes*, pp. 27–8; tr. Joseph P. Clancy, *Medieval Welsh Poems* (2003), p. 139; 'Marwnad Hywel ab Owain' (Elegy for Hywel ab Owain), tr. Ifor Williams, *Anglesey Antiquarian Society and Field Club Transactions* (1923), pp. 51–5; tr. Robert Gurney, *Bardic Heritage*, pp. 46–7.

PHYLIP BRYDYDD (c. 1222)

Individual Translations
'Dadolwch Rhys Gryg' (The Poet Phylip's appeal to his Lord Rhys Gryg), tr. Thomas Stephens, *The Literature of the Kymry*, pp. 166–70 (1876: pp. 156–61); tr. Robert Gurney, *Bardic Heritage*, p. 66.

SYPYN CYFEILIOG (Dafydd Bach ap Madog Wladaidd; *fl. c.*1340–*c.* 1390)

Individual Translations
'Croeso mewn Llys' (Christmas Revels), tr. Joseph P. Clancy, *The Earliest Welsh Poetry*, p. 189; tr. Joseph P. Clancy, *Oxford Book*, p. 34; tr. Gwyn Williams, *To Look for a Word*, p. 64; tr. Joseph P. Clancy, *Medieval Welsh Poems* (2003), pp. 254–5; 'Cywydd Serch' (To a Girl), tr. Gwyn Williams, *To Look for a Word*, pp. 62–3.

Y PRYDYDD BYCHAN (*fl.* 1222–68)

Individual Translations
'Marwnad Rhys Gryg' (Elegy for Rhys Gryg), tr. Tony Conran, *The Penguin Book of Welsh Verse*, p. 126; tr. Tony Conran, *Welsh Verse*, pp. 159–60; 'Englynion a gant y Prydydd Bychan o Ddeheubarth i Owain Goch fab Gruffudd ap Llywelyn' (Englynion: Sung by the

Prydydd Bychan, of South Wales, to Owen the Red, son of Gruffydd ab Llywelyn), tr. Thomas Stephens, *The Literature of the Kymry*, pp. 373–5 (1876: pp. 357–9); tr. unsigned, *The History of the Literature of Wales*, p. 6.

BEIRDD YR UCHELWYR:
MEDIEVAL POETRY

Critical Editions

Catherine A. McKenna, *The Medieval Welsh Religious Lyric* (Belmont, Massachusetts: Ford & Bailie, 1991).
[*The Medieval Welsh Religious Lyric*]

Anthologies

Joseph P. Clancy, *Medieval Welsh Lyrics* (London: St. Martin's Press, 1965).
[*Medieval Welsh Lyrics*]

Dafydd Johnston, *Canu Maswedd yr Oesoedd Canol: Medieval Welsh Erotic Poetry* (Cardiff: Tafol, 1991). Reprinted (Seren, 1998).
[*Medieval Welsh Erotic Poetry*][1]

Richard Loomis and Dafydd Johnston, *Medieval Welsh Poems: An Anthology* (Binghamton, New York: Medieval & Renaissance Texts & Studies, 1992).
[*Medieval Welsh Poems*]

Dafydd Johnston, *Galar y Beirdd: Marwnadau Plant/Poets' Grief: Medieval Welsh Elegies for Children* (Cardiff: Tafol, 1993).
[*Poets' Grief*]

Joseph P. Clancy, *Medieval Welsh Poems* (Dublin: Four Courts Press, 2003).
[*Medieval Welsh Poems* (2003)]

---

[1] Where page numbers differ for this edition they have been noted in brackets.

ANON.

Individual Translations

'Dychan i Dre'r Fflint ac i'r Pibydd' (A Visit to Flint), tr. Joseph P. Clancy, *Medieval Welsh Lyrics*, pp. 166–8; tr. Joseph P. Clancy, *Medieval Welsh Poems* (2003), pp. 281–2; '**Englyn i'r Gal**' (Englyn to the Penis), tr. Dafydd Johnston, *Medieval Welsh Erotic Poetry*, p. 31 (1998: p. 27); '**Y Gwielyn**' (The Rod), tr. Dafydd Johnston, *Medieval Welsh Erotic Poetry*, p. 85 (1998: p. 81); '**Y Llances Lysti**' (The Lusty Lass), tr. Dafydd Johnston, *Medieval Welsh Erotic Poetry*, pp. 81–3 (1998: pp. 77–9).

BEDO AEDDREN (*fl.* 1500)

Individual Translations

'**Y Grawys**' (From Lent to Summer), tr. Gwyn Williams, *The Burning Tree*, pp. 141–3; tr. Joseph P. Clancy, *Medieval Welsh Lyrics*, pp. 169–70; tr. Gwyn Williams, *Welsh Poems: Sixth Century to 1600*, pp. 76–7; tr. Gwyn Williams, *To Look for a Word*, pp. 112–13; tr. Joseph P. Clancy, *Medieval Welsh Poems* (2003), pp. 283–4.

DAFYDD AB EDMWND (*fl.* 1450–97)

Individual Translations

'**Awdl Foliant i Rys o Fôn**' (Ode to Rhys o Fôn), tr. unsigned, *The History of the Literature of Wales*, pp. 134–5; '**Cywydd Merch**' (To a Girl), tr. A. P. Graves, *Welsh Poetry Old and New*, p. 36; tr. Gwyn Williams, *The Burning Tree*, pp. 125–7; tr. Gwyn Williams, *Welsh Poems: Sixth Century to 1600*, pp. 68–9; '**Dan Bared**' (Under the Eaves), tr. Joseph P. Clancy, *Medieval Welsh Lyrics*, pp. 227–8; tr. Gwyn Williams, *To Look for a Word*, pp. 101–2; tr. Joseph P. Clancy, *Medieval Welsh Poems* (2003), pp. 331–2; '**Dychan i Geilliau Guto'r Glyn**' (Satire on Guto'r Glyn's Testicles), tr. Dafydd Johnston, *Medieval Welsh Erotic Poetry*, pp. 125–9; '**Enwi'r Ferch**' (Naming the Girl), tr. Gwyn Williams, *The Burning Tree*, pp. 133–5; tr. Gwyn Williams, *Welsh Poems: Sixth Century to 1600*, pp. 72–2; tr. Gwyn Williams, *To Look for a Word*, pp. 195–6; '**I Wallt Merch**' (To a Girl's

Hair), tr. H. Idris Bell, *Transactions of the Honourable Society of Cymmrodorion* (1942), 143; tr. Gwyn Williams, *The Burning Tree*, pp. 129–31; tr. Joseph P. Clancy, *Medieval Welsh Lyrics*, pp. 226–7; tr. Tony Conran, *The Penguin Book of Welsh Verse*, pp. 183–4; tr. Gwyn Williams, *Welsh Poems: Sixth Century to 1600*, pp. 70–1; tr. Gwyn Williams, *To Look for a Word*, pp. 103–4; tr. Gwyn Williams, *Oxford Book*, pp. 64–5; tr. Gwyn Williams, *A Book of Wales* (1987), pp. 25–6; tr. Tony Conran, *Welsh Verse*, pp. 208–9; tr. Joseph P. Clancy, *Medieval Welsh Poems* (2003), pp. 329–30; '**Marwnad Siôn Eos**' (Lament for Siôn Eos), tr. Gwyn Williams, *The Burning Tree*, pp. 137–9; tr. Joseph P. Clancy, *Medieval Welsh Lyrics*, pp. 229–31; tr. Gwyn Williams, *To Look for a Word*, pp. 107–9; tr. Gwyn Williams, *Welsh Poems: Sixth Century to 1600*, pp. 74–5; tr. Joseph P. Clancy, *Medieval Welsh Poems*, pp. 129–31; tr. Joseph P. Clancy, *Medieval Welsh Poems* (2003), pp. 332–4.

DAFYDD AP GWILYM (*fl.* 1315/20–50/70)

Collections

Arthur James Johnes (Maelog), *Translations in to English from the Poems of Davyth ap Gwilym* (London: Henry Hooper, 1834).
[*Translations in to English from the Poems of Davyth ap Gwilym*]

Barddoniaeth Dafydd ap Gwilym o Grynhoad Owen Jones (Owain Myfyr), William Owen (Dr. W. Owen Pughe), Edward Williams (Iolo Morganwg) yn nghydag amryw gyfieithiadau i'r Seisnig, ed. Robert Ellis (Cynddelw) (Liverpool: I. Foulkes, 1873).
[*Barddoniaeth Dafydd ap Gwilym*]

Evelyn Lewes, *Life and Poems of Dafydd ap Gwilym* (London: David Nutt, 1914).
[*Life and Poems*]

W. J. Gruffydd, *Dafydd ap Gwilym* (Cardiff: University of Wales Press, 1935).
[*Dafydd ap Gwilym*]

H. Idris Bell, *Dafydd ap Gwilym: Fifty Poems* (London: Cymmrodorion Society, 1942).
[*Fifty Poems*]

Nigel Heseltine, *Dafydd ap Gwilym: Selected Poems* (Dublin: The Cuala Press, 1944). Reprinted as *25 Poems by Dafydd ap Gwilym* (Banbury: The Piers Press, 1968).[2]
[*Selected Poems*]

Rachel Bromwich, *Dafydd ap Gwilym: A Selection of Poems* (Llandysul: Gomer Press, 1982).
[*A Selection of Poems*]

Richard Loomis, *Dafydd ap Gwilym: The Poems* (Binghamton, New York: Medieval & Renaissance Texts & Studies, 1982).
[*The Poems*]

Martin Green, *Homage to Dafydd ap Gwilym* (Lewiston, N.Y.; Lampeter: Edwin Mellen, 1993).
[*Homage*]

A House of Leaves: Selected Poems of Dafydd ap Gwilym, ed. David Rowe (Castell Newydd Emlyn: Gweithdy'r Gair, 1995).
[*House of Leaves*]

Gwyn Thomas, *Dafydd ap Gwilym: His Poems* (Cardiff: University of Wales Press, 2001).
[*His Poems*]

Critical Editions

Rachel Bromwich, *Writers of Wales: Dafydd ap Gwilym* (Cardiff: University of Wales Press, 1974).
[*Writers of Wales*]

---

[2] Page numbers for this edition are noted in brackets.

Miscellaneous

Poetry Wales: Dafydd ap Gwilym Number, 8.4 (1973).
[*Poetry Wales: Dafydd ap Gwilym*]

Gwyn Thomas, *Dafydd ap Gwilym: Chwe Cherdd, Six Poems*
(Newtown: Gwasg Gregynog, 1985).

Individual Translations[3]
'**Amnaid**' (A Sign), tr. Robert Gurney, *Bardic Heritage*, pp. 103–4;
'**Angof**' (Being forgetful), tr. Richard Loomis, *Medieval Welsh
Poems*, pp. 72–3; '**Athrodi ei Was**' (Insulting his Servant), tr. Joseph
P. Clancy, *Medieval Welsh Lyrics*, pp. 64–5, tr. Richard Loomis,
Medieval Welsh Poems, pp. 59–61; '**Basaleg**', tr. Patrick K. Ford, *The
Celtic Poets*, pp. 256–8; '**Cyngor gan Frawd Llwyd**' (Advice from a
Greyfriar), tr. Robert Gurney, *Bardic Heritage*, p. 132; '**Cywydd i
Ifor Hael**' (To Ivor the Generous), tr. Joseph P. Clancy, *Medieval
Welsh Lyrics*, pp. 27–8; tr. Richard Loomis, *Medieval Welsh Poems*,
pp. 15–16; tr. Patrick K. Ford, *The Celtic Poets*, pp. 250–2; '**Cywydd
y Gal**' (Reproach to his Penis), tr. Dafydd Johnston, *Medieval Welsh
Erotic Poetry*, pp. 29–31 (1998: pp. 25–7); tr. Dafydd Johnston,
Medieval Welsh Poems, pp. 81–2; tr. Dafydd Johnston, *World
Poetry: An Anthology of Verse from Antiquity to our Time*, ed.
Katharine Washburn and John S. Major (New York; London:
Norton, 1998), pp. 449–50; tr. Joseph P. Clancy, *Medieval Welsh
Poems* (2003), pp. 192–3; '**Dewis un o Bedair**' (Four Women), tr.
Joseph P. Clancy, *Medieval Welsh Lyrics*, pp. 67–9; '**Diolch am Fenig**'
(Giving Thanks for Gloves), tr. Edward Williams (Iolo Morganwg),
Poems, Lyric and Pastoral (London: Printed for the author by
J. Nichols, 1794), pp. 192–8; tr. Richard Loomis, *Medieval Welsh
Poems*, pp. 16–17; '**Dychan i Rys Meigen**' (A Satire on Rhys
Meigen), tr. Patrick K. Ford, *The Celtic Poets*, pp. 151–4;
'**Edifeirwch**' (The Judgement), tr. Joseph P. Clancy, *Medieval Welsh
Lyrics*, p. 89; tr. Richard Loomis, *Medieval Welsh Poems*, p. 44;

---

[3] It would be wise to remind readers again that, with the exception of a
small selection printed separately here, individual translations within
collections of translations of Dafydd ap Gwilym's poems are not listed.
It should therefore be borne in mind that there are dozens of additional
translations of the above poems within the collections.

'**Englynion i Ifor Hael**' (Englynion to Ifor Hael), tr. Patrick K. Ford, *The Celtic Poets*, pp. 253–5; '**Englynion yr Offeren**' (Verses for the Mass), tr. Leslie Norris, *Leslie Norris: Collected Poems* (Bridgend: Seren, 1996), pp. 161–3; '**Galw ar Ddwynwen**' (Invoking Dwynwen), tr. Joseph P. Clancy, *Medieval Welsh Lyrics*, pp. 73–5; tr. Richard Loomis, *Medieval Welsh Poems*, pp. 42–4; tr. Rachel Bromwich, *An Anglesey Anthology*, ed. Dewi Roberts (Gwasg Carreg Gwalch, 1999), pp. 63–4; '**Gerlant o Blu Paun**' (A Garland of Peacock Feathers), tr. Joseph P. Clancy, *Medieval Welsh Lyrics*, pp. 50–1; tr. Robert Gurney, *Bardic Heritage*, pp. 100–1; tr. Richard Loomis, *Medieval Welsh Poems*, pp. 87–8; '**Gwadu iddo fod yn Fynach**' (Denying that he's a Monk), tr. Richard Loomis, *Medieval Welsh Poems*, pp. 27–8; '**Gwallt Morfudd**' (Morfudd's Hair), tr. Richard Loomis, *Medieval Welsh Poems*, pp. 40–1; '**I Iesu Grist**' (To Jesus Christ), tr. Leslie Norris, *Leslie Norris: Collected Poems* (Bridgend: Seren, 1996), pp. 160–1; '**Llw Morfudd**' (Morfudd's Oath), tr. Joseph P. Clancy, *Medieval Welsh Lyrics*, pp. 46–7; tr. Richard Loomis, *Medieval Welsh Poems*, pp. 31–3; '**Llychwino pryd y ferch**' (Beauty's Ruin), tr. Joseph P. Clancy, *Medieval Welsh Lyrics*, pp. 99–100; tr. Richard Loomis, *Medieval Welsh Poems*, pp. 52–3; '**Marwnad Angharad**' (Funeral ode to Angharad), tr. H. Idris Bell, *A History of Welsh Literature*, pp. 100–1; '**Marwnad Ifor a Nest**' (Elegy for Ifor and Nest), tr. Patrick K. Ford, *The Celtic Poets*, pp. 259–61; '**Morfudd a Dyddgu**' (Morfudd and Dyddgu), tr. Joseph P. Clancy, *Medieval Welsh Lyrics*, pp. 96–8; tr. Joseph P. Clancy, *Medieval Welsh Poems* (2003), pp. 199–200; '**Noson Olau**' (A Moonlit Night), tr. Joseph P. Clancy, *Medieval Welsh Lyrics*, pp. 76–8; '**Penwisg Merch**' (A Girl's Headdress), tr. Richard Loomis, *Medieval Welsh Poems*, pp. 63–4; '**Rhag Hyderu ar y Byd**' (The World's Brittleness), tr. Joseph P. Clancy, *Medieval Welsh Lyrics*, pp. 53–4; '**Rhagoriaeth y Bardd ar Arall**' (The Poet's Superiority over his Rival), tr. Joseph P. Clancy, *Medieval Welsh Lyrics*, pp. 91–2; tr. Richard Loomis, *Medieval Welsh Poems*, pp. 50–2; '**Saethu'r Ferch**' (Shooting the Girl), tr. Richard Loomis, *Medieval Welsh Poems*, p. 75; '**Siom**' (Disappointment), tr. Joseph P. Clancy, *Medieval Welsh Lyrics*, pp. 51–3; tr. Richard Loomis, *Medieval Welsh Poems*, pp. 41–2; '**Taeru**' (Insisting), tr. Richard Loomis, *Medieval Welsh Poems*, p. 67; '**Tri Phorthor Eiddig**' (Eiddig's Three Doormen), tr. Joseph P. Clancy, *Medieval Welsh Lyrics*, pp. 78–80; tr. Richard Loomis, *Medieval Welsh Poems*, pp. 56–7; '**Y Cariad a Wrthodwyd**' (Morfudd's

Fickleness), tr. Joseph P. Clancy, *Medieval Welsh Lyrics*, pp. 95–6; '**Y Ceiliog Bronfraith**' (The Thrushcock), tr. Tony Conran, *The Penguin Book of Welsh Verse*, pp. 144–5; tr. Robert Gurney, *Bardic Heritage*, pp. 86–8; tr. Gwyn Williams, *Choose Your Stranger* (Port Talbot: Alun Books, 1979), pp. 54–5; tr. Tony Conran, *Welsh Verse*, pp. 176–7; tr. Richard Loomis, *Medieval Welsh Poems*, p. 85; '**Y Cleddyf**' (The Sword), tr. Joseph P. Clancy, *Medieval Welsh Lyrics*, pp. 89–91; '**Y Deildy**' (A House All of Leaves), tr. Patrick K. Ford, *The Celtic Poets*, pp. 276–7; '**Y Dylluan**' (The Owl), tr. Joseph P. Clancy, *Medieval Welsh Lyrics*, pp. 30–1; tr. Joseph P. Clancy, *Poetry Wales: Dafydd ap Gwilym*, pp. 68–9; tr. Richard Loomis, *Medieval Welsh Poems*, pp. 83–5; '**Y Gwayw**' (The Spear), tr. Joseph P. Clancy, *Medieval Welsh Lyrics*, p. 60; tr. Leslie Norris, *Leslie Norris: Collected Poems* (Bridgend: Seren, 1996), p. 157; '**Y Llwynog**' (The Fox), tr. Gwyn Williams, *To Look for a Word*, pp. 47–8; tr. Leslie Norris, *Leslie Norris: Collected Poems* (Bridgend: Seren, 1996), p. 155; '**Ymryson Dafydd ap Gwilym a Gruffudd Gryg: Cywydd Cyntaf Dafydd**' (Dafydd's Reply), tr. Patrick K. Ford, *The Celtic Poets*, pp. 321–3; '**Y Mwdwl Gwair**' (The Haycock), tr. Richard Loomis, *Medieval Welsh Poems*, pp. 88–9; '**Y Seren**' (The Star), tr. Joseph P. Clancy, *Medieval Welsh Lyrics*, pp. 84–5; tr. Richard Loomis, *Medieval Welsh Poems*, pp. 36–7; tr. Patrick K. Ford, *The Celtic Poets*, pp. 286–7; '**Yr Annerch**' (The Greeting), tr. Robert Gurney, *Bardic Heritage*, p. 76; '**Yr Euryches**' (The Lady Goldsmith), tr. Richard Loomis, *Medieval Welsh Poems*, p. 29; '**Yr Het Fedw**' (The Birch Hat), tr. Joseph P. Clancy, *Medieval Welsh Lyrics*, pp. 73–5; tr. Richard Loomis, *Medieval Welsh Poems*, pp. 35–6.

Selection

Breichiau Morfudd (Morfudd's Arms)
David Bell, *Fifty Poems*, pp. 115–19; Joseph P. Clancy, *Medieval Welsh Lyrics*, pp. 44–6; Robert Gurney, *Bardic Heritage*, pp. 98–9; Rolfe Humphries, *Oxford Book*, pp. 35–7; Richard Loomis, *The Poems*, pp. 133–5; Rolfe Humphries, *House of Leaves*, pp. 37–8; Richard Loomis, *Medieval Welsh Poems*, pp. 33–4; Gwyn Thomas, *His Poems*, pp. 112–13; Joseph P. Clancy, *Medieval Welsh Poems* (2003), pp. 195–7.

Cyngor y Biogen (The Magpie's Advice)
H. Idris Bell, *Fifty Poems*, pp. 217–21; Kenneth Hurlstone Jackson, *A Celtic Miscellany* (1951), pp. 229–30 (1971: pp. 211–13); H. Idris Bell, *A History of Welsh Literature*, p. 109; Joseph P. Clancy, *Medieval Welsh Lyrics*, pp. 101–3; Robert Gurney, *Bardic Heritage*, pp. 127–9; Richard Loomis, *The Poems*, pp. 146–8; Rachel Bromwich, *A Selection of Poems*, pp. 80–2; Richard Loomis, *Medieval Welsh Poems*, pp. 89–91; Patrick K. Ford, *The Celtic Poets*, pp. 308–10; Gwyn Thomas, *His Poems*, pp. 129–31; Joseph P. Clancy, *Medieval Welsh Poems* (2003), pp. 202–4.

Cyrchu Lleian (To the Nun)
Arthur James Johnes (Maelog), *Translations in to English from the Poems of Davyth ap Gwilym*, pp. 8–9; Nigel Heseltine, *Selected Poems*, pp. 25–6 (1968: pp. 37–8); Joseph P. Clancy, *The Anglo-Welsh Review*, 12.29 (1962), 29–30; Gwyn Williams, *The Rent that's Due to Love*, pp. 33–5; Robert Gurney, *Bardic Heritage*, pp. 112–13; Rachel Bromwich, *A Selection of Poems*, pp. 52–4; Richard Loomis, *The Poems*, pp. 214–15; Patrick K. Ford, *The Celtic Poets*, pp. 306–7; Gwyn Thomas, *His Poems*, p. 220.

Cystudd y Bardd (The Poet's Affliction)
Arthur James Johnes (Maelog), *Translations in to English from the Poems of Davyth ap Gwilym*, p. 93; Arthur James Johnes (Maelog), *The Poetry of Wales* (1873), pp. 137–8; Evelyn Lewes, *Life and Poems*, pp. 87–8; David Bell, *Fifty Poems*, p. 215; Joseph P. Clancy, *Medieval Welsh Lyrics*, pp. 70–1; Rachel Bromwich, *A Selection of Poems*, pp. 194–5; Richard Loomis, *The Poems*, pp. 203–4; Gwyn Thomas, *His Poems*, p. 203.

Cystudd Cariad (The Pain of Love)
H. Idris Bell, *Fifty Poems*, p. 303; Robert Gurney, *Bardic Heritage*, pp. 141–2; Rachel Bromwich, *A Selection of Poems*, p. 194; Richard Loomis, *The Poems*, p. 187; Joseph P. Clancy, *Medieval Welsh Lyrics*, p. 106; Tony Conran, *The Penguin Book of Welsh Verse*, p. 146; Tony Conran, *Welsh Verse*, pp. 177–8; Richard Loomis, *Medieval Welsh Poems*, pp. 71–2; Rolfe Humphries, *A House of Leaves*, pp. 55–6; Gwyn Thomas, *His Poems*, p. 182.

Dan y Bargod (Under the Eaves)
Nigel Heseltine, *Selected Poems*, pp. 26–8 (1968: pp. 39–40); Joseph P. Clancy, *Medieval Welsh Lyrics*, pp. 36–7; Rachel Bromwich, *A Selection of Poems*, pp. 144–6; Richard Loomis, *The Poems*, pp. 185–6; Martin Green, *Homage*, pp. 24–5; Rachel Bromwich, *A House of Leaves*, pp. 49–50; Patrick K. Ford, *The Celtic Poets*, pp. 288–90; Gwyn Thomas, *His Poems*, pp. 180–1.

Dyddgu
Arthur James Johnes (Maelog), *Translations in to English from the Poems of Davyth ap Gwilym*, pp. 9–10; Joseph P. Clancy, *Medieval Welsh Lyrics*, pp. 58–9; Robert Gurney, *Bardic Heritage*, pp. 77–8; Rachel Bromwich, *A Selection of Poems*, pp. 38–40; Richard Loomis, *The Poems*, pp. 120–1; Richard Loomis, *Medieval Welsh Poems*, pp. 22–3; Rolfe Humphries, *A House of Leaves*, pp. 27–8; Gwyn Thomas, *His Poems*, pp. 94–5.

Ei Gysgod (His Shadow)
Arthur James Johnes (Maelog), *Translations in to English from the Poems of Davyth ap Gwilym*, pp. 28–31; unsigned, *Barddoniaeth Dafydd ap Gwilym*, pp. 387–9; Nigel Heseltine, *Selected Poems*, pp. 33–5 (1968: pp. 46–8); David Bell, *Fifty Poems*, pp. 285–9; Joseph P. Clancy, *Medieval Welsh Lyrics*, pp. 56–8; Bryan Walters, *From the Welsh*, pp. 21–4; Rachel Bromwich, *A Selection of Poems*, pp. 190–2; Richard Loomis, *The Poems*, pp. 254–5; Richard Loomis, *Medieval Welsh Poems*, pp. 79–81; Martin Green, *Homage*, pp. 31–2; Patrick K. Ford, *The Celtic Poets*, pp. 315–17; Gwyn Thomas, *His Poems*, pp. 276–7.

I Ddymuno Boddi'r Gŵr Eiddig (To Wish *Jaloux* Drowned)
Arthur James Johnes (Maelog), *Translations in to English from the Poems of Davyth ap Gwilym*, pp. 55–7; Arthur James Johnes (Maelog), *Transactions of the Honourable Society of Cymmrodorion* (1907–8), 146; David Bell, *Fifty Poems*, pp. 129–31; Joseph P. Clancy, *Medieval Welsh Lyrics*, pp. 80–2; Robert Gurney, *Bardic Heritage*, pp. 133–5; Richard Loomis, *The Poems*, pp. 165–6; Rolfe Humphries, *A House of Leaves*, pp. 51–2; Gwyn Thomas, *His Poems*, pp. 154–5.

I Wahodd Dyddgu (An Invitation to Dyddgu)
Arthur James Johnes (Maelog), *Translations in to English from the Poems of Davyth ap* Gwilym, pp. 13–14; H. Idris Bell, *Fifty Poems*, pp. 271–5; Nigel Heseltine, *Selected Poems*, pp. 44–5 (1968: pp. 61–2); Joseph P. Clancy, *Medieval Welsh Lyrics*, pp. 66–7; Robert Gurney, *Bardic Heritage*, pp. 78–9; Joseph P. Clancy, *Poetry Wales: Dafydd ap Gwilym*, pp. 69–70; Bryan Walters, *From the Welsh*, pp. 19–20; Richard Loomis, *The Poems*, pp. 223–4; Richard Loomis, *Medieval Welsh Poems*, pp. 24–5; Rolfe Humphries, *A House of Leaves*, pp. 31–2; Gwyn Thomas, *His Poems*, pp. 231–2.

Marwnad Gruffudd ab Adda (Elegy for Gruffudd ab Adda)
H. Idris Bell, *Fifty Poems*, pp. 293–7; Kenneth Hurlstone Jackson, *A Celtic Miscellany* (1951), pp. 284–5 (1971: pp. 258–9); H. Idris Bell, *A History of Welsh Literature*, p. 101; Joseph P. Clancy, *Medieval Welsh Lyrics*, pp. 54–6; Richard Loomis, *The Poems*, pp. 79–81; Rachel Bromwich, *A Selection of Poems*, pp. 172–4; Richard Loomis, *Medieval Welsh Poems*, pp. 18–19; Gwyn Thomas, *His Poems*, pp. 50–1.

Mawl i'r Haf (In Praise of Summer)
David Bell, *Fifty Poems*, pp. 253–5; Joseph P. Clancy, *Medieval Welsh Lyrics*, pp. 26–7; Rachel Bromwich, *A Selection of Poems*, pp. 8–10; Richard Loomis, *The Poems*, pp. 95–6; Patrick K. Ford, *The Celtic Poets*, pp. 262–4; Richard Loomis, *Medieval Welsh Poems*, pp. 92–4; Gwyn Thomas, *His Poems*, pp. 59–60; Joseph P. Clancy, *Medieval Welsh Poems* (2003), pp. 187–8.

Merch yn Edliw ei Lyfrdra (The Coward)
David Bell, *Fifty Poems*, pp. 121–5; Joseph P. Clancy, *Medieval Welsh Lyrics*, pp. 42–3; Robert Gurney, *Bardic Heritage*, p. 121; Rachel Bromwich, *A Selection of Poems*, pp. 134–6; Richard Loomis, *The Poems*, pp. 140–1; Richard Loomis, *Medieval Welsh Poems*, pp. 67–9; Rolfe Humphries, *A House of Leaves*, pp. 33–4; Gwyn Thomas, *His Poems*, pp. 120–1.

Merch Gyndyn (A Stubborn Girl)
unsigned, *The Cambrian Wreath*, pp. 135–7; Joseph P. Clancy, *Medieval Welsh Lyrics*, pp. 31–2; Rachel Bromwich, *A Selection of Poems*, pp. 50–2; Richard Loomis, *The Poems*, pp. 114–15; Richard

Loomis, *Medieval Welsh Poems*, pp. 62–3; Patrick K. Ford, *The Celtic Poets*, pp. 303–4; Gwyn Thomas, *His Poems*, pp. 85–6.

Merch yn Ymbincio (A Girl Dressing Up)
unsigned, *The Cambrian Wreath*, pp. 133–5; Arthur James Johnes (Maelog), *Translations in to English from the Poems of Davyth ap Gwilym*, p. 92; David Bell, *Fifty Poems*, pp. 143–5; Kenneth Hurlstone Jackson, *A Celtic Miscellany* (1951), pp. 225–6 (1971: pp. 208–9); Joseph P. Clancy, *Medieval Welsh Lyrics*, pp. 35–6; Richard Loomis, *The Poems*, pp. 127–8; Richard Loomis, *Medieval Welsh Poems*, pp. 66–7; Gwyn Thomas, *His Poems*, pp. 103–4.

Merched Llanbadarn (The Girls of Llanbadarn)
Nigel Heseltine, *Selected Poems*, pp. 20–2 (1968: pp. 31–2); H. Idris Bell, *Fifty Poems*, pp. 197–9; Kenneth Hurlstone Jackson, *A Celtic Miscellany* (1951), pp. 226–7 (1971: pp. 209–10); Gwyn Williams, *The Burning Tree*, pp. 93–5; Joseph P. Clancy, *Medieval Welsh Lyrics*, pp. 29–30; Tony Conran, *Poetry Wales*, 3.1 (1967), 22–3; Tony Conran, *The Penguin Book of Welsh Verse*, pp. 141–2; Robert Gurney, *Bardic Heritage*, pp. 74–5; Gwyn Williams, *Welsh Poems: Sixth Century to 1600*, pp. 52–3; Gwyn Williams, *To Look for a Word*, pp. 49–50; Bryan Walters, *From the Welsh*, pp. 10–11; Rachel Bromwich, *A Selection of Poems*, pp. 136–8; Richard Loomis, *The Poems*, pp. 125–6; Rolfe Humphries, *Oxford Book*, pp. 37–8; Tony Conran, *Welsh Verse*, pp. 173–4; Rolfe Humphries, *A Book of Wales* (1987), pp. 26–7; Carl Lofmark, *Bards and Heroes*, pp. 97–8; *Harri Webb: Collected Poems* (Llandysul: Gomer, 1995), pp. 178–9; Glyn Jones, *Glyn Jones: Collected Poems*, ed. Meic Stephens (Cardiff: University of Wales Press, 1996), p. 225; *Leslie Norris: Collected Poems* (Bridgend: Seren, 1996), pp. 159–60; Richard Loomis, *Medieval Welsh Poems*, pp. 64–6; Martin Green, *Homage*, pp. 22–3; Rolfe Humphries, *A House of Leaves*, pp. 29–30; Patrick K. Ford, *The Celtic Poets*, pp. 292–3; Tony Conran, *Wales: A Celebration*, ed. Dewi Roberts (Llanrwst: Gwasg Carreg Gwalch, 2000), pp. 55–6; Gwyn Thomas, *His Poems*, pp. 101–2; Joseph P. Clancy, *Medieval Welsh Poems* (2003), pp. 186–7.

Mis Mai (May)
Arthur James Johnes (Maelog), *Translations in to English from the Poems of Davyth ap Gwilym*, p. 18; unsigned, *Barddoniaeth Dafydd*

ap Gwilym, p. 386; Ernest Rhys, *A Celtic Anthology*, p. 266; Robert Gurney, *Bardic Heritage*, pp. 85–6; Rachel Bromwich, *A Selection of Poems*, pp. 4–6; Richard Loomis, *The Poems*, pp. 89–90; Richard Loomis, *Medieval Welsh Poems*, pp. 82–3; Ernest Rhys, *The Bardic Source Book*, p. 243; Patrick K. Ford, *The Celtic Poets*, pp. 265–7; Gwyn Thomas, *His Poems*, pp. 51–2.

Mis Mai a Mis Ionawr (May and January)
Arthur James Johnes (Maelog), *The Poetry of Wales* (1873), p. 143; H. Idris Bell, *The Nationalist*, 4.36 (1911), 11; H. Idris Bell, *Fifty Poems*, pp. 257–9; *A Celtic Miscellany* (1951), pp. 79–80 (1971: pp. 75–6); Joseph P. Clancy, *Medieval Welsh Lyrics*, pp. 85–6; Robert Gurney, *Bardic Heritage*, pp. 107–8; Joseph P. Clancy, *Poetry Wales: Dafydd ap Gwilym*, pp. 70–1; Rachel Bromwich, *A Selection of Poems*, p. 2; Richard Loomis, *The Poems*, pp. 156–7; Richard Loomis, *Medieval Welsh Poems*, pp. 37–8; Gwyn Thomas, *His Poems*, pp. 142–3.

Morfudd fel yr Haul (Morfudd Compared to the Sun)
Joseph P. Clancy, *Medieval Welsh Lyrics*, pp. 93–5; Joseph P. Clancy, *Poetry Wales: Dafydd ap Gwilym*, pp. 73–5; Rachel Bromwich, *A Selection of Poems*, pp. 26–8; Richard Loomis, *The Poems*, pp. 116–17; Richard Loomis, *Medieval Welsh Poems*, pp. 30–1; Patrick K. Ford, *The Celtic Poets*, pp. 297–9; Gwyn Thomas, *His Poems*, pp. 87–8; Joseph P. Clancy, *Medieval Welsh Poems* (2003), pp. 197–9.

Morfudd yn Hen (Morfudd Grown Old)
Joseph P. Clancy, *Medieval Welsh Lyrics*, pp. 103–4; Rachel Bromwich, *A Selection of Poems*, pp. 48–50; Richard Loomis, *The Poems*, pp. 251–2; Richard Loomis, *Medieval Welsh Poems*, pp. 48–9; Gwyn Thomas, *His Poems*, pp. 272–3; Joseph P. Clancy, *Medieval Welsh Poems* (2003), pp. 204–5.

Offeren y Llwyn (The Mass of the Grove)
Arthur James Johnes (Maelog), *Translations in to English from the Poems of Davyth ap Gwilym*, pp. 31–2; unsigned, *Barddoniaeth Dafydd ap Gwilym*, pp. 391–2; unsigned, *The Nationalist*, 1.5 (1907), 32; Evelyn Lewes, *Life and Poems*, pp. 121–2; H. Idris Bell, *Fifty Poems*, pp. 263–5; Nigel Heseltine, *Selected Poems*, pp. 32–3 (1968: pp. 44–5); Gwyn Williams, *The Burning Tree*, pp. 89–91; Gwyn

Williams, *Presenting Welsh Poetry*, pp. 28–9; Joseph P. Clancy, *Medieval Welsh Lyrics*, pp. 49–50; Robert Gurney, *Bardic Heritage*, pp. 92–3; Gwyn Williams, *Welsh Poems: Sixth Century to 1600*, pp. 50–1; Gwyn Williams, *To Look for a Word*, pp. 51–2; Gwyn Williams, *Oxford Book*, pp. 40–1; Rachel Bromwich, *A Selection of Poems*, pp. 78–80; Richard Loomis, *The Poems*, pp. 227–8; Richard Loomis, *Medieval Welsh Poems*, pp. 46–7; Patrick K. Ford, *The Celtic Poets*, pp. 273–4; Gwyn Thomas, *His Poems*, p. 237; Joseph P. Clancy, *Medieval Welsh Poems* (2003), pp. 194–5.

Pererindod Merch (A Girl's Pilgrimage)

unsigned, *Beauties of British Poetry*, selected by Sidney Melmoth (Huddersfield: sold by Vernor L. Hood, Crosby & Letterman, London, 1801), pp. 181–4; Edward Williams (Iolo Morganwg), *The Cambrian Wreath*, pp. 125–9; Edward Williams (Iolo Morganwg), *Cambrian Quarterly Magazine*, 5 (1833), 175–8; Arthur James Johnes (Maelog), *Translations in to English from the Poems of Davyth ap Gwilym*, pp. 35–41; Professor Cowell, *Y Cymmrodor*, 2 (1878), 120–1; Nigel Heseltine, *Selected Poems*, pp. 1–2 (1968: pp. 6–7); Rachel Bromwich, *Selected Poems*, pp. 1–2; Richard Loomis, *The Poems*, pp. 200–1; Richard Loomis, *Medieval Welsh Poems*, pp. 73–5; Martin Green, *Homage*, pp. 3–5; Gwyn Thomas, *His Poems*, pp. 198–9.

Taith i Garu (Journeying for Love)

Nigel Heseltine, *Selected Poems*, pp. 40–1 (1968: pp. 55–7); Rachel Bromwich, *A Selection of Poems*, pp. 130–2; Richard Loomis, *The Poems*, pp. 176–8; Martin Green, *Homage*, pp. 37–9; Gwyn Thomas, *His Poems*, pp. 169–70; Joseph P. Clancy, *Medieval Welsh Poems* (2003), pp. 205–6.

Talu Dyled (Paying a Debt)

Edward Jones, *The Bardic Museum*, p. 43; David Bell, *Fifty Poems*, pp. 203–7; Robert Gurney, *Bardic Heritage*, pp. 140–1; Rachel Bromwich, *A Selection of Poems*, pp. 30–2; Richard Loomis, *The Poems*, pp. 105–6; Richard Loomis, *Medieval Welsh Poems*, pp. 25–6; Gwyn Thomas, *His Poems*, pp. 72–3.

Trafferth Mewn Tafarn (Trouble at a Tavern)

David Bell, *Fifty Poems*, pp. 229–33; Nigel Heseltine, *Selected Poems*, pp. 17–20 (1968: pp. 28–30); Kenneth Hurlstone Jackson, *A Celtic Miscellany* (1951), pp. 227–8 (1971: pp. 210–11); Joseph P. Clancy, *Medieval Welsh Lyrics*, pp. 24–6; Tony Conran, *Poetry Wales*, 3.1 (1967), 20–2; Tony Conran, *The Penguin Book of Welsh Verse*, pp. 142–4; Joseph P. Clancy, *Poetry Wales: Dafydd ap Gwilym*, pp. 66–7; Gwyn Williams, *To Look for a Word*, pp. 57–8; Bryan Walters, *From the Welsh*, pp. 13–14; Joseph P. Clancy, *A Book of Wales* (1987), pp. 29–30; Rachel Bromwich, *A Selection of Poems*, pp. 142–4; Richard Loomis, *The Poems*, pp. 230–1; Tony Conran, *Welsh Verse*, pp. 174–6; Martin Green, *Homage*, pp. 16–17; Richard Loomis, *Medieval Welsh Poems*, pp. 57–9; Rolfe Humphries, *A House of Leaves*, pp. 24–6; Patrick K. Ford, *The Celtic Poets*, pp. 300–2; Gwyn Thomas, *His Poems*, pp. 241–2; Joseph P. Clancy, *Medieval Welsh Poems* (2003), pp. 190–1.

Tri Phorthor Eiddig (*Jaloux's* Three Porters)

Evelyn Lewes, *Life and Poems*, pp. 77–9; David Bell, *Fifty Poems*, pp. 235–9; Joseph P. Clancy, *Medieval Welsh Lyrics*, pp. 78–80; Richard Loomis, *The Poems*, pp. 172–4; Richard Loomis, *Medieval Welsh Poems*, pp. 56–7; Rolfe Humphries, *A House of Leaves*, pp. 39–41; Gwyn Thomas, *His Poems*, pp. 163–4.

Y Bardd a'r Brawd Llwyd (The Poet and the Grey Friar)

Arthur James Johnes (Maelog), *Translations in to English from the Poems of Davyth ap Gwilym*, pp. 26–7; unsigned, *The Cambrian Wreath*, pp. 139–42; Evelyn Lewes, *Life and Poems*, pp. 106–8; H. Idris Bell, *Fifty Poems*, pp. 155–61; Nigel Heseltine, *Selected Poems*, pp. 28–31 (1968: pp. 41–3); Edwin S. James, *Wales*, 6.23 (1946), 107–9; Kenneth Hurlstone Jackson *A Celtic Miscellany* (1951), pp. 230–2 (1971: pp. 213–14); D. M. Lloyd, *A Book of Wales* (1953), pp. 318–20; Joseph P. Clancy, *Medieval Welsh Lyrics*, pp. 38–40; Tony Conran, *The Penguin Book of Welsh Verse*, pp. 137–9; Robert Gurney, *Bardic Heritage*, pp. 132–3; Tony Conran, *Welsh Verse*, pp. 169–71; Rachel Bromwich, *A Selection of Poems*, pp. 150–2; Richard Loomis, *The Poems*, pp. 247–9; Carl Lofmark, *Bards and Heroes*, pp. 90–1; Tony Conran, *Transactions of the Honourable Society of Cymmrodorion* (1992), 26; Richard Loomis, *Medieval Welsh Poems*, pp. 19–22; Martin Green, *Homage*, pp. 26–9; Patrick

K. Ford, *The Celtic Poets*, pp. 311–14; Gwyn Thomas, *His Poems*, pp. 267–9.

Y Breuddwyd (The Dream)

Arthur James Johnes (Maelog), *Translations in to English from the Poems of Davyth ap Gwilym*, pp. 48–50; W. J. Gruffydd, *The Nationalist*, 1.4 (1907), 17; H. Idris Bell, *Fifty Poems*, pp. 165–7; Joseph P. Clancy, *Medieval Welsh Lyrics*, pp. 43–4; Robert Gurney, *Bardic Heritage*, pp. 101–3; Rachel Bromwich, *A Selection of Poems*, pp. 108–10; Richard Loomis, *The Poems*, pp. 112–13; Richard Loomis, *Medieval Welsh Poems*, pp. 61–2; Gwyn Thomas, *His Poems*, pp. 82–3.

Y Don ar Afon Dyfi (To the Wave on the River Dyfi)

Arthur James Johnes (Maelog), *Cambrian Quarterly Magazine*, 3 (1831), 26; Arthur James Johnes (Maelog), *Translations in to English from the Poems of Davyth ap Gwilym*, pp. 15–16; H. Idris Bell, *Fifty Poems*, pp. 125–9; Arthur James Johnes (Maelog), *A Book of Wales* (1953), pp. 62–3; Joseph P. Clancy, *Medieval Welsh Lyrics*, pp. 48–9; Rachel Bromwich, *A Selection of Poems*, pp. 112–14; Richard Loomis, *The Poems*, pp. 160–1; Richard Loomis, *Medieval Welsh Poems*, pp. 39–40; Gwyn Thomas, *His Poems*, pp. 146–7.

Y Drych (The Mirror)

Arthur James Johnes (Maelog), *Translations in to English from the Poems of Davyth ap Gwilym*, pp. 94–5; Nigel Heseltine, *Selected Poems*, pp. 39–40 (1968: p. 54); Joseph P. Clancy, *Medieval Welsh Lyrics*, pp. 62–3; Robert Gurney, *Bardic Heritage*, p. 117; Rachel Bromwich, *A Selection of Poems*, pp. 188–90; Richard Loomis, *The Poems*, pp. 207–8; Carl Lofmark, *Bards and Heroes*, p. 96; Richard Loomis, *Medieval Welsh Poems*, p. 76; Martin Green, *Homage*, p. 36; Rolfe Humphries, *A House of Leaves*, p. 48; Daniel Huws, *World Poetry: An Anthology of Verse from Antiquity to our Time*, ed. Katharine Washburn and John S. Major (New York; London: Norton, 1998), pp. 447–8; Patrick K. Ford, *The Celtic Poets*, pp. 294–5; Gwyn Thomas, *His Poems*, pp. 208–9.

Y Ffenestr (The Window)

F. S., *The Cambrian* (16 January 1808), 4; Nigel Heseltine, *Selected Poems*, pp. 43–4 (1968: pp. 59–60); Richard Loomis, *The Poems*, pp.

148–50; Richard Loomis, *Medieval Welsh Poems*, pp. 69–70; Martin Green, *Homage*, pp. 40–1; Rolfe Humphries, *A House of Leaves*, pp. 35–6; Gwyn Thomas, *His Poems*, pp. 132–3.

Y Fun o Eithinfynydd (The Girl of Eithinfynydd)
David Bell, *Fifty Poems*, pp. 113–15; Leonard Owen, *The London Welshman*, 19.4 (1964), 18; Joseph P. Clancy, *Medieval Welsh Lyrics*, pp. 31–2; Robert Gurney, *Bardic Heritage*, pp. 111–12; Richard Loomis, *The Poems*, pp. 139–40; Richard Loomis, *Medieval Welsh Poems*, pp. 34–5; Gwyn Thomas, *His Poems*, p. 119.

Y Gwynt (The Wind)
Edward Jones, *The Bardic Museum*, pp. 54–5; Arthur James Johnes (Maelog), *Translations in to English from the Poems of Davyth ap Gwilym*, pp. 50–1; Evelyn Lewes, *The Life and Poems*, pp. 53–5; W. J. Gruffydd, *Dafydd ap Gwilym*, pp. 77–9; Nigel Heseltine, *Selected Poems*, pp. 9–11 (1968: pp. 17–19); H. Idris Bell, *Fifty Poems*, p. 189–93; Joseph P. Clancy, *Medieval Welsh Lyrics*, pp. 71–2; Tony Conran, *The Penguin Book of Welsh Verse*, pp. 147–8; Joseph P. Clancy, *Poetry Wales: Dafydd ap Gwilym*, pp. 75–6; Joseph P. Clancy, *Oxford Book*, pp. 38–40; Rachel Bromwich, *A Selection of Poems*, pp. 104–6; Richard Loomis, *The Poems*, pp. 220–2; Tony Conran, *Welsh Verse*, pp. 178–80; Martin Green, *Homage*, pp. 9–10; Richard Loomis, *Medieval Welsh Poems*, pp. 45–6; Rachel Bromwich, *A House of Leaves*, pp. 44–6; Daniel Huws, *World Poetry: An Anthology of Verse from Antiquity to our Time*, ed. Katharine Washburn and John S. Major (New York; London: Norton, 1998), pp. 446–7; Gwyn Thomas, *His Poems*, pp. 227–8; Joseph P. Clancy, *Medieval Welsh Poems* (2003), pp. 200–2.

Y Llwyn Celyn (The Holly Grove)
Arthur James Johnes (Maelog), *Translations in to English from the Poems of Davyth ap Gwilym*, pp. 79–80; Arthur James Johnes (Maelog), *The Poetry of Wales* (1873), pp. 141–2; Ernest Rhys, *A Celtic Anthology*, p. 268; Joseph P. Clancy, *Medieval Welsh Lyrics*, pp. 40–1; Rachel Bromwich, *A Selection of Poems*, p. 16; Richard Loomis, *The Poems*, pp. 98–9; Richard Loomis, *Medieval Welsh Poems*, pp. 86–7; Ernest Rhys, *The Bardic Source Book*, p. 244; Patrick K. Ford, *The Celtic Poets*, pp. 271–2; Gwyn Thomas, *His Poems*, pp. 62–3.

Y Niwl (The Mist)
Arthur James Johnes (Maelog), *Cambrian Quarterly Magazine*, 1 (1829), 415; Arthur James Johnes (Maelog), *Translations in to English from the Poems of Davyth ap Gwilym*, pp. 20–1; Professor Cowell, *Y Cymmrodor*, 2 (1878), 124–5; Joseph P. Clancy, *Medieval Welsh Lyrics*, pp. 61–2; Rachel Bromwich, *A Selection of Poems*, pp. 132–4; Richard Loomis, *The Poems*, pp. 155–6; Richard Loomis, *Medieval Welsh Poems*, pp. 91–2; Glyn Jones, *Glyn Jones: Collected Poems*, ed. Meic Stephens (Cardiff: University of Wales Press, 1996), pp. 54–5; Gwyn Thomas, *His Poems*, pp. 140–1.

Y Rhugl Groen (The Rattle Bag)
Gwyn Williams, *The Burning Tree*, pp. 97–9; Joseph P. Clancy, *Medieval Welsh Lyrics*, pp. 34–5; Gwyn Williams, *Welsh Poems: Sixth Century to 1600*, pp. 54–5; Gwyn Williams, *To Look for a Word*, pp. 53–4; Joseph P. Clancy, *The Rattle Bag*, ed. Seamus Heaney and Ted Hughes (London: Faber & Faber, 1982), pp. 354–5; Richard Loomis, *The Poems*, pp. 232–3; Gwyn Thomas, *His Poems*, pp. 244–5; Joseph P. Clancy, *Medieval Welsh Poems* (2003), pp. 189–90.

Y Serch Lledrad (Secret Love)
David Bell, *Transactions of the Honourable Society of Cymmrodorion* (1941), 34; David Bell, *Fifty Poems*, pp. 139–43; Nigel Heseltine, *Selected Poems*, pp. 24–5 (1968: pp. 35–6); Kenneth Hurlstone Jackson, *A Celtic Miscellany* (1951), pp. 105–6 (1971: p. 99); Joseph P. Clancy, *Medieval Welsh Lyrics*, pp. 98–9; Gwyn Williams, *To Look for a Word*, pp. 55–6; Bryan Walters, *From the Welsh*, pp. 15–18; Rachel Bromwich, *A Selection of Poems*, pp. 32–4; Richard Loomis, *The Poems*, pp. 163–4; Rachel Bromwich, *A House of Leaves*, pp. 53–4; Richard Loomis, *Medieval Welsh Poems*, pp. 70–1; Martin Green, *Homage*, pp. 20–1; Patrick K. Ford, *The Celtic Poets*, pp. 280–2; Gwyn Thomas, *His Poems*, pp. 152–3.

Y Wawr (Dawn)
Prof. W. Lewis Jones, *Transactions of the Honourable Society of Cymmrodorion* (1907–8), 142; David Bell, *Fifty Poems*, pp. 145–9; Nigel Heseltine, *Selected Poems*, pp. 22–3 (1968: pp. 33–4); Melville Richards, in *Eos: An Inquiry into the Theme of Lovers' Meetings and Partings at Dawn in Poetry*, ed. A. T. Hatto (The Hague: Mouton, 1965), pp. 187–93; Joseph P. Clancy, *Medieval Welsh Lyrics*, pp.

82–4; Rachel Bromwich, *A Selection of Poems*, pp. 146–8; Richard Loomis, *The Poems*, pp. 238–9; Carl Lofmark, *Bards and Heroes*, pp. 94–5; Richard Loomis, *Medieval Welsh Poems*, pp. 78–9; Martin Green, *Homage*, pp. 18–19; Rolfe Humphries, *A House of Leaves*, pp. 57–8; Gwyn Thomas, *His Poems*, pp. 253–4.

Yr Adfail (The Ruin)
Arthur James Johnes (Maelog), *Translations in to English from the Poems of Davyth ap Gwilym*, pp. 104–5; Joseph P. Clancy, *Medieval Welsh Lyrics*, pp. 104–5; Tony Conran, *The Penguin Book of Welsh Verse*, pp. 149–50; Joseph P. Clancy, *Poetry Wales: Dafydd ap Gwilym*, pp. 72–3; Tony Conran, *Welsh Verse*, pp. 180–1; Rachel Bromwich, *A Selection of Poems*, p. 186; Richard Loomis, *The Poems*, pp. 258–9; Rolfe Humphries, *House of Leaves*, pp. 61–2; Patrick K. Ford, *The Celtic Poets*, pp. 278–9; Gwyn Thomas, *His Poems*, pp. 282–3; Joseph P. Clancy, *Medieval Welsh Poems* (2003), pp. 206–7.

Yr Ehedydd (To the Lark)
Arthur James Johnes (Maelog), *Cambrian Quarterly Magazine*, 1 (1829), 15; Arthur James Johnes (Maelog), *Translations in to English from the Poems of Davyth ap Gwilym*, p. 91; Arthur James Johnes (Maelog), *The Poetry of Wales* (1873), p. 55; Arthur James Johnes (Maelog), *The Red Dragon*, 5 (1884), 270; unsigned, *Wales*, 1.1 (1894), 21; Elizabeth Sharp (Lyra Celtica), *Young Wales*, 2.21 (1896), 227; H. Idris Bell, *The Nationalist*, 4.33 (1910), 39–41; Evelyn Lewes, *Life and Poems*, pp. 119–21; Arthur James Johnes (Maelog), *A Celtic Anthology*, p. 278; David Bell, *Fifty Poems*, pp. 173–7; Nigel Heseltine, *Selected Poems*, pp. 11–13 (1968: pp. 20–2); Joseph P. Clancy, *Medieval Welsh Lyrics*, pp. 87–8; Robert Gurney, *Bardic Heritage*, pp. 125–6; Rachel Bromwich, *A Selection of Poems*, pp. 74–8; Richard Loomis, *The Poems*, pp. 215–17; Richard Loomis, *Medieval Welsh Poems*, pp. 54–5; Martin Green, *Homage*, pp. 11–13; Gwyn Thomas, *His Poems*, pp. 221–2.

Yr Haf (Summer)
Arthur James Johnes, *The Poetry of Wales* (1873), pp. 41–3; Arthur James Johnes, *The Red Dragon*, 1 (1882), 153–5; Joseph P. Clancy, *Medieval Welsh Lyrics*, pp. 69–70; Robert Gurney, *Bardic Heritage*, pp. 97–8; Rachel Bromwich, *A Selection of Poems*, pp. 6–8; Richard Loomis, *The Poems*, pp. 91–2; Richard Loomis, *Medieval Welsh*

Poems, pp. 49–50; Patrick K. Ford, *The Celtic Poets*, pp. 268–70; Gwyn Thomas, *His Poems*, pp. 53–4.

Yr Wylan (The Seagull)
Arthur James Johnes (Maelog), *Cambrian Quarterly Magazine*, 1 (1829), 331; Arthur James Johnes (Maelog), *Translation in to English from the Poems of Davyth ap Gwilym*, pp. 11–12; William Owen Pughe, *The Cambrian Journal*, 5 (1858), 106–7; unsigned, *The Poetry of Wales* (1873), p. 54; Evelyn Lewes, *The Nationalist*, 1.3 (1907), 32; Evelyn Lewes, *Life and Poems*, pp. 48–9; David Bell, *Fifty Poems*, pp. 177–9; Nigel Heseltine, *Selected Poems*, pp. 31–2 (1968: pp. 4–5); Kenneth Hurlstone Jackson, *A Celtic Miscellany* (1951), pp. 107–8 (1971: pp. 100–1); Arthur James Johnes (Maelog), *A Book of Wales* (1953), pp. 320–1; Joseph P. Clancy, *Medieval Welsh Lyrics*, p. 23; Robert Gurney, *Bardic Heritage*, pp. 130–1; Tony Conran, *The Penguin Book of Welsh Verse*, pp. 139–40; Joseph P. Clancy, *Poetry Wales: Dafydd ap Gwilym*, p. 65; Glyn Jones, *Oxford Book*, p. 34; Tony Conran, *Welsh Verse*, p. 172; Rachel Bromwich, *A Selection of Poems*, p. 74; Richard Loomis, *The Poems*, pp. 222–3; Glyn Jones, *A Book of Wales* (1987), p. 28; Tony Conran, *Transactions of the Honourable Society of Cymmrodorion* (1992), 20; Richard Loomis, *Medieval Welsh Poems*, p. 77; Martin Green, *Homage*, pp. 1–2; Glyn Jones, *Glyn Jones: Collected Poems*, ed. Meic Stephens (Cardiff: University of Wales Press, 1996), p. 52; Leslie Norris, *Leslie Norris: Collected Poems* (Bridgend: Seren, 1996), p. 158; Patrick K. Ford, *The Celtic Poets*, pp. 284–5; Gwyn Thomas, *His Poems*, p. 229.

POEMS OF UNCERTAIN AUTHORSHIP ATTRIBUTED TO DAFYDD AP GWILYM[4]

Collections

Selections from the Dafydd ap Gwilym Apocrypha, ed. & tr. Helen Fulton (Llandysul: Gomer Press, 1996).
[*Apocrypha*]

---

[4] Thomas Parry in *Gwaith Dafydd ap Gwilym* (1952) made the first attempt to distinguish between genuine works by Dafydd ap Gwilym and the works of other, medieval and later, poets attributed to Dafydd ap Gwilym. This work was lately expanded by Helen Fulton, *Apocrypha* (1996).

Individual Translations

'**Ceirw'n Ymgydio**' (Deer Coupling), tr. Dafydd Johnston, *Medieval Welsh Erotic Poetry*, p. 111; '**Chwedl Blodeuwedd**' (The Pedigree of the Owl), tr. Arthur James Johnes (Maelog), *Cambrian Quarterly Magazine*, 1 (1829), 166–7; '**Cywydd i Anfon y Gal a'r Ceilliau'n Llatai**' (The Poet sends his Genitals as a Love Messenger), tr. Dafydd Johnston, *Medieval Welsh Erotic Poetry*, pp. 33–5 (1998: pp. 29–31); '**Cyngor Hen Wraig**' (An Old Woman's Advice), tr. Dafydd Johnston, *Medieval Welsh Erotic Poetry*, pp. 47–9 (1998: pp. 43–5); '**Cywydd y Cydio**' (Sexual Intercourse), tr. Dafydd Johnston, *Medieval Welsh Erotic Poetry*, pp. 55–7 (1998: pp. 51–3); '**I Forfudd**' (Englynion: To Morfudd), tr. Tony Conran, *The Penguin Book of Welsh Verse*, p. 271; tr. Gwyn Williams, *To Look for a Word*, p. 61; tr. Tony Conran, *Welsh Verse*, p. 308; '**I Seina**' (Gwilymiana: a Dialogue between the Bard and a Maid), tr. Rhydychenwr, *Cambrian Wreath*, pp. 138–9; tr. unsigned, *Barddoniaeth Dafydd ap Gwilym*, pp. 380–1; '**Y Cywydd Diwethaf**' (The Last Cywydd), tr. A. P. Graves, *Welsh Poetry Old and New*, pp. 27–8; tr. A. P. Graves, *A Celtic Psaltery*, p. 77; tr. Robert Gurney, *Bardic Heritage*, pp. 142–3; '**Y Llwyn Bedw**' (The Birch Grove), tr. Ernest Rhys, *Transactions of the Honourable Society of Cymmrodorion* (1892–3), 36–7; tr. Grace Rhys, *A Celtic Anthology*, pp. 268–70; tr. Kenneth Hurlstone Jackson, *A Celtic Miscellany* (1951), pp. 80–3 (1971: pp. 76–9); tr. Robert Gurney, *Bardic Heritage*, pp. 108–9; tr. Grace Rhys, *The Bardic Source Book*, p. 246; '**Y Fun Dawel**' (A Reproach to Morfudd), tr. H. Idris Bell, *The Nationalist*, 4.33 (1910), 39; tr. H. Idris Bell, *A Celtic Anthology*, pp. 263–4; tr. H. Idris Bell, *The Bardic Source Book*, p. 241; '**Y Dyn dan y Gerwyn**' (The Man Under the Tub), tr. Dafydd Johnston, *Medieval Welsh Erotic Poetry*, pp. 87–9; '**Y Ferch yn Ymladd yn ôl**' (The Girl Fights Back), tr. Dafydd Johnston, *Medieval Welsh Erotic Poetry*, pp. 71–3 (1998: pp. 67–9); '**Yr Eog**' (The Salmon), tr. William Lewis Jones, *Land of My Fathers*, pp. 55–6; tr. Joseph P. Clancy, *Medieval Welsh Lyrics*, pp. 163–5; tr. Robert Gurney, *Bardic Heritage*, pp. 83–4; tr. Joseph P. Clancy, *Medieval Welsh Lyrics* (2003), pp. 278–80; '**Yr Oed**' (The Love-Tryst), tr. Dafydd Johnston, *Medieval Welsh Erotic Poetry*, pp. 67–9 (1998: pp. 63–7).

Selection

Claddu'r Bardd o Gariad (The Burial of the Poet, Dead for Love)
Arthur James Johnes (Maelog), *Translations in to English from the Poems of Davyth ap Gwilym*, pp. 33–5; unsigned, *Barddoniaeth Dafydd ap Gwilym*, pp. 383–4; Arthur James Johnes (Maelog), *The Red Dragon*, 1 (1882), 248–9; Evelyn Lewes, *Life and Poems*, pp. 50–1;[5] William Lewis Jones, *Land of my Fathers*, pp. 56–7; A. P. Graves, *A Celtic Psaltery*, p. 76; A. P. Graves, *Welsh Poetry Old and New*, pp. 26–7; W. J. Gruffydd, *Dafydd ap Gwilym*, pp. 75–7; H. Idris Bell, *Fifty Poems*, pp. 221–5; Kenneth Hurlstone Jackson, *A Celtic Miscellany* (1951), pp. 85–6 (1971: pp. 81–2); Tony Conran, *The Penguin Book of Welsh Verse*, pp. 159–60; Nigel Heseltine, *25 Poems*, pp. 26–7; Robert Gurney, *Bardic Heritage*, pp. 109–11; Tony Conran, *Welsh Verse*, pp. 188–9; Martin Green, *Homage*, p. 15; Helen Fulton, *Apocrypha*, pp. 68–70.

I'r Lleian (To the Nun)
Evelyn Lewes, *Life and Poems*, pp. 34–5; H. Idris Bell, *Fifty Poems*, pp. 153–5; Joseph P. Clancy, *The Anglo-Welsh Review*, 12.29 (1962), 29–30; Joseph P. Clancy, *Medieval Welsh Lyrics*, pp. 165–6; Tony Conran, *The Penguin Book of Welsh Verse*, pp. 160–1; Gwyn Williams, *To Look for a Word*, p. 79; Tony Conran, *Welsh Verse*, pp. 189–90; Helen Fulton, *Apocrypha*, p. 52; Joseph P. Clancy, *Medieval Welsh Poems* (2003), pp. 280–1.

Llys y Banhadlwyn (The Bower of Broom)
Arthur James Johnes (Maelog), *Translations in to English from the Poems of Davyth ap Gwilym*, pp. 73–5; Arthur James Johnes (Maelog), *The Poetry of Wales* (1873), pp. 138–40; Arthur James Johnes (Maelog), *A Book of Wales* (1953), pp. 316–17; Joseph P. Clancy, *Medieval Welsh Lyrics*, pp. 151–3; Robert Gurney, *Bardic Heritage*, pp. 95–6; Helen Fulton, *Apocrypha*, pp. 64–8; Joseph P. Clancy, *Medieval Welsh Poems* (2003), pp. 269–71.

---

[5] Lewes makes reference to a translation of this poem by H. Elvet Lewis (Elfed). I have been unable to locate this translation.

Saith Gusan (Seven Kisses)
Gwyn Williams, *The Rent that's Due to Love*, pp. 29–31; Joseph P. Clancy, *The Anglo-Welsh Review*, 12.29 (1962), 28–9; Joseph P. Clancy, *Medieval Welsh Lyrics*, pp. 158–9; Robert Gurney, *Bardic Heritage*, pp. 90–1; Gwyn Williams, *To Look for a Word*, pp. 59–60; Joseph P. Clancy, *Oxford Book*, pp. 50–1; Helen Fulton, *Apocrypha*, pp. 62–4.

Y Dilyw/Y Daran (The Thunder Storm)
Edward Williams (Iolo Morganwg), *Poems, Lyric and Pastoral* (London: Printed for the author by J. Nichols, 1794), pp. 20–2; Edward Williams (Iolo Morganwg), *The Cambrian Wreath*, pp. 113–14; Edward Williams (Iolo Morganwg), *Barddoniaeth Dafydd ap Gwilym*, pp. 379–80; Arthur James Johnes (Maelog), *Translations in to English from the Poems of Davyth ap Gwilym*, pp. 42–3; Nigel Heseltine, *Selected Poems*, pp. 7–9 (1968: pp. 14–16); Robert Gurney, *Bardic Heritage*, pp. 114–15; Martin Green, *Homage*, p. 6; Helen Fulton, *Apocrypha*, pp. 122–4.

Y Niwl Hudolus (The Mist)
George Borrow, *Transactions of the Honourable Society of Cymmrodorion* (1892–3), 36; George Borrow, *Welsh Poems & Ballads*, pp. 59–60; David Bell, *Fifty Poems*, pp. 245–9; Kenneth Hurlstone Jackson, *A Celtic Miscellany* (1951), pp. 82–3 (1971: pp. 78–9); George Borrow, *A Book of Wales* (1953), pp. 315–16; George Borrow, *Presenting Welsh Poetry*, pp. 30–1; Robert Gurney, *Bardic Heritage*, pp. 81–3; Helen Fulton, *Apocrypha*, pp. 118–20.

Y Sêr (The Stars)
Arthur James Johnes (Maelog), *Translations in to English from the Poems of Davyth ap Gwilym*, pp. 22–5; Arthur James Johnes (Maelog), *Barddoniaeth Dafydd ap Gwilym*, pp. 381–3; H. Idris Bell, *Transactions of the Honourable Society of Cymmrodorion* (1941), 34–5; H. Idris Bell, *Fifty Poems*, pp. 239–45; *A Celtic Miscellany* (1951), pp. 83–5 (1971: pp. 79–80); Joseph P. Clancy, *Medieval Welsh Lyrics*, 154–6; Robert Gurney, *Bardic Heritage*, pp. 118–20; Helen Fulton, *Apocrypha*, pp. 108–12; Gwyn Thomas, *His Poems*, pp. 307–9; Joseph P. Clancy, *Medieval Welsh Poems* (2003), pp. 271–3.

Y Tŷ Bedwen (The Birch-tree House)
H. Idris Bell, *Fifty Poems*, pp. 133–5; Gwyn Williams, *The Rent that's Due to Love*, pp. 37–9; Joseph P. Clancy, *Medieval Welsh Lyrics*, p. 161; Gwyn Williams, *To Look for a Word*, p. 80; Helen Fulton, *Apocrypha*, pp. 32–4; Joseph P. Clancy, *Medieval Welsh Poems* (2003), pp. 276–7.

Yr Alarch (The Swan)
unsigned, *Barddoniaeth Dafydd ap Gwilym*, pp. 385–6; Arthur James Johnes (Maelog), *Translations in to English from the Poems of Davyth ap Gwilym*, pp. 63–4; Arthur James Johnes (Maelog), *The Poetry of Wales* (1873), pp. 142–3; unsigned, *The Nationalist*, 1.5 (1907), 32; H. Idris Bell, *Fifty Poems*, pp. 169–73; H. Idris Bell, *A Book of Wales* (1953), pp. 44–5; Joseph P. Clancy, *Medieval Welsh Lyrics*, pp. 156–8; Robert Gurney, *Bardic Heritage*, pp. 135–6; Helen Fulton, *Apocrypha*, pp. 84–6; R. Williams Parry, *Cerddi R. Williams Parry: Y Casgliad Cyflawn*, ed. Alan Llwyd (Denbigh: Gwasg Gee, 1998), p. 240; Joseph P. Clancy, *Medieval Welsh Poems* (2003), pp. 275–6.

Yr Eira[6] (The Snow)
Arthur James Johnes (Maelog), *Translations in to English from the Poems of Davyth ap Gwilym*, pp. 89–90; Evelyn Lewes, *The Nationalist*, 2.13 (1908), 11; H. Idris Bell, *The Nationalist*, 4.36 (1911), 12; Evelyn Lewes, *Life and Poems*, pp. 4–5; H. Idris Bell, *A Celtic Anthology*, pp. 264–6; H. Idris Bell, *Fifty Poems*, pp. 275–9; Nigel Heseltine, *Selected Poems*, pp. 5–7 (1968: pp. 12–13); Kenneth Hurlstone Jackson, *A Celtic Miscellany* (1951), pp. 81–2 (1971: pp. 77–8); Robert Gurney, *Bardic Heritage*, pp. 104–6; Martin Green, *Homage*, pp. 7–8; Helen Fulton, *Apocrypha*, pp. 112–14; R. Williams Parry, *Cerddi R. Williams Parry: Y Casgliad Cyflawn*, ed. Alan Llwyd (Dinbych: Gwasg Gee, 1998), p. 239; H. Idris Bell, *The Bardic Source Book*, p. 242; Rolfe Humphries, *World Poetry: An*

---

[6] There is some debate over the authorship of this poem. Some academics maintain that it is the work of Dafydd ap Gwilym. It was not included in Thomas Parry's edition but strong arguments have been put forward in recent years for Dafydd ap Gwilym as author.

Anthology of Verse from Antiquity to our Time, ed. Katharine Washburn and John S. Major (New York; London: Norton, 1998), pp. 448–9; Gwyn Thomas, *His Poems*, pp. 310–11; Joseph P. Clancy, *Medieval Welsh Poems* (2003), pp. 267–9.

DAFYDD LLWYD AP LLYWELYN AP GRUFFUDD (Dafydd Llwyd of Mathafarn; *c.* 1395–1486)

Individual Translations
'Cywydd y Fedwen' (The Birchtree), tr. Dafydd Johnston, *Medieval Welsh Poems*, pp. 135–7; 'Dialedd y Bardd' (The Poet's Revenge), tr. Dafydd Johnston, *Medieval Welsh Erotic Poetry*, pp. 99–101 (1998: pp. 95–7).

Gwerfyl Mechain and Dafydd Llwyd of Mathafarn, 'Ymddiddan Rhwng Dau Fardd' (A Conversation between Two Poets), tr. Dafydd Johnston, *Medieval Welsh Erotic Poetry*, p. 45 (1998: p. 41).

'SIR' DAFYDD LLWYD THE SCHOLAR (*fl.* 1550–70)

Individual Translations
'Y Clerigwr a'r Forwyn' (The Cleric and the Virgin), tr. Dafydd Johnston, *Medieval Welsh Erotic Poetry*, pp. 107–9 (1998: pp. 103–5); 'Merch o Swydd Lincoln' (A Lincolnshire Lass), tr. Dafydd Johnston, *Medieval Welsh Erotic Poetry* (1998), pp. 107–9.[7]

DAFYDD NANMOR (*fl.* 1450–90)

Individual Translations
'Bonedd Rhys ap Rhydderch ap Rhys' (The Nobility of Rhys ap Rhydderch ap Rhys), tr. A. P. Graves (after Borrow), *Welsh Poetry Old and New*, p. 22; tr. George Borrow, *Welsh Poems & Ballads*, p. 129; tr. Joseph P. Clancy, *Medieval Welsh Lyrics*, pp. 194–6; tr. Tony

---

[7] This translation is the only addition to the 1998 Seren edition of *Medieval Welsh Erotic Poetry*.

Conran, *The Penguin Book of Welsh Verse*, pp. 180–2; tr. Gwyn Williams, *To Look for a Word*, pp. 110–11; tr. Tony Conran, *Welsh Verse*, pp. 206–7; tr. Tony Conran, *Medieval Welsh Poems*, pp. 132–3; tr. Joseph P. Clancy, *Medieval Welsh Poems* (2003), pp. 306–7; 'Cywydd i Wallt Llio Rhydderch' (Llio's Hair), tr. Robert Gurney, *Bardic Heritage*, pp. 152–4; tr. Dafydd Johnston, *Medieval Welsh Poetry*, pp. 134–5; 'I'r Paun' (The Peacock), tr. Joseph P. Clancy, *Medieval Welsh Lyrics*, pp. 192–3; tr. Joseph P. Clancy, *Medieval Welsh Poems* (2003), pp. 302–3; 'I Rys o'r Tywyn' (Ode to Rhys ap Maredudd of Tywyn), tr. H. Idris Bell, *A History of Welsh Literature*, p. 137; tr. H. Idris Bell, *Presenting Welsh Poetry*, pp. 32–4; tr. Tony Conran, *The Penguin Book of Welsh Verse*, pp. 178–80; tr. H. Idris Bell, *Oxford Book*, pp. 60–2; tr. H. Idris Bell, *Transactions of the Honourable Society of Cymmrodorion* (1982), 37; tr. Tony Conran, *Welsh Verse*, pp. 203–5; tr. Joseph P. Clancy, *Medieval Welsh Poems* (2003), pp. 203–5; 'I Syr Dafydd ap Thomas Offeiriad o'r Faenawr' (To Sir Dafydd ap Thomas), tr. H. Idris Bell, *A History of Welsh Literature*, p. 152; 'Marwnad Bun' (Elegy for a Maiden), tr. H. Idris Bell, *Transactions of the Honourable Society of Cymmrodorion* (1942), 142; tr. Joseph P. Clancy, *Medieval Welsh Lyrics*, pp. 193–4; tr. Robert Gurney, *Bardic Heritage*, pp. 154–5; tr. Joseph P. Clancy, *Medieval Welsh Poems* (2003), pp. 305–6.

DING MOEL (*fl.* fifteenth century)

Individual Translations
'Cyngor i Gyfaill' (Advice to a Friend), tr. Dafydd Johnston, *Medieval Welsh Erotic Poetry*, pp. 51–3 (1998: pp. 47–9).

THOMAS EVANS OR THOMAS AB IFAN (*fl.* 1580–1633)

Individual Translations
'Aelodau Rhywiol Mab a Merch' (The Male and Female Sexual Organs), tr. Dafydd Johnston, *Medieval Welsh Erotic Poetry*, p. 135; 'I Ferch' (To a Girl), tr. Dafydd Johnston, *Medieval Welsh Erotic Poetry*, p. 135; 'Rhoi'r Ffidil yn y To' (Farewell to Arms), tr. Dafydd Johnston, *Medieval Welsh Erotic Poetry*, p. 135.

GRONW GYRIOG (*fl.* 1320)

Individual Translations
'**Marwnad Gwenhwyfar**' (Lament for Gwenhwyfar), tr. Joseph P. Clancy, *Medieval Welsh Poems* (2003), pp. 185–6.

GRUFFUDD AB ADDA AP DAFYDD (*fl.* 1340–70)

Individual Translations
'**Lleidr Serch**' (The Thief of Love), tr. Gwyn Williams, *Introduction to Welsh Poetry*, p. 98; tr. Gwyn Williams, *The Burning Tree*, p. 87; tr. Joseph P. Clancy, *Medieval Welsh Lyrics*, p. 109; tr. Gwyn Williams, *Welsh Poems: Sixth Century to 1600*, p. 49; tr. Gwyn Williams, *To Look for a Word*, p. 65; tr. Joseph P. Clancy, *Medieval Welsh Poems* (2003), pp. 209–10; '**Y Fedwen yn Bawl Haf**' (The Maypole), tr. Arthur James Johnes (Maelog), *Translations into English Verse from the Poems of Davyth ap Gwilym* (London: Henry Hooper, 1834), pp. 71–2; tr. H. Idris Bell, *Transactions of the Honourable Society of Cymmrodorion* (1940), 227–9; tr. Kenneth Hurlstone Jackson, *A Celtic Miscellany* (1951), pp. 87–9 (1971: pp. 82–4); tr. Joseph P. Clancy, *Medieval Welsh Lyrics*, pp. 107–8; tr. Joseph P. Clancy, *Medieval Welsh Poems*, pp. 94–6; tr. Joseph P. Clancy, *Medieval Welsh Poems* (2003), pp. 208–9.

GRUFFUDD AB IEUAN AP LLYWELYN FYCHAN (*c.* 1485–1553)

Individual Translations
'**Marwnad Tudur Aled**' (Elegy on Tudur Aled), tr. H. Idris Bell, *The Nationalist*, 4.34 (1911), 30–2; '**Cywydd yn erbyn braint delwau**' (Cywydd against the privileges of images), tr. Glanmor Williams, *Transactions of the Honourable Society of Cymmrodorion* (1991), 94.

GRUFFUDD GRYG (1357–70)

Individual Translations
'Cywydd i Dduw' (Christ the King), tr. Joseph P. Clancy, *Medieval Welsh Lyrics*, pp. 131–2; tr. Joseph P. Clancy, *Medieval Welsh Poems* (2003), pp. 218–19; 'Cywydd Marwnad Rhys ap Tudur o Fôn' (Lament for Rhys ap Tudur), tr. Joseph P. Clancy, *Medieval Welsh Lyrics*, pp. 124–6; tr. Joseph P. Clancy, *Medieval Welsh Poems* (2003), pp. 212–14; 'I'r Don' (The Wave), tr. H. Idris Bell, *Transactions of the Honourable Society of Cymmrodorion* (1942), 135–6; 'I'r Lleuad' (The April Moon), tr. Joseph P. Clancy, *Medieval Welsh Lyrics*, pp. 122–4; tr. Joseph P. Clancy, *Medieval Welsh Poems* (2003), pp. 210–12; 'Y Ferch Anwadal' (The Fickle Girl), tr. Joseph P. Clancy, *Medieval Welsh Lyrics*, pp. 128–9; tr. Joseph P. Clancy, *Medieval Welsh Poems* (2003), pp. 215–17; 'Ymryson Dafydd ap Gwilym a Gruffudd Gryg' (The Verse Debate Between Dafydd ap Gwilym and Gruffudd Gryg) ['Cywydd Cyntaf Gruffudd' (Gruffudd's First Cywydd)], tr. Arthur James Johnes (Maelog), *Cambrian Quarterly Magazine*, 2 (1830), 434; tr. Arthur James Johnes (Maelog), *Translations into English Verse from the Poems of Davyth ap Gwilym* (London: Henry Hooper, 1834), pp. 67–8; tr. Joseph P. Clancy, *Medieval Welsh Lyrics*, pp. 126–7; tr. Richard Loomis, *Dafydd ap Gwilym: The Poems* (Binghamton, New York: Medieval & Renaissance Texts & Studies, 1982), pp. 263–4; tr. Patrick K. Ford, *The Celtic Poets*, pp. 319–20; tr. Gwyn Thomas, *Dafydd ap Gwilym: His Poems* (Cardiff: University of Wales Press, 2001), pp. 288–9; tr. Joseph P. Clancy, *Medieval Welsh Poems* (2003), pp. 214–15; ['Ail Gywydd Gruffudd' (Gruffudd's Second Cywydd)], tr. Richard Loomis, *Dafydd ap Gwilym: The Poems* (Binghamton, New York: Medieval & Renaissance Texts & Studies, 1982), pp. 266–8; tr. Gwyn Thomas, *Dafydd ap Gwilym: His Poems* (Cardiff: University of Wales Press, 2001), pp. 293–4; ['Trydydd Cywydd Gruffudd' (Gruffudd's Third Cywydd)], tr. Richard Loomis, *Dafydd ap Gwilym: The Poems* (Binghamton, New York: Medieval & Renaissance Texts & Studies, 1982), pp. 270–1; tr. Gwyn Thomas, *Dafydd ap Gwilym: His Poems* (Cardiff: University of Wales Press, 2001), pp. 297–8; ['Pedwerydd Cywydd Gruffudd' (Gruffudd's Fourth Cywydd)], tr. Richard Loomis, *Dafydd ap Gwilym: The Poems* (Binghamton, New York: Medieval & Renaissance Texts & Studies, 1982), pp. 273–5; tr. Gwyn Thomas, *Dafydd ap Gwilym: His Poems*

(Cardiff: University of Wales Press, 2001), pp. 302–3; '**Yr Ywen Uwchben Bedd Dafydd ap Gwilym**' (The Yew-Tree above the grave of Dafydd ap Gwilym), tr. David Bell, *Dafydd ap Gwilym: Fifty Poems*, ed. H. Idris Bell (London: Cymmrodorion Society, 1942), pp. 307–9; tr. David Bell, *Transactions of the Honourable Society of Cymmrodorion* (1949–51), 42–3; tr. Joseph P. Clancy, *Medieval Welsh Lyrics*, pp. 129–30; tr. Tony Conran, *The Penguin Book of Welsh Verse*, pp. 157–8; tr. Robert Gurney, *Bardic Heritage*, pp. 148–9; tr. Leslie Norris, *Poetry Wales*, 6.3 (1970), 27–8; tr. Tony Conran, *Welsh Verse*, pp. 186–7; tr. Leslie Norris, *Leslie Norris: Collected Poems* (Bridgend: Seren, 1996), p. 91; tr. Joseph P. Clancy, *Medieval Welsh Poems* (2003), pp. 217–18.

GRUFFUDD LLWYD AP DAFYDD AB EINION LLYGLIW (*c.* 1380–*c.* 1420)

Individual Translations

'**I Ddanfon yr Haul i Annerch Morgannwg**' (Sending the Sun to Morgannwg), tr. Arthur James Johnes (Maelog), *Translations in to English Verse from the Poems of Davyth ap Gwilym* (London: Henry Hooper, 1834), pp. 96–9; tr. unsigned, *Barddoniaeth Dafydd ap Gwilym o Grynhoad Owen Jones (Owain Myfyr), William Owen (Dr. W. Owen Pughe), Edward Williams (Iolo Morganwg) yn nghydag amryw gyfieithiadau i'r Seisnig*, ed. Robert Ellis (Cynddelw) (Liverpool: I. Foulkes, 1873), pp. 389–91; tr. unsigned, *The Poetry of Wales* (1873), pp. 55–6; tr. W. Lewis Jones, *Transactions of the Honourable Society of Cymmrodorion* (1907–8), 129; tr. Evelyn Lewes, *Life and Poems of Dafydd ap Gwilym* (London: David Nutt, 1914), pp. 71–4; tr. George Borrow, *Welsh Poems & Ballads*, pp. 153–4; tr. A. P. Graves, *Welsh Poetry Old and New*, pp. 23–6; tr. unsigned, *Cymru Heroica: An Anthology of Welsh Verse*, ed. Owen Watkin (London: James Brodie & Co., [1919?]), pp. 14–15; tr. Joseph P. Clancy, *Medieval Welsh Lyrics*, pp. 147–9; tr. Joseph P. Clancy, *Medieval Welsh Poems* (2003), pp. 263–5; '**I Hywel ap Meurig Fychan o Nannau a Meurig Llwyd ei Frawd**' (To Hywel and Meurig, Sons of Meurig Fychan of Nannau), tr. Dafydd Johnston, *Medieval Welsh Poems*, pp. 117–19; '**I Owain Glyndŵr**' (To Owain Glyndŵr), tr. Edward Jones, *The Musical, Poetical, and Historical Relicks*, pp. 21–4; tr. unsigned, in Thomas Pennant, *A Tour in Wales Vol. I,*

(London: Benjamin White, 1784), pp. 334–8; tr. Dafydd Johnston, *Medieval Welsh Poems*, pp. 115–17; tr. Mr Williams of Vron, *The Bardic Source Book*, pp. 211–14; tr. Joseph P. Clancy, *Medieval Welsh Poems* (2003), pp. 265–7; '**Marwnad Hywel ap Meurig Fychan o Nannau**' (Elegy for Hywel ap Meurig of Nannau), tr. Dafydd Johnston, *Medieval Welsh Poems*, pp. 120–1; '**Mawl i Hywel ap Meurig Fychan o Nannau a Meurig Llwyd ei Frawd**' (In Defence of Praise), tr. Joseph P. Clancy, *Medieval Welsh Poems* (2003), pp. 261–3; '**Y Cwest ar Forgan ap Dafydd o Rydodyn**' (An Ode on Morgan ap Dafydd), tr. Taliesin Williams (ab Iolo), *Iolo Manuscripts*, pp. 680–1; tr. unsigned, *The History of the Literature of Wales*, pp. 18–20.

GUTO'R GLYN (*c.* 1412–*c.* 1493)

Collections

R. Gerallt Jones, *Guto'r Glyn* (Market Drayton: Tern Press, 1976).

Individual Translations

'**Ateb i Lywelyn ap Gutun**' (The Drunken Dream of Llywelyn), tr. Joseph P. Clancy, *Medieval Welsh Lyrics*, pp. 205–6; tr. Joseph P. Clancy, *Medieval Welsh Poems* (2003), pp. 311–13; '**Canmol Croesoswallt**' (In Praise of Oswestry), tr. Howel W. Lloyd, *Archaeologia Cambrensis*, 11 (5th series, 1894), 67; tr. D. M. Lloyd, *A Book of Wales* (1953), pp. 95–7; tr. Joseph P. Clancy, *Medieval Welsh Lyrics*, pp. 219–21; tr. Richard Loomis, *Medieval Welsh Poems*, pp. 175–7; tr. Joseph P. Clancy, *Medieval Welsh Poems* (2003), pp. 324–5; '**Cywydd Clod Matthew Goch**' (Encomium Matthew Goch), tr. Howel W. Lloyd, *The History of the Literature of Wales*, pp. 87–8; '**Cywydd i Ieuan ab Einion ap Gruffydd o'r Cryniarth**' (To Ieuan ab Einion), tr. Howel W. Lloyd, *Archaeologia Cambrensis*, 3 (5th series, 1886), 259–61; '**Dychan i Gal Dafydd ab Edmwnd**' (Satire on Dafydd ab Edmwnd's Penis), tr. Dafydd Johnston, *Medieval Welsh Erotic Poetry*, pp. 131–3; '**I Dafydd, Abad Glyn Egwestl**' (To Dafydd ab Ieuan), tr. H. Idris Bell, *Transactions of the Honourable Society of Cymmrodorion* (1940), 249–53; tr. Joseph P. Clancy, *Medieval Welsh Lyrics*, pp. 224–5; tr. Tony Conran, *The Penguin Book of Welsh Verse*, pp. 175–77; tr. Tony Conran, *Welsh*

Verse, pp. 201–3; tr. Richard Loomis, *Medieval Welsh Poems*, pp. 193–5; tr. Joseph P. Clancy, *Medieval Welsh Poems* (2003), pp. 325–7; '**I Ddafydd Llwyd o Aber Tanad**' (To Dafydd Llwyd), tr. Howel Wm. Lloyd, *Archaeologia Cambrensis*, 7 (4th series, 1876), 33; '**I Ddafydd Llwyd ap Dafydd ab Einion**' (Ode to Dafydd Llwyd ap Dafydd ab Einion), tr. Taliesin Williams (ab Iolo), *Iolo Manuscripts*, pp. 694–6; tr. unsigned, *The History of the Literature of Wales*, pp. 89–91; '**I Ddiolch am Farch i Ddafydd ap Meurig Fychan o Nannau**' (A Horse for Guto: for Dafydd ap Meurig Fychan of Nannau), tr. Richard Loomis, *Medieval Welsh Poems*, pp. 187–9; '**I Erchi Llyfr y Greal**' (A Request to Trahaearn ab Ieuan for a Loan of 'The Holy Grail'), tr. Taliesin Williams (ab Iolo), *Iolo Manuscripts*, pp. 704–6; tr. Thomas Stephens, *The Literature of the Kymry*, pp. 443–5 (1876: pp. 424–6); tr. Ernest Rhys, *A Celtic Anthology*, pp. 274–5; tr. H. Idris Bell, *Transactions of the Honourable Society of Cymmrodorion* (1942), 146–7; tr. Richard Loomis, *Medieval Welsh Poems*, pp. 198–200; '**I Feibion Llywelyn ap Hwlcyn o Fôn**' (Jewels of Môn), tr. Richard Loomis, *Medieval Welsh Poems*, pp. 151–3; '**I Harri Ddu o Eos**' (Harri Ddu), tr. Richard Loomis, *Medieval Welsh Poems*, pp. 179–81; '**I Hywel ab Ifan Fychan**' (To Hywel ab Ifan Fychan), tr. Tony Conran, *The Penguin Book of Welsh Verse*, pp. 173–5; tr. Tony Conran, *Welsh Verse*, pp. 199–201; '**I Hywel ap Ieuan o Foelyrch**' (Moelyrch), tr. Richard Loomis, *Medieval Welsh Poems*, pp. 157–9; '**I Hywel o Foelyrch pan Friwiasai ei Lin**' (A Healing Cywydd, for Hywel of Moelyrch), tr. Richard Loomis, *Medieval Welsh Poems*, pp. 159–61; '**I Ofyn Ffaling gan Elen Gwraig Gr. Ap. Lln. Ap Gruffudd**' (A Cloak from Elen of Llŷn), tr. Richard Loomis, *Medieval Welsh Poems*, pp. 185–6; '**I'r Brenin Edward**' (King Edward IV), tr. Richard Loomis, *Medieval Welsh Poems*, pp. 171–3; '**I'r Deon Cyffin i Ddiolch am Baderau**' (The Rosary), tr. Richard Loomis, *Medieval Welsh Poems*, pp. 189–91; '**I Rys Abad Ystrad Fflur**' (Defending His Privileges), tr. Richard Loomis, *Medieval Welsh Poems*, pp. 196–7; '**I Sieffrai Cyffin Cwnstabl Croesoswallt**' (Geoffrey Cyffin, Constable of Oswestry), tr. Richard Loomis, *Medieval Welsh Poems*, pp. 177–9; '**I Wiliam Herbart**' (To William Herbert), tr. Joseph P. Clancy, *Medieval Welsh Lyrics*, pp. 207–9; tr. Richard Loomis, *Medieval Welsh Poems*, pp. 166–8; tr. Joseph P. Clancy, *Medieval Welsh Poems* (2003), pp. 318–20; '**I Wladys Hael**' (Courting Gwladus Hael), tr. Richard Loomis, *Medieval Welsh Poems*, pp. 181–2; tr. Joseph P. Clancy,

Medieval Welsh Lyrics (2003), pp. 315–16; 'Marwnad Edward ap Dafydd o'r Waun' (Edward ap Dafydd of Chirkland), tr. Richard Loomis, *Medieval Welsh Poems*, pp. 153–5; 'Marwnad Gwerful Ferch Fadog o Fro Danad' (Gwerful of Tanat-Vale), tr. Richard Loomis, *Medieval Welsh Poems*, pp. 173–5; 'Marwnad Harri Ddu o Eos' (The Death of Harri Ddu), tr. Richard Loomis, *Medieval Welsh Poems*, pp. 183–4; 'Marwnad Llywelyn ab y Moel' (Lament for Llywelyn ab y Moel), tr. Joseph P. Clancy, *Medieval Welsh Lyrics*, pp. 209–11; tr. Gwyn Williams, *To Look for a Word*, pp. 83–5; tr. Richard Loomis, *Medieval Welsh Poems*, pp. 148–51; tr. Joseph P. Clancy, *Medieval Welsh Poems* (2003), pp. 313–14; 'Marwnad Rhys Abad Ystrad Fflur' (The Kiss of Peace), tr. Richard Loomis, *Medieval Welsh Poems*, pp. 191–3; 'Marwnad Siôn ap Madog Pilstwn' (Lament for Siôn ap Madog Pilstwn), tr. Joseph P. Clancy, *Medieval Welsh Lyrics*, pp. 215–17; tr. Richard Loomis, *Medieval Welsh Poems*, pp. 155–7; Joseph P. Clancy, *Medieval Welsh Lyrics* (2003), pp. 322–4; 'Moliant i Siân Gwraig Siôn Bwch' (Lady Jane Burrough of Mawddwy), tr. Richard Loomis, *Medieval Welsh Poems*, pp. 161–3; 'Moliant Llaw Arian Siôn Dafi' (The Silver Hand of Siôn Dafi), tr. Richard Loomis, *Medieval Welsh Poems*, pp. 163–5; 'Moliant Tomas ap Watcyn Fychan' (The Drinking Bout), tr. Richard Loomis, *Medieval Welsh Poems*, pp. 146–8; 'Porthmona' (Sheep-Dealing), tr. Joseph P. Clancy, *Medieval Welsh Lyrics*, pp. 211–13; tr. Joseph P. Clancy, *Medieval Welsh Poems* (2003), pp. 320–2; 'Serch Offeiriad ar ei Nawddsant' (A Priest's Love), tr. Joseph P. Clancy, *Medieval Welsh Lyrics*, pp. 213–15; tr. Joseph P. Clancy, *Medieval Welsh Poems* (2003), pp. 316–18; 'Ystyriaeth Bywyd' (Meditation), tr. Joseph P. Clancy, *Medieval Welsh Lyrics*, pp. 221–3; tr. Richard Loomis, *Medieval Welsh Poems*, pp. 200–2; tr. Joseph P. Clancy, *Medieval Welsh Poems* (2003), pp. 327–9.

GUTUN OWAIN or GRUFFUDD AP HUW AB OWAIN (*fl.* 1450–98)

Individual Translations
'Cywydd dros Maredydd ap Gruffydd ap Ednyfed i Ofyn March i'r Abad Siôn ap Rhisiart Abad Llanegwystl' (Asking a Stallion), tr. Tony Conran, *The Penguin Book of Welsh Verse*, pp. 187–8; tr. Tony Conran, *Welsh Verse*, pp. 211–13; 'Gofyn Cŵn Hela' (The Hounds),

tr. Joseph P. Clancy, *Medieval Welsh Lyrics*, pp. 236–7; tr. Joseph P. Clancy, *Medieval Welsh Poems* (2003), pp. 341–3; 'Y Ddyn a'r Santaidd Anwyd' (Love's Language), tr. Joseph P. Clancy, *Medieval Welsh Lyrics*, pp. 237–9; tr. Joseph P. Clancy, *Medieval Welsh Poems* (2003), pp. 343–4; 'Y Fun Uchel o Fonedd' (To a Noble Girl), tr. Dafydd Johnston, *Medieval Welsh Poems*, pp. 205–6; 'Awdl i Ddafydd (ap Ieuan) ap Iorwerth abad Llan Egwestl' (Ode in Praise of the Abbot of Glynegwestl), tr. Dafydd Johnston, *Medieval Welsh Poems*, pp. 203–5; tr. Joseph P. Clancy, *Medieval Welsh Poems* (2003), pp. 344–6.

GWERFUL MECHAIN (*fl.* 1462–1500)

Individual Translations
'Cywydd i ofyn Telyn' (Asking for a Harp), tr. Margaret Lloyd, *Poetry Wales*, 29.4 (1994), 44; 'Cywydd y Cedor' (Vivat Vagina), tr. Dafydd Johnston, *Medieval Welsh Erotic Poetry*, pp. 41–3 (1998: pp. 37–9); tr. Joseph P. Clancy, *Medieval Welsh Poems* (2003), pp. 338–9; 'I Wragedd Eiddigeddus' (To Jealous Wives), tr. Dafydd Johnston, *Medieval Welsh Erotic Poetry*, pp. 37–9 (1998: pp. 33–5).

Gwerful Mechain and Dafydd Llwyd of Mathafarn, 'Ymddiddan Rhwng Dau Fardd' (A Conversation between Two Poets), tr. Dafydd Johnston, *Medieval Welsh Erotic Poetry*, p. 45 (1998: p. 41).

POEMS OF UNCERTAIN AUTHORSHIP ATTRIBUTED TO GWERFUL MECHAIN[8]

'Gwerful wyf o gwr y lan' (The Hostess of the Ferry Inn), tr. H. Idris Bell, *A Celtic Anthology*, p. 275; tr. Joseph P. Clancy, *Medieval Welsh Lyrics*, pp. 232–3; tr. H. Idris Bell, *Oxford Book*, p. 66; Joseph P. Clancy, *Medieval Welsh Poems*, pp. 206–7; tr. Joseph P. Clancy, *Medieval Welsh Poems* (2003), pp. 337–8; 'Yr Eira' (The Snowfall), tr. Kenneth Hurlstone Jackson, *A Celtic Miscellany* (1951), p. 139

---

[8] For more information on works attributed to Gwerful Mechain but possibly the work of Gwerful Fychan and others, see *Gwaith Gwerful Mechain ac Eraill*, ed. Nerys Ann Howells (Aberystwyth: University of Wales Centre for Advanced Welsh and Celtic Studies, 2001), p. 3.

(1971: p. 128); tr. Kenneth Hurlstone Jackson, *Oxford Book*, p. 66; 'Ysbiwch farch glas buan' (The Grey Steed), tr. A. P. Graves, *Welsh Poetry Old and New*, p. 40; tr. A. P. Graves, *A Celtic Anthology*, pp. 275–6.[9]

GWILYM AP SEFNYN (*fl.* 1435–70)

Individual Translations
'Marwnad i'w Ddeg Plentyn' (Elegy for His Ten Children), tr. Dafydd Johnston, *Poets' Grief*, pp. 63–7.

HUW ARWYSTLI (*fl.* 1542–78)

Individual Translations
'Mab wedi Ymwisgo mewn Dillad Merch' (A Boy Dressed in Girl's Clothes), tr. Dafydd Johnston, *Medieval Welsh Erotic Poetry*, pp. 121–3.

HUW CAE LLWYD (*fl.* 1455–1505)

Individual Translations
'Crog Aberhodni' (The Cross), tr. Joseph P. Clancy, *Medieval Welsh Lyrics*, pp. 240–2; tr. Joseph P. Clancy, *Medieval Welsh Poems* (2003), pp. 347–8.

HUW LLWYD O GYNFAL (1568?–1630?)

Individual Translations
'Cyngor y Llwynog' (The Fox's Counsel), tr. Joseph P. Clancy, *Medieval Welsh Lyrics*, pp. 204–7; tr. Joseph P. Clancy, *Oxford Book*, pp. 86–9.

---

[9] This poem has been attributed to Gwerful Mechain, Huw Cae Llwyd, Maredudd ap Rhys, Ieuan Brydydd Hir, Llywelyn Goch ap Meurig Hen, Syr Phylip Emlyn, Rhys Goch Eryri and Dafydd Nanmor. See *Gwaith Gwerful Mechain*.

HYWEL AP DAFYDD AB IEUAN AP RHYS (Hywel Dafi; *fl.* 1450–80)

Individual Translations
'**Ffantasi**' (Fantasy), tr. Dafydd Johnston, *Medieval Welsh Erotic Poetry*, pp. 59–61 (1998: pp. 55–7); '**Rhwystredigaeth**' (Frustration), tr. Dafydd Johnston, *Medieval Welsh Erotic Poetry*, pp. 59–61 (pp. 63–5).

'SIR' HYWEL OF BUILTH (*fl.* middle sixteenth century)

Individual Translations
'**Gofyn Clo Cont**' (To Request a Chastity Belt), tr. Dafydd Johnston, *Medieval Welsh Erotic Poetry*, pp. 117–19.

IEUAN AP RHYDDERCH (fifteenth century)

Individual Translations
'**Gorhoffedd**' (Ieuan's Boast), tr. Gwyn Williams, *To Look for a Word*, pp. 88–92; tr. Patrick K. Ford, *The Celtic Poets*, pp. 218–22.

IEUAN BRYDYDD HIR HYNAF (*fl.* 1450–85)

Individual Translations
'**Cywydd i Henaint**' (Old Age), tr. Joseph P. Clancy, *Medieval Welsh Poems* (2003), pp. 335–6; '**Elen Deg o Landaf**' (Fair Elen of Llandaf), tr. Dafydd Johnston, *Medieval Welsh Erotic Poetry*, pp. 103–5 (1998: pp. 99–101); '**Cywydd i Ffynnon Gwenfrewi**' (Saint Winefride's Well), tr. Joseph P. Clancy, *Medieval Welsh Poems* (2003), pp. 334–5.

IEUAN DEULWYN (*fl.* 1460)

Individual Translations
'**I'r Fedwen**' (The Birch-Tree), tr. H. Idris Bell, *The Nationalist*, 4.34 (1911), 29–30.

IEUAN GETHIN AP IEUAN AP LLEISION (*fl.* 1437–90)

Individual Translation
'Cywydd y Bydafe', tr. unsigned, *Archaeologia Cambrensis*, 139 (1990), 56; '**Marwnad Ieuan Dowr**' (Elegy for Ieuan Dowr), tr. William Owen Pughe, *The Cambrian Journal*, 5 (1858), 109; tr. unsigned, *The History of the Literature of Wales*, p. 112; '**Marwnad i'w Fab**' (Elegy for His Son), tr. Dafydd Johnston, *Poets' Grief*, pp. 73–5; '**Marwnad i'w Ferch**' (Elegy for His Daughter), tr. Dafydd Johnston, *Poets' Grief*, pp. 81–7; '**Y Chwarae'n Troi'n Chwerw**' (A Misadventure), tr. Dafydd Johnston, *Medieval Welsh Erotic Poetry* (1998: pp. 91–3).

IOCYN DDU AB ITHEL GRACH (*fl. c.* 1350–1400)

Individual Translations
'**Ymffrost Clerwr**' (A Minstrel's Boast), tr. Dafydd Johnston, *Medieval Welsh Erotic Poetry*, pp. 87–9 (1998: pp. 83–5).

IOLO GOCH (*c.* 1325–*c.* 1398)

Collections

Dafydd Johnston, *Iolo Goch: Poems* (Llandysul: Gomer, 1993).

Individual Translations
'**Cywydd y Llong**' (The Ship), tr. Joseph P. Clancy, *Medieval Welsh Lyrics*, pp. 142–4; tr. Joseph P. Clancy, *Medieval Welsh Poems* (2003), pp. 236–7; '**Dewi Sant**' (A Pilgrimage to Saint David's), tr. Joseph P. Clancy, *Medieval Welsh Poems* (2003), pp. 240–3; '**I Ferch**' (Portrait of a Maiden), tr. Joseph P. Clancy, *Medieval Welsh Lyrics*, pp. 140–2; tr. Joseph P. Clancy, *Medieval Welsh Poems* (2003), pp. 233–5; '**I Ofyn March gan Ithel ap Robert o Goedymynydd**' (The Horse), tr. Joseph P. Clancy, *Medieval Welsh Poems* (2003), pp. 238–40; '**I'r Farf**' (Bard and Beard), tr. Joseph P. Clancy, *Medieval Welsh Lyrics*, pp. 144–5; tr. Bryan Walters, *From the Welsh*, p. 28; tr. Joseph P. Clancy, *Medieval Welsh Poems* (2003), pp. 230–1; '**Llys Ieuan, Esgob Llanelwy**' (The Poet's Welcome: At Llanelwy), tr.

Gwyn Williams, *To Look for a Word*, p. 67; '**Llys Owain Glyndŵr yn Sycharth**' (The Court of Owain Glyndŵr at Sycharth), tr. Edward Jones, *The Bardic Museum*, p. 57; tr. Howel W. Lloyd, *The History of the Literature of Wales*, pp. 63–5; tr. Howel W. Lloyd, *Y Cymmrodor*, 5 (1882), 265–73; tr. George Borrow, *Archaeologia Cambrensis*, 11 (5th series, 1894), 240–1; tr. George Borrow, *Welsh Poems & Ballads*, pp. 27–30; tr. George Borrow, *A Book of Wales* (1953), pp. 92–4; tr. Joseph P. Clancy, *Medieval Welsh Lyrics*, pp. 135–8; tr. Tony Conran, *The Penguin Book of Welsh Verse*, pp. 153–6; tr. Gwyn Williams, *To Look for a Word*, pp. 66–7; tr. Tony Conran, *Welsh Verse*, pp. 183–6; tr. Carl Lofmark, *Bards and Heroes*, p. 100; tr. Dafydd Johnston, *Medieval Welsh Poems*, pp. 99–101; tr. Joseph P. Clancy, *Medieval Welsh Poems* (2003), pp. 249–51; '**Marwnad Dafydd ap Gwilym**' (Elegy for Dafydd ap Gwilym), tr. Joseph P. Clancy, *Medieval Welsh Lyrics*, pp. 145–6; tr. Robert Gurney, *Bardic Heritage*, pp. 146–7; tr. Joseph P. Clancy, *Medieval Welsh Poems* (2003), pp. 235–6; '**Marwnad Ithel ap Robert**' (Elegy for Ithel ap Robert), tr. Dafydd Johnston, *Medieval Welsh Poems*, pp. 102–5; tr. Joseph P. Clancy, *Medieval Welsh Poems* (2003), pp. 245–9; '**Marwnad Llywelyn Goch ap Meurig Hen**' (Lament for Llywelyn Goch ap Meurig Hen), tr. Joseph P. Clancy, *Medieval Welsh Poems* (2003), pp. 251–3; '**Moliant i Feibion Tudur Fychan**' (Praise of Tudur Fychan's Sons), tr. Dafydd Johnston, *An Anglesey Anthology*, ed. Dewi Roberts (Gwasg Carreg Gwalch, 1999), pp. 104–6; '**Moliant Syr Rosier Mortimer**' (Praise of Sir Roger Mortimer), tr. Dafydd Johnston, *Medieval Welsh Poems*, pp. 106–9; '**Syr Hywel y Fwyall**' (Sir Hywel of the Axe), tr. Gwyn Williams, *The Burning Tree*, pp. 113–17; tr. Joseph P. Clancy, *Medieval Welsh Lyrics*, pp. 133–5; tr. Gwyn Williams, *Welsh Poetry: Sixth Century to 1600*, pp. 62–4; tr. Gwyn Williams, *To Look for a Word*, pp. 71–3; tr. Dafydd Johnston, *Medieval Welsh Poems*, pp. 96–9; tr. Joseph P. Clancy, *Medieval Welsh Poems* (2003), pp. 243–5; '**Y Llafurwr**' (The Ploughman), tr. H. Idris Bell, *The Nationalist*, 4.34 (1911), 28–9; tr. A. P. Graves, *Welsh Poetry Old and New*, pp. 34–6; tr. A. P. Graves, *A Celtic Psaltery*, pp. 78–9; tr. unsigned, *Cymru Heroica: An Anthology of Welsh Verse*, ed. Owen Watkin (London: James Brodie & Co., [1919?]), p. 12; tr. H. Idris Bell, *A Celtic Anthology*, p. 272; tr. H. Idris Bell, *Transactions of the Honourable Society of Cymmrodorion* (1942), 137–8; tr. D. M. Lloyd, *A Book of Wales* (1953), pp. 151–2; tr. Gwyn Williams, *The Burning Tree*, pp. 107–11; tr. Joseph P.

Clancy, *Medieval Welsh Lyrics*, pp. 138–40; tr. Gwyn Williams, *Welsh Poems: Sixth Century to 1600*, pp. 59–61; tr. Gwyn Williams, *To Look for a Word*, pp. 68–70; tr. Gwyn Williams, *Oxford Book*, pp. 45–7; tr. Dafydd Johnston, *Medieval Welsh Poems*, pp. 109–11; tr. H. Idris Bell, *The Bardic Source Book*, p. 244; tr. Joseph P. Clancy, *Medieval Welsh Poems* (2003), pp. 231–3.

IORWERTH AB Y CYRIOG (*c.* 1360)

Individual Translations
'**I Ddiolch am gae**' (The Brooch), tr. Joseph P. Clancy, *Medieval Welsh Poems* (2003), pp. 222–3.

IORWERTH BELI (*fl.* early fourteenth century)

Individual Translations
'**Cwyn yn erbyn Esgob Bangor**' (Complaint against the Bishop of Bangor), Joseph P. Clancy, *Medieval Welsh Poems* (2003), pp. 183–4.

LEWYS DARON (*fl. c.* 1497–*c.* 1530)

Individual Translations
'**I Bedr yn Rhosyr**' (Praise to Saint Peter and his Church in the town of Rhosyr, namely Newborough, Anglesey), tr. Hugh Owen, *Archaeologia Cambrensis*, 19 (6th series, 1919), 141–3.

LEWYS GLYN COTHI or LLYWELYN Y GLYN (*c.* 1420–89)

Individual Translations
'**Awdl Briodas Robert Hwitnai ac Elis ferch Tomas Fychan**' (Epithalamium), tr. Howel W. Lloyd, *The History of the Literature of Wales*, pp. 117–20; '**Cywydd y Farf**' (The Poet's Beard), tr. Dafydd Johnston, *Medieval Welsh Poems*, pp. 142–3; tr. Joseph P. Clancy, *Medieval Welsh Poems* (2003), pp. 297–8; '**Englynion i Dduw**' (Stanzas to the Trinity), tr. Gwyn Williams, *Introduction to Welsh*

Poetry, p. 158; tr. Gwyn Williams, *To Look for a Word*, p. 114; '**I Ofyn Cleddyf gan Ddafydd ap Gutun**' (The Sword), tr. Joseph P. Clancy, *Medieval Welsh Lyrics*, pp. 186–8; '**I Ofyn Gwely gan Bedair Gwraig**' (Request for a Bed), tr. Dafydd Johnston, *Medieval Welsh Poems*, pp. 140–2; '**I Ofyn Huling Gwely gan Elin Ferch Lywelyn**' (The Coverlet), tr. Joseph P. Clancy, *Medieval Welsh Lyrics*, pp. 188–90; tr. Joseph P. Clancy, *Medieval Welsh Poems* (2003), pp. 299–300; '**Marwnad Gwenllian Ferch Rhys**' (Elegy on Gwenllian), tr. Ernest Rhys, *A Celtic Anthology*, p. 274; tr. Ernest Rhys, *The Bardic Source Book*, p. 245; '**Marwnad Siôn y Glyn**' (Lament for Siôn y Glyn), tr. A. P. Graves, *Welsh Poetry Old and New*, pp. 37–9; tr. A. P. Graves, *A Celtic Psaltery*, pp. 80–1; tr. H. Idris Bell, *Transactions of the Honourable Society of Cymmrodorion* (1942), 145; tr. Gwyn Williams, *The Burning Tree*, pp. 145–7; tr. Joseph P. Clancy, *The Anglo-Welsh Review*, 12.29 (1962), 30–1; tr. Joseph P. Clancy, *Medieval Welsh Lyrics*, pp. 190–1; tr. Tony Conran, *The Penguin Book of Welsh Verse*, pp. 185–6; tr. Gwyn Williams, *Welsh Poetry: Sixth Century to 1600*, pp. 78–9; tr. Gwyn Williams, *To Look for a Word*, pp. 115–16; tr. Bryan Walters, *From the Welsh*, pp. 25–7; tr. Joseph P. Clancy, *Oxford Book*, pp. 62–4; tr. Tony Conran, *Welsh Verse*, pp. 209–11; tr. Joseph P. Clancy, *A Book of Wales* (1987), pp. 171–2; tr. Dafydd Johnston, *Medieval Welsh Poems*, pp. 144–5; tr. Dafydd Johnston, *Poets' Grief*, pp. 103–5; tr. Joseph P. Clancy, *Medieval Welsh Poems* (2003), pp. 300–2; *from* '**Moliant Dafydd ap Tomas Fychan**' (Plynlimmon), tr. George Borrow, *Welsh Poems & Ballads*, p. 137; A. P. Graves, *Welsh Poetry Old and New*, p. 39; '**Moliant Gruffudd ap Nicolas**' (An Ode to Gruffydd ab Nicholas of Newtown), tr. Howel W. Lloyd, *Archaeologia Cambrensis*, 9 (4th series, 1878), 207–11; '**Moliant Ieuan ap Lewys a Thanglwyst**' (To Thank Ieuan ap Lewys and his Wife Tanglwyst), tr. Dafydd Johnston, *Medieval Welsh Poems*, pp. 138–9; '**Moliant Meredudd ap Hywel a Thref Groesoswallt**' (To Meredydd ap Hywel and to the Town of Oswestry), tr. Howel Wm. Lloyd, *Archaeologia Cambrensis*, 11 (5th series, 1894), 64–5; '**Moliant Owain ap Gruffudd ap Nicolas**' (An Ode to Owen ab Gruffydd ab Nicholas of Kydweli), tr. Howel W. Lloyd, *Archaeologia Cambrensis*, 9 (4th series, 1878), 215–17; '**Moliant Siôn ap Dafydd a Mawd**' (His Boast of Siôn ap Dafydd and His Wife, Maud), tr. Tony Conran, *A Swansea Anthology*, ed. James A. Davies (Bridgend: Seren, 1996), pp. 14–15.

[Lewys Glyn Cothi?] 'Dychan Gŵr Caer' (A Satire on the English Residing in Flint), tr. H. L. J. J. W, *Archaeologia Cambrensis*, 1 (1846), 59–60; tr. Mrs M. C. Llewelyn, *Archaeologia Cambrensis*, 1 (1846), 153–5; tr. Mrs M. C. Llewelyn, *The Literature of the Kymry*, pp. 68–9 (1876: pp. 59–61); tr. Mrs M. C. Llewelyn, *The History of the Literature of Wales*, pp. 122–4; tr. H. Idris Bell, *Transactions of the Honourable Society of Cymmrodorion* (1942), 143–4; tr. Kenneth Hurlstone Jackson, *A Celtic Miscellany* (1951), pp. 234–5 (1971: pp. 216–17); tr. Mrs M. C. Llewelyn, *Presenting Welsh Poetry*, pp. 35–7; tr. Mrs M. C. Llewelyn, *Oxford Book*, pp. 51–3.

LLAWDDEN or IEUAN LLAWDDEN (*fl.* 1450)

Individual Translations
'Myned Adref' (No Place Like Home), tr. Tony Conran, *The Penguin Book of Welsh Verse*, p. 269; tr. Gwyn Jones, *Oxford Book*, p. 66; tr. Tony Conran, *Welsh Verse*, p. 306.

LLYWELYN AP GUTUN AP IEUAN LYDAN (*fl.* 1480)

Individual Translations
'Dychan i Uto'r Glyn' (Mock Elegy for Guto'r Glyn), tr. Joseph P. Clancy, *Medieval Welsh Lyrics*, pp. 203–4; tr. Gwyn Williams, *To Look for a Word*, pp. 86–7; tr. Joseph P. Clancy, *Medieval Welsh Poems* (2003), pp. 309–11; 'Mab a Merch yn Caru' (A Man and a Woman Making Love), tr. Dafydd Johnston, *Medieval Welsh Erotic Poetry*, pp. 113–15; 'Marwnad Gruffudd' (Elegy for Gruffudd), tr. Dafydd Johnston, *Poets' Grief*, pp. 95–7.

LLYWELYN AP MOEL Y PANTRI (d. 1440)

Individual Translations
'I Frwydr Waun Gaseg' (The Battle of Waun Gaseg), tr. H. Idris Bell, *Transactions of the Honourable Society of Cymmrodorion* (1940), 231–33; tr. Joseph P. Clancy, *Medieval Welsh Lyrics*, pp. 183–5; tr. Gwyn Williams, *To Look for a Word*, pp. 81–2; tr. H. Idris Bell, *Oxford Book*, pp. 59–60; tr. Joseph P. Clancy, *Medieval Welsh*

Poems (2003), pp. 294–5; 'I Goed y Graig Lwyd' (To the Greyrock Woods), tr. H. Idris Bell, *Transactions of the Honourable Society of Cymmrodorion* (1940), 233–5; tr. Joseph P. Clancy, *Medieval Welsh Lyrics*, pp. 182–3; tr. Tony Conran, *The Penguin Book of Welsh Verse*, pp. 171–2; tr. Tony Conran, *Welsh Verse*, pp. 198–9; tr. Tony Conran, *Medieval Welsh Poems*, pp. 127–9; tr. Joseph P. Clancy, *Medieval Welsh Poems* (2003), pp. 295–7.

LLYWELYN AP RHISIART or LEWYS MORGANNWG (*fl.* 1520–65)

Individual Translations
'Cywydd i Illtud Sant' (Cywydd to St Illtud), tr. Taliesin Williams (ab Iolo), *Iolo Manuscripts*, pp. 683–5; tr. unsigned, *The History of the Literature of Wales*, pp. 140–1; 'Ir Wyry Vair o Ben Rhys' ['ferch vyry'] (To the Virgin Mary of Penrhys), tr. Llywarch Reynolds, *Archaeologia Cambrensis*, 11 (4th series, 1880), 73–4; tr. Ifano Jones, *Archaeologia Cambrensis*, 14 (6th series, 1914), 395–6; 'Ir Wyry Vair o Ben Rhys' ['mae nawnef mewn un ynys'] (To the Virgin Mary of Penrhys), tr. Llywarch Reynolds, *Archaeologia Cambrensis*, 11 (4th series, 1880), 75–6; tr. Ifano Jones and G. H. J., *Archaeologia Cambrensis*, 14 (6th series, 1914), 400–2.

LLYWELYN FYCHAN (*fl. c.* 1360)

Individual Translations
'Haint y Nodau' (The Pestilence), tr. Dafydd Johnston, *Poets' Grief*, pp. 51–5.[10]

LLYWELYN GOCH AP MEURIG HEN (*fl.* 1350–90)

Individual Translations
'Awdl Gyffes' (Confession), tr. Joseph P. Clancy, *Medieval Welsh Poems* (2003), pp. 229–30; 'Cywydd i'r Benglog' (To the Skull), tr.

---

[10] See Dafydd Johnston's note on the poem for the academic debate over authorship.

Gwyn Williams, *Introduction to Welsh Poetry*, p. 125; tr. Joseph P. Clancy, *Medieval Welsh Lyrics*, pp. 113–14; tr. Robert Gurney, *Bardic Heritage*, pp. 150–1; '**I ddiolch i Dduw am arbed bywyd Llywelyn Fychan ap Llywelyn, Abad Ystrad-fflur**' (To Llywelyn Fychan ap Llywelyn Abbot of Strata Florida), tr. Revd John Williams, *Archaeologia Cambrensis*, 3 (1848), 129–30; '**Marwnad Lleucu Llwyd**' (Lament for Lleucu Llwyd), tr. Richard Llwyd, Cwrtmawr Manuscript 12.B, National Library of Wales; tr. unsigned, *The Bardic Museum*, p. 51; tr. Evan Evans (Ieuan Fardd, Ieuan Brydydd Hir), *Gwaith y Parchedig Evan Evans (Ieuan Brydydd Hir)*, ed. D. Silvan Evans (Caernarfon: H. Humphreys, 1876), pp. 150–2; tr. Ernest Rhys, *A Celtic Anthology*, p. 273; tr. David Bell, *Transactions of the Honourable Society of Cymmrodorion* (1942), 138–40; tr. Gwyn Williams, *The Burning Tree*, pp. 101–5; tr. Joseph P. Clancy, *The Anglo-Welsh Review*, 12.29 (1962), 26–8; tr. Joseph P. Clancy, *Medieval Welsh Lyrics*, pp. 116–19; tr. Gwyn Williams, *Welsh Poetry: Sixth Century to 1600*, pp. 56–8; tr. Gwyn Williams, *To Look for a Word*, pp. 74–6; tr. Joseph P. Clancy, *Oxford Book*, pp. 42–5; tr. Joseph P. Clancy, *A Book of Wales* (1987), pp. 185–7; tr. Dafydd Johnston, *Medieval Welsh Poems*, pp. 112–14; tr. Ernest Rhys, *The Bardic Source Book*, p. 245; tr. Joseph P. Clancy, *Medieval Welsh Poems* (2003), pp. 224–7; '**Moliant Hywel a Meurig Llwyd o Nannau**' (The Snow), tr. Joseph P. Clancy, *Medieval Welsh Lyrics*, pp. 119–21; Joseph P. Clancy, *Medieval Welsh Poems* (2003), pp. 227–9; '**Y Penloyn**' (The Coal-tit), tr. H. Idris Bell, *Dafydd ap Gwilym: Fifty Poems* (London: Cymmrodorion Society, 1942), pp. 179–83; tr. Joseph P. Clancy, *Medieval Welsh Lyrics*, pp. 114–16; tr. Tony Conran, *The Penguin Book of Welsh Verse*, pp. 151–2; tr. Robert Gurney, *Bardic Heritage*, pp. 123–5; tr. Tony Conran, *Welsh Verse*, pp. 181–3; tr. Helen Fulton, *Selections from the Dafydd ap Gwilym Apocrypha* (Llandysul: Gomer Press, 1996), pp. 80–2; tr. Joseph P. Clancy, *Medieval Welsh Poems* (2003), pp. 223–4.

MADOG BENFRAS (*fl.* 1320–60)

Individual Translations
'**Yr Halaenwr**' (The Saltman), tr. Joseph P. Clancy, *Medieval Welsh Lyrics*, pp. 110–12; tr. Joseph P. Clancy, *Medieval Welsh Poems* (2003), pp. 219–21; '**Pregeth y Brawd Du**' (The Black Friar's

Sermon), tr. Helen Fulton, *Selections from the Dafydd ap Gwilym Apocrypha* (Llandysul: Gomer Press, 1996), p. 10.

MAREDUDD AP RHYS (*fl.* 1440–83)

Individual Translations
'Cywydd i ofyn rhwyd bysgota gan Ifan ap Tudur o Lanufudd' (A Poem to Request a Fishing Net, with a Description of it), tr. Taliesin Williams (ab Iolo), *Iolo Manuscripts*, pp. 700–2; tr. unsigned, *The History of the Literature of Wales*, pp. 94–6; 'Cywydd i Ifan ap Tudur o Lanufudd i ddiolch am y rhwyd' (A Poem to Return Thanks for the Net), tr. Taliesin Williams (ab Iolo), *Iolo Manuscripts*, pp. 702–4.

ROBIN CLIDRO (*fl.* 1545–80)

Individual Translations
'Coed Marchan' (Marchan Wood), tr. Gwyn Williams, *The Burning Tree*, pp. 163–5; tr. Gwyn Williams, *Welsh Poetry: Sixth Century to 1600*, pp. 87–8; tr. Gwyn Williams, *To Look for a Word*, pp. 127–8.

RHYS GOCH ERYRI (*fl.* 1385–1448)

Individual Translations
'I Robert ap Meredudd' (Ode, in Praise of Robert ab Meredith), tr. Revd Rd Williams, *The Bardic Museum*, pp. 59–60; 'I Feuno Sant' (The Vision of Saint Beuno), tr. Joseph P. Clancy, *Medieval Welsh Lyrics*, pp. 198–202; 'Ymryson Rhys a Siôn Cent: Ateb Rhys Goch' (Answer to Siôn Cent), tr. Tony Conran, *The Penguin Book of Welsh Verse*, p. 170; tr. Tony Conran, *Welsh Verse*, p. 197.

[Rhys Goch?] 'I'r Llwynog, i Erchi iddo Ladd Paun Dafydd Nanmor' (To the Fox), tr. unsigned, *Cambrian Quarterly Magazine*, 2 (1830), 56; tr. Arthur James Johnes (Maelog), *Translations in to English Verse from the Poems of Davyth ap Gwilym* (London: Henry Hooper, 1834), pp. 68–9; tr. unsigned, *The History of the Literature of Wales*, pp. 70–1; tr. Joseph P. Clancy, *Medieval Welsh Lyrics*, pp. 197–8; tr. Joseph P. Clancy, *Medieval Welsh Poems* (2003), pp. 308–9.

SIÔN CENT (*c.* 1400–30/45)

Individual Translations
'**Gobeithiaw a Ddaw Ydd Wyf**' (My Hope is on what is to Come), tr.
D. M. Lloyd, *A Book of Wales* (1953), p. 133; '**Gwagedd Ymffrost
Dyn**' (Man's Vanity), tr. Dafydd Johnston, *Medieval Welsh Poems*,
pp. 122–3; '**Hud a Lliw y Byd**' (The Illusion of this World), tr. Gwyn
Williams, *The Burning Tree*, pp. 119–23; tr. Gwyn Williams, *Welsh
Poetry: Sixth Century to 1600*, pp. 65–7; tr. Gwyn Williams, *To Look
for a Word*, pp. 98–100; '**I'r Byd**' (Ghostly Counsel), tr. H. Idris Bell,
Transactions of the Honourable Society of Cymmrodorion (1942),
140–1; '**I'r Saith Bechod Marwol**' (Repentance), tr. Joseph P. Clancy,
Medieval Welsh Lyrics, pp. 175–6; tr. Tony Conran, *The Penguin
Book of Welsh Verse*, pp. 165–6; tr. Tony Conran, *Welsh Verse*, pp.
193–4; tr. Joseph P. Clancy, *Medieval Welsh Poems* (2003), pp.
286–7; '**I Wagedd ac Oferedd y Byd**' (The Vanity and Worthlessness
of the World), tr. H. Idris Bell, *The Nationalist*, 4.32 (1910), 41–3; tr.
A. P. Graves, *Welsh Poetry Old and New*, p. 41; tr. A. P. Graves, *A
Celtic Psaltery*, p. 82; tr. H. Idris Bell, *A Celtic Anthology*, pp. 270–1;
tr. Gwyn Williams, *The Rent that's Due to Love*, pp. 41–9; tr. Gwyn
Williams, *Introduction to Welsh Poetry*, pp. 135–6; tr. Joseph P.
Clancy, *Medieval Welsh Lyrics*, pp. 177–81; tr. Gwyn Williams, *To
Look for a Word*, pp. 93–7; tr. Joseph P. Clancy, *Oxford Book*, pp.
54–8; tr. Joseph P. Clancy, *Medieval Welsh Poems*, pp. 123–7; tr. H.
Idris Bell, *The Bardic Source Book*, pp. 246–7; tr. Joseph P. Clancy,
Medieval Welsh Poems (2003), pp. 290–3; '**Nid Oes Iawn Gyfaill Ond
Un**' (He Alone Faithful), tr. H. Idris Bell, *Transactions of the
Honourable Society of Cymmrodorion* (1940), 241–5; '**Rhag Digio
Duw**' (The Passion), tr. Illtud Evans, *Wales*, 5, 8 & 9 (1945), 16;
'**Ymryson Siôn Cent a Rhys Goch Eryri: Dychan Siôn Cent i'r Awen
Gelwyddog**' (The Lying Muse), tr. H. Idris Bell, *A History of Welsh
Literature*, pp. 159–60; tr. Joseph P. Clancy, *Medieval Welsh Lyrics*,
pp. 171–2; tr. Tony Conran, *The Penguin Book of Welsh Verse*, pp.
167–9; tr. Tony Conran, *Welsh Verse*, pp. 194–6; tr. Joseph P. Clancy,
Medieval Welsh Poems (2003), pp. 284–6.

[Siôn Cent?] '**Fy Mhwrs, Gramersi am Hyn**' (My Purse, Gramercy to
You for This!), tr. H. Idris Bell, *Transactions of the Honourable
Society of Cymmrodorion* (1940), 237–41; tr. Kenneth Hurlstone
Jackson, *A Celtic Miscellany* (1951), pp. 232–3 (1971: pp. 214–16);

tr. Joseph P. Clancy, *Medieval Welsh Lyrics*, pp. 173–5; tr. Joseph P. Clancy, *Medieval Welsh Poems* (2003), pp. 288–9.

SIÔN PHYLIP (d. 1620)

Individual Translations
'**Yr Wylan**' (The Seagull), tr. Joseph P. Clancy, *Medieval Welsh Lyrics*, pp. 268–70; tr. Joseph P. Clancy, *Oxford Book*, pp. 79–81.

SIÔN TUDUR (*c.* 1522–1602)

Individual Translations
'**Cywydd i Ladd ar y Beirdd**' (To Denounce the Bards), tr. Gwyn Williams, *Introduction to Welsh Poetry*, pp. 184–5; tr. H. Idris Bell, *A History of Welsh Literature*, p. 206; tr. Joseph P. Clancy, *Medieval Welsh Lyrics*, pp. 256–8; tr. Tony Conran, *The Penguin Book of Welsh Verse*, pp. 197–9; tr. Tony Conran, *Welsh Verse*, pp. 220–23; '**Prognosticasiwn Doctor Powel**' (Doctor Powel's Prognostication), tr. H. Idris Bell, *A History of Welsh Literature*, pp. 180–1; tr. Gwyn Williams, *Introduction to Welsh Poetry*, pp. 190–2; '**Cywydd i ofyn March**' (The Nag), tr. Joseph P. Clancy, *Medieval Welsh Lyrics*, pp. 258–60; '**Englynion y Misoedd**', tr. Gwyn Williams, *Introduction to Welsh Poetry*, pp. 193–4.

TRAHAEARN BRYDYDD MAWR (first half of the fourteenth century)

Individual Translations
'**Marwnad Hywel o Landingad yn Ystrad Tywi**' (Elegy for Hywel), tr. Edward Davies, *The Mythology and Rites of the British Druids*, pp. 67–71.

TUDUR ALED (*c.* 1465–*c.* 1525)

Individual Translations
'**Bonedd**' (Nobility), tr. Gwyn Williams, *Introduction to Welsh Poetry*, p. 175; tr. Tony Conran, *The Penguin Book of Welsh Verse*,

p. 270; tr. Tony Conran, *Welsh Verse*, p. 307; 'Caws Drwg' (Bad Cheese), tr. Gwyn Williams, *Introduction to Welsh Poetry*, p. 175; 'I Ofyn March' (To Ask for a Stallion), tr. Gwyn Williams, *The Burning Tree*, pp. 149–53; tr. Joseph P. Clancy, *Medieval Welsh Lyrics*, pp. 243–5; tr. Gwyn Williams, *Welsh Poetry: Sixth Century to 1600*, pp. 80–2; tr. Gwyn Williams, *To Look for a Word*, pp. 117–19; tr. Joseph P. Clancy, *Oxford Book*, pp. 67–9; tr. Joseph P. Clancy, *Medieval Welsh Poems*, pp. 210–13; tr. Joseph P. Clancy, *Medieval Welsh Poems* (2003), pp. 351–3; 'Cywydd Heddwch i Wynedd' (A Plea for Peace), tr. Edwin Stanley James, *Wales*, 5.7 (1945), 18; tr. Joseph P. Clancy, *Medieval Welsh Lyrics*, pp. 246–9; tr. Joseph P. Clancy, *Medieval Welsh Poems* (2003), pp. 353–7; *from* 'Marwnad Siân Stradling' (Elegy for Siân Stradling), tr. Gwyn Williams, *Introduction to Welsh Poetry*, pp. 172–3; 'Serch a Rois ar Chwaer Esyllt' (Love's Frustration), tr. Joseph P. Clancy, *Medieval Welsh Lyrics*, pp. 250–2; 'Tad Haelioni: Cywydd i Syr Roser Salbri' (Advice to Roger Salesbury), tr. Dafydd Johnston, *Medieval Welsh Poems*, pp. 208–10; 'Yr Englyn Olaf' (The Last Englyn), tr. Gwyn Williams, *Introduction to Welsh Poetry*, p. 176; tr. Tony Conran, *The Penguin Book of Welsh Verse*, pp. 272; tr. Tony Conran, *Welsh Verse*, pp. 309.

TUDUR PENLLYN (*c.* 1420–85)

Individual Translations

'I Ruffudd Fychan o Gorsygedol' (To Gruffydd Vaughan, Cors y Cedol), tr. Howel W. Lloyd, *Archaeologia Cambrensis*, 9 (4th series, 1878), 62–3; 'Moliant Dafydd ap Siancyn' (The Outlaw), tr. Glyn Davies, *The Nationalist*, 1.3 (1907), 15–16; tr. H. Idris Bell, *Transactions of the Honourable Society of Cymmrodorion* (1940), 245–9; tr. H. Idris Bell, *A History of Welsh Literature*, p. 157; tr. Joseph P. Clancy, *Medieval Welsh Lyrics*, pp. 234–5; tr. Joseph P. Clancy, *Medieval Welsh Poems* (2003), pp. 340–1; 'Ymddiddan Rhwng Cymro a Saesnes' (A Conversation Between a Welshman and an Englishwoman), tr. Dafydd Johnston, *Medieval Welsh Erotic Poetry*, pp. 75–7 (1998: pp. 71–3).

WILIAM LLŶN (1534/5–80)

Individual Translations
'**Marwnad Gruffydd Hiraethog**' (Elegy for Gruffydd Hiraethog), tr. A. P. Graves, *Welsh Poetry Old and New*, p. 40; tr. Dafydd Johnston, *Medieval Welsh Poems*, pp. 213–16; '**Pibyddion**' (Englyn to Pipers), tr. Gwyn Williams, *Introduction to Welsh Poetry*, p. 182; '**Tawelwch**' (Abiding), tr. H. Idris Bell, *A Celtic Anthology*, p. 282; '**Awdl Farwnad ar ôl Huw ap Siôn ap Hywel o Lan Fendigaid**' (Elegy for Huw ap Siôn), tr. Edwin Stanley James, *Wales*, 5, 8 & 9 (1945), 90; '**Marwnad Syr Owain ap Gwilym**' (Lament for Sir Owain ap Gwilym), tr. Joseph P. Clancy, *Medieval Welsh Lyrics*, pp. 253–5; tr. Tony Conran, *The Penguin Book of Welsh Verse*, pp. 189–91; tr. Tony Conran, *Welsh Verse*, pp. 213–15; *from* '**Marwnad Huw ap Rhisiart o Fodwrda**' (Elegy for Huw ap Rhisiart), tr. Evan Richard, *The Cambrian Register*, 3 (1818), 197; tr. Evan Richard, *The History of the Literature of Wales*, pp. 148–52; '**Ystyriaeth Bywyd**' ['Naked, little and weak'], tr. Gwyn Williams, *Introduction to Welsh Poetry*, p. 182.

RHYDDIAITH Y CYFNOD CANOL: MEDIEVAL PROSE

The Mabinogi and Native Welsh Tales

Charlotte Guest, *The Mabinogion from the Llyfr Coch o Hergest, and other ancient Welsh manuscripts* (London: Longman, 1836–49).

Sidney Lanier, *The Boy's Mabinogion* (London: Sampson Low & Co., 1881).

Padraic Colum, *The Island of the Mighty* (New York: The Macmillan Company, 1924).

W. J. Gruffydd, *Math vab Mathonwy: an inquiry into the origins and development of the fourth branch of the Mabinogi with the text and a translation* (Cardiff: University of Wales Press, 1928).

T. P. Ellis and John Lloyd, *The Mabinogion: A New Translation* (Oxford: Clarendon Press, 1929).

Evangeline Walton, *The Virgin and the Swine* (New York: Willet Clark, 1936). Reprinted as *The Island of the Mighty* (London: Pan/Ballantine Books, 1972).

Gwyn Jones and Thomas Jones, *The Mabinogion* (London: Everyman Library, J. M. Dent & Sons, 1949).

W. J. Gruffydd, *Branwen* (Cardiff: University of Wales Press, 1953).

Gwyn Jones, *Welsh Legends and Folk-Tales* (London: Oxford University Press, 1955).

Wyn Griffith, *The Adventures of Pryderi: taken from the Mabinogion* (Cardiff: University of Wales Press, 1962).

Beryl Jones, *Tales of Magic and Romance* (Cardiff: University of Wales Press, 1964).

Barbara Leonie Picard, *Celtic Tales: Legends of Tall Warriors and Old Enchantments* (London: Edmund Ward, 1964).

Olwen Bowen, *Tales from the Mabinogion* (London: Victor Gollancz, 1969).

Jeffrey Gantz, *The Mabinogion* (London and New York: Penguin Books, 1976).

Patrick K. Ford, *The Mabinogion and Other Medieval Welsh Tales* (Berkeley: University of California Press, 1977).

Marilyn Jenkins, *The Four Branches of the Mabinogi* (Treforest: The National Language Unit of Wales, 1981).

Gwyn Thomas and Kevin Crossley-Holland, *Tales from the Mabinogion* (Gollancz Children's, 1984).

John Lovat, *Welsh Tales: the Four Branches of the Mabinogion . . . and Culhwch and Olwen/dramatised for radio* (Cardiff: BBC Cymru, 1996).

Jenny Nimmo, *Branwen*, with illustrations by Jac Jones (Llandysul: Pont, 1997).

Wyn Griffith, *Pryderi* (Newtown: Gwasg Gregynog, 1998).

Otherworld, animated feature of the *Mabinogi* (Dir. Derek Hayes and Marc Evans for S4C, 2002).

Other Medieval Welsh Prose Works

Thomas Jones, *Brut y Tywysogion: The Chronicle of the Princes: Red Book of Hergest Version* (Cardiff: University of Wales Press, 1955).

Arthur Jones, *Historia Gruffudd fab Cynan: The History of Gruffydd ap Cynan* (Manchester: Manchester University Press, 1910).

D. Simon Evans, *Historia Gruffudd fab Cynan: Medieval Prince of Wales: the Life of Gruffudd ap Cynan* (Llanerch: Llanerch Enterprises, 1990).

Individual Translations

from '**Breuddwyd Rhonabwy**' (The Dream of Rhonabwy), tr. Kenneth Hurlstone Jackson, *A Celtic Miscellany* (1951), pp. 194–5 (1971: pp. 179–80); tr. Lady Charlotte Guest, *The Bardic Source Book*, pp. 248–56; *from* '**Culhwch and Olwen**', tr. Kenneth Hurlstone Jackson, *A Celtic Miscellany* (1951), pp. 197, 213–14, 217–21 (1971: pp. 182, 197–8, 201–4); *from* '**Gereint fab Erbin**', tr. Kenneth Hurlstone Jackson, *A Celtic Miscellany* (1951), pp. 191–2 (1971: pp. 177–8); *from* '**Historia Gruffudd fab Cynan**', tr. Kenneth Hurlstone Jackson, *A Celtic Miscellany* (1951), pp. 197–8 (1971: p. 183); *from* '**Lludd and Llefelys**', tr. Kenneth Hurlstone Jackson, *A Celtic Miscellany* (1951), pp. 157–63 (1971: pp. 145–50); *from* '**Math fab Mathonwy**', tr. Idrison, *Cambrian Quarterly Magazine*, 1 (1829), pp. 170–9, 395–10 [sic], 416–28; tr. John Rhŷs, *Y Cymmrodor*, 18 (1905), 137; tr. Kenneth Hurlstone Jackson, *A Celtic Miscellany* (1951), p. 164 (1971: pp. 151–2); tr. Tony Conran, *Welsh Verse*, pp. 135–6; tr. Robert Graves, *World Poetry: An Anthology of Verse from Antiquity to our Time*, ed. Katharine Washburn and John S. Major (New York; London: Norton, 1998), pp. 336–7; *from* '**Peredur**', tr. William Owen Pughe, NLW Manuscripts 13244; tr. Kenneth Hurlstone Jackson, *A Celtic Miscellany* (1951), p. 173 (1971: p. 160); tr. John K. Bollard, *The Romance of Arthur II*, ed. James J. Wilhelm (New York & London: Garland Publishing, 1986), pp. 32–61; *from* '**Pwyll**', tr. William Owen Pughe, *The Cambrian Register*, 1 (1796), 177–87; tr. William Owen Pughe, *The Cambrian Register*, 2 (1799), 322–7; tr. William Owen Pughe, *The Cambrian Register*, 3 (1818), 230–46; tr. William Owen Pughe, *The Cambro-Briton*, 2 (1821), 271–5.[1]

---

[1] For further information regarding William Owen Pughe's ill-fated translation of the *Mabinogi* see Arthur Johnston, 'William Owen-Pughe and the Mabinogion', *National Library of Wales Journal*, 10 (1957–8), 323–8.

YR UNFED GANRIF AR BYMTHEG A'R AIL GANRIF AR BYMTHEG: THE SIXTEENTH AND SEVENTEENTH CENTURIES

ANON.

Hen Benillion (Traditional Folk Verses)

Collections

H. Idris Bell, *Caseg Broadsheet No. 2: Penillion* (Caseg Press, 1941).

Aneirin Talfan Davies, *Welsh Folk Verse* (Llandysul: Gwasg Gomer, 1942).

Glyn Jones, *When the Rose-bush brings forth Apples: Fourteen Old Welsh Verses Translated with Introduction* (Newtown: Gwasg Gregynog, 1980).

Glyn Jones, *Honeydew on the Wormwood* (Newtown: Gwasg Gregynog, 1984).

Glyn Jones, *A People's Poetry: Hen Benillion* (Bridgend: Seren, 1997).

Joseph P. Clancy, *Where there's Love: Welsh Folk Poems of Love and Marriage* (Aberystwyth: Northgate Books, 1995). Second edition (2000).

Miscellaneous

Tony Conran, *Dacw 'Nghariad* [There's my darling] (Penygroes: Cwmni Cyhoeddi Gwynn Cyf, 1983).

Tony Conran, *Deryn y Bwn o'r Banna* [Bittern he took a bundle] (Penygroes: Cwmni Cyhoeddi Gwynn Cyf, 1983).

Tony Conran, *Hela'r Sgyfarnog* [Hunting the Hare] (Penygroes: Cwmni Cyhoeddi Gwynn Cyf, 1983).

Tony Conran, *Mae 'nghariad i'n Fenws* [My Darling's a Venus] (Penygroes: Cwmni Cyhoeddi Gwynn Cyf, 1983).

Tony Conran, *Rew di ranno* (Penygroes: Cwmni Cyhoeddi Gwynn Cyf, 1983).

Individual Translations

tr. Edward Jones, *The Musical, Poetical, and Historical Relicks*, pp. 31–8, 40; tr. unsigned, *The Cambro-Briton*, 1 (1820), 32–4, 70–1, 73, 92–3, 110–11, 50–1, 91–2, 233, 353, 436; tr. unsigned, *The Cambro-Briton*, 2 (1820/21), 38, 74, 137–8, 233–4, 328–9, 374–5, 424; tr. unsigned, *The Cambro-Briton*, 3 (1821/22), 51, 122, 250, 314; tr. unsigned, *Cambrian Quarterly Magazine*, 2 (1830), 58; tr. J. Ceiriog Hughes, *Gems of Welsh Melody* (London & Wrexham: Simpkin, Marshall & Co; Hughes & Son, 1860), pp. 36–9; tr. John Pughe, *Archaeologia Cambrensis*, 11 (1865), 397; tr. unsigned, *The Poetry of Wales* (1873), pp. 110–12; tr. H. Idris Bell, *The Nationalist*, 2.18 (1908), 20; tr. H. Idris Bell, *The Nationalist*, 4.35 (1911), 47; tr. H. Idris Bell and C. C. Bell, *Poems from the Welsh*, pp. 29, 53, 56–7, 64; tr. Ernest Rhys, *A Celtic Anthology*, p. 323; tr. Aneirin Talfan Davies, *The Welsh Review*, 3.4 (1944), 268; tr. Gwyn Williams, *The Welsh Review*, 4.4 (1945), 284; tr. Pennar Davies, *Wales*, 5.7 (1945), 20; tr. Keidrych Rhys, *Wales*, 5.7 (1945), 21; tr. Gwyn Williams, *The Welsh Review*, 5.4 (1946), 257; tr. Gwyn Williams, *The Welsh Review*, 7.1 (1948), pp. 37–47; tr. R. S. Thomas, *Wales*, 6.22 (1946), 7; tr. R. S. Thomas, *The Stones of the Field* (Carmarthen: Druid Press, 1946), p. 18; tr. Gwyn Williams, *The Rent that's Due to Love*, pp. 57–73, 75, 79–91, 101; tr. Kenneth Hurlstone Jackson, *A Celtic Miscellany* (1951), pp. 114, 120–1, 123, 137–8, 140–46, 287 (1971: pp. 112–15, 127, 129–34, 261–2); tr. Gwyn Williams, *Introduction to Welsh Poetry*, pp. 196, 211–14; tr. H. Idris Bell, *A History of Welsh Literature*, pp. 233, 235–7; tr. Gwyn Williams, *The Burning Tree*, pp. 157, 167–9, 219; tr. Leonard Owen, *The London Welshman*, 20.1 (1965), 17; tr. Tony Conran, *Poetry Wales*, 3.1 (1967), 29; tr. Tony Conran, *The Penguin Book of Welsh Verse*, pp. 192–3, 206, 269; tr. Gwyn Williams, *Welsh Poems: Sixth century to 1600*, pp. 84, 89–90, 115; tr. Glyn Jones, *Aquarias*, 8 (1976); tr. Gwyn Williams, *To Look for a Word*, pp. 121, 125–6, 129–35, 146, 179–86; tr. Gwyn Williams, Tony Conran, Kenneth Hurlstone Jackson, C. C. Bell, Aneirin Talfan Davies, *Oxford Book*, pp. 70–8, 90; tr. Tony Conran, *Welsh Verse*, pp. 216–17, 228–9, 243–9, 306; tr. Aneirin Talfan Davies, *A Book of Wales* (1987), pp. 166, 311–12; tr. Siân James, *Love from Wales: An Anthology*, ed. Tony Curtis and Siân James (Bridgend: Seren Books, 1991), pp. 45, 104; tr. Harri Webb, *Harri Webb: Collected Poems* (Llandysul: Gomer, 1995), pp. 212–14; tr. R. S. Thomas, in Jason Walford Davies, *Gororau'r Iaith: R. S. Thomas a'r Traddodiad Llenyddol Cymraeg* (Cardiff: University of Wales Press, 2003), p. 95; tr. unsigned (Glyn Jones's personal copy of *The Stones of the Field* [1946]), MS in Canolfan Ymchwil R. S. Thomas, University of Wales, Bangor.[1]

Canu Rhydd Cynnar [sixteenth century, popular song]
'**Ffeind i Law a'i Lygad**' (He Whose Hand and Eye are Gentle), tr. Kenneth Hurlstone Jackson, *A Celtic Miscellany* (1951), pp. 120–1 (1971: pp. 112–13); tr. Kenneth Hurlstone Jackson, *Oxford Book*, p. 73; tr. Kenneth Hurlstone Jackson, *Love from Wales: An Anthology*, ed. Tony Curtis and Siân James (Bridgend: Seren Books, 1991), pp. 104–5.

[sixteenth century, anonymous poem]
'**Araith ddichan ir Gwragedd**' (Against Women), tr. Gwyn Williams, *The Welsh Review*, 7, 1 (1948), 37–47; tr. Gwyn Williams, *The Rent that's Due to Love*, pp. 57–73; tr. Gwyn Williams, *Against Women* (London: Golden Cockerel Press, 1953); tr. Gwyn Williams, *To Look for a Word*, pp. 129–35; tr. Gwyn Williams, *Oxford Book*, pp. 74–7.

c. 1600 Tragedy
from **Troelus a Chressyd** (Troilus and Cressida), tr. Gwyn Williams, *The Welsh Review*, 5.4 (1946), 246–9; tr. Gwyn Williams, *The Rent that's Due to Love*, pp. 51–5; tr. Gwyn Williams, *The Burning Tree*, pp. 171–9; tr. Gwyn Williams, *Presenting Welsh Poetry*, pp. 42–3; tr. Gwyn Williams, *Welsh Poems: Sixth century to 1600*, pp. 91–5; tr. Gwyn Williams, *To Look for a Word*, pp. 147–55.

[1]   See Jason Walford Davies, *Gororau'r Iaith: R. S. Thomas a'r Traddodiad Llenyddol Cymraeg* (Cardiff: University of Wales Press, 2003), p. 94.

WILIAM CYNWAL (d. 1587/8)

Individual Translations *Po.*
'Cyfaill Marw' (To a Dead Friend), tr. H. Idris Bell, *The Welsh Review*, 5.2 (1946), 117; 'O Blaid y Gwragedd' (In Defence of Woman), tr. Gwyn Williams, *The Burning Tree*, pp. 181–97; tr. Gwyn Williams, *Province*, 3.4 (1956), 137–8; tr. Gwyn Williams, *In Defence of Woman* (London: Golden Cockerel Press, 1958); tr. Gwyn Williams, *Welsh Poems: Sixth Century to 1600*, pp. 96–104; tr. Gwyn Williams, *To Look for a Word*, pp. 136–44.

CHARLES EDWARDS (1628–91?)

Individual Translations *Pr.*
from **Y Ffydd Ddi Ffuant** (The Sincere Faith), tr. Grahame Davies, *The Chosen People: Wales & The Jews*, ed. Grahame Davies (Bridgend: Seren, 2002), pp. 21–2.

THEOPHILUS EVANS (1693–1767)

Prose
Drych y Prif Oesoedd, *A View of the Primitive Ages*, tr. Revd George Roberts (Ebensburg [Pa.]: Printed for the publishers, by Canan & Scott, 1834). Reprinted (Llanidloes: John Pryse, [1863?]).

Individual Translations *Pr.*
from **Drych y Prif Oesoedd** (Mirror of the First Ages), tr. Grahame Davies, *The Chosen People: Wales & The Jews*, ed. Grahame Davies (Bridgend: Seren, 2002), pp. 22–5.

SIÔN GRUFFUDD (d. 1586?)

Individual Translations *Po.*
'Hiraeth am Gaernarfon' (Longing for Caernarfon), tr. Tony Conran, *The Penguin Book of Welsh Verse*, pp. 195–6; tr. Gwyn Williams, *To Look for a Word*, pp. 122–3; tr. Tony Conran, *Welsh Verse*, pp. 218–20.

RICHARD HUGHES (d. 1618)

Individual Translations *Po.*
'**Boreuddydd**' (Break of Day), tr. Gwyn Williams, *The Rent that's Due to Love*, p. 77; tr. Gwyn Williams, *To Look for a Word*, p. 156; *from* '**Cyfres o Garolau Serch**' (Love songs), tr. C. C. Bell, *Poems from the Welsh*, p. 27; tr. Gwyn Williams, *Introduction to Welsh Poetry*, pp. 223–6; tr. Gwyn Williams, *To Look for a Word*, pp. 157–60; '**I Candish a Drâk**' (To Cavendish and Drake), tr. Gwyn Williams, *Introduction to Welsh Poetry*, p. 222.

HUW MACHNO or HUW OWEN (*c.* 1560–1637)

Individual Translations *Po.*
'**Marwnad Owain ap Huw Machno**' (Elegy for Owain ap Huw Machno), tr. Dafydd Johnston, *Galar y Beirdd: Marwnadau Plant/Poets' Grief: Medieval Welsh Elegies for Children* (Cardiff: Tafol, 1993), pp. 113–19.

MORRIS KYFFIN (*c.* 1555–98)

Individual Translations *Po.*
'**Y Gôg**' (The Cuckoo), tr. Robert Gurney, *Bardic Heritage*, p. 157.

MORGAN LLWYD (1619–59)

Prose
Gair o'r Gair, *A Discourse of the Word of God*, tr. Griffith Rudd (London: John Oswald, 1739).

Llyfr y Tri Aderyn, 'The Book of the Three Birds', tr. L. J. Parry, *Winning Compositions in the Llandudno Eisteddfod 1896*, ed. E. Vincent Evans (Liverpool: 1898), pp. 195–274.

Individual Translations *Po.*
'**Duw a'i Eglwys**' (God and His Church), tr. Tony Conran, *The Penguin Book of Welsh Verse*, p. 200; tr. Gwyn Williams, *To Look for a Word*, p. 176; tr. Tony Conran, *Welsh Verse*, p. 176.

HUW MORYS (Eos Ceiriog; 1622–1709)[2]

Individual Translations *Po.*
'**Bore Gaeaf**' (Thick Snow), tr. Kenneth Hurlstone Jackson, *A Celtic Miscellany* (1951), p. 138 (1971: p. 128); '**Byrder Einioes**' (That Our Life is Brief), tr. Robert Gurney, *Bardic Heritage*, pp. 173–4; '**Carol Plygain Dydd Nadolig Crist**' (Carol for the Morning of Christ's Nativity), tr. Robert Gurney, *Bardic Heritage*, pp. 174–6; '**Cyffes y Bardd ar Wely Clefyd**' (The Bard's Death-bed Confession), tr. A. P. Graves, *Welsh Poetry Old and New*, pp. 117–19; tr. A. P. Graves, *A Celtic Psaltery*, pp. 83–4; '**I Hyfawl Riain**' (In Praise of a Girl), tr. H. Idris Bell, *The Nationalist*, 4.35 (1911), 47–8; tr. A. P. Graves, *Welsh Poetry Old and New*, pp. 43–5; tr. Gwyn Williams, *The Welsh Review*, 5.4 (1946), 249–53; tr. Gwyn Williams, *The Rent that's Due to Love*, pp. 95–9; tr. Gwyn Williams, *A Book of Wales* (1953), pp. 326–7; tr. Gwyn Williams, *Presenting Welsh Poetry*, pp. 46–8; tr. Tony Conran, *The Penguin Book of Welsh Verse*, pp. 202–3; tr. Gwyn Williams, *To Look for a Word*, pp. 188–90; tr. Gwyn Williams, *Oxford Book*, pp. 107–9; tr. Tony Conran, *Welsh Verse*, pp. 225–6; tr. Gwyn Williams, *Love from Wales: An Anthology*, ed. Tony Curtis and Siân James (Bridgend: Seren Books, 1991), p. 15.

WILLIAM PEILYN (c. 1570)

Individual Translations *Po.*
'**Hanes bagad o Gymry a aethant, yn amser y Frenhines Elsbeth, drwy ei gorchymyn hi, i'r Gorllewin India i ddial ar, ac i anrheithio'r**

---

[2] There is a translation entitled 'Quick, Death!' by A. P. Graves [*Welsh Poetry Old and New*, p. 119; *A Celtic Psaltery*, p. 85 and *A Celtic Anthology*, p. 290]. Thematically it resembles Huw Morys's 'Oes Fer' but the translator's interpretation is so different that I cannot verify this as the original source text.

Hisbaenwyr' (The Ballad of the Welsh Buccaneers), tr. J. Glyn Davies, *Y Cymmrodor*, 26 (1916), 230–2; tr. A. P. Graves, *The Welsh Outlook* (St David's Day 1917), 135–7; tr. A. P. Graves, *A Book of Wales* (1953), pp. 146–7; **'Ymddiddan rhwng Gŵr a Pelican'** (Conversation between a Man and a Pelican), tr. Gwyn Williams, *Introduction to Welsh Poetry*, pp. 219–20.

WILIAM PHYLIP (1579–1669)

Individual Translations *Po.*
'Ffarwel i Hendre Fechan' (Farewell to Hendre Fechan), tr. H. Idris Bell, *A History of Welsh Literature*, pp. 224–5; tr. Tony Conran, *The Penguin Book of Welsh Verse*, p. 201; tr. H. Idris Bell, *Oxford Book*, p. 101; tr. Tony Conran, *Welsh Verse*, pp. 224–5.

RHYS PRICHARD (Yr Hen Ficer; 1579–1644)

Collections

William Shepard Prisbiter, *Cambrias Light, being two of Mr Rees Prichard's British Divine Gems* (Shrewsbury: Thomas Durston, 1716).

Revd William Evans, *The Welshman's Candle: or the divine poems of Mr Rees Pritchard* (Llawhaden) (Carmarthen: printed for the translator, 1771).

John Bulmer, *Beauties of the Vicar of Llandovery; or, Light from the Welshman's Candle* (London: Holdsworth and Ball, 1830).

R. Brinley Jones, *'A Lanterne to their Feete': remembering Rhys Prichard 1579–1644 Vicar of Llandovery* (Porthyrhyd, Llanwrda: Drovers Press, 1994).

Individual Translations *Po.*
from **Canwyll y Cymry**, tr. unsigned, in *A Collection of Hymns to the Children of God in All Ages* (London: printed; and to be held at all the Brethren Chapels, 1754); tr. Revd William Evans, *The History of the Literature of Wales*, pp. 229–37; tr. unsigned, *Cambrian Quarterly*

Magazine, 3 (1831), 328; tr. Revd William Evans, *The Poetry of Wales* (1873), pp. 160–6; tr. A. P. Graves, *Welsh Poetry Old and New*, p. 43; tr. George Borrow, *Welsh Poems & Ballads*, pp. 151–2; tr. A. P. Graves, *A Celtic Psaltery*, p. 89; tr. unsigned, *A Celtic Anthology*, pp. 279–80; tr. Gwyn Williams, *To Look for a Word*, pp. 177–8.

EDMWND PRYS (1543/4–1623)

Individual Translations *Po.*
'**Balet Cymraeg**' (A Welsh Ballad), tr. Kenneth Hurlstone Jackson, *A Celtic Miscellany* (1951), pp. 89–90 (1971: pp. 84–5); tr. Gwyn Williams, *The Burning Tree*, pp. 213–7; tr. Gwyn Williams, *Welsh Poems: Sixth Century to 1600*, pp. 112–14; tr. Gwyn Williams, *To Look for a Word*, pp. 172–4.

TOMOS PRYS (*c.* 1564–1634)

Individual Translations *Po.*
'**Cywydd i Ddangos mai uffern yw Llundain**' (London is Hell), tr. Gwyn Williams, *To Look for a Word*, pp. 161–3; '**Danfon Chwannen yn Llatai at ei Gariad**' (A Poem to Send a Flea as Messenger to a Pretty Girl), tr. Gwyn Williams, *Choose Your Stranger* (Port Talbot: Alun Books, 1979), pp. 56–8; '**Heldrin ar y Môr**' (Trouble at Sea), tr. Gwyn Williams, *Introduction to Welsh Poetry*, pp. 199–200; tr. Gwyn Williams, *The Burning Tree*, pp. 199–203; tr. Gwyn Williams, *Presenting Welsh Poetry*, pp. 38–41; tr. Gwyn Williams, *Welsh Poems: Sixth Century to 1600*, pp. 105–7; tr. Gwyn Williams, *To Look for a Word*, pp. 168–70; tr. Gwyn Williams, *Oxford Book*, pp. 84–6; '**I Merch Lân**' (To a Pretty Girl), tr. Gwyn Williams, *The Burning Tree*, p. 205; tr. Gwyn Williams, *Welsh Poems: Sixth Century to 1600*, p. 108; tr. Gwyn Williams, *To Look for a Word*, p. 171; '**Marwnad Hanibol Prys**' (Elegy for Hanibol Prys), tr. Dafydd Johnston, *Galar y Beirdd: Marwnadau Plant/Poets' Grief: Medieval Welsh Elegies for Children* (Cardiff: Tafol, 1993), pp. 125–9; '**Y Llamhidydd**' (The Porpoise), tr. Gwyn Williams, *The Burning Tree*, pp. 207–11; tr. Joseph P. Clancy, *Medieval Welsh Lyrics*, pp. 261–3; tr. Gwyn Williams, *Welsh Poems: Sixth Century to 1600*, pp. 109–11; tr. Gwyn Williams, *To Look for a Word*, pp. 164–7.

WILIAM THOMAS (*c.* 1586)

Individual Translations *Po.*
'**Englynion i'r Delyn**' (Stanzas to the Harp), tr. Gwyn Williams, *The Burning Tree*, p. 161; tr. Gwyn Williams, *Welsh Poems: Sixth Century to 1600*, p. 86; tr. Gwyn Williams, *To Look for a Word*, p. 124.

ELLIS WYNNE (1671–1734)

Prose

Gweledigaetheu y Bardd Cwsc

George Borrow, *The Sleeping Bard: Or, Visions of the World, Death, and Hell, translated from the Cambrian British* (London: Murray, 1860).

Robert Gwyneddon Davies, *The Visions of the Sleeping Bard* (London: Simpkin, Marshall & Co., 1897).

T. Gwynn Jones, *Visions of the Sleeping Bard* (Newtown: Gwasg Gregynog, 1940).

Individual Translations *Pr.*
*from **Gweledigaetheu y Bardd Cwsc***, tr. George Borrow, *Welsh Poems & Ballads*, pp. 109–11, 121–5; tr. George Borrow, *A Book of Wales* (1953), pp. 297–8; tr. T. Gwynn Jones, *A Book of Wales* (1953), pp. 298–99, pp. 304–5.

Individual Translations *Po.*
from '**Angau**' (Counsel in View of Death), tr. A. P. Graves, *Welsh Poetry Old and New*, pp. 120–1; tr. George Borrow, *Welsh Poems & Ballads*, pp. 115–18; tr. George Borrow, *Land of My Fathers*, pp. 61–72; tr. A. P. Graves, *A Celtic Psaltery*, p. 86; tr. George Borrow, *A Celtic Anthology*, p. 289; tr. Gwyn Williams, *To Look for a Word*, pp. 191–2.

Individual Translations *hymns*
'**Myfi yw'r Atgyfodiad Mawr**' (The Resurrection and the Life Am I), tr. M. J. H. Ellis, *Welsh Hymns and their Tunes*, pp. 89–90.

Y DDEUNAWFED GANRIF: THE EIGHTEENTH CENTURY

ANON.

Folk Song [attributed to Wil Hopcyn, b. 1701] '**Bugeilio'r Gwenith Gwyn**' (Watching the Wheat), tr. A. P. Graves, *Welsh Poetry Old and New*, pp. 50–1; tr. C. C. Bell, *Poems from the Welsh*, pp. 28–9; tr. C. C. Bell, *Land of My Fathers*, p. 74.

DAVID CHARLES (1762–1834)

Individual Translations *hymns*
'**Mae Ffrydiau'n Gorfoledd yn tarddu**' (From God's throne of glory there floweth), tr. Revd R. Parry, *Hymns of the Welsh Revival*, pp. 27–9; Revd Lemuel John Hopkin James (Hopcyn), *Welsh Melodies in the Old Notation for Hymns in English Translated and Original*, n.p. [hymn 30] (1912: pp. 31–2); tr. Jane Owen, *Welsh Hymns and their Tunes*, pp. 115–16; tr. Revd J. W. Wynne Jones, *Wales*, 2.12 (1895), 163; tr. H. Elvet Lewis, *Sweet Singers of Wales*, pp. 89–90; '**O Iesu mawr rho d'anian bur**' ('Grant Thy pure Spirit, Jesu hear!'), tr. Jane Owen, *Welsh Hymns and their Tunes*, p. 115.

WALTER DAVIES (Gwallter Mechain; 1761–1849)

Individual Translations *Po.*
'**Cyfnos**' (Nightfall), tr. John Rhŷs, *Y Cymmrodor*, 18 (1905), 144; tr. Kenneth Hurlstone Jackson, *A Celtic Miscellany* (1951), p. 137 (1971: p. 127); tr. Tony Conran, *The Penguin Book of Welsh Verse*, p. 266; tr. Tony Conran, *Oxford Book*, p. 203; tr. Tony Conran, *Welsh Verse*, p. 303.

EVAN EVANS (Ieuan Fardd, Ieuan Brydydd Hir; 1731–88)

Individual Translations *Po.*
'**Beddargraff Dyn Celwyddog**' (The Epitaph of a Deceitful Man), tr. author, *Gwaith y Parchedig Evan Evans (Ieuan Brydydd Hir)*, ed. D. Silvan Evans (Caernarfon: H. Humphreys, 1876), p. 149; *from* '**Cynydd Hiraeth y Bardd am ei Wlad**' (The Unhappy Pilgrim), tr. Robert Gurney, *Bardic Heritage*, p. 171; '**Englynion i Ddewi Fardd ac i'w Lyfr**' (Englynion to the poet Dewi and to his book called *Blodeugerdd Cymru*), tr. Robert Gurney, *Bardic Heritage*, pp. 171–2; '**Llys Ifor Hael**' (The Hall of Ifor Hael), tr. W. Lewis Jones, *Land of My Fathers*, p. 29; tr. Gwyn Williams, *The Welsh Review*, 5.4 (1946), 255; tr. Gwyn Williams, *The Rent that's Due to Love*, p. 109; tr. Kenneth Hurlstone Jackson, *A Celtic Miscellany* (1951), p. 149 (1971: pp. 137–8); tr. Tony Conran, *The Penguin Book of Welsh Verse*, p. 218; tr. Robert Gurney, *Bardic Heritage*, p. 172; tr. Gwyn Williams, *To Look for a Word*, p. 197; tr. Harri Webb, *Triad: thirty three poems by Peter Griffith, Harri Webb, Meic Stephens* (Merthyr Tydfil: The Triskel Press, 1963), p. 49; tr. Gwyn Williams, *Oxford Book*, p. 137; tr. Tony Conran, *Welsh Verse*, p. 238; tr. Harri Webb, *Harri Webb: Collected Poems* (Llandysul: Gomer, 1995), p. 64.

ANN GRIFFITHS (1776–1805)

Collections

George Richard Gould Pughe, *The Hymns of Ann Griffiths of Dolwar Fechan* (Blackburn: Geo. H. Durham, Exchange Works, 1900).

Evan Richards, *A Short Memoir of Ann Griffiths with a Translation of Her Letters and Hymns* (Cadoxton-Barry: E. J. Llewellin, Printer & Stationer, 1916).

R. R. Williams, *The Hymns of Ann Griffiths* (Liverpool: The Brython Press, [1948]).

Homage to Ann Griffiths: A Special Bicentenary Publication, with translations by H. A. Hodges (Penarth: Church in Wales Publications, 1976).

Robert O. F. Wynne and John Ryan, *The Hymns of Ann Griffiths*, ed. John Ryan (Caernarfon: Tŷ ar y Graig, 1980).

A. M. Allchin, *Songs to her God* (Cambridge, Mass: Cowley Publications, *c.* 1987).

Alan Gaunt and Alan Luff, *Hymns and Letters: Ann Griffiths* (London: Stainer and Bell, 1999).

Critical Editions

A. M. Allchin, *Ann Griffiths*, Writers of Wales (Cardiff: University of Wales Press, 1976); Second Edition: *Ann Griffiths: The Furnace and the Fountain* (Cardiff: University of Wales Press, 1987).

Individual Translations *hymns*
'**Am fy mod i mor llygredig**' (Expecting the Lord), tr. Tony Conran, *Welsh Verse*, pp. 238–9; '**A raid i'm sêl, oedd farwor tanllyd**' (Must my zeal, like glowing embers), tr. Joseph P. Clancy, *Other Words*, p. 28; '**Ei law aswy sy'n fy nghynnal**' (My Beloved), tr. H. Idris Bell, *Poems from the Welsh*, p. 40; tr. H. Elvet Lewis, *A Celtic Anthology*, p. 302; '**Er cryfed ydyw'r stormydd**' (The Boat), tr. Ernest Rhys, *A Celtic Anthology*, p. 302; '**Gwna fi fel pren planedig, O fy Nuw**' (Make me Like a Tree Planted), tr. Revd Lemuel John Hopkin James (Hopcyn), *Welsh National Supplement of Hymns*, pp. 53–4; tr. Gwyn Williams, *To Look for a Word*, p. 205; '**Mae bod yn fyw o fawr ryfeddod**' (What a wonder! to be living), tr. Joseph P. Clancy, *Other Words*, p. 52; '**Mae'r dydd yn dod i'r had brenhinol**' (Comes the day the royal offspring), tr. H. Elvet Lewis, *Sweet Singers of Wales*, p. 69; '**Melys gofio y cyfamod**' (Mysteries of Grace), tr. Revd R. Parry, *Hymns of the Welsh Revival*, pp. 61–3; tr. H. Elvet Lewis, *Sweet Singers of Wales*, pp. 64–5; '**O! am dreiddio i'r adnabyddiaeth**' (O to penetrate the knowledge), tr. Joseph P. Clancy, *Other Words*, p. 51; '**O am gael ffydd i edrych**' (O! for faith to see), tr. H. A. Hodges, *Welsh Hymns and their Tunes*, p. 123; tr. Joseph P. Clancy, *Other Words*, p. 24; '**O! ddedwydd awr! tragwyddol orffwys**' (O Day of Bliss), tr. H. Elvet Lewis, *Sweet Singers of Wales*, p. 57; tr. R. Bryan, *Wales*, 3.23 (1896), 100; '**O'm blaen mi wela' ddrws agored**' (See, an open door before me), tr. Joseph P. Clancy, *Other Words*, pp. 53–4;

'**Os rhaid wynebu'r afon donnog**' (Must I face the stormy river), tr. H. Elvet Lewis, *Sweet Singers of Wales*, pp. 66–7; tr. Joseph P. Clancy, *Other Words*, pp. 52–3; '**Pan fo'r enaid mwya' gwresog**' ('When the soul at its most fervent'), tr. Joseph P. Clancy, *Other Words*, p. 52; '**Rhyfedd, rhyfedd gan Angylion**' (Wonder! Wonder to the Angels), tr. Tony Conran, *Welsh Verse*, pp. 240–1; tr. H. A. Hodges, *Welsh Hymns and their Tunes*, pp. 120–1; tr. Rowan Williams, *After Silent Centuries* (Oxford: The Perpetua Press, 1994), pp. 44–5; tr. Joseph P. Clancy, *Other Words*, pp. 29–30; '**Wele'n sefyll rhwng y myrtwydd**' (See Him Stand Among the Myrtles), tr. A. P. Graves, *Welsh Poetry Old and New*, p. 124; tr. H. Idris Bell, *A Book of Wales* (1953), p. 361; tr. Gwyn Williams, *The Rent that's Due To Love*, p. 111; tr. Gwyn Williams, *To Look for a Word*, p. 204; tr. Revd J. Harris Hughes, *The Treasury*, 101.4 (1977), 11; tr. H. Idris Bell, *Oxford Book*, pp. 139–40; tr. Tony Conran, *Welsh Verse*, p. 239; tr. H. A. Hodges, *Welsh Hymns and their Tunes*, pp. 124–5; tr. Rowan Williams, *After Silent Centuries* (Oxford: The Perpetua Press, 1994), p. 46; tr. Joseph P. Clancy, *Other Words*, p. 27.

[attributed to Ann Griffiths] '**Nid oes gwrthrych ar y ddaear**' (There can be no earthly object), tr. Joseph P. Clancy, *Other Words*, p. 51.
[attributed to Ann Griffiths] '**O Arglwydd Dduw rhagluniaeth**' (O Lord and God, Salvation), tr. Revd Lemuel John Hopkin James (Hopcyn), *Welsh National Supplement of Hymns*, p. 62.

JOHN HUGHES (1775–1854)

Individual Translations *hymns*
'**O! anfon Di yr Ysbryd Glân**' (O! Send me the Holy Spirit), tr. Revd Lemuel John Hopkin James (Hopcyn), *Welsh National Supplement of Hymns*, pp. 64–5.

DAFYDD JONES (1711–77)

Individual Translations *hymns*
'**Dewch, frodyr, un fryd**' (Come, brethren, unite), tr. H. Elvet Lewis, *Sweet Singers of Wales*, pp. 27–8; tr. H. Elvet Lewis, *Welsh Hymns and their Tunes*, p. 104; '**Y Dyn anianol nid yw yn deall y pethau sydd**

o **Dduw'** ['Mae plant y byd yn holi . . .'] ('Men of the world are asking . . .'), tr. H. Elvet Lewis, *Sweet Singers of Wales*, pp. 26–7.

EDWARD JONES (1761–1836)

Individual Translations *hymns*
'**Mae'n llond y nefoedd, llond y byd**' (Majestas Dei), tr. H. Elvet Lewis, *Sweet Singers of Wales*, pp. 93–5; tr. R. Bryan, *Wales*, 3.25 (1896), 194; tr. Jane Owen (verse 1) and H. Elvet Lewis (verse 2), *Welsh Hymns and their Tunes*, pp. 111–12.

HUGH JONES (1749–1825)

Individual Translations *hymns*
'**O tyn y gorchudd yn y mynydd hyn**' ('Remove the veil in this dear mount of love'), tr. H. Elvet Lewis, *Sweet Singers of Wales*, pp. 92–3; tr. Revd Lemuel John Hopkin James (Hopcyn), *Welsh Melodies in the Old Notation for Hymns in English Translated and Original*, n.p. [hymn 51] (1912: pp. 46–7).

THOMAS JONES (1756–1820)

Individual Translations *hymns*
'**A oes obaith am achubiaeth?**' (A Door of Hope), tr. Revd R. Parry, *Hymns of the Welsh Revival*, pp. 55–7; '**Mi wn fod fy Mhrynwr yn fyw**' (I know that my Redeemer lives), tr. Revd Lemuel John Hopkin James (Hopcyn), *Welsh National Supplement of Hymns*, pp. 52–3; '**O arwain fy enaid i'r dyfroedd**' (O lead Thou my soul to the waters), tr. Revd Lemuel John Hopkin James (Hopcyn), *Welsh Melodies in the Old Notation for Hymns in English Translated and Original*, n.p. [hymn 14] (1912: p. 19).

LÉWIS MORRIS (Llewelyn Ddu o Fôn; 1701–65)

Individual Translations *Po.*
'**Caniad y Gôg i Feirionnydd**' (The Cuckoo's Address to Merioneth), tr. William Vaughan [printed as 'a member of the Society'], *Diddanwch*

Teuluaidd, Y Llyfr Cyntaf: yn cynnwys gwaith y Parchedig Mr Goronwy Owen, Lewis Morris, Esq.; a Mr Huw Huws, &c . . . (London: Wiliam Roberts, 1763), pp. 185–6; tr. A. P. Graves, *Welsh Poetry Old and New*, pp. 51–2; tr. George Borrow, *Welsh Poems & Ballads*, pp. 63–5; tr. George Borrow, *Land of My Fathers*, pp. 12–13; tr. William Vaughan, in Hugh Owen, *The Life and Works of Lewis Morris* (Anglesey Antiquarian Society: 1951), pp. 295–7; tr. Gwyn Williams, *To Look for a Word*, pp. 193–4; '**Cywydd y Rhew a'r Eira**' (Poem of the Frost and Snow), tr. Leonard Owen, *The London Welshman*, 19.3 (1963), 7; tr. Tony Conran, *The Penguin Book of Welsh Verse*, p. 207; tr. Tony Conran, *Oxford Book*, pp. 115–16; tr. Tony Conran, *Welsh Verse*, pp. 229–30; '**Morwynion Glân Meirionydd**' (The Fair Maids of Meirionnydd), tr. Richard Llwyd, *Poems, Tales, Odes, Sonnets, Translations from the British*, pp. 202–5; tr. Howel William Lloyd, *Y Cymmrodor*, 5 (1882), 145–7.

WILLIAM LEWIS (*fl.* 1754–94)

Individual Translations *hymns*
'**Cof am y cyfiawn Iesu**' (Thoughts of Gethsemane), tr. Revd R. Parry, *Hymns of the Welsh Revival*, pp. 51–3.

DAFYDD NICOLAS (1705?–74)

Individual Translations *Po.*
'**Ffani Blodeu'r Ffair**' (Fanny, Blooming Fair), tr. unsigned, *The Cambrian Register*, 2 (1796), 564–6; tr. unsigned, *The Red Dragon*, 5 (1884), 78–9; tr. William Davies, *The Cambrian Wreath*, pp. 115–17.

GORONWY OWEN (Goronwy Ddu o Fôn; 1723–69)

Individual Translations *Po.*
from '**Caniad i'r Cymmrodorion**' (Upon Welsh), tr. Robert Gurney, *Bardic Heritage*, p. 166; '**Cywydd Hiraeth am Fôn**' (Wearying for Mona), tr. Robert Gurney, *Bardic Heritage*, pp. 160–5; '**Cywydd Hiraeth am Wlad Fôn, atteb i Gywydd Huw Bardd Coch**' (Exiled from Mona), tr. A. P. Graves, *Welsh Poetry Old and New*, p. 49; tr. Robert Gurney, *Bardic Heritage*, pp. 159–60; '**Cywydd y Nennawr**'

(Ode to a London Garret), tr. Ernest Rhys, *A Celtic Anthology*, pp. 298–9; '**Bonedd a Chyneddfau'r Awen**' (The Pedigree of the Muse), tr. George Borrow, *Welsh Poems and Ballads*, pp. 79–83; '**Briodasgerdd Elin Morys**' (Bridal Song for Elin Morys), tr. Robert Gurney, *Bardic Heritage*, pp. 166–9; '**Dau Englyn o Glod i'r Delyn**' (The Harp), tr. George Borrow, *Welsh Poems and Ballads*, p. 87; *from* '**Dydd y Farn**' (The Day of Judgment), tr. author, *The Poetry of Wales* (1873), pp. 26–9; tr. A. P. Graves, *The Nationalist*, 4.31 (1910), 64; tr. A. P. Graves, *Welsh Poetry Old and New*, pp. 122–3, tr. A. P. Graves, *A Celtic Psaltery*, pp. 87–8; '**Gofuned Goronwy Ddu o Fôn**' (The Wish), tr. Gwyn Williams, *The Rent that's Due to Love*, pp. 103–7; tr. Tony Conran, *Dock Leaves*, 8.21 (1957), 50–1; tr. Tony Conran, *The Penguin Book of Welsh Verse*, pp. 213–14; tr. Gwyn Williams, *To Look for a Word*, pp. 195–6; tr. Tony Conran, *Welsh Verse*, pp. 233–5; tr. Tony Conran, *An Anglesey Anthology*, ed. Dewi Roberts (Gwasg Carreg Gwalch, 1999), pp. 118–19; '**Gwahodd**' (The Invitation), tr. George Borrow, *Welsh Poems & Ballads*, pp. 73–6; tr. George Borrow, *Presenting Welsh Poetry*, pp. 50–2; tr. Tony Conran, *The Penguin Book of Welsh Verse*, pp. 215–17; tr. George Borrow, *Oxford Book*, pp. 134–6; tr. Tony Conran, *Welsh Verse*, pp. 235–7; tr. George Borrow, *An Anglesey Anthology*, ed. Dewi Roberts (Gwasg Carreg Gwalch, 1999), pp. 115–17; '**Marwnad Elin**' (Elegy for Elin), tr. Kenneth Hurlstone Jackson, *A Celtic Miscellany* (1951), pp. 292–3 (1971: pp. 266–7); tr. Robert Gurney, *Bardic Heritage*, pp. 169–70; tr. Kenneth Hurlstone Jackson, *Oxford Book*, p. 136.

WILLIAM OWEN PUGHE (1759–1835)

Individual Translations *Po.*
'**Ymadaw Corf ac Enaid**' (The Dying Christian to his Soul), tr. unsigned, *The Cambro-Briton*, 2 (1820/21), 86.[1]

HYWEL RHYS (d. 1799)

Individual Translations *Po.*
'**Cân y Darfochyn**' (The Badger Hunt), tr. Theophilus Jones, *The Cambrian Wreath*, pp. 130–3.

[1] The Welsh original is itself a 'very happy translation' of Pope's 'The Dying Christian to His Soul'.

MORGAN RHYS (1716–79)

Individual Translations *hymns*
'**Beth sydd i mi yn y Byd**' (What have I on earth to gain), tr. Revd J. W. Wynne Jones, *Wales*, 2.12 (1895), 163; tr. Revd Lemuel John Hopkin James (Hopcyn), *Welsh National Supplement of Hymns*, p. 61; '**Capten mawr ein hiachawdwriaeth**' (Victories of the Cross), tr. Revd R. Parry, *Hymns of the Welsh Revival*, p. 61; '**Dewch, hen ac ieuainc, dewch**' (Come, old and young now come), tr. Revd R. Parry, *Hymns of the Welsh Revival*, p. 67; tr. Revd Lemuel John Hopkin James (Hopcyn), *Welsh Melodies in the Old Notation for Hymns in English Translated and Original*, n.p. [hymn 53] (1912: pp. 49–50); '**Dy Hen addewid Rasol**' (Thy gracious ancient promise), tr. H. Elvet Lewis, *Sweet Singers of Wales*, p. 142; '**Dyma Geidwad i'r colledig**' (Lo! a Saviour for the lost ones), tr. Revd R. Parry, *Hymns of the Welsh Revival*, p. 37; tr. Revd Lemuel John Hopkin James (Hopcyn), *Welsh Melodies in the Old Notation for Hymns in English Translated and Original*, n.p. [hymn 48] (1912: p. 44); '**Fe welir Seion fel y wawr**' ('Fair as the dawn shall Zion be'), tr. Ll. M. W., *Welsh National Supplement of Hymns*, p. 43; '**Gwnes addunedau fil**' ('I promise every day'), tr. H. Elvet Lewis, *Sweet Singers of Wales*, pp. 71–2; '**Henffych i'r bore hyfryd**' (Hail the beautiful morning), tr. H. Elvet Lewis, *Sweet Singers of Wales*, p. 74; '**O! agor fy llygaid i weled**' ('Lord, open mine eyes to behold'), tr. H. Elvet Lewis, *Sweet Singers of Wales*, p. 73; tr. Revd R. Parry, *Hymns of the Welsh Revival*, p. 61; tr. H. Elvet Lewis, *Welsh Hymns and their Tunes*, pp. 106–7; '**O anllygredig Ddinas**' ('O undefilèd city'), tr. Revd Lemuel John Hopkin James (Hopcyn), *Welsh National Supplement of Hymns*, p. 56; '**Pechadur wyf, O Arglwydd**' ('O Lord, I am a sinner'), tr. Revd Lemuel John Hopkin James (Hopcyn), *Welsh National Supplement of Hymns*, p. 57; '**Peraidd ganodd Sêr y Bore**' ('All the morning stars were singing'), tr. Jane Owen, *Welsh Hymns and their Tunes*, p. 106; '**Tragwyddol glod i'r cyfiawn**' ('All praise to Christ the Righteous'), tr. H. Elvet Lewis, *Sweet Singers of Wales*, p. 72.

DAVID RICHARDS (Dafydd Ionawr; 1751–1827)

Individual Translations *Po.*
'**Beddargraff Geneth Fach**' (Epitaph on a Little Girl), tr. H. Idris Bell, *Transactions of the Honourable Society of Cymmrodorion*

(1941), 37; tr. Kenneth Hurlstone Jackson, *A Celtic Miscellany* (1951), p. 147 (1971: p. 135); 'Cywydd y Daran' (An Ode to the Thunder), tr. Revd R. Harries Jones, *The Poetry of Wales* (1873), pp. 32–4; tr. M. Samuel, *The Red Dragon*, 2 (1882), 416–17; *from* 'Cywydd y Drindod' [Cân Gwenfron] (A Prayer), tr. J. Bodvan Anwyl, *Young Wales*, 4.38 (1898), 39.

JOHN ROBERTS (Siôn Robert Lewis; 1731–1806)

'Braint, braint' (Bless'd, bless'd), tr. Revd Lemuel John Hopkin James (Hopcyn), *Welsh Melodies in the Old Notation for Hymns in English Translated and Original*, n.p. [hymn 23] (1912: p. 26).[2]

EVAN THOMAS (*c.* 1710–*c.* 1770)

Individual Translations *Po.*
'I Wraig Fonheddig Neuadd Llanarth' (To the Noble Woman of Llanarth Hall), tr. Tony Conran, *The Penguin Book of Welsh Verse*, p. 208; tr. Gwyn Williams, *To Look for a Word*, p. 197; tr. Gwyn Jones, *Oxford Book*, p. 117; tr. Tony Conran, *Welsh Verse*, p. 230.

JOHN THOMAS (1730–1804?)

Individual Translations *hymns*
'Am fod fy Iesu'n byw' ('Because my Jesus rose'), tr. unsigned, *Welsh Hymns and their Tunes*, p. 109.

DAFYDD WILLIAM (1720/1–94)

Individual Translations *hymns*
'Anghrediniaeth, gad fi'n llonydd' (Unbelief, let me have quiet), tr. H. Elvet Lewis, *Sweet Singers of Wales*, pp. 75–6; 'Arglwydd, gwrando'r gwan yn griddfan' (Hear my grief), tr. H. Elvet Lewis, *Sweet Singers of Wales*,

---

[2] The first verse (the well-known 'Braint, braint') is attributed to John Roberts, but the following two verses are anonymous.

pp. 76–7; '**O anfeidrol rym y cariad**' (The Omnipotence of Love) tr. H. Elvet Lewis, *Sweet Singers of Wales*, p. 78; '**O Arglwydd, dyro awel**' ('Lord, let the gladdening breezes revive'), tr. H. Elvet Lewis, *Sweet Singers of Wales*, p. 77; '**Yn y dyfroedd mawr a'r tonnau**' (When I'm passing through the waters), tr. H. Elvet Lewis, *Sweet Singers of Wales*, p. 79; tr. Revd J. W. Wynne Jones, *Wales*, 2.12 (1895), 163; tr. Revd Lemuel John Hopkin James (Hopcyn), *Welsh Melodies in the Old Notation for Hymns in English Translated and Original*, n.p. [hymn 41] (1912: pp. 40–1); tr. H. Elvet Lewis, *Welsh Hymns and their Tunes*, p. 108.

THOMAS WILLIAM (1761–1844)

Individual Translations *hymns*
'**Adenydd fel c'lomen pe cawn**' (All for the wings of a dove), tr. Revd R. Parry, *Hymns of the Welsh Revival*, p. 25; tr. W. H. D., *Welsh National Supplement of Hymns*, p. 53; '**Llef Eliseus ar ôl Elias**' (The Cry of Elish after Elijah), tr. H. Elvet Lewis, *Sweet Singers of Wales*, pp. 83–4; tr. R. S. Thomas, *Wales*, 5.7 (1945), 16, tr. R. S. Thomas, *The Stones of the Field* (Carmarthen: The Druid Press, 1946), p. 39; tr. R. S. Thomas, *Selected Poems* (Newcastle Upon Tyne: Bloodaxe Books, 1986), p. 13; '**Mae pren y bwyd wedi'i gael yng nghanol anial dir**' (The tree of life in barren soil), tr. H. Elvet Lewis, *Sweet Singers of Wales*, pp. 84–5; '**O'th flaen, O Dduw! 'rwy'n dyfod**' (O God, I come before Thee), tr. Revd R. Parry, *Hymns of the Welsh Revival*, pp. 45–6; tr. Revd Lemuel John Hopkin James (Hopcyn), *Welsh Melodies in the Old Notation for Hymns in English Translated and Original*, n.p. [hymn 55] (1912: pp. 48–9); tr. John Mainwaring, *The Evangelical Magazine of Wales* (February/March, 1985), 15; '**Rwyf innau'n un o'r lliaws sy'n gorwedd wrth y llyn**' (I am among the multitude who lie beside the lake), tr. H. Elvet Lewis, *Sweet Singers of Wales*, pp. 82–3; tr. H. Elvet Lewis, *Welsh Hymns and their Tunes*, p. 110; '**Y Gŵr wrth ffynnon Jacob**' (He who at Jacob's fountain), tr. Elvet Lewis, *Sweet Singers of Wales*, p. 135;[3] tr. Revd R. Parry, *Hymns of the Welsh Revival*, p. 25; tr. Revd Lemuel John Hopkin

---

[3] This verse was made popular during the Revival of 1904–5 and it has often been published independently of the other two verses in the original hymn.

James (Hopcyn), *Welsh Melodies in the Old Notation for Hymns in English Translated and Original*, n.p. [hymn 49].

EDWARD WILLIAMS (Iolo Morganwg; 1747–1826)

Collections

Taliesin Williams (ab Iolo) (ed.), *The Iolo Manuscripts: A Selection of Ancient Welsh Manuscripts* (Llandovery: Welsh Manuscripts Society, 1848).

Individual Translations *Po.*
'**Cân y Maensaer** *neu* **Y Maensaer Mwyn**' (The Stone-Mason), tr. Gwyn Williams, *To Look for a Word*, pp. 206–7.

Individual Translations *hymns*
'**Mawr ddyled arnom sydd i foli Iôr y nef**' (Constrained by love are we), tr. Revd Lemuel John Hopkin James (Hopcyn), *Welsh Melodies in the Old Notation for Hymns in English Translated and Original*, n.p. [hymn 31] (1912: p. 32); '**Mawr yw daioni'r Duw a'n gwnaeth**' ('How great is God's benevolence'), tr. Revd Lemuel John Hopkin James (Hopcyn), *Welsh National Supplement of Hymns*, pp. 66–7.

Individual Translations *Pr.*
Barddas, vol 1 The Book of Bardism, tr. J. Williams ab Ithel, *The Bardic Source Book*, pp. 310–28.

Rhys Goch ap Rhiccert forgeries[4]

Individual Translations *Po.*
from '**Cân Eiddig**' (The Jealous Lover), tr. Thomas Stephens, *The Literature of the Kymry*, p. 481 (1876: pp. 461–2); '**Cân i Ddanfon yr Adar yn Lateion at Ferch**' (Song to send the Birds with Messages to a Maid), tr. Thomas Stephens, *The Literature of the Kymry*, pp.

---

[4] Twenty poems were attributed to Rhys Goch ap Rhiccert ab Einion ap Collwyn in the *Iolo Manuscripts*. Later scholarship uncovered that around fifteen of these were forged by Iolo Morganwg and an additional five poems made up of a mixture of older manuscript poems.

483–5 (1876: pp. 464–6); '**Cân i Wallt Merch**' (Song to a Maiden's Hair), tr. Thomas Stephens, *The Literature of the Kymry*, pp. 477–80 (1876: pp. 457–60); tr. unsigned, *A Celtic Anthology*, p. 263; tr. Ernest Rhys, *The Bardic Source Book*, p. 241; '**Cân i Yrru'r Wylan yn Llatai**' (Song to the Sea Gull), tr. Thomas Stephens, *The Literature of the Kymry*, pp. 486–8 (1876: pp. 467–8); '**Canu'r Marw o'i Serch**' (A Song to Her for Whom I am Dying), tr. John Thomas (Ieuan Ddu), *The Literature of the Kymry*, pp. 358–9 (1876: pp. 342–4); tr. A. P. Graves, *Welsh Poetry Old and New*, pp. 31–3; '**Cân Serch, o'r Hen Ganiad**' ['Gorthrwm a thrwm a thrist fyddaf'] (The Poet's Arbour in the Birch-Wood), tr. Thomas Stephens, *The Literature of the Kymry*, pp. 482–3 (1876: pp. 462–3); tr. Kenneth Hurlstone Jackson, *A Celtic Miscellany* (1951), p. 87 (1971: p. 82); tr. Kenneth Hurlstone Jackson, *Oxford Book*, p. 139; '**Cân y Fronfraith**' (The Song of the Thrush), tr. unsigned, *The History of the Literature of Wales*, pp. 29–31; tr. A. P. Graves, *Welsh Poetry Old and New*, pp. 29–31; '**Cân y Fwyalch**' (The Song of the Thrush), tr. Thomas Stephens, *The Literature of the Kymry*, pp. 487–9 (1876: pp. 468–70); *from* '**Cân yr Haf**' (Song to the Summer), tr. Thomas Stephens, *The Literature of the Kymry*, pp. 356–8 (1876: pp. 340–2).

Morgan Gruffudd forgeries[5]

Individual Translations *Po.*
'**Cân**' ['*codais foreddydd i rodio'r gweunydd*'] (Song), tr. Iolo Morganwg, *Poems, Lyric and Pastoral* (London: J. Nichols, 1794), pp. 70–3; tr. Iolo Morganwg, *Cambrian Quarterly Magazine*, 5 (1833), 413–14; tr. Iolo Morganwg, *The Red Dragon*, 1 (1882), 424–5.

JOHN WILLIAMS (*c*. 1728–1806)

Individual Translations *hymns*
'**Pwy welaf o Edom yn dod**' (What warrior from Edom is He?), tr. Revd R. Parry, *Hymns of the Welsh Revival*, p. 55; tr. Revd Lemuel John Hopkin James (Hopcyn), *Welsh Melodies in the Old Notation for Hymns in English Translated and Original*, n.p. [hymn 1] (1912: p. 8).

---

[5] Another of Iolo Morganwg's pseudonyms.

WILLIAM WILLIAMS (Williams Pantycelyn or Pantycelyn; 1717–91)

Collections

William Williams, *Hosannah to the Son of David, or, Hymns of praise to God for our glorious redemption by Christ: and, Gloria in excelsis, or, Hymns of praise to God & the Lamb/by William Williams; with an introductory sketch/by E. Morgan* (London: D. Sedgwick, 1859).

Holl Weithiau, Prydyddawl a Rhyddieithol, Y Diweddar Barch. William Williams, Pant-y-Celyn, ed. Revd J. R. Kilsby Jones (London: William MacKenzie, 1867).

Robert Jones, *A view of the Kingdom of Christ, or, Christ is all, and in all: a poem by way of exposition of Col. iii. 11, 1 Cor. xv. 25* (London: William Clowes & Sons, 1878).

R. R. Williams, *Popular Hymns of Pantycelyn* (Liverpool: The Brython Press, 1948).

Critical Editions

Bethan Lloyd-Jones, *Drws y Society Profiad: The Experience Meeting* (Evangelical Movement of Wales, 1973).

Eifion Evans, *Pursued by God: a selective translation with notes of the Welsh religious classic Theomemphus/by William Williams of Pantycelyn (first published in Welsh in 1764); together with a brief survey of the author's life and work* (Bryntyrion, Bridgend: Evangelical Press of Wales, 1996).

Individual Translations *hymns*

'**Af at yr orsedd fel yr wyf**' (To Jesu's throne, unclean I go), tr. Mrs Penderel Llewelyn, *Hymns Translated from the Welsh*, p. 9; '**Angylion doent yn gyson**' (Angelic Throngs Unnumbered), tr. unsigned, *The Poetry of Wales* (1873), pp. 154–5; '**Anweledig, rwy'n dy garu**' (Hidden from my sight, I love you), tr. Joseph P. Clancy, *Other*

Words, pp. 47–8; '**Arglwydd, arwain trwy'r anialwch**' (Guide me, O thou great Jehovah), tr. author and Peter Williams, *A Book of Wales* (1987), pp. 316–7; tr. Joseph P. Clancy, *Other Words*, pp. 49–50; '**Arnat, Iesu, boed fy meddwl**' (Let my mind be on you – Jesus), tr. Joseph P. Clancy, *Planet*, 88 (1991), 50–5; tr. Joseph P. Clancy, *Other Words*, p. 44; '**Awn bechaduriaid at y Dŵr**' (Ho! haste, ye sinners, to the stream), tr. Mrs Penderel Llewelyn, *Hymns Translated from the Welsh*, p. 11; '**Blinais ar afonydd Babel**' (Hasten, Israel! From the Desert), tr. unsigned, *The Poetry of Wales* (1873), pp. 149–50; '**Cariad Crist a Phechod Sion**' (Jesu's Love and Zion's sinning), tr. Mrs Penderel Llewelyn, *Hymns Translated from the Welsh*, p. 13; '**Cheisiais, Arglwydd, ddim ond hynny**' (I have asked, Lord, nothing further), tr. Joseph P. Clancy, *Other Words*, pp. 45–6; '**Cofia, f'enaid, cyn it' dreulio**' ('O my soul do thou consider'), tr. Revd Lemuel John Hopkin James (Hopcyn), *Welsh National Supplement of Hymns*, p. 71; '**Cyfarwydda f'enaid**' (Lord, direct me as I journey), tr. H. Elvet Lewis, *Sweet Singers of Wales*, p. 43; tr. Revd R. Parry, *Hymns of the Welsh Revival*, p. 49; tr. Revd Lemuel John Hopkin James (Hopcyn), *Welsh Melodies in the Old Notation for Hymns in English Translated and Original*, n.p. [hymn 54] (1912: p. 48); '**Cymer, Iesu, fi fel'r ydwyf**' (Victory by the Cross), tr. Revd R. Parry, *Hymns of the Welsh Revival*, pp. 47–9; '**Dal fi, fy Nuw, dal fi i'r lan**' (Uphold me, Lord! thine aid I seek), tr. Mrs Penderel Llewelyn, *Hymns Translated from the Welsh*, p. 15; '**Dechrau canu, dechrau canmol**' (Begin to sing, Begin to praise), tr. Revd Lemuel John Hopkin James (Hopcyn), *Welsh National Supplement of Hymns*, p. 56; '**Disgyn, Iesu, o'th gynteddoedd**' (Oh! bow down, thou mighty Saviour), tr. Mrs Penderel Llewelyn, *Hymns Translated from the Welsh*, p. 17; '**Draw mi wela'r nos yn darfod**' (Yonder is the night departing), tr. Revd Lemuel John Hopkin James (Hopcyn), *Welsh Melodies in the Old Notation for Hymns in English Translated and Original*, n.p. [hymn 34] (1912: p. 34); '**Duw, teyrnasa ar y ddaear**' (O'er the earth, in every nation), tr. Mrs Penderel Llewelyn, *Hymns Translated from the Welsh*, p. 19; '**Dyn dieithir ydwyf yma**' (In this land I am a stranger), tr. Joseph Morris, *Favourite Welsh Hymns Translated into English*, pp. 33–4; tr. unsigned, *The Poetry of Wales* (1873), p. 150; tr. H. Elvet Lewis, *Sweet Singers of Wales*, p. 41; '**Fe welir rhyw ddyddiau**' (The glory is coming), tr. H. Elvet Lewis, *Sweet Singers of Wales*, pp. 48–9; '**Fy meiau trymion, luoedd maith**' (The pardoned sinner), tr. Revd R. Parry, *Hymns of the Welsh Revival*, pp. 53–5; '**Fy ngweddi,** dos i'r nef' (Direct unto my God), tr. unsigned, *The Poetry of Wales* (1873), p. 155; 'Gwaed dy groes sy'n codi 'fyny' (Jesu's blood can raise the feeble), tr. H. Elvet Lewis, *Sweet Singers of Wales*, p. 141; tr. Revd R. Parry, *Hymns of the Welsh Revival*, p. 37; tr. Revd Lemuel John Hopkin James (Hopcyn), *Welsh National Supplement of Hymns*, p. 44; 'Iesu, dlfyrrwch fy enaid drud' (Jesus, My Preciouo Soul's Delight), tr. Mrs Penderel Llewelyn, *Hymns Translated from the Welsh*, p. 21; tr. unsigned, *The Poetry of Wales* (1873), p. 154; tr. Gwyn Williams, *To Look for a Word*, p. 199; tr. Joseph P. Clancy, *Planet*, 88 (1991), 50–5; tr. Joseph P. Clancy, *Other Words*, pp. 48–9; 'Iesu, Iesu, 'rwyt Ti'n ddigon' (Jesus – though my only pleasure), tr. Mrs Penderel Llewelyn, *Hymns Translated from the Welsh*, p. 23; tr. unsigned, *The Poetry of Wales* (1873), p. 150; 'Mae addewid nef o'm hochr' (The prayer of the penitent), tr. Revd R. Parry, *Hymns of the Welsh Revival*, pp. 21–3; 'Mae'r faner fawr ymlaen' (The standard is ahead), tr. H. Elvet Lewis, *Sweet Singers of Wales*, pp. 43–5; 'Mae'r iachawdwriaeth fel y môr' (Salvation free is like the sea), tr. Revd Lemuel John Hopkin James (Hopcyn), *Welsh Melodies in the Old Notation for Hymns in English Translated and Original*, n.p. [hymn 29] (1912: pp. 30–1); 'Marchog, Iesu, yn llwyddiannus' (Ride on, Jesus, ride in triumph), tr. unsigned, *The Poetry of Wales* (1873), p. 152; tr. H. Elvet Lewis, *Sweet Singers of Wales*, pp. 45–7; tr. Revd R. Parry, *Hymns of the Welsh Revival*, pp. 19–21; tr. Revd Lemuel John Hopkin James (Hopcyn), *Welsh Melodies in the Old Notation for Hymns in English Translated and Original*, n.p. [hymn 35] (1912: pp. 34–5); tr. A. P. Graves, *Welsh Poetry Old and New*, pp. 125–6; tr. A. P. Graves, *A Celtic Psaltery*, p. 90; tr. G. O. Williams, *Welsh Hymns and their Tunes*, p. 102; 'Mewn anial dyrys le' (In a lonely desert place), tr. H. Elvet Lewis, *Sweet Singers of Wales*, pp. 47–8; 'Mi dafla' 'maich oddi ar fy ngwar' (The Intercessor), tr. Revd R. Parry, *Hymns of the Welsh Revival*, p. 51; 'Mi wela'r cwmwl du' (Peace after Storm), tr. H. Elvet Lewis, *Sweet Singers of Wales*, p. 40; tr. H. Elvet Lewis, *A Celtic Anthology*, p. 301; tr. Tony Conran, *The Penguin Book of Welsh Verse*, pp. 211–12; tr. Tony Conran, *Welsh Verse*, pp. 232–3; tr. Joseph P. Clancy, *Other Words*, pp. 46–7; 'N'ad i'r gwynt-oedd cryf dychrynllyd: Disgwyl wyf trwy hyd yr hirnos' (I am through the lone night waiting), tr. unsigned, *The Poetry of Wales* (1873), p. 151; tr. H. Elvet Lewis, *Sweet Singers of Wales*, pp. 38–9; 'Ni chollwyd gwaed y groes' (The blood of Jesu's cross), tr. H. Elvet Lewis, *Sweet Singers of Wales*, pp. 43–5; 'Nis gall angylion pur y nef'

(The Brightest Angels of the Skies), tr. Mrs Penderel Llewelyn, *Hymns Translated from the Welsh*, p. 27; '**O! am nerth i dreulio 'nyddiau'**[6] (Aid me, Lord, always to tarry), tr. unsigned, *The Poetry of Wales* (1873), p. 153; tr. Revd Lemuel John Hopkin James (Hopcyn), *Welsh National Supplement of Hymns*, p. 52; tr. Gwladys A. Charles-Jones, *Y Ddinas*, 4.9 (1950), 7; '**O! dyrchafa f'enaid egwan**' (Communion with God), tr. Revd R. Parry, *Hymns of the Welsh Revival*, pp. 43–5; '**O! Golch fi beunydd**' (O wash me daily), tr. Jane Owen, *Welsh Hymns and their Tunes*, pp. 98–9; '**O! lefara, addfwyn Iesu**' (Gentle Jesus, speak, speak to me), tr. Revd R. Parry, *Hymns of the Welsh Revival*, p. 59; tr. Robert Bryan, *Y Greal*, 3.10 (1910), 164; tr. Revd Lemuel John Hopkin James (Hopcyn), *Welsh Melodies in the Old Notation for Hymns in English Translated and Original*, n.p. [hymn 51] (1912: 45–6); '**O! sancteiddia f'enaid, Arglwydd**' (The cleansed heart), tr. Revd R. Parry, *Hymns of the Welsh Revival*, p. 57; tr. Revd Lemuel John Hopkin James (Hopcyn), *Welsh National Supplement of Hymns*, p. 45; '**O Tyred Arglwydd mawr**' (The Virtues of the Cross), tr. W. H., *Wales*, 3.26 (1896), 286; tr. unsigned, *Wales*, 3.32 (1896), 570; '**Pam y caiff bwystfilod rheibus**' (Why should beasts of prey be suffered to destroy the tender blade?), tr. H. Elvet Lewis, *Sweet Singers of Wales*, pp. 34–5; [verse 2: '**Gosod Babell yng ngwlad Goshen**'] (Fix, O Lord, a tent in Goshen), tr. unsigned, *The Poetry of Wales* (1873), pp. 150–1; '**Pererin wyf mewn anial dir**' (A Pilgrim in a Desert Land), tr. Tony Conran, *The Penguin Book of Welsh Verse*, p. 210; tr. Gwyn Williams, *To Look for a Word*, p. 198; tr. Tony Conran, *Welsh Verse*, pp. 231–2; '**Pwy ddyry i'm falm o Gilead**' (Who will give me Gilead's balm), tr. Mrs Penderel Llewelyn, *Hymns Translated from the Welsh*, p. 31; tr. H. Elvet Lewis, *Sweet Singers of Wales*, pp. 50–2; '**Rwy'n edrych dros y bryniau pell**' (I Look Beyond the Distant Hills), tr. unsigned, *The Poetry of Wales* (1873), pp. 153–4; tr. H. Elvet Lewis, *Sweet Singers of Wales*, p. 38; tr. H. Idris Bell, *A Book of Wales* (1953), p. 360; tr. Tony Conran, *The Penguin Book of Welsh Verse*, pp. 209–10; tr. H. Idris Bell, *Oxford Book*, p. 118; tr. Tony Conran, *Welsh Verse*, pp. 230–1; tr. H. Idris Bell, *A Book of Wales* (1987), pp. 315–16; tr. H. Idris Bell, *Welsh Hymns and their Tunes*, p. 101; tr. Joseph P. Clancy,

---

[6] Williams Pantycelyn is the author of the first verse but when a second is published, 'Yn dy waith y mae fy mywyd', Evan Griffiths (1795–1873) is the author.

Planet, 88 (1991), 50–5; tr. Joseph P. Clancy, *Other Words*, p. 50; **'Rwy'n dewis Iesu a'i farwol glwy'** (The Happy Choice), tr. Revd R. Parry, *Hymns of the Welsh Revival*, p. 45; **'Yn Eden, cofiaf hynny byth'** (Cwymp Eden a chodiad Calfaria: Eden and Calvary), tr. Revd R. Parry, *Hymns of the Welsh Revival*, pp. 29–31; tr. H. A. Hodges, *Welsh Hymns and their Tunes*, p. 98; **'Tyred, Iesu, i'r ardaloedd'** (O'er the Earth, in Every Nation), tr. unsigned, *The Poetry of Wales* (1873), p. 152; **'Tyred, Iesu, i'r anialwch'** (Jesus, come, into the wasteland), tr. Joseph P. Clancy, *Other Words*, pp. 44–5; **'Yn Eden, cofiaf hynny byth'** (Eden and Calvary), tr. John Morgan, *The Red Dragon*, 7 (1885), 221–2.

Individual Translations *Po.*
'Duw, os wyt am ddibennu'r byd' (If Thou would'st end the world, O Lord), tr. H. Elvet Lewis, *Sweet Singers of Wales*, p. 144; *from* **Theomemphus** (The Farwell Song of Theomemphus), tr. Gwyn Williams, *To Look for a Word*, pp. 200–2; *from* **Golwg ar Deyrnas Crist** (A View of Christ's Kingdom), tr. Saunders Lewis and Gwyn Jones, *Oxford Book*, pp. 119–22.

Y BEDWAREDD GANRIF AR BYMTHEG: THE NINETEENTH CENTURY

Anthologies

Edmund O. Jones, *Welsh Lyrics of the Nineteenth Century* (London: Simpkin, Marshall & Co, 1896).
[*Welsh Lyrics of the Nineteenth Century*]

H. Idris Bell and C. C. Bell, *Welsh Poems of the Twentieth Century in English Verse* (Wrexham: Hughes & Son, 1925).[1]
[*Welsh Poems of the Twentieth Century*]

ANON.

Individual Translations *Po.*
'**Hiraeth**' (Not Divided in Death), tr. Kenneth Hurlstone Jackson, *A Celtic Miscellany* (1951), p. 146 (1971: p. 134).

Individual Translations *hymns*
'**Bydd myrdd o ryfeddodau**' ('There shall be a thousand wonders'), tr. H. Elvet Lewis, *Sweet Singers of Wales*, p. 143; '**Draw mi welaf ryfeddodau**' (Love Divine), tr. Revd R. Parry, *Hymns of the Welsh Revival*, pp. 37–9; '**Dyma Feibl annwyl Iesu**' ('Here's the Bible of my Saviour'), Revd Lemuel John Hopkin James (Hopcyn), *Welsh Melodies in the Old Notation for Hymns in English Translated and Original*, n.p. [hymn 33] (1912: pp. 33).[2]

WILLIAM AMBROSE (Emrys; 1813–73)

Individual Translations *Po.*
'**Y Blodeuyn Olaf**' (The Last Flower), tr. Francis Edwards, *Translations from the Welsh*, p. 25.

---

[1] Though published in 1925 many of the translated poems are by writers represented in this section.
[2] This hymn first appeared in 1820 and the translation that appears in the second edition reflects the slight variation that appeared in 1821.

JOHN BLACKWELL (Alun; 1797–1841)

Individual Translations *Po.*
'**Cân Gwraig y Pysgotwr**' (The Song of the Fisherman's Wife), tr. Revd Robert Jones, *Y Cymmrodor*, 2 (1878), 21–3; tr. unsigned, *The Poetry of Wales* (1873), p. 133; tr. Edmund O. Jones, *Wales*, 1.4 (1894), 161; tr. N. Bennett, *Wales*, 2.14 (1895), 281; tr. Edmund O. Jones, *Welsh Lyrics of the Nineteenth Century*, pp. 3–4; '**Cathl i'r Eos**' (Song to the Nightingale), tr. unsigned, *The Poetry of Wales* (1873), p. 46; tr. R. Drury, *Wales*, 1.7 (1894), 304; tr. R. A. Griffith, *Young Wales*, 1.5 (1895), 113; tr. Edmund O. Jones, *Welsh Lyrics of the Nineteenth Century*, p. 8; tr. R. L. Davies, *Cambrian Lyrics*, pp. 2–3; tr. Tony Conran, *The Penguin Book of Welsh Verse*, p. 221; tr. Tony Conran, *Welsh Verse*, p. 249; '**Doli**' (Dolly), tr. A. P. Graves, *Welsh Poetry Old and New*, pp. 86–7; tr. Edmund O. Jones, *Welsh Lyrics of the Nineteenth Century*, pp. 5–6; '**Abaty Tintern**' (Tintern Abbey), tr. Edmund O. Jones, *Welsh Lyrics of the Nineteenth Century*, p. 7; '**Rhywun**' (Lassie), tr. Robert Bryan, *The Nationalist*, 1.10 (1907), 31; '**Y Ddeilen Grin**' (The Withered Leaf), tr. unsigned, *The Poetry of Wales* (1873), p. 134.

ROBERT BRYAN (1858–1920)

Individual Translations *Po.*
'**Cân Medi**' (A Reaping Song), tr. Francis Edwards, *Translations from the Welsh*, p. 61; '**Clychau Aberdyfi**' (The Bells of Aberdovey), tr. Francis Edwards, *Translations from the Welsh*, pp. 51–3; '**Gwen fy Mun**' (Gwen my Love), tr. Francis Edwards, *Translations from the Welsh*, p. 55; '**Hun y Prydydd**' (The Bard's Last Sleep), tr. Francis Edwards, *Translations from the Welsh*, p. 63; '**O Noson Gu**' (Beloved Night), tr. Francis Edwards, *Translations from the Welsh*, p. 49; '**Orpheus**', tr. Francis Edwards, *Translations from the Welsh*, pp. 39–47; '**Suo-gân**' (Lullaby), tr. A. P. Graves, *Welsh Poetry Old and New*, pp. 114–15; tr. Francis Edwards, *Translations from the Welsh*, p. 65; '**Trai a Llanw**' (Ebb and Flow), tr. Francis Edwards, *Translations from the Welsh*, p. 57; '**Y Gwcw Fach**' (The Little Cuckoo), tr. A. P. Graves, *Welsh Poetry Old and New*, pp. 90–1; '**Y Nos sydd yn Agos**' (The Night is Nigh), tr. Francis Edwards, *Translations from the Welsh*, p. 59; '**Y Seren**' (The Star), tr. Francis Edwards, *Translations from the Welsh*, p. 37.

COSLETT COSLETT (Carnelian; 1834–1910)

Individual Translations *Po.*
'**Seren y Gogledd**' (The Pole Star), tr. Kenneth Hurlstone Jackson, *A Celtic Miscellany* (1951), p. 137 (1971: p. 127); tr. Kenneth Hurlstone Jackson, *Oxford Book*, p. 203.

JOHN DAVIES (Ossian Gwent; 1839–92)

Individual Translations *Po.*
'**Y Cyfarchiad Boreuol**' (A Morning Greeting), tr. Edmund O. Jones, *Welsh Lyrics of the Nineteenth Century*, pp. 109–11; '**Y Bibl**' (The Bible), tr. Edmund O. Jones, *Welsh Lyrics of the Nineteenth Century*, p. 106; '**Y Dryw**' (The Wren), tr. unsigned, *The Nationalist*, 1.9 (1907), 32; '**Y Llyn**' (The Lake), tr. Edmund O. Jones, *Welsh Lyrics of the Nineteenth Century*, pp. 107–8; '**Yr Uchedydd**' (The Lark), tr. Edmund O. Jones, *Welsh Lyrics of the Nineteenth Century*, p. 105.

RICHARD DAVIES (Tafolog; 1830–1904)

Individual Translations *hymns*
'**Iddo Ef**' (Unto Him), tr. H. Elvet Lewis, *Sweet Singers of Wales*, pp. 151–3.

RICHARD DAVIES (Mynyddog; 1833–77)

Individual Translations *Po.*
'**Geirian Cariad**' (Love Foresworn), tr. Rhys D. Morgan, *The Red Dragon*, 1 (1882), 341; '**Gweno Fwyn**' (Gwenny Dear), tr. Ifano Jones, *The Welsh Review*, 1.4 (1906), 80; '**Hwyrgân**' (A Nocturne), tr. Edmund O. Jones, *Welsh Lyrics of the Nineteenth Century*, p. 97; tr. Francis Edwards, *Translations from the Welsh*, p. 31; '**Mae Cân yn Llond yr Awel**' (Music Fills the Breeze), tr. Jeannie S. Popham, *The Nationalist*, 1.4 (1907), 32; tr. Francis Edwards, *Translations from the Welsh*, p. 29; '**Mae Dau yn well nag un**' (Better two than one), tr. M. S. Merthyr, *Caneuon Mynyddog* (Wrexham: Hughes & Son, 1882), pp. 106–7; '**Mae Tri yn well na Dau**' (Better three than two),

tr. M. S. Merthyr, *Caneuon Mynyddog* (Wrexham: Hughes & Son, 1882), pp. 108–9; '**Nid Dyna'r Dyn i mi**' (That's not the man for me), tr. unsigned, *Caneuon Mynyddog* (Wrexham: Hughes & Son, 1882), pp. 41–3; '**Pan ddaw fy Ngwen**' (When Comes my Gwen), tr. Edmund O. Jones, *Wales*, 1,7 (1894), 321; tr. Edmund O. Jones *Welsh Lyrics of the Nineteenth Century*, pp. 95–6; '**Rhyfelgyrch Capten Morgan**' (Captain Morgan's March), tr. M. C. Gillington, *Treasury of Welsh Songs*, pp. 18–19; tr. M. C. Gillington, *Pencader Poems: A Collection of Patriotic Verse published on the day of the Rally at Pencader September 27th 1952* (Cardiff: J. E. Jones, Plaid Cymru, 1952), n.p. [p. 13]; '**Rosa Hesterna**', tr. H. Idris Bell, *Welsh Poems of the Twentieth Century*, p. 56; '**Tyred i'r Bad, Gariad**' (Come to the Boat, Love), tr. Edmund O. Jones, *Welsh Lyrics of the Nineteenth Century*, pp. 98–9; '**Wrth Droed y Grisiau**' (At the Foot of the Stairs), tr. Edmund O. Jones, *Welsh Lyrics of the Nineteenth Century*, pp. 100–1; '**Y Fynwent yn ymyl y Môr**' (The Churchyard by the Sea), tr. R. L. Davies, *Cambrian Lyrics*, pp. 34–9.

THOMAS ESSILE DAVIES (Dewi Wyn o Esyllt; 1820–91)

Individual Translations *Po.*
'**Beth Ganaf yn Awr**' (What Shall I Sing Now?) tr. Rhiauon, *The Red Dragon*, 2 (1882), 363.

O. M. EDWARDS (1858–1920)

Prose
Cartrefi Cymru, *Homes of Wales*, tr. T. Eurfyl Jones (Wrexham: Hughes & Son, 1931).

Individual Translations *Pr.*
from **Clych Atgof** (The Bells of Memory), tr. Meic Stephens, *A Book of Wales* (1987), pp. 55–6; tr. Meic Stephens, *Illuminations*, pp. 1–7; from **Er Mwyn Cymru** (The Soul of a Nation), tr. D. M. Lloyd, *A Book of Wales* (1953), pp. 264–5; from **Llynnoedd Llonydd** (Owain Glyn Dŵr), tr. D. M. Lloyd, *A Book of Wales* (1953), p. 132; tr. D. M. Lloyd, *A Book of Wales* (1987), pp. 54–5; from **O'r Bala i Geneva** (From Bala to Geneva), tr. D. M. Lloyd, *A Book of Wales* (1953),

pp. 63–4; tr. D. M. Lloyd, *A Book of Wales* (1987), p. 57; tr. Grahame Davies, *The Chosen People: Wales & The Jews*, ed. Grahame Davies (Bridgend: Seren, 2002), pp. 158–65; '**Yn y Wlad**' (Tregaron Bog), tr. D. M. Lloyd, *A Book of Wales* (1953), pp. 56–8.

ROGER EDWARDS (1811–86)

Individual Translations *Po.*
'**Yr Afonig**' (The Streamlet), tr. Francis Edwards, *Translations from the Welsh*, pp. 19–23.

Individual Translations *hymns*
'**Beth yw'r adsain o Ephrata?**' ('What is in Ephrata heard?'), tr. H. Elvet Lewis, *Sweet Singers of Wales*, pp. 128–9; '**Crefydd Foreuol**' ('Dear is the advent of the spring'), tr. H. Elvet Lewis, *Sweet Singers of Wales*, pp. 127–8.

RICHARD FOULKES EDWARDS (Risiart Ddu o Wynedd; 1836–70)

Individual Translations *Po.*
'**Cân Bugail Morgannwg**' (The Glamorgan Shepherd's Song), tr. M. C. Gillington, *Treasury of Welsh Songs*, pp. 68–9.

ROBERT ELLIS (Cynddelw; 1812–75)

Individual Translations *Po.*
'**Awr Cwsg**' (The Hour of Sleep), tr. H. Idris Bell, *The Welsh Review*, 5.2 (1946), 119; tr. H. Idris Bell, *Poems from the Welsh*, p. 73; tr. H. Idris Bell, *Oxford Book*, p. 205; *from* '**Cywydd Berwyn**' (Betimes to Berwyn), tr. John Young Evans, *Wales*, 3.27 (1896), 319.

CHRISTMAS EVANS (1776–1838)

Individual Translations *hymns*
'**Dwy fflam ar ben Calfaria**' ('On Calvary together two flames were seen to shine'), tr. Paxton Hood, *Sweet Singers of Wales*, pp. 133–4.

DANIEL EVANS (Daniel Ddu o Geredigion; 1792–1846)

Individual Translations *Po.*
from '**Annerch i Lygad y Dydd**' (To the Daisy), tr. unsigned, *The Poetry of Wales* (1873), pp. 51–2; *from* '**Cân y Mab Maeth a elwir Cariad**' (Song of the Foster-son, Love), tr. unsigned, *Poetry of Wales* (1873), pp. 108–10; '**Cestyll Cymru**' (The Castles of Wales), tr. unsigned, *Poetry of Wales* (1873), pp. 89–90; '**Gwlad fy Ngenedigaeth**' (The Country of my Birth), tr. Lydia Jones, in Daniel Evans, *Gwinllan y Bardd; sef Prydyddwaith ar Amrywiol Destunau a Gwahanol Fesurau* (Lampeter: J. Davis, 1872), pp. 242–6; tr. Lydia Jones, *Poetry of Wales* (1873), pp. 70–3; '**Menyw**' (Woman), tr. unsigned, *Poetry of Wales* (1873), pp. 128–9; *from* '**Mis Mai**' (To May), tr. unsigned, *Poetry of Wales* (1873), pp. 49–50; *from* '**Torriad y Dydd**' (The Dawn), tr. unsigned, *Poetry of Wales* (1873), pp. 50–1; '**Y Ddafad**' (The Ewe), tr. unsigned, *Poetry of Wales*, (1873), pp. 131–2; '**Y Fam i'w Maban, yn ôl claddu ei Dad**' (The Mother to her child after its Father's Death), tr. unsigned, *Poetry of Wales* (1873), pp. 126–7; '**Yr Eneth Ffyddlon**' (The Faithful Maiden), tr. unsigned, *Poetry of Wales* (1873), pp. 129–31.

Individual Translations *hymns*
'**Dychweliad yr Afradlon**' ('Who is yonder weary pilgrim'), tr. H. Elvet Lewis, *Sweet Singers of Wales*, pp. 100–1.

EVAN EVANS (Ieuan Glan Geirionydd; 1795–1855)

Miscellaneous

Morfa Rhuddlan: or the Battle of Rhuddlan Marsh; with an English version of Ieuan Glan Geirionydd's Celebrated Ode and Historical illustrations by Alfred (Ruthin: Isaac Clarke, 1862).

Individual Translations *Po.*
'Beati Mortui' (Epigram), tr. Gwyn Williams, *To Look for a Word*, p. 208; '**Caniad y Gog i Arfon**' (In Praise of Arvon), tr. unsigned, *Poetry of Wales* (1873), pp. 44–5; tr. Edmund O. Jones, *Welsh Poets of To-day and Yesterday*, pp. 11–14; '**Cydmariaeth rhwng y byd a'r Môr**' (The World and the Sea: A Comparison) [misprinted as the work of John Blackwell (Alun)], tr. unsigned, *The Poetry of Wales* (1873), p. 135; '**Cyflafan Morfa Rhuddlan**' (The Battle of Rhuddlan Marsh), tr. Alfred, in *Geirionydd: Cyfansoddiadau barddonol, cerddorol, a rhyddieithol, y diweddar Barch Evan Evans (Ieuan Glan Geirionydd)*, ed. W. J. Roberts and Gwalchmai (Rhythyn [Rhuthin]: I. Clarke, 1862), p. 187; tr. R. Bellis Jones, *Wales*, 1.5 (1894), 222; tr. Edmund O. Jones, *Welsh Lyrics of the Nineteenth Century*, pp. 11–14; tr. Professor Rushton, *Treasury of Welsh Songs*, pp. 60–1; tr. A. P. Graves, *Welsh Poetry Old and New*, pp. 55–6; tr. A. P. Graves, *Land of my Fathers*, pp. 31–2; *from* '**Cywydd y Bedd**' (Mankind's Procession to the Grave), tr. John Young Evans, *Wales*, 2.11 (1895), 120; '**Glan Geirionydd**', tr. unsigned, *Poetry of Wales* (1873), pp. 125–6; '**Glan Llyn Geirionydd**' (Lake Geirionydd), tr. Edmund O. Jones, *Welsh Poets of To-day and Yesterday*, pp. 18–20; '**Hen Forgan a'i Wraig**' (Old Morgan and His Wife), tr. T. W. Harris, *Gems of Welsh Melody* (London & Wrexham: Simpkin, Marshall & Co; Hughes & Son, 1860), pp. 28–30; tr. T. W. Harris and another, *Poetry of Wales* (1873), pp. 105–7; '**Rhieingerdd Bugail Cwmdyli**' (The Shepherd of Cwmdyli), tr. Edmund O. Jones, *Welsh Lyrics of the Nineteenth Century*, pp. 15–16; *from* '**Ymdrech Serch a Rheswm**' (Love and Reason), tr. Edmund O. Jones, *Welsh Poets of To-day and Yesterday*, pp. 14–18; '**Ysgoldy Rhad Llanrwst**' (Llanrwst Free School), tr. A. P. Graves, *Welsh Poetry Old and New*, p. 54; tr. Tony Conran, *The Penguin Book of Welsh Verse*, pp. 219–20; tr. Gwyn Williams, *Choose Your Stranger* (Port Talbot: Alun Books, 1979), pp. 59–60; tr. Tony Conran, *Welsh Verse*, pp. 241–3.

Individual Translations *hymns*
'**Ar lan Iorddonen ddofn**' (Deep Jordan's banks I tread), Revd Lemuel John Hopkin James (Hopcyn), *Welsh Melodies in the Old Notation for Hymns in English Translated and Original*, n.p. [hymn 38]; '**Croesi yr Iorddonen**' (The Crossing of Jordan), tr. Cariadfab, *Wales*, 3.28 (1896), 358; '**Fy Nhad sydd wrth y llyw**' (My father at the helm), tr. Revd Lemuel John Hopkin James (Hopcyn), *Welsh Melodies in the*

Old Notation for Hymns in English Translated and Original, n.p. [hymn 4] (1912: pp. 10–12); 'Glan yr Iorddonen' (On the banks of Jordan), tr. H. Elvet Lewis, *Sweet Singers of Wales*, pp. 107–8; 'Angau yn Ymyl' ['Mae'm rhedfa îs y rhod/Yn nesu at y nôd'] (Death awaits), tr. H. Elvet Lewis, *Sweet Singers of Wales*, pp. 106–7; tr. Revd Lemuel John Hopkin James (Hopcyn), *Welsh National Supplement of Hymns*, pp. 55–6; tr. H. Elvet Lewis, *Welsh Hymns and their Tunes*, p. 117; 'Mae 'nghyfeillion adre'n myned' (To their home my friends are taken), tr. R. Bryan, *Wales*, 2.10 (1895), 80; tr. Revd R. Parry, *Hymns of the Welsh Revival*, pp. 41–3; tr. Revd Lemuel John Hopkin James (Hopcyn), *Welsh Melodies in the Old Notation for Hymns in English Translated and Original*, n.p. [hymn 7] (1912: pp. 13–14); 'Mor ddedwydd yw y rhai trwy ffydd' (Hymn) ['Happy are they through faith'], tr. Gwyn Williams, *The Rent that's Due to Love*, p. 113; 'Na Wrthod Fi' ('Turn not away from me'), tr. H. Elvet Lewis, *Sweet Singers of Wales*, pp. 105–6; 'O Dowch! ieuenctid hoff, yn awr' (Cofio tragwyddoldeb: Eternity), tr. Revd R. Parry, *Hymns of the Welsh Revival*, p. 23; 'Rwy'n sefyll ar dymhestlog lan yr hen Iorddonen ddu' ('On Jordan's dark, tempestuous shore'), tr. J. P. Owen, *Wales*, 2.18 (1895), 448; tr. H. Idris Bell, *The Nationalist*, 2.22 (1908), 17; tr. H. Idris Bell, *Poems from the Welsh*, p. 41; tr. Revd Lemuel John Hopkin James (Hopcyn), *Welsh National Supplement of Hymns*, pp. 32–3; 'Yr Ochor Draw' (Why Should we Weep), tr. Edmund O. Jones, *Welsh Lyrics of the Nineteenth Century*, pp. 17–18.

HUGH EVANS (1854–1934)

Prose (Novel)
Cwm Eithin, *The Gorse Glen*, tr. E. Morgan Humphreys (Liverpool: Brython Press, 1948).

Individual Translations *Pr.*
from **Cwm Eithin** (What will you have for Supper?), tr. E. Morgan Humphreys, *A Book of Wales* (1953), pp. 69–71; (The Little Old Cottages), tr. E. Morgan Humphreys, *A Book of Wales* (1953), pp. 152–4; (Knitting), tr. E. Morgan Humphreys, *A Book of Wales* (1953), p. 154; (Beti Jones's Supper), tr. E. Morgan Humphreys, *A Book of Wales* (1953), pp. 245–7.

THOMAS EVANS (Telynog; 1840–65)

Individual Translations *Po.*
'**Prudd-gân**' (A Lament), tr. A. P. Graves, *The Nationalist*, 3.29 (1909), 59; tr. Alfred Perceval Graves, *Welsh Poetry Old and New*, pp. 130–1; '**Yr Haf**' (Winter and Summer), tr. Kenneth Hurlstone Jackson, *A Celtic Miscellany* (1951), p. 93 (1971: p. 87).

ROBERT ARTHUR GRIFFITH (Elphin; 1860–1936)

Individual Translations *Po.*
'**Anwylyd, Oni ddoi?**' (Song) ['Beloved, let's away'], tr. H. Idris Bell, *Poems from the Welsh*, p. 30; *from* ***Sonedau y Nos*** 'III' (Sonnet), tr. H. Idris Bell, *The Nationalist*, 4.32 (1910), 5; tr. H. Idris Bell, *Poems from the Welsh*, p. 44; *from* ***Sonedau y Nos*** 'V' (Sonnet), tr. H. Idris Bell, *Poems from the Welsh*, p. 67.

DAVID C. HARRIS (Caeronwy; 1846–85)

Individual Translations *Po.*
'**Hen Walia Anwylaidd**' (Adieu to Dear Cambria), tr. Miss Lawrence, *Treasury of Welsh Songs*, pp. 56–7.

GERARD MANLEY HOPKINS (1844–89)

Individual Translations *Po.*
'**Cywydd**' (Cywydd of Greeting), tr. Tony Conran, *Planet*, 78 (1989/90), 59; tr. unsigned, in Norman White, *Gerard Manley Hopkins in Wales* (Bridgend: Seren, 1998), pp. 134–5.

ELLEN HUGHES (1862–1927)

Individual Translations *Po.*
'**Cân y Gwcw**' (Cuckoo), tr. unsigned, *Wales*, 2.20 (1895), 565; '**Fy Ngoreu Bychan i**' (My Little Best), tr. unsigned, *Wales*, 2.15 (1895), 324.

HUGH DERFEL HUGHES (1816–90)

Individual Translations *hymns*
'Y Cyfamod Disigl' (The Immovable Covenant), tr. Revd David
Lewis Pughe, *Poetry of Wales* (1873), pp. 29–32; tr. Revd David
Lewis Pughe, *Wales*, 1.1 (1894), 10–11; tr. Revd R. Parry, *Hymns of
the Welsh Revival*, p. 69; tr. A. P. Graves, *Welsh Poetry Old and New*,
pp. 126–7; 'Y Gŵr a fu gynt o dan hoelion' (The Christ who was nailed
to the crossbeam), tr. Revd Lemuel John Hopkin James (Hopcyn),
*Welsh Melodies in the Old Notation for Hymns in English Translated
and Original*, n.p. [hymn 58].

JOHN CEIRIOG HUGHES (Ceiriog; 1832–87)

Collections

A. P. Graves, *English Verse Translations of the Welsh Poems of
Ceiriog Hughes* (Wrexham: Hughes & Son, 1926).

Individual Translations *Po.*
from 'Alun Mabon', tr. unsigned and tr. Glanmor, in John Ceiriog
Hughes, *Oriau'r Bore sef Parhad o 'Oriau'r Hwyr'* (Rhuthyn: I.
Clarke, 1862), pp. 116, 117; tr. Edmund O. Jones, *Welsh Lyrics of the
Nineteenth Century*, pp. 55, 59, 60; tr. A. P. Graves, *The Nationalist*,
3.29 (1909), 61; tr. Edmund O. Jones, *The Nationalist*, 4.35 (1911),
30–3; tr. H. Idris Bell, *Poems from the Welsh*, p. 78; tr. Francis
Edwards, *Translations from the Welsh*, pp. 9, 11; tr. A. P. Graves,
Welsh Poetry Old and New, pp. 68–9, 82–3; tr. H. Idris Bell, *Land of
My Fathers*, p. 13; tr. Gwyn Williams, *The Rent that's Due to Love*,
pp. 115–17; tr. H. Idris Bell, *Presenting Welsh Poetry*, p. 59; tr. Tony
Conran, *The Penguin Book of Welsh Verse*, p. 227; tr. Gwyn
Williams, *To Look for a Word*, pp. 217–18; tr. H. Idris Bell, *Oxford
Book*, p. 142; tr. Tony Conran, *Welsh Verse*, pp. 255–6; tr. H. Idris
Bell, *A Book of Wales* (1987), p. 99; tr. Tony Conran, *Wales: A
Celebration*, ed. Dewi Roberts (Llanrwst: Gwasg Carreg Gwalch,
2000), pp. 134–5; 'Anhawdd Rhoddi Hen Delynau' (On the Willow's
Branches Tender), tr. M. C. Gillington, *Treasury of Welsh Songs*, pp.
70–1; 'Ar Hyd y Dolydd Eang' (Along the Spacious Meadows), tr.
Francis Edwards, *Translations from the Welsh*, p. 13; 'Ar Hyd y Nos'

(All Through the Night), tr. Robert Bryan, *The Nationalist*, 1.12 (1908), 12; tr. A. P. Graves, *The Nationalist*, 2.22 (1908), 32; tr. A. P. Graves, *Welsh Poetry Old and New*, p. 78; tr. A. P. Graves, *A Celtic Psaltery*, p. 97; '**Bedd Llywelyn**' (Llewelyn's Grave), tr. Edmund O. Jones, *Welsh Lyrics of the Nineteenth Century*, pp. 71–2; '**Breuddwyd y Bardd**' (The Bard's Dream), tr. A. P. Graves, *The Nationalist*, 2.21 (1908), 31; tr. A. P. Graves, *Welsh Poetry Old and New*, pp. 74–5; '**Bugail yr Hafod**' (The Shepherd of the Shieling), tr. A. P. Graves, *The Nationalist*, 2.21 (1908), 32; tr. A. P. Graves, *Welsh Poetry Old and New*, pp. 71–2; tr. Tony Conran, *Welsh Verse*, p. 254; '**Carnfradwyr ein Gwlad**' (The Traitors of Wales), tr. Edmund O. Jones, *Welsh Lyrics of the Nineteenth Century*, pp. 65–7; '**Caru'r Lleuad**' (The Moon's Charms), tr. J. Phillips, *The Red Dragon*, 10 (1886), 331; '**Codiad yr Haul**' (The Rising of the Sun), tr. Edmund O. Jones, *Welsh Lyrics of the Nineteenth Century*, p. 62; tr. A. P. Graves, *The Nationalist*, 2.22 (1908), 32; tr. A. P. Graves, *Welsh Poetry Old and New*, pp. 79–80; '**Cyfoedion Cofadwy**' (Remembered Friends), tr. Henry Rowland, *Wales*, 3.30 (1896), 454; '**Dafydd y Garreg Wen**' (David of the White Rock), tr. Professor Rushton, *Gems of Welsh Melody* (London & Wrexham: Simpkin, Marshall & Co; Hughes & Son, 1860), pp. 20–1; tr. Alfred, in John Ceiriog Hughes, *Oriau'r Bore sef Parhad o 'Oriau'r Hwyr'* (Rhuthyn: I. Clarke, 1862), p. 113; tr. Edmund O. Jones, *Welsh Lyrics of the Nineteenth Century*, pp. 63–4; tr. A. P. Graves, *Welsh Poetry Old and New*, p. 80; tr. A. P. Graves, *A Celtic Psaltery*, p. 98; '**Dwfin yw'r Môr**' (Deep the Sea), tr. A. P. Graves, *The Nationalist*, 2.23 (1909), 25; '**Dychweliad yr Hen Filwr**' (The Return of the Veteran), tr. R. L. Davies, *Cambrian Lyrics*, pp. 8–13; '**Gofidiau Serch**' (Love-Grief), tr. C. C. Bell, *Poems from the Welsh*, pp. 63–4; '**I Blas Gogerddan**' (Plas Gogerddan), tr. A. P. Graves, *Welsh Poetry Old and New*, pp. 73–4; tr. A. P. Graves, *A Celtic Psaltery*, p. 96; tr. A. P. Graves, *Land of my Fathers*, p. 37; '**Jerusalem**', tr. D. M. Lloyd, *A Book of Wales* (1953), pp. 368–9; *from Jona* ['Gweddi Daer'] (Fervent Prayer from *Jonah*), tr. Mynorydd, *Wales*, 3.24 (1896), 178; '**Maes Crogen**' (The Field of Crogen), tr. Ernest Rhys, *Land of my Fathers*, pp. 35–6; '**Morfa Rhuddlan**' (The Strand of Rhuddlan), tr. Edmund O. Jones, *Welsh Lyrics of the Nineteenth Century*, p. 73; '**Myfanwy Fychan**', tr. Edmund O. Jones, *Welsh Lyrics of the Nineteenth Century*, p. 56; tr. R. L. Davies, *Cambrian Lyrics*, pp. 14–21; tr. A. P. Graves, *The Nationalist*, 2.24 (1909), 31–2; tr. Francis Edwards, *Translations* *from the Welsh*, pp. 5–7; '**Nant y Mynydd**' (The Mountain Stream), tr. Edmund O. Jones, *Welsh Lyrics of the Nineteenth Century*, p. 70; tr. R. L. Davies, *Cambrian Lyrics*, pp. 4–5; tr. Edmund O. Jones, *Land of My Fathers*, p. 101; tr. H. Idris Bell and C. C. Bell, *Poems from the Welsh*, p. 25; tr. Francis Edwards, *Translations from the Welsh*, p. 7; tr. D. Vaughan Thomas, *The Welsh Outlook*, 8 (1921), 259; tr. Kenneth Hurlstone Jackson, *A Celtic Miscellany* (1951), p. 92 (1971: pp. 86–7); tr. Kenneth Hurlstone Jackson, *Oxford Book*, p. 141; '**Pan Gyfyd yr Heulwen**' (The Pass of Llanberis), tr. A. P. Graves, *The Nationalist*, 2.23 (1909), 26; '**Rhyddid**' (Liberty), tr. Edmund O. Jones, *Welsh Lyrics of the Nineteenth Century*, pp. 57–8; tr. Edmund O. Jones, *Pencader Poems: A Collection of Patriotic Verse published on the day of the Rally at Pencader September 27th 1952* (Cardiff: J. E. Jones, Plaid Cymru, 1952), n.p. [p. 15]; '**Rhyfelgyrch Cadben Morgan**' (Forth to Battle), tr. A. P. Graves, *Welsh Poetry Old and New*, p. 76; '**Serch Hudol**' (Alluring Love), tr. Francis Edwards, *Translations from the Welsh*, pp. 15–17; tr. A. P. Graves, *Welsh Poetry Old and New*, pp. 69–70; tr. A. P. Graves, *A Celtic Psaltery*, p. 95; '**Syr Harri Ddu**' (Black Sir Harry), tr. M. C. Gillington, *Treasury of Welsh Songs*, pp. 24–5; '**Ti wyddost beth Ddywed fy Nghalon**' (A Mother's Message), tr. Edmund O. Jones, *Welsh Lyrics of the Nineteenth Century*, pp. 68–9; '**Tros y Garreg**' (Over the Stone), tr. M. C. Gillington, *Treasury of Welsh Songs*, pp. 80–1; tr. A. P. Graves, *Welsh Poetry Old and New*, pp. 77–8; '**Tuag Adre**' (Homeward Bound), tr. Edmund O. Jones, *Welsh Lyrics of the Nineteenth Century*, p. 61; tr. R. L. Davies, *Cambrian Lyrics*, pp. 6–7; '**Y Bardd yn ei Awen**' (The Inspired Bard), tr. Mrs C. B. Wilson, *Treasury of Welsh Songs*, pp. 44–5; '**Y Gadlys**' (The War-Camp), tr. Edmund O. Jones, *Treasury of Welsh Songs*, pp. 30–1; '**Y Gwcw**' (The Cuckoo), tr. C. C. Bell, *Poems from the Welsh*, pp. 55–6; '**Y March a'r Gwddw Brith**' (The Steed of Dapple Grey), tr. Edmund O. Jones, *Welsh Lyrics of the Nineteenth Century*, p. 74; tr. A. P. Graves, *The Nationalist*, 2.22 (1908), 31; '**Ymdaith Gwŷr Harlech**' (March of the Men of Harlech), tr. John Jones (Talhaiarn), *Treasury of Welsh Songs*, pp. 40–1; tr. A. P. Graves, *Welsh Poetry Old and New*, pp. 67–8; tr. A. P. Graves, *Land of my Fathers*, pp. 36–7; tr. John Jones (Talhaiarn), *Pencader Poems: A Collection of Patriotic Verse Published on the day of the Rally at Pencader September 27th 1952* (Cardiff: J. E. Jones, Plaid Cymru, 1952), n.p. [p. 5]; '**Yn Nyffryn Clwyd**' (The Vale of Clwyd), tr. A. P. Graves, *Welsh Poetry Old and*

New, pp. 72–3; '**Yn Nyffryn Llangollen**' (The Vale of Llangollen), tr. A. P. Graves, *The Nationalist*, 2.23 (1909), 26; '**Yn Ynys Môn fe Safai Gŵr** (On Mona's Isle), tr. Glanmor, *Oriau'r Bore sef Parhad o 'Oriau'r Hwyr', gan John Ceiriog Hughes* (Rhuthyn: I. Clarke, 1862), p. 115–16; '**Yr Arad Goch**' (The Red Plough), tr. A. P. Graves, *The Nationalist*, 3.28 (1909), 62; tr. A. P. Graves, *Welsh Poetry Old and New*, pp. 64–6; '**Y Teulu Cysglyd**' (A Pothersome Pair), tr. Tony Conran, *Welsh Verse*, p. 255; '**Y Trên**' (The Train), tr. W. H. Baker, *Gems of Welsh Melody* (London & Wrexham: Simpkin, Marshall & Co; Hughes & Son, 1860), pp. 79–83; tr. W. H. Baker, in John Ceiriog Hughes, *Oriau'r Bore sef Parhad o 'Oriau'r Hwyr'* (Rhuthyn: I. Clarke, 1862), p. 114.

EVAN JAMES (Ieuan ap Iago; 1809–78)

Individual Translations (*Welsh National Anthem*)
'**Hen Wlad fy Nhadau**' (Land of My Fathers), tr. Eben Fardd, *Baledi Cymraeg: Welsh Ballads* (Pontypridd: F. Evans, c. 1855); tr. John Owen (Owain Alaw), *Gems of Welsh Melody* (London & Wrexham: Simpkin, Marshall & Co; Hughes & Son, 1860), pp. 24–5; tr. R. L. Davies, *Cambrian Lyrics*, pp. 66–7; tr. W. Lewis Jones, *Land of my Fathers*, pp. 14–15; tr. unsigned, in Edward Thomas, *Wales* (London: A & C Black Ltd [1924]), pp. 158–9; tr. A. P. Graves, *Pencader Poems: A Collection of Patriotic Verse published on the day of the Rally at Pencader September 27th 1952* (Cardiff: J. E. Jones, Plaid Cymru, 1952), n.p. [p. 16]; tr. Eben Fardd, *National Library of Wales Journal*, 3, 1 & 2 (1943), 6; tr. A. P. Graves, in Norman Davies, *The Isles: A History* (London: Macmillan, 1999), pp. 1163–4.

DAVID JONES (1805–68)

Individual Translations *hymns*
'**Mae Duw yn llon'd pob lle**' (God filleth all in all), tr. H. Elvet Lewis, *Sweet Singers of Wales*, pp. 124–6; tr. Revd R. Parry, *Hymns of the Welsh Revival*, pp. 39–41; tr. Revd Lemuel John Hopkin James (Hopcyn), *Welsh Melodies in the Old Notation for Hymns in English Translated and Original*, n.p. [hymn 56] (1912: p. 49).

EVAN JONES (Ieuan Gwynedd; 1820–52)

Individual Translations *Po.*
'**Bythod Cymru**' (The Cottages of Wales), tr. Edmund O. Jones, *Welsh Lyrics of the Nineteenth Century*, pp. 47–9; tr. R. L. Davies, *Cambrian Lyrics*, pp. 22–5; '**Ewch a Chloddiwch Fedd i mi**' (Go and Dig a Grave for me), tr. Edmund O. Jones, *Welsh Lyrics of the Nineteenth Century*, pp. 50–1.

EVAN PAN JONES (1834–1922)

Individual Translations *Po.*
'**Af Adref, Af**' (Homeward), tr. H. Idris Bell, *Welsh Poems of the Twentieth Century*, pp. 74–5; '**Mae'r Gaua'n D'od**' (Winter's Coming), tr. H. Idris Bell, *Welsh Poems of the Twentieth Century*, p. 41; '**Nos Da**' (Good-Night), tr. H. Idris Bell, *Poems from the Welsh*, p. 77; '**Y Ffynon**' (The Well), tr. H. Idris Bell, *Poems from the Welsh*, p. 31; '**Y Fynwent Iuddewig**' (Jewish Cemetery), tr. H. Idris Bell, *Poems from the Welsh*, p. 51; '**Yr Ystorm ar Plimlimon**' (A Storm on Plinlimmon), tr. H. Idris Bell, *Poems from the Welsh*, pp. 65–6.

JOHN JONES (Ioan Emlyn; 1820–73)

Individual Translations *Po.*
'**Bedd y Dyn Tylawd**' (The Poor Man's Grave), tr. Edmund O. Jones, *Welsh Lyrics of the Nineteenth Century*, pp. 27–8; tr. R. L. Davies, *Cambrian Lyrics*, pp. 30–3; tr. A. P. Graves, *Welsh Poetry Old and New*, pp. 59–60.

JOHN JONES (Ioan Tegid, Tegid; 1792–1852)

Individual Translations *Po.*
'**Fy Nghariad**' (My Lady Love), tr. Hal, *Cambrian Quarterly Magazine*, 4 (1832), 37; '**Ymddiddanion fy Mam**' (My Mother), tr. E. Davies, *Cambrian Quarterly Magazine*, 1 (1829), 384; '**Ymweliad y Bardd**' (The Bard's Visit), tr. Lady Charlotte Schreiber,[3] *Gems of*

---

[3] Formerly known as Lady Charlotte Guest.

Welsh Melody (London & Wrexham: Simpkin, Marshall & Co; Hughes & Son, 1860), pp. 26–7.

JOHN JONES (Talhaiarn; 1810–69)[4]

Individual Translations *Po.*

'**Castell Caerffili**' (Caerphilly Castle), tr. unsigned, *Treasury of Welsh Songs*, pp. 50–1; '**Codiad yr Hedydd**' (The Rising of the Lark), tr. R. L. Davies, *Cambrian Lyrics*, pp. 56–7; tr. Francis Edwards, *Translations from the Welsh*, p. 33; '**Dewch i'r Frwydr**' (Come to Battle), tr. M. C. Gillington, *Treasury of Welsh Songs*, pp. 36–7; '**Eilonwy**', tr. H. Idris Bell, *The Nationalist*, 2.15 (1908), 20; tr. H. Idris Bell, *Poems from the Welsh*, pp. 29–30; '**Galar Gwraig y Milwr**' (The Lament of the Soldier's Wife), tr. unsigned, *Treasury of Welsh Songs*, pp. 76–7; '**I Aderyn**' (To a Bird), tr. R. L. Davies, *Cambrian Lyrics*, pp. 58–9; '**Merch Megan**' (The Daughter of Megan), tr. unsigned, *Treasury of Welsh Songs*, pp. 48–9; '**Molawd Cymru**' (In Praise of Wales), tr. A. P. Graves, *Welsh Poetry Old and New*, pp. 57–8; '**Plygeingân**' (A Morning Song), tr. Edmund O. Jones, *Welsh Poets of To-day and Yesterday*, p. 25; tr. Francis Edwards, *Translations from the Welsh*, p. 35; '**Plygiad y Bedol**' (Bending the Shoe), tr. unsigned, *Treasury of Welsh Songs*, pp. 4–5; '**Rhyfelgyrch Gwŷr Harlech**' (March of the Men of Harlech), tr. John Oxenford, *Land of my Fathers*, pp. 116–19; *from* '**Tal ar Ben Bodran**' (Tal on the Summit of Bodran), tr. Gwyn Williams, *To Look for a Word*, pp. 209–12; '**Tros y Garreg**' (O'er the Rocks), tr. Edmund O. Jones, *Welsh Poets of To-day and Yesterday*, pp. 24–5; '**Y Deryn Pur**' (The Gentle Bird), tr. unsigned, *Treasury of Welsh Songs*, pp. 22–3.

LEWIS DAVIES JONES (Llew Tegid; 1851–1928)

Individual Translations *Po.*

'**Pant-y-Pistyll**' (Waterfall Hollow), tr. A. P. Graves, *Welsh Poetry Old and New*, pp. 89–90.

---

[4] 'The Shake of the Hand' is published as a translation by the author in *The Red Dragon*, 1 (1882), 66. But it is published alongside his original English-language poems in *Gwaith Talhaiarn* Vol. I, p. 366, and has not been listed below.

OWEN WYNNE JONES (Glasynys; 1828–70)

Individual Translations *Po.*
'**Bugeileg**' (Blodeuwedd and Hywel), tr. Edmund O. Jones, *Welsh Lyrics of the Nineteenth Century*, pp. 21–4; '**Bugeilgerdd Gŵyl Ifan**' (A Pastoral), tr. Edmund O. Jones, *Wales*, 1.3 (1894), 129–30, u. Edmund O. Jones, *Welsh Poets of To-day and Yesterday*, pp. 21–2; '**Cân Eisteddfod**' (St. David's Day), tr. Henry Davies, *Treasury of Welsh Songs*, pp. 8–9; '**Cân Serch**' (Gwen), tr. R. A. Griffith, *Young Wales*, 1.7 (1895), 158; *from* '**Myfanwy Fychan**' (Myfanwy), tr. Edmund O. Jones, *Welsh Poets of To-day and Yesterday*, pp. 22–3.

Individual Translations *Pr.*
from **Cymru Fu** (A Merry Evening at the Hafod), tr. D. M. Lloyd, *A Book of Wales* (1953), pp. 158–62.

PETER JONES (Pedr Fardd; 1775–1845)

Individual Translations *hymns*
'**Cyn llunio'r byd, cyn lledu'r nefoedd wen**' (The Counsels of God), tr. Revd R. Parry, *Hymns of the Welsh Revival*, pp. 35–7; tr. Edmund Tudor Owen, *Welsh Hymns and their Tunes*, p. 114; '**Cysegrwn flaenffrwyth ddyddiau'n hoes**' (Come, consecrate our early days), tr. H. Elvet Lewis, *Sweet Singers of Wales*, p. 96; tr. Revd R. Parry, *Hymns of the Welsh Revival*, pp. 65–7; tr. Revd Lemuel Hopkin James (Hopcyn), *Welsh Melodies in the Old Notation for Hymns in English Translated and Original*, n.p. [hymn 63] (1912: p. 47); '**Rhyfedd Ras**' ('Sweet streams of pleasantness'), tr. H. Elvet Lewis, *Sweet Singers of Wales*, pp. 96–7; '**Un ydyw'r Eglwys oll**' (The Church of God is One), tr. Revd Lemuel John Hopkin James (Hopcyn), *Welsh National Supplement of Hymns*, pp. 65–6.

ROBERT AMBROSE JONES (Emrys ap Iwan; 1848–1906)

Individual Translations *Pr.*
'**Paham y Gorfu'r Undebwyr**' (The True Welshman), tr. D. R. Walden-Jones, *Planet*, 9 (1971–2), 21–4; '**Homiliau**' (Keep Yourselves a Nation), tr. Meic Stephens, *A Book of Wales* (1987), p. 167.

THOMAS TUDNO JONES (Tudno; 1844–95)

Individual Translations *Po.*
'**Beddargraff Cadben Owen Owens**' (Epitaph on Capt. Owen Owens), tr. H. Idris Bell, *Poems from the Welsh*, p. 75; '**Beddargraff Cymraes yn Lloegr**' (Epitaph on a Welshwoman Buried in England), tr. H. Idris Bell, *Poems from the Welsh*, p. 75; '**Beddargraff Morwr**' (A Sailor's Epitaph), tr. H. Idris Bell, *Poems from the Welsh*, p. 75; tr. Keidrych Rhys, *Wales*, 5.7 (1945), 20; *from* '**Mae Arnaf Eisiau Marw**' (I would like to die), tr. R. L. Davies, *Wales*, 2.16 (1895), 380.

WILLIAM JONES (Ehedydd Iâl; 1815–99)

Individual Translations *hymns*
'**Er Nad yw 'Nghnawd ond Gwellt**' (Although my Flesh is Straw), tr. H. Elvet Lewis, *Sweet Singers of Wales*, pp. 139–40; tr. R. S. Thomas, *Planet*, 98 (1993), 42.

HOWELL ELVET LEWIS (Elfed; 1860–1953)

Individual Translations *Po.*
'**Cofio**' (Remembrance), tr. Francis Edwards, *Translations from the Welsh*, p. 129; '**Cwmeisian**', tr. Francis Edwards, *Translations from the Welsh*, pp. 115–17; '**Gobaith Dibrofiad**' (Life's Morning), tr. H. Idris Bell, *The Welsh Review*, 5.2 (1946), 117; tr. H. Idris Bell, *Oxford Book*, p. 205; '**Gyda'r Bore Bach**' (In the Early Morn), tr. Francis Edwards, *Translations from the Welsh*, p. 127; *from* '**Llewelyn ein Llyw Olaf**' (Llewelyn, Our Last Leader), tr. Francis Edwards, *Translations from the Welsh*, pp. 119–25; '**Llyn y Morwynion**' (The Maidens' Lake), tr. author, *Welsh Poets of To-day and Yesterday*, pp. 30–45; '**Nid da rhy o ddim**' (Summer's Satiety), tr. H. Idris Bell, *Poems from the Welsh*, p. 74; '**O Navis!**' tr. Francis Edwards, *Translations from the Welsh*, pp. 131–3; '**Paid Rhoi Fyny!**' (Never Despair), tr. Francis Edwards, *Translations from the Welsh*, pp. 107–13; '**Pan Ddaw'r Nos**' (When Night Comes), tr. Francis Edwards, *Translations from the Welsh*, p. 93; '**Peidiwch Holi Heddyw**' (Question not at Present), tr. T. M. Rees, *Young Wales*, 5.54 (1899), 130; '**Rhagorfraint y Gweithiwr**' (The Worker's Prerogative), tr.

Francis Edwards, *Translations from the Welsh*, pp. 97–105; '**Sub Rosa**' (Young Wales), tr. A. P. Graves, *Welsh Poetry Old and New*, pp. 97–8; '**Y Gân Brydlon**' (The Seasonable Song), tr. Francis Edwards, *Translations from the Welsh*, p. 95; '**Y Glowr**' (The Miner), tr. H. Idris Bell, *Poems from the Welsh*, p. 74; tr. Ernest Rhys, *A Celtic Anthology*, p. 296; '**Y Llanw**' (The High Tide), tr. A. P. Graves, *Welsh Poetry Old and New*, pp. 98–100; tr. A. P. Graves, *A Celtic Psaltery*, pp. 99–100; '**Y Seren a'r Mynydd**' (The Star and the Mountain), tr. Francis Edwards, *Translations from the Welsh*, pp. 89–91; '**Yr Hauwr**' (The Sower), tr. H. Idris Bell, *Poems from the Welsh*, p. 74; '**Yr Ywen**' (The Yew Tree), tr. H. Idris Bell, *Poems from the Welsh*, p. 74.

Individual Translations *hymns*
'**Ar y mynydd gyda'r Iesu**' (On the mountain with the Saviour), tr. Revd Lemuel John Hopkin James (Hopcyn), *Welsh National Supplement of Hymns*, pp. 62–3; '**Rho im yr hedd**' (Give me that peace), tr. Revd Lemuel John Hopkin James (Hopcyn), *Welsh National Supplement of Hymns*, p. 69.

EDWARD MATTHEWS (1813–92)

Individual Translations *Pr.*
from Hanes Bywyd Siencyn Penhydd (A Methodist 'Exhorter'), tr. D. M. Lloyd, *A Book of Wales* (1953), pp. 209–11.

ELUNED MORGAN (1870–1938)

Individual Translations *Pr.*
from Gwymon y Môr (A Daughter of the Sea), tr. D. M. Lloyd, *A Book of Wales* (1953), pp. 221–3; (Fear of the Sea), tr. Meic Stephens, *Illuminations: an Anthology of Welsh Short Prose* (Cardiff: Welsh Academic Press, 1998), pp. 7–9.

JOHN MORRIS-JONES (1864–1929)

Miscellaneous

Cwyn y Gwynt: The Plaint of the Wind, tr. W. Lewis Jones (London: Rowland's [*c.* 1928]). *Part song for mixed voices.*

Cwyn y Gwynt: The Wind's Complaint, tr. H. Idris Bell (Llangollen: Gwynn Publishing Co., 1948).

Cymru Rydd: My Land, tr. A. P. Graves (Swansea: Snell & Sons, [1932]). *Part song for Children.*

Fy Mreuddwyd: In Dreamland, tr. Wil Ifan (Cardiff: University Council for Music and the University of Wales Press Board [1938]). *Part song for Male Voices.*

Y Wenwlad: The Fairland, tr. David Bell (Llangollen: Gwynn Publishing Co. [1938]). *Cân unsain/unison.*

Individual Translations *Po.*

'**Arianwen**', tr. Evan Jones Roberts, National Library of Wales Archives, 19981E; '**Cwyn y Gwynt**' (The Wind's Lament), tr. W. Lewis Jones, *Land of my Fathers*, p. 101; tr. A. E. Z., *The Welsh Outlook* (September 1921), 216; tr. J. R. Williams, *The Welsh Outlook*, 12.11 (1925), 292;[5] tr. R. Williams Parry, *The Magazine of the University College of North Wales*, 38.1 (1929), 27; tr. Tony Conran, *The Penguin Book of Welsh Verse*, p. 228; tr. Tony Conran, *Oxford Book*, p. 143; tr. Tony Conran, *Welsh Verse*, p. 256; tr. Glyn Jones, *Glyn Jones: Collected Poems*, ed. Meic Stephens (Cardiff: University of Wales Press, 1996), p. 188; tr. R. Williams Parry, *Cerddi R. Williams Parry: Y Casgliad Cyflawn*, ed. Alan Llwyd (Dinbych: Gwasg Gee, 1998), pp. 216–17; '**Y Cwmwl**' (The Cloud), tr. H. Idris Bell, *Poems from the Welsh*, p. 32; '**Cymru Rydd**' (My Land), tr. A. P. Graves, *Welsh Poetry Old and New*, pp. 103–4; '**Fy Mreuddwyd**' (My Dream), tr. A. E. Z., *The Welsh Outlook*, 8 (1921), 216; '**Fy Ngardd**' (My Garden), tr. A. P. Graves, *Welsh Poetry Old and New*, p. 106; '**Henaint**' (Old Age), tr. Kenneth Hurlstone Jackson, *A Celtic*

---

[5] Williams publishes two different translations of this poem.

Miscellany (1951), p. 144 (1971: p. 133); tr. Tony Conran, *The Penguin Book of Welsh Verse*, p. 272; tr. Tony Conran, *Oxford Book*, p. 204; tr. Tony Conran, *Welsh Verse*, p. 309; tr. R. Williams Parry, *Cerddi R. Williams Parry*, ed. Alan Llwyd (Dinbych: Gwasg Gee, 1998), p. 219; '**Seren y Gogledd**' (The North Star), tr. Francis Edwards, *Translations from the Welsh*, p. 151; tr. A. E. Z., *The Welsh Outlook*, 8 (1921), 216; tr. Tony Conran, *The Penguin Book of Welsh Verse*, pp. 228–9; tr. Tony Conran, *Oxford Book*, p. 143; tr. Tony Conran, *Welsh Verse*, p. 257; '**Toriad y Dydd**' (The Dawn of Day), tr. Francis Edwards, *Translations from the Welsh*, pp. 145–7; '**Y Gwylanod**' (Seagulls), tr. H. Idris Bell, *A Celtic Anthology*, p. 309; tr. H. Idris Bell, *Poems from the Welsh*, p. 55; tr. Gwyn Williams, *Presenting Welsh Poetry*, p. 60; tr. Gwyn Williams, *To Look for a Word*, p. 223; tr. Glyn Jones, *Glyn Jones: Collected Poems*, ed. Meic Stephens (Cardiff: University of Wales Press, 1996), p. 233; '**Yn y Cwch**' (In the Boat), tr. Francis Edwards, *Translations from the Welsh*, p. 149; '**Yr Afonig**' (The Little River), tr. H. Idris Bell, *Poems from the Welsh*, p. 44; tr. Francis Edwards, *Translations from the Welsh*, p. 153; '**Yr Hwyr Tawel**' (The Peaceful Night), tr. Lella M. Thomas, *Hanes a Chyfansoddiadau Arobryn Eisteddfod Gadeiriol Môn 1926* (Llanfair Pwllgwyngyll, 1926), p. 73; '**Y Seren Unig**' (The Lonely Star), tr. A. E. Z., *The Welsh Outlook*, 8 (1921), 216.

DANIEL OWEN (1836–95)

Prose (Novels)
Gwen Tomos, *Gwen Tomos*, tr. T. Ceiriog Williams and E. R. Harries (Wrexham: Hughes & Son, 1963).

Hunangofiant Rhys Lewis, *Rhys Lewis, Minister of Bethel: An Autobiography*, tr. James Harris (Wrexham: Hughes, 1888). 2nd edition 1915.

Individual Translations *Pr.*
from **Enoc Huws** (*Enoch Hughes*) [serial: chapters 2–52], tr. Claud Vivian, *Wales*, 1–3 (July 1894–December 1896); tr. D. M. Lloyd, *A Book of Wales* (1953), pp. 288–91; *from* **Gwen Tomos** (*The Maid of Wernddu*) [serial], tr. Revd J. Talog Davies, *The Treasury* (January 1918–July 1919); tr. D. M. Lloyd, *A Book of Wales* (1953), pp.

165–6; tr. D. M. Lloyd, *A Book of Wales* (1987), pp. 206–7; *from* **Hunangofiant Rhys Lewis** (*The Autobiography of Rhys Lewis*), tr. James Harris, *Land of My Fathers*, pp. 87–95; tr. James Harris, *Land of My Fathers*, pp. 95–100; tr. D. M. Lloyd, *A Book of Wales* (1953), pp. 175–7, 243–5, 300–1, 305, 306–7, 366–7; tr. D. M. Lloyd, *A Book of Wales* (1987), p. 206; tr. James Harris, *Wales: A Celebration*, ed. Dewi Roberts (Llanrwst: Gwasg Carreg Gwalch, 2000), pp. 162–3; *from* **Y Dreflan** (*The Hamlet: Its Dwellers and Doings*) [serial], tr. unsigned, *The Treasury* (January 1916–October 1917).

DAVID OWEN (Dewi Wyn; 1784–1841)

Individual Translations *Po.*
'**Elusengarwch**' (An Ode to Charity), tr. Griffith George, *Wales*, 2.10 (1895), 67–9.

ELLIS OWEN (1789–1868)

Individual Translations *Po.*
'**Beddargraff Gwraig Gelwyddog**' (A Lying Woman), tr. H. Idris Bell, *The Welsh Review*, 5.2 (1946), 119; tr. Tony Conran, *The Penguin Book of Welsh Verse*, p. 269; tr. Tony Conran, *Welsh Verse*, p. 206.

OWEN GRIFFITH OWEN (Alafon; 1847–1916)

Individual Translations *Po.*
'**Beddargraff Dr Roberts**' (Epitaph on Dr Roberts), tr. R. Williams Parry, *Cerddi R. Williams Parry: Y Casgliad Cyflawn*, ed. Alan Llwyd (Denbigh: Gwasg Gee, 1998), p. 223; '**Gwerddon y Ffridd**' (Upland Green), tr. H. Idris Bell, *Welsh Poems of the Twentieth Century*, p. 39; '**Nos o Haf**' (A Summer Night), tr. H. Idris Bell, *Welsh Poems of the Twentieth Century*, p. 38; '**Tros y Ffin**' (Revenant), tr. H. Idris Bell, *The Welsh Outlook*, 1 (1914), 312; tr. H. Idris Bell, *Welsh Poems of the Twentieth Century*, p. 65.

ROBERT OWEN (Eryron Gwyllt Walia; 1803–70)

Individual Translations *hymns*
'**Bydd gwel'd gogoniant Iesu**' (The exalted Jesus), tr. Revd R. Parry, *Hymns of the Welsh Revival*, pp. 33–5.

ROBERT OWEN (1858–85)

Individual Translations *Po.*
from '**Myfyrdod mewn Unigedd**' (A Prayer), tr. Edmund O. Jones, *Welsh Lyrics of the Nineteenth Century*, p. 117; '**O'r Dyfnder**' (De Profundis), tr. Edmund O. Jones, *Welsh Lyrics of the Nineteenth Century*, pp. 115–16.

RICHARD PARRY (Gwalchmai, Monwysiad; 1803–97)

Individual Translations *Po.*
'**Canu'n Iach i Arfon**' (Good-Bye to Arvon), tr. A. P. Graves, *Welsh Poetry Old and New*, pp. 85–6; '**Mewn Awen Fwyn Lawen**' (Oh! Let the Kind Minstrel), tr. John Parry, *Treasury of Welsh Songs*, pp. 6–7.

EVAN PUGHE (1806–69)

Individual Translations *hymns*
'**I Dad y Trugareddau**' (Thanksgiving), tr. Revd Lemuel John Hopkin James (Hopcyn), *Welsh Melodies in the Old Notation for Hymns in English Translated and Original*, n.p. [hymn 17] (1912: pp. 20–1).

EVAN REES (Dyfed; 1850–1923)

Individual Translations *Po.*
'**Awdwr Byw Dan Flodeu'r Bedd**' (The Shadow of Death), tr. H. Idris Bell, *Poems from the Welsh*, pp. 48–9; '**Y Dragoman**' (The Dragoman), tr. A. P. Graves, *Welsh Poetry Old and New*, pp. 101–2.

Individual Translations *hymns*
'**Ar ei ben bo'r goron**' (Upon his head he wears a crown), tr. W. H.
D., *Welsh National Supplement of Hymns*, p. 60; '**Pen Calfaria**' (To
Mount Calvary I'm looking), tr. H. Elvet Lewis, *Sweet Singers of
Wales*, pp. 150–1; tr. Revd Lemuel John Hopkin James (Hopcyn),
Welsh National Supplement of Hymns, p. 55.

WILLIAM REES (Gwilym Hiraethog; 1802–83)

Prose (Novel)
Helyntion Bywyd Hen Deiliwr, *Gwen and Gwladys*, tr. W. Rees Evans
(London: Elliot Stock, 1896).

Miscellaneous
from '**Heddwch**', William Rees (Gwilym Hiraethog), *Love and death:
translation of an extract from a Welsh ode (awdl) on 'Peace'*
(Swansea: Cambrian, 1886).

Individual Translations *Po.*
'**Atgofion Mebyd**' (The Memories of Youth), tr. J. Bodvan Anwyl,
Young Wales, 40.41 (1898), 103; *from* '**Emmanuel**', tr. author, *Wales*,
3.25 (1896), 227–8; tr. A. P. Graves, *Welsh Poetry Old and New*, p.
134; tr. A. P. Graves, *A Celtic Psaltery*, p. 93; '**Job**' (The Angel's
Song), tr. R. Morris Lewis, *Wales*, 1.3 (1894), 125; '**Y Gôf Du**' (The
Blacksmith), tr. R. L. Davies, *Cambrian Lyrics*, pp. 52–5.

Individual Translations *hymns*
'**Dyma Gariad fel y Moroedd**' (Here is Love that's like the Ocean), tr.
Talnant Llewelyn, *Young Wales*, 9.101 (1903), 101; tr. Revd R. Parry,
Hymns of the Welsh Revival, p. 27; tr. Revd Lemuel John Hopkin
James (Hopcyn), *Welsh Melodies in the Old Notation for Hymns in
English Translated and Original*, n.p. [hymn 40] (1912: pp. 40–1);
'**Gwisg dy Gleddyf llym, daufiniog**' (Gird Thy two-edged sword), tr.
Revd Lemuel John Hopkin James (Hopcyn), *Welsh Melodies in the
Old Notation for Hymns in English Translated and Original*, n.p.
[hymn 36] (1912: p. 33); '**Y Waredigol dorf o Saint**' (The host of
Saints Redeemed), tr. Ll. M. W., *Welsh National Supplement of
Hymns*, pp. 59–60.

ABSALOM ROBERTS (1780?–1864)

Individual Translations *Po.*
'**Tri phennill i Drawsfynydd**' (Three verses to Trawsfynydd), tr. H.
Idris Bell, *A History of Welsh Literature*, p. 299.

EDWARD ROBERTS (Iorwerth Glan Aled; 1819–67)

Individual Translations *Po.*
'**Codiad yr Hedydd**' (The Rising of the Lark), tr. John Thomas,
Treasury of Welsh Songs, pp. 66–7; '**Y Lili**' (The Lily), tr. J. Bodvan
Anwyl, *Young Wales*, 5.51 (1899), 72.

JOHN ROBERTS (Minimus; 1808–80)

Individual Translations *hymns*
'**Bywha Dy Waith**' ('Revive Thy Work'), tr. Revd Lemuel John
Hopkin James (Hopcyn), *Welsh National Supplement of Hymns*, p.
65.

ROBERT ROBERTS (Silyn; 1871–1930)

Individual Translations *Po.*
'**Ar Lannau'r Tawelfor**' (By the Pacific), tr. H. Idris Bell, *Poems from
the Welsh*, p. 26; '**Blodau**' (Flowers), tr. Glyn Jones, *Glyn Jones:
Collected Poems*, ed. Meic Stephens (Cardiff: University of Wales
Press, 1996), p. 232; '**Cerdd i Fro Morgannwg**' (In Glamorgan), tr. C.
C. Bell, *Welsh Poems of the Twentieth Century*, p. 43; '**Llwybrau
Bywyd**' (The Paths of Life), tr. F. E., *The Welsh Outlook*, 2 (1915),
102; '**Priflys y Gwylnos**' (The Palace of Darkness), tr. H. Idris Bell,
Poems from the Welsh, p. 42; '**Siom**' (Disillusion), tr. H. Idris Bell,
Poems from the Welsh, p. 47; '**Tir-Na'n Og**' (In Tir-N'an Og), tr. F.
E., *The Welsh Outlook*, 2 (1915), 102; tr. H. Idris Bell, *Welsh Poems
of the Twentieth Century*, p. 48; '**Y Gwyliwr**' (The Watchman), tr. H.
Idris Bell, *Poems from the Welsh*, p. 70.

WILLIAM JOHN ROBERTS (Gwilym Cowlyd; 1828–1904)

Individual Translations *Po.*
'Llynnoedd Eryri' (Mountain Lakes), tr. H. Idris Bell, *Poems from the Welsh*, p. 73; tr. unsigned, *Wales*, 5.7 (1945), 21; tr. Kenneth Hurlstone Jackson, *A Celtic Miscellany* (1951), p. 136 (1971: p. 126); tr. H. Idris Bell, *Transactions of the Honourable Society of Cymmrodorion* (1941), 36.

EBENEZER THOMAS (Eben Fardd; 1802–63)

Individual Translations *Po.*
from 'Cywydd i Langybi' (Cywydd to Llangybi), tr. H. Idris Bell, *A History of Welsh Literature*, p. 342; *from* 'Dinistr Jerusalem' (Jerusalem Destroyed), tr. A. P. Graves, *Welsh Poetry Old and New*, pp. 132–3; tr. A. P. Graves, *A Celtic Psaltery*, pp. 91–2; tr. Tony Conran, *The Penguin Book of Welsh Verse*, pp. 222–3; tr. Tony Conran, *Welsh Verse*, pp. 250–1; tr. Grahame Davies, *The Chosen People: Wales & The Jews*, ed. Grahame Davies (Bridgend: Seren, 2002), pp. 63–5.

JOHN THOMAS (Ieuan Ddu; 1795–1871)

Individual Translations *Po.*
'Hedydd Lon' (Gwenny Dear), tr. unsigned, *Treasury of Welsh Songs*, pp. 28–9; 'Rhiban Morfudd' (Morfudd's Ribbon), tr. J. H. Wiffen, *Treasury of Welsh Songs*, pp. 20–1; 'Trewch, Trewch y Tant' (Strike, Strike the Harp), tr. unsigned, *Treasury of Welsh Songs*, pp. 58–9.

WILLIAM THOMAS (Gwilym Marles; 1834–79)

Individual Translations *Po.*
'Golygfa' (Scene), tr. Gwyn Williams, *To Look for a Word*, p. 220; 'Pwy Gleddir Gyntaf' (Who in this new God's acre?), tr. Edmund O. Jones, *Welsh Lyrics of the Nineteenth Century*, pp. 42–3; 'Hen Lwnc Destyn Cymreig "I Arad a Dafad a Llong"' (An Old Welsh Toast),

tr. Gwyn Williams, *To Look for a Word*, p. 219; '**Ymholiad**' (Enquiry), tr. Gwyn Williams, *To Look for a Word*, p. 220; '**Ym Mrig yr Hwyr**' (The Night-Fall), tr. T. C. U., *Wales*, 3.32 (1896), 535.

WILLIAM THOMAS (Islwyn; 1832–78)

Collection

Meurig Walters, *Islwyn: Man of the Mountain* (Llandybïe: Salesbury [The Islwyn Memorial Society], 1983).

Individual Translations *Po.*[6]

'**Angel**' (The Angel), tr. C. C. Bell, *Poems from the Welsh*, pp. 36–7; '**Beirdd Cymru**' (The Poets of Wales), tr. Edmund O. Jones, *Welsh Lyrics of the Nineteenth Century*, pp. 89–90; *from* '**Cymru**' (Wales), tr. Edmund O. Jones, *Welsh Lyrics of the Nineteenth Century*, p. 85; tr. J. Bodvan Anwyl, *Young Wales*, 2.20 (1896), 189–90; H. Idris Bell, *Poems from the Welsh*, pp. 52–3; tr. Edmund O. Jones, *Pencader Poems: A Collection of Patriotic Verse published on the day of the Rally at Pencader September 27th 1952* (Cardiff: J. E. Jones, Plaid Cymru, 1952), n.p. [p. 14]; tr. Tony Conran, *A Swansea Anthology*, ed. James A. Davies (Bridgend: Seren, 1996), p. 33; '**David Bach**' (Davie), tr. Peter Hughes Griffiths, *A Celtic Anthology*, pp. 307–8; '**Saboth Gartref**' (The Sick Minister), tr. Edmund O. Jones, *Welsh Lyrics of the Nineteenth Century*, pp. 86–7; '**Seren Heddwch**' (Star of Peace), tr. Edmund O. Jones, *Welsh Poets of To-day and Yesterday*, pp. 4–5; tr. Francis Edwards, *Translations from the Welsh*, p. 27; tr. Francis Edwards, *Land of my Fathers*, p. 44; '**Y Breuddwyd**' (The Dream), tr. Tony Conran, *A Swansea Anthology*, ed. James A. Davies (Bridgend: Seren, 1996), pp. 33–4; '**Y Dylanwad**' (Inspiration), tr. Edmund O. Jones, *Welsh Lyrics of the Nineteenth Century*, pp. 81–2; tr. H. Idris Bell, *Poems from the Welsh*, pp. 20–1; '**Y Fodrwy Briodasol**' (The Wedding Ring), tr. T. M. Rees, *Young Wales*, 4.47

---

[6] The recording of translations from the poetry of Islwyn is problematic because of the way in which he lifted whole sections from the two poems called *Y Storm* (The Storm), publishing them as individual poems, different poems, to which he added variations and so on.

(1898), 264; '**Yr Hen Weinidog**' (The Old Minister), tr. R. Morris Lewis, *Wales*, 1.4 (1894), frontispiece.

From **Y Storm I** (originally published or translated as individual poems) '**Fe Welai y Graig**' (The Lighthouse), tr. Edmund O. Jones, *Welsh Lyrics of the Nineteenth Century*, p. 91; '**Mae Bywyd fel y Nef**' (Life, like the heavens), tr. Edmund O. Jones, *Welsh Lyrics of the Nineteenth Century*, p. 88; '**Mae'r Oll yn Gysygredig**' (All is Sacred), tr. T. Z. Jones, *Wales*, 2.19 (1895), 484; tr. Edwin Stanley James, *Wales*, 5.7 (1945), 17; tr. Tony Conran, *The Penguin Book of Welsh Verse*, pp. 224–5; tr. Gwyn Williams, *Presenting Welsh Poetry*, pp. 54–5; tr. Gwyn Williams, *To Look for a Word*, p. 214; tr. Tony Conran, *Welsh Verse*, pp. 251–2; '**Mynwent Ystormus**' (The Sea), tr. C. C. Bell, *Poems from the Welsh*, p. 34; tr. C. C. Bell, *A Celtic Anthology*, p. 307; '**O Hapus Luddedig**' (Blest Weary One), tr. S. Williams, *Wales*, 3.23 (1896), 111–12; '**Tybiaeth**' (Intimations), tr. Edmund O. Jones, *Welsh Lyrics of the Nineteenth Century*, pp. 83–4; tr. D. M. Lloyd, *A Book of Wales* (1953), pp. 369–70; '**Y Nos**' (The Night), tr. Edmund O. Jones, *Welsh Lyrics of the Nineteenth Century*, pp. 79–80; tr. T. M. Rees, *Young Wales*, 5.59 (1899), 264; tr. Edmund O. Jones, *Welsh Poets of To-day and Yesterday*, pp. 5–10; tr. D. J. Davies, in David James (Defynnog), *A Primer of Kymric Literature* (Cardiff: The Educational Publishing Co. Ltd, [1913]), pp. 160–2; *from* **Y Storm II**, tr. Tony Conran, *The Penguin Book of Welsh Verse*, pp. 225–6; tr. Tony Conran, *Welsh Verse*, pp. 252–3.

Individual Translations *hymns*
'**Gwêl uwchlaw cymylau amser**' (See beyond our time's horizon), tr. H. Elvet Lewis, *Sweet Singers of Wales*, pp. 117–18; tr. Revd Lemuel John Hopkin James (Hopcyn), *Welsh Melodies in the Old Notation for Hymns in English Translated and Original*, n.p. [hymn 22] (1912: p. 25); tr. Gwyn Williams, *Presenting Welsh Poetry*, pp. 55–6; tr. Gwyn Williams, *To Look for a Word*, pp. 215–16.

ELISEUS WILLIAMS (Eifion Wyn; 1867–1926)

Individual Translations *Po.*
'**Bardd a Blodeuyn**' (The Daisy), tr. C. C. Bell, *Welsh Poems of the Twentieth Century*, pp. 34–5; '**Blodau a Serch**' (Love and Apple-

blossom), tr. Robert Gurney, *Bardic Heritage*, p. 177; '**Blodau'r Grug**' (Heather), tr. Kenneth Hurlstone Jackson, *A Celtic Miscellany* (1951), p. 136 (1971: p. 126); tr. Tony Conran, *The Penguin Book of Welsh Verse*, p. 266; tr. Kenneth Hurlstone Jackson, *Oxford Book*, p. 203; tr. Tony Conran, *Welsh Verse*, p. 303; '**Cantre'r Gwaelod**', tr. C. C. Bell, *Welsh Poems of the Twentieth Century*, p. 30; '**Chwefror**' (February), tr. Francis Edwards, *Translations from the Welsh*, p. 79; '**Credo**', tr. C. C. Bell, *Welsh Poems of the Twentieth Century*, p. 68; '**Cynnig Calon**' (The Offer of a Heart), tr. Francis Edwards, *Translations from the Welsh*, p. 77; '**Gobaith**' (Hope), tr. Francis Edwards, *Translations from the Welsh*, p. 71; '**Gwylan**' (Seagull), tr. Francis Edwards, *Translations from the Welsh*, pp. 67–9; '**Gŵyl Ifan**' (St John's Day), tr. H. Idris Bell, *Welsh Poems of the Twentieth Century*, p. 37; '**Hwiangerdd Sul y Blodau**' (Flower Sunday Lullaby), tr. R. L. Davies, *Cambrian Lyrics*, pp. 44–7; tr. J. W. Wynne-Jones, in Eifion Wyn, *Telynegion Maes a Môr* (Cardiff: Educational Publishing Co. Ltd, 1906), pp. 11–12; tr. A. P. Graves, *Welsh Poetry Old and New*, pp. 108–10; tr. A. P. Graves, *A Celtic Psaltery*, pp. 103–4; '**Hydref**' (October), tr. Francis Edwards, *Translations from the Welsh*, p. 83; '**Lliw Dydd: Lliw Nos**' (By Day: By Night), tr. Francis Edwards, *Translations from the Welsh*, p. 85; '**Mab y Mynydd**' (Son of the Mountain), tr. Gwyn Williams, *Presenting Welsh Poetry*, pp. 57–8; tr. Gwyn Williams, *To Look for a Word*, pp. 221–2; '**Mehefin**' (June), tr. Francis Edwards, *Translations from the Welsh*, p. 81; tr. H. Idris Bell, *Welsh Poems of the Twentieth Century*, p. 36; '**Men**', tr. Francis Edwards, *Translations from the Welsh*, p. 73; '**Ora Pro Nobis**', tr. J. W. Wynne-Jones, in Eifion Wyn, *Telynegion Maes a Môr* (Cardiff: Educational Publishing Co. Ltd, 1906), pp. 22–3; tr. A. P. Graves, *Welsh Poetry Old and New*, pp. 107–8; tr. A. P. Graves, *A Celtic Psaltery*, pp. 101–2; '**Paradwys y Bardd**' (Little Wales for me), tr. Robert Gurney, *Bardic Heritage*, p. 178; '**Pe Bai Gennyt Serch**' (A Love Song), tr. H. Idris Bell, *The Nationalist*, 1.11 (1908), 8; tr. H. Idris Bell, *Poems from the Welsh*, p. 32; tr. H. Idris Bell, *A Book of Wales* (1953), p. 340; '**Serch**' (Love), tr. Robert Gurney, *Bardic Heritage*, pp. 177–8; '**Tan dy Lewyrch, Leuad Ieuanc**' (In the Moonlight), tr. H. Idris Bell, *Poems from the Welsh*, p. 68; '**Y Blodyn Glas**' (Forget-Me-Not), tr. Francis Edwards, *Translations from the Welsh*, p. 75; '**Y Mabinogi**', tr. H. Idris Bell, *Welsh Poems of the Twentieth Century*, pp. 31–2; '**Yr Afal Melyn**' (The Yellow Apple), tr. H. Idris Bell, *Welsh Poems of the Twentieth*

Century, p. 47; '**Yr Afon**' (The River), tr. Francis Edwards, *Translations from the Welsh*, p. 87; '**Ystyriwch y Lili**' (Consider the Lily), tr. R. L. Davies, *Cambrian Lyrics*, pp. 48–51.

ROBERT WILLIAMS (Robert ap Gwilym Ddu; 1766–1850)

Individual Translations *Po.*
'**Crist Gerbron Peilat**' (Christ Before Pilate), tr. Kenneth Hurlstone Jackson, *A Celtic Miscellany* (1951), p. 148 (1971: p. 136); tr. Tony Conran, *The Penguin Book of Welsh Verse*, p. 268; tr. Tony Conran, *Welsh Verse*, p. 305; '**Gobeithio**' (Hope), tr. Tony Conran, *The Penguin Book of Welsh Verse*, p. 270; tr. Tony Conran, *Welsh Verse*, p. 307; '**Merch y Bardd**' (An Only Child), tr. Tony Conran, *The Penguin Book of Welsh Verse*, p. 271; tr. Tony Conran, *Welsh Verse*, p. 308; '**Llwybr y Bedd**' (Old Age and Death), tr. H. Idris Bell, *Poems from the Welsh*, p. 75; tr. Kenneth Hurlstone Jackson, *A Celtic Miscellany* (1951), p. 145 (1971: p. 133).

Individual Translations *hymns*
'**Mae'r Gwaed a Redodd ar y Groes**' (Jesu's Blood), tr. H. Elvet Lewis, *Sweet Singers of Wales*, p. 98; tr. Griffith Jones (Glan Menai), *Wales*, 3.27 (1896), 319; tr. Jane Owen, *Welsh Hymns and their Tunes*, pp. 112–13.

ROBERT WILLIAMS (Trebor Mai; 1830–77)

Individual Translations *Po.*
'**Beddargraff Gwraig**' (On a Woman), tr. H. Idris Bell, *The Welsh Review*, 5.2 (1946), 117; tr. H. Idris Bell, *Oxford Book*, p. 204; '**Bugail y Garnedd**' (The Shepherd's Love), tr. Edmund O. Jones, *Welsh Lyrics of the Nineteenth Century*, pp. 31–2; '**Fry yn y Nef**' (In Heaven Above), tr. R. Drury, *Wales*, 2.11 (1895), 133.

ROWLAND WILLIAMS (Hwfa Môn; 1823–1905)

Individual Translations *Po.*
'**Yr Ystorm**' (The Storm), tr. Revd Robert Jones, *Y Cymmrodor* (1877), 127–9.

TALIESIN WILLIAMS (Taliesin ab Iolo; 1787–1847)

Individual Translations *Po.*
'**Y Derwyddon**' (The British Druids), tr. Lord Aberdare, *Red Dragon*, 5 (1883), 240–8.

THOMAS MARCHANT WILLIAMS (1845–1914)

Individual Translations *Po.*
'**Alarch Llyn Llandrindod**' (The Swan of Llandrindod Wells), tr. '**Balarch**', *The Nationalist*, 1.10 (1907), 32; tr. Evan Morgan, *The Nationalist*, 1.11 (1908), 33; '**Gwalia Wen**' (Dear Old Wales), tr. Edmund O. Jones, in Sir Thomas Marchant Williams, *Odlau Serch a Bywyd* (Cardiff: The Educational Publishing Co. Ltd, 1907), pp. 9–13; tr. Edmund O. Jones, *The Nationalist*, 1.2 (1907), 26; '**Y Bedd**' (The Grave), tr. Edmund O. Jones, in Sir Thomas Marchant Williams, *Odlau Serch a Bywyd* (Cardiff: The Educational Publishing Co. Ltd, 1907), p. 5; '**Y Cwmwl**' (The Cloud), tr. H. Idris Bell, *Poems from the Welsh*, pp. 39–40; '**Yr Haul**' (The Sun), tr. H. Idris Bell, *Poems from the Welsh*, p. 74.

WILLIAM WILLIAMS (Caledfryn; 1801–69)

Individual Translations *Po.*
from '**Awdl ar Ddrylliad yr Agerlong Rothsay Castle gerllaw Beaumaris, Awst, 17, 1831**' (The Shipwreck), tr. unsigned, *The Poetry of Wales* (1873), pp. 36–8; '**Bywyd Dyn**' (Man's Life), tr. H. Idris Bell, *Welsh Poems of the Twentieth Century*, p. 63; tr. H. Idris Bell, *A Celtic Anthology*, p. 305; '**Diwedd y Cynhaeaf**' (Harvest End), tr. R. S. Thomas, *Experimenting with an Amen* (London: Macmillan, 1986), p. 15; tr. R. S. Thomas, *Collected Poems: 1945–1990* (London: Phoenix Giant, 1995), p. 487; '**Y Gog**' (The Cuckoo), tr. Edmund O. Jones, *Welsh Lyrics of the Nineteenth Century*, pp. 37–8.

YR UGEINFED GANRIF:
THE TWENTIETH CENTURY

Anthologies

Poetry

H. Idris Bell and C. C. Bell, *Welsh Poems of the Twentieth Century in English Verse* (Wrexham: Hughes & Son, 1925).
[*Welsh Poems of the Twentieth Century*]

R. Gerallt Jones, *Poetry of Wales 1930–1970* (Llandysul: Gwasg Gomer, 1974).
[*Poetry of Wales 1930–1970*]

Joseph P. Clancy, *Twentieth Century Welsh Poems* (Llandysul: Gomer, 1982).
[*Twentieth Century Welsh Poems*]

Modern Poetry in Translation (with Dafydd Johnston as guest editor), 7 (1995).
[*Modern Poetry in Translation*]

Menna Elfyn and John Rowlands (eds), *The Bloodaxe Book of Modern Welsh Poetry: 20th century Welsh language poetry in translation* (Newcastle Upon Tyne: Bloodaxe Books, 2003).
[*Bloodaxe Book*]

Prose

Welsh Short Stories (London: Faber & Faber, 1937).
[*Welsh Short Stories* (1937)]

George Ewart Evans (ed.), *Welsh Short Stories* (London: Faber & Faber, 1959).
[*Welsh Short Stories* (1959)]

Gwyn Jones and Islwyn Ffowc Elis (eds), *Twenty-Five Welsh Short Stories* (London: Oxford University Press, 1971). Reprinted as *Classic Welsh Short Stories* (Oxford: Oxford University Press, 1992). [*Twenty-Five Welsh Short Stories*][1]

Alun Richards (ed.), *The Penguin Book of Welsh Short Stories* (Middlesex: Penguin Books, 1976).
[*The Penguin Book of Welsh Short Stories*]

Alun Richards (ed.), *The New Penguin Book of Welsh Short Stories* (Harmondsworth: Penguin Books, 1994).
[*The New Penguin Book of Welsh Short Stories*]

Meic Stephens, *Illuminations: an Anthology of Welsh Short Prose* (Welsh Academic Press, 1998).
[*Illuminations*]

GLYN M. ASHTON (Wil Cwch Angau; 1910–91)

Individual Translations *Pr.*
'**Hynafiaid**' (Ancestors), tr. Meic Stephens, *Illuminations*, pp. 133–7.

EUROS BOWEN (1904–88)

Collections

Euros Bowen, *Poems* (Llandysul: Gomer, 1974).

Cynthia and Saunders Davies (eds), *Euros Bowen: Priest-Poet/ Bardd-Offeiriad* (Penarth: Church in Wales Publications, 1993).

Individual Translations *Po.*
'**Adar Rhiannon**' (The Birds of Rhiannon), tr. Gwyn Williams, *Presenting Welsh Poetry*, p. 66; tr. Gwyn Williams, *To Look for a Word*, p. 249; '**Amser Eira**' (Snow Time), tr. Joseph P. Clancy, *Twentieth Century Welsh Poems*, p. 149; '**Asgellaid o Aur**' (Winged in

---

[1] Page numbers remain the same.

Gold), tr. author, *Oxford Book*, pp. 214–15; tr. R. Gerallt Jones, *Planet*, 71 (1988), 46–7; '**Brain**' (Crows), tr. Frank Olding, *Poetry Wales*, 24.1 (1988), 57; '**Brodor o Baradwys**' (Native of Paradise), tr. author, *Poetry Wales*, 19.1 (1983), 62–4; '**Bugail Kares**' (The Shepherd of Kares), tr. Tom Earley, *Poetry Wales*, 20.3 (1985), 54; '**Clywais Anadl**' (I Heard a Breath), tr. Joseph P. Clancy, *Twentieth Century Welsh Poems*, p. 139; '**Costrel yn y Mwg**' (A Costrel in the Smoke), tr. author, *Poetry Wales*, 11.1 (1975), 65–7; '**Danadl ym Mai**' (Nettles in May), tr. Joseph P. Clancy, *Twentieth Century Welsh Poems*, pp. 139–40; tr. author, *Oxford Book*, p. 215; tr. Joseph P. Clancy, *Bloodaxe Book*, p. 135; '**Diferion**' (Drops), tr. R. Gerallt Jones, *Poetry of Wales 1930–1970*, p. 177; '**Dylan Thomas**', tr. Tony Conran, *The Penguin Book of Welsh Verse*, p. 270; tr. Tony Conran, *Welsh Verse*, p. 307; '**Y Ddraenen Ddu**' (Blackthorn), tr. author, *Oxford Book*, p. 216; tr. author, *A Book of Wales* (1987), p. 10; '**Eirlysiau**' (Snowdrops), tr. Joseph P. Clancy, *Twentieth Century Welsh Poems*, p. 147; tr. Joseph P. Clancy, *Other Words*, pp. 6–7; '**Yr Eos**' (The Nightingale), tr. R. Gerallt Jones, *Poetry of Wales 1930–1970*, p. 171; tr. R. Gerallt Jones, *Bloodaxe Book*, pp. 134–5; '**Gloywad**' (Glint), tr. Tony Conran, *The Penguin Book of Welsh Verse*, pp. 256–7; tr. Tony Conran, *Welsh Verse*, pp. 287–8; tr. Tony Conran, *Love from Wales: An Anthology*, ed. Tony Curtis and Siân James (Bridgend: Seren Books, 1991), p. 67; '**Golau**' (Light), tr. Joseph P. Clancy, *Twentieth Century Welsh Poems*, pp. 143–6; '**Hwyaid Gwylltion**' (Wild Ducks), tr. Tony Conran, *The Penguin Book of Welsh Verse*, p. 266; tr. Tony Conran, *Welsh Verse*, p. 303; '**Hyn**' (This), tr. Joseph P. Clancy, *Twentieth Century Welsh Poems*, p. 154; '**Ieuenctid yr Iaith**' (The Youth of the Language), tr. Joseph P. Clancy, *Twentieth Century Welsh Poems*, pp. 149–50; tr. Joseph P. Clancy, *Bloodaxe Book*, pp. 136–7; '**Y Llyn Llonydd**' (The Quiet Lake), tr. Joseph P. Clancy, *Twentieth Century Welsh Poems*, pp. 153–4; '**Llysywen**' (Eel), tr. R. Gerallt Jones, *Poetry of Wales 1930–1970*, pp. 187–9; tr. Joseph P. Clancy, *Twentieth Century Welsh Poems*, p. 148; '**Maniach**' (Bits and Pieces), tr. Joseph P. Clancy, *Twentieth Century Welsh Poems*, p. 142; '**Marmor Carrara**' (Carrara Marble), tr. R. Gerallt Jones, *Poetry of Wales 1930–1970*, pp. 183–5; tr. Joseph P. Clancy, *Twentieth Century Welsh Poems*, pp. 152–3; '**Mewn Arena**' (In an Arena), tr. Frank Olding, *Poetry Wales*, 24.1 (1988), 58–9; '**Mewn Ffald**' (In a Pound), tr. author, *Poetry Wales*, 12.1 (1976), 29–30; '**Mynyddoedd**' (Mountains), tr. author, *Poetry Wales*, 12.1 (1976), 31–2; '**Ogof Wag**' (An Empty Cave), tr. Joseph P.

Clancy, *Twentieth Century Welsh Poems*, p. 150; **'Pan fo'r Gwynt'** (When the Wind), tr. R. Gerallt Jones, *Poetry of Wales 1930–1970*, p. 175; tr. Tom Earley, *Planet*, 49/50 (1980), 70; **'Pŵer y Gerdd'** (The Power of Song), tr. Joseph P. Clancy, *Trivium*, 8 (1973), 116; tr. Joseph P. Clancy, *Twentieth Century Welsh Poems*, p. 141; tr. author, *Bloodaxe Book*, p. 136; **'Reredos'**, tr. author, *New England Review and Bread Loaf Quarterly*, 10.4 (1988), 477; tr. Joseph P. Clancy, *Poetry Wales*, 29.4 (1994), 40; tr. Joseph P. Clancy, *Other Words*, pp. 64–5; **'Saliwt'** (Salute), tr. Frank Olding, *Poetry Wales*, 24.1 (1988), 59–60; **'Y Tair Colomen'** (The Three Doves), tr. R. Gerallt Jones, *Poetry of Wales 1930–1970*, pp. 179–81; **'Torheulo'** (Sunbathing), tr. Joseph P. Clancy, *Twentieth Century Welsh Poems*, p. 151; **'Tywod Sacara'** (The Sand at Saqqara), tr. author, *Poetry Wales*, 10.2 (1974), 106–8; **'Ymwacáu'** (Kenosis), tr. author, *Poetry Wales*, 16.3 (1981), 5–6; **'Yn Chartres'** (In Chartres), tr. author, *Bloodaxe Book*, pp. 137–8; **'Yr Alarch'** (The Swan), tr. Tony Conran, *The Penguin Book of Welsh Verse*, p. 256; tr. R. Gerallt Jones, *Poetry of Wales 1930–1970*, p. 173; tr. Joseph P. Clancy, *Twentieth Century Welsh Poems*, p. 140; tr. Joseph P. Clancy, *A Book of Wales* (1987), p. 9; tr. Tony Conran, *Welsh Verse*, p. 287; tr. author, *Planet*, 71 (1988), 44–5.

GERAINT BOWEN (1915–)

Individual Translations *Po.*
from **'Awdl Foliant i Amaethwr'** (Ode in Praise of the Farmer) [**'Gosteg y Bardd'** (The Poet's Prelude)], tr. Gillian Clarke, *Bloodaxe Book*, pp. 168–9.

DILYS CADWALADR (1902–79)

Individual Translations *Po.*
'Y Llen' (The Veil), tr. Colonel R. C. Ruck, *Dock Leaves*, 4.12 (1953), 8–16.

Individual Translations *Pr.*
'Y Gwesteion' (The Guests), tr. R. S. Thomas, *Wales*, 8.29 (1948), 541–3.

ANEIRIN TALFAN DAVIES (1908–80)

Individual Translations *Po.*
'**Edrychais yn dy Wyneb Neithiwr, Angau**' (I Looked you in the Face Last Night), tr. Joseph P. Clancy, *Twentieth Century Welsh Poems*, p. 155; tr. Joseph P. Clancy, *Bloodaxe Book*, pp. 138–9; '**Llyfrau**' (Books), tr. Catherine Fisher, *Bloodaxe Books*, pp. 139–40.

E. TEGLA DAVIES (1880–1967)

Prose (Novel)
Gŵr Pen y Bryn, *The Master of Pen y Bryn*, tr. Nina Watkins (Llandybie: Christopher Davies, 1975).

Individual Translations *Pr.*
from **Gŵr Pen y Bryn** (Awakening), tr. Nina Watkins, *Wales: A Celebration*, ed. Dewi Roberts (Llanrwst: Gwasg Carreg Gwalch, 2000), pp. 113–15; '**Nedw**' (Nedw and his Nuts), tr. Meic Stephens, *A Book of Wales* (1987), pp. 30–2; '**O'r Pulpud**' (From the Pulpit), tr. Meic Stephens, *Illuminations*, pp. 72–7; '**Samuel Jones yr Hendre yn diolch am ei gynhaeaf**' (Samuel Jones's Harvest Thanksgiving), tr. Dafydd Jenkins, *The Welsh Review*, 1.2 (1939), 63–8; tr. Dafydd Jenkins, *Twenty-Five Welsh Short Stories*, pp. 189–96; '**Yr Epaddyn Rhyfedd**' (The Strange Apeman), tr. Wyn Griffith, *Welsh Short Stories* (1937), pp. 144–51; tr. Wyn Griffith, *The Penguin Book of Welsh Short Stories*, pp. 140–5.

GARETH ALBAN DAVIES (1926–)

Individual Translations *Po.*
'**Angau yn Fenis**' (Death in Venice), tr. author, *Modern Poetry in Translation*, pp. 16–17; tr. author, *Bloodaxe Book*, p. 199; '**Artá, Majorca – Pasg 1991**' (Artá, Majorca – Easter 1991), tr. author, *Modern Poetry in Translation*, pp. 21–2; '**Bethesda, Ton**', tr. author, *Modern Poetry in Translation*, pp. 24–6; '**Caer Bwlch-y-clawdd**', tr. Joseph P. Clancy, *Twentieth Century Welsh Poems*, pp. 187–8; '**Cerdyn Nadolig at Gyfaill nad yw efallai'n fyw**' (Christmas Card to a Friend who Might be Dead), tr. Mike Jenkins and author, *Bloodaxe*

Book, pp. 197–8; '**Cwm Mabws**', tr. author, *Modern Poetry in Translation*, pp. 27–8; '**Diptych**', tr. author, *Quaderno 2 di Lettera* (March, 1977), 25; tr. author, *Modern Poetry in Translation*, pp. 18–19; '**Er cof am Ernest Longfield**' (In Memory of Ernest Longfield), tr. author, *Modern Poetry in Translation*, pp. 22–4; '**Er Cof am J. R. R.**' (In Memory of J. R. R.), tr. R. Gerallt Jones, *Poetry of Wales 1930–1970*, pp. 297–9; '**Fethard, Swydd Wexford, Iwerddon**' (Fethard, County Wexford, Ireland), tr. author, *Modern Poetry in Translation*, pp. 25–6; '**Gwerin Chile**' (The Chilean People), tr. author, *Modern Poetry in Translation*, pp. 20–1; tr. author, *Bloodaxe Book*, pp. 196–7; '**Huw Owen, Gwenynog, Môn**' (Huw Owen, Gwenynog, Anglesey), tr. author, *Modern Poetry in Translation*, pp. 17–18; tr. author, *An Anglesey Anthology*, ed. Dewi Roberts (Gwasg Carreg Gwalch, 1999), pp. 107–9; '**Hydref**' (Autumn), tr. author, *Quaderno 2 di Lettera* (March, 1977), 23; '**Mewnlifwyr**' (Incomers), tr. Mike Jenkins and author, *Bloodaxe Book*, pp. 200–1; '**Mudandod Amser**' (Time's Muteness), tr. Joseph P. Clancy, *Twentieth Century Welsh Poems*, p. 188; tr. Joseph P. Clancy, *Bloodaxe Book*, p. 200; '**Poitiers: Medi 1978**' (Poitiers: September 1978), tr. author, *Poetry Wales*, 17.1 (1981), 13; '**Siarl y Pumed yn Yuste**' (Charles the Fifth in Yuste), tr. author, *Modern Poetry in Translation*, pp. 26–7; '**Villahermosa: Madrid, 1976**', tr. author, *Quaderno 2 di Lettera* (March, 1977), 21; '**Y Ddawns**' (The Dance), tr. R. Gerallt Jones, *Poetry of Wales 1930–1970*, pp. 293–5; tr. Gwyn Jones, *Oxford Book*, pp. 274–5; '**Y Gwyddau Gwylltion**' (The Wild Geese), tr. author, *Modern Poetry in Translation*, pp. 19–20; tr. author, *Bloodaxe Book*, pp. 195–6; '**Y Trên Pedwar i Valladolid**' (The Four O'Clock Train to Valladolid), tr. R. Gerallt Jones, *Poetry of Wales 1930–1970*, p. 301.

Individual Translations *Pr.*
'**Y Got Ffwr**' (The Fur Coat), tr. Meic Stephens, *Illuminations*, pp. 207–14.

J. EIRIAN DAVIES (1918–98)

Individual Translations *Po.*
'**Draenen Ddu**' (The Black Thorn), tr. Siôn Eirian, *Bloodaxe Book*, p. 190; '**Penbleth**' (Bafflement), tr. Siôn Eirian, *Bloodaxe Book*, pp.

189–90; '**Cân Galed**' (Hard Song), tr. Siôn Eirian, *Bloodaxe Book*, pp. 190–2.

JAMES KITCHENER DAVIES (1902–52)

Individual Translations *Po.*
'**Sŵn y Gwynt sy'n Chwythu**' (The Sound of the Wind that is Blowing), tr. Joseph P. Clancy, *Poetry Wales* (Special feature on James Kitchener Davies), 17.3 (1982), 9–19; tr. Joseph P. Clancy, *Twentieth Century Welsh Poems*, pp. 109–19; *from* '**Sŵn y Gwynt sy'n Chwythu**', tr. R. Gerallt Jones, *Poetry of Wales 1930–1970*, pp. 133–45; tr. Joseph P. Clancy, *Oxford Book*, pp. 207–13; tr. Joseph P. Clancy, *The Valleys*, ed. John Davies and Mike Jenkins (Poetry Wales Press, 1984), pp. 35–6; tr. Joseph P. Clancy, *A Book of Wales* (1987), pp. 36–7; tr. Joseph P. Clancy, *A Rhondda Anthology*, ed. Meic Stephens (Bridgend: Seren, 1993), pp. 88–91; tr. Joseph P. Clancy, *Transactions of the Honourable Society of Cymmrodorion*, 6 (1999), 126–34; tr. Joseph P. Clancy, *Bloodaxe Book*, pp. 104–11.

PENNAR DAVIES (Davies Aberpennar; 1911–96)

Individual Translations *Po.*
'**Aletheia**', tr. R. Gerallt Jones, *Poetry of Wales 1930–1970*, p. 239; '**Ave Atque Vale**', tr. Joseph P. Clancy, *Bloodaxe Book*, pp. 143–4; '**Cathl i'r Almonwydden**' (A Song for the Almond Tree), tr. R. Gerallt Jones, *Poetry of Wales 1930–1970*, pp. 235–7; '**Chwilen y Dom**' (The Dung-Beetle), tr. Joseph P. Clancy, *Trivium*, 8 (1973), 118–19; tr. Joseph P. Clancy, *Twentieth Century Welsh Poems*, pp. 156–7; tr. Joseph P. Clancy, *Bloodaxe Book*, pp. 144–5; '**Disgyrchiant**' (Gravity), tr. Gwilym Rees Hughes, *Poetry Wales*, 7.1 (1971), 36–7; tr. Gwilym Rees Hughes, *A Book of Wales* (1987), pp. 38–9; '**Dwy Soned**' (Two Sonnets), tr. R. Gerallt Jones, *Poetry of Wales 1930–1970*, p. 233; '**Llanddwyn**', tr. Joseph P. Clancy, *Twentieth Century Welsh Poems*, pp. 158–9; '**Mi a fûm gydag Ulysses**' (I was with Ulysses), tr. Joseph P. Clancy, *Bloodaxe Book*, pp. 141–3; '**Nicé Adeiniog Samothracia**' (The Winged Niké of Samothrace), tr. Joseph P. Clancy, *Twentieth Century Welsh Poems*, pp. 157–8; '**Newtrino**' (Neutrino), tr. author, *Quaderno 2 di Lettera* (March,

1977), 27; '**Pan Oeddwn Fachgen**' (When I was a Boy), tr. Joseph P. Clancy, *Bloodaxe Book*, pp. 140–1; '**Smaldod y Dewin**' (The Wizard's Jest), tr. Joseph P. Clancy, *Twentieth Century Welsh Poems*, pp. 159–60; '**Wrth Hel Llus**' (While Picking Whimberries), tr. author, *Quaderno 2 di Lettera* (March, 1977), 29.

Individual Translations *Pr.*
'**Gazeles**' (Gazelle), tr. author, *The Anglo-Welsh Review*, 20.45 (1972), 115–21.

T. GLYNNE DAVIES (1926–88)

Individual Translations *Po.*
'**Adfeilion**' (Ruins), tr. R. Gerallt Jones, *Poetry of Wales 1930–1970*, pp. 305–23; tr. Joseph P. Clancy, *Bloodaxe Book*, pp. 203–5; '**Brawddegau wrth gofio Hiraethog**' (Sentences while remembering Hiraethog), tr. R. Gerallt Jones, *Poetry of Wales 1930–1970*, p. 325; tr. R. Gerallt Jones, *Oxford Book*, pp. 276–7; '**Caernarfon, Gorffennaf 2, 1969**' (Caernarfon, 2 July, 1969), tr. Joseph P. Clancy, *Twentieth Century Welsh Poems*, p. 186; tr. Joseph P. Clancy, *Oxford Book*, pp. 277–8; tr. Joseph P. Clancy, *Bloodaxe Book*, p. 206; '**Dydd Diolch**' (Thanksgiving Day), tr. Joseph P. Clancy, *Twentieth Century Welsh Poems*, p. 184; '**Margiad Elin**', tr. R. Gerallt Jones, *Poetry of Wales 1930–1970*, p. 327; '**Yr Hwsmon**' (The Bailiff), tr. R. Gerallt Jones, *Poetry of Wales 1930–1970*, pp. 329–31; tr. Joseph P. Clancy, *Twentieth Century Welsh Poems*, pp. 184–5; tr. author, *Oxford Book*, pp. 275–6; tr. Joseph P. Clancy, *Bloodaxe Book*, pp. 201–2.

J. M. EDWARDS (1903–78)

Individual Translations *Po.*
'**Nadolig Ewrop 1945**' (Christmas in Europe: 1945), tr. Robert Minhinnick, *Bloodaxe Book*, pp. 114–15; '**Pentrefi Cymru**' (Villages of Wales), tr. Joseph P. Clancy, *Twentieth Century Welsh Poems*, pp. 121–2; '**Y Cae Gwenith**' (The Wheat Field), tr. Gwyn Williams, *To Look for a Word*, pp. 252–3; '**Y Gof**' (The Blacksmith), tr. Joseph P. Clancy, *Twentieth Century Welsh Poems*, pp. 122–3; tr. Joseph P. Clancy, *The Heart of Wales: An Anthology*, ed. James A. Davies

(Bridgend: Seren, 1994), pp. 79–80; '**Y Gweddill**' (The Remainder), tr. R. Gerallt Jones, *Poetry of Wales 1930–1970*, p. 155; tr. Robert Minhinnick, *Bloodaxe Book*, pp. 113–14; '**Yr Einioes**' (Life), tr. R. Gerallt Jones, *Poetry of Wales 1930–1970*, p. 157.

ISLWYN FFOWC ELIS (1924–2004)

Prose (Novel)
Cysgod y Cryman, *Shadow of the Sickle*, tr. Meic Stephens (Llandysul: Gomer, 1998).

Individual Translations *Pr.*
'**Cyn Oeri'r Gwaed**' (Before I go), tr. author, *A Book of Wales* (1987), pp. 59–62; '**Hunandosturi**' (Self-Pity), tr. author, *The New Penguin Book of Welsh Short Stories*, pp. 265–76; '**Wythnos yng Nghymru Fydd**' (The Old Woman of Bala), tr. Meic Stephens, *A Book of Wales* (1987), pp. 57–8; '**Y Ddafad**' (Black Barren), tr. author, *The Penguin Book of Welsh Short Stories*, 309–17; '**Y Polyn**' (Song of a Pole), tr. author, *Twenty-Five Welsh Short Stories*, pp. 67–74; '**Y Rhaid sydd Arnaf**' (The Imperative upon Me), tr. Meic Stephens, *Illuminations*, pp. 88–91; '**Y Tyddyn**' (The Girl in the Heather), tr. author, *Welsh Short Stories* (1959), pp. 123–30.

EINION EVANS (1926–)

Individual Translations *Po.*
'**Merch Fach Gaddafi**' (Gadafi's Little Daughter), tr. Mike Jenkins, *Bloodaxe Book*, p. 207.

ELLIS HUMPHREY EVANS (Hedd Wyn; 1887–1917)

Individual Translations *Po.*
'**Atgo**' (Memory), tr. Gwyn Williams, *To Look for a Word*, p. 228; '**Rhyfel**' (War), tr. Gwyn Williams, *Presenting Welsh Poetry*, p. 62; tr. Gwyn Williams, *To Look for a Word*, p. 228; tr. Alan Llwyd, *Poetry Wales*, 28.2 (1992), 51; tr. Gillian Clarke, *Bloodaxe Book*, p. 67; '**Y Blotyn Du**' (The Black Blot), tr. Gillian Clarke, *Bloodaxe Book*, p. 67.

ELWYN EVANS (1912–)

Individual Translations *Po.*
'**Iddewes**' ['Wele yr Iddewon lân/Mae ei bronnau . . .'] (A Jewess), tr.
Grahame Davies, *The Chosen People: Wales & The Jews*, ed.
Grahame Davies (Bridgend: Seren, 2002), p. 293; '**Iddewes**' ['Wele yr
Iddewon lân/Deufin meddal . . .'] (The Jewess), pp. 293–4;
'**Jerusalem Ranedig**' (Jerusalem Divided), tr. Grahame Davies, *The
Chosen People: Wales & The Jews*, ed. Grahame Davies (Bridgend:
Seren, 2002), pp. 103–7; '**Taith yn ôl**' (Return Journey), tr. Grahame
Davies, *The Chosen People: Wales & The Jews*, ed. Grahame Davies
(Bridgend: Seren, 2002), pp. 107–13.

WILLIAM EVANS (Wil Ifan; 1882–1968)

Individual Translations *Po.*
from '**Bro fy Mebyd**' (The Vale of my Youth), tr. Elin ap Hywel,
Bloodaxe Book, pp. 57–9; '**Drannoeth**' (The Day After), tr. Francis
Edwards, *Translations from the Welsh*, p. 139; tr. H. Idris Bell, *The
Welsh Outlook*, 17.8 (1930), 212; tr. H. Idris Bell, *A History of Welsh
Literature*, pp. 406–7; '**Glan Môr**' (Beside the Sea), tr. Francis
Edwards, *Translations from the Welsh*, p. 141; '"**Gwiriwyd hi'n
Wraig i arall**"' (The Ring), tr. H. Idris Bell and C. C. Bell, *Welsh
Poems of the Twentieth Century*, p. 53; '**Gwyn a Gwridog**' (White and
Red), tr. Francis Edwards, *Translations from the Welsh*, p. 134;
'**Pelydr a Chwmwl**' (Sunshine and Cloud), tr. Francis Edwards,
Translations from the Welsh, p. 143; '**Y Deffro**' (The Awakening), tr.
Francis Edwards, *Translations from the Welsh*, p. 137; '**Ym
Mhorthcawl**' (In Porthcawl), tr. Robert Minhinnick, *Bloodaxe Book*,
p. 57.

ALBERT EVANS-JONES (Cynan; 1895–1970)

Individual Translations *Po.*
'**Aberdaron**', tr. author, *Cerddi Cynan: y Casgliad Cyflawn*
(Llandysul: Gomer, 1987), p. 188; '**Anfon y Nico**' (A Message
Home), tr. Harri Webb, *The Anglo-Welsh Review*, 22.50 (1973),
117–18; '**Dos**' (Vain Flight), tr. H. Idris Bell, *Welsh Poems of the*

Twentieth Century, p. 52; '**Eirlysiau**' (Snowdrops), tr. A. G. Prys-Jones, *A Book of Wales* (1953), pp. 342–3; tr. Joseph P. Clancy, *Twentieth Century Welsh Poems*, p. 89; '**Aberdaron**', tr. Joseph P. Clancy, *Twentieth Century Welsh Poems*, pp. 89–90; tr. Joseph P. Clancy, *A Book of Wales* (1987), pp. 71–2; tr. Joseph P. Clancy, *Wales: A Celebration*, ed. Dewi Roberts (Llanrwst: Gwasg Carreg Gwalch, 2000), pp. 39–40; '**Monastîr**', tr. Sally Roberts Jones, *Bloodaxe Book*, pp. 88–90; *from* '**Mab y Bwthyn**' (The Prodigal Son), tr. Sally Roberts Jones, *Bloodaxe Book*, p. 87; '**Teifi**', tr. author, *Cerddi Cynan: y Casgliad Cyflawn* (Llandysul: Gomer, 1987), p. 186; '**Y Llwybrau Gynt lle bu'r Gân**' (The Better Part), tr. H. Idris Bell, *Welsh Poems of the Twentieth Century*, p. 59.

W. R. P. GEORGE (1912–)

Individual Translations *Po.*
'**Armstrong ac Aldrin ar y Lleuad**' (Armstrong and Aldrin on the Moon), tr. Richard Poole, *Bloodaxe Book*, p. 150; '**Delffi**' (Delphi), tr. author, *Poetry Wales*, 9.1 (1973), 56–8; '**Calangaeaf 1975**' (All Saints Day 1975), tr. Bryan Martin Davies, *Poetry Wales*, 12.1 (1976), 34–5.

J. GWYN GRIFFITHS (1911–2004)

Individual Translations *Po.*
'**Abw Simbel**' (Abu Simbel), tr. Joseph P. Clancy, *Twentieth Century Welsh Poems*, pp. 161–2; '**Antaios**', tr. R. Gerallt Jones, *Poetry of Wales 1930–1970*, p. 249; '**Bryn y Baedd, Rhydychen**' (Boar's Hill, Oxford), tr. R. Gerallt Jones, *Poetry of Wales 1930–1970*, p. 247; '**Dim ond Croesi**' (Merely Crossing), tr. R. Gerallt Jones, *Poetry of Wales 1930–1970*, pp. 243–5; '**Mae Dau'n Cofleidio**' (Two are Embracing), tr. Richard Poole, *Bloodaxe Book*, pp. 147–8; '**Mae Ffiniau i Gariad Brawdol**' (There are Limits to Brotherly Love), tr. Richard Poole, *Bloodaxe Book*, p. 146; '**Parasitiaid**' (Parasites), tr. Richard Poole, *Bloodaxe Book*, p. 148; '**Rosa Mystica**', tr. Richard Poole, *Bloodaxe Book*, pp. 146–7; '**Yr Heniaith**' (The Old Language), tr. Joseph P. Clancy, *Twentieth Century Welsh Poems*, pp. 162–3.

W. J. GRUFFYDD (1881–1954)

Hen Atgofion, *The Years of the Locust*, tr. D. Myrddin Lloyd
(Llandysul: Gomer, 1976).

Individual Translations *Pr.*
from **Hen Atgofion** (Exile in Cardiff), tr. D. M. Lloyd, *A Book of
Wales* (1987), pp. 95–6; tr. D. M. Lloyd, *A Cardiff Anthology*, ed.
Meic Stephens (Bridgend: Seren, 1987), pp. 99–100; '**Y Diweddar
Lemuel Parry, Ysw., Y.H., O.B.E.**' (The Late Lemuel Parry, Esq.,
J.P., O.B.E), tr. Meic Stephens, *Illuminations*, pp. 12–17.

Individual Translations *Po.*[2]
from '**Ar yr Allt**' (Stanzas in Imitation of Omar Khayyam),[3] tr. H.
Idris Bell, *Poems from the Welsh*, pp. 69–70; '**Bethesda'r Fro**', tr.
H. Idris Bell, *Wales*, 1 (1943), 45–50; '**Breuddwyd**' (A Dream), tr. H.
Idris Bell, *Welsh Poems of the Twentieth Century*, p. 57; '**Capten John
Huws**' (Captain John Huws of the Oriana), tr. Joseph P. Clancy,
Twentieth Century Welsh Poems, pp. 39–40; '**Cerdd Hen Lanc Tyn y
Mynydd**' (The Ballad of the Old Bachelor of Tyn y Mynydd), tr. A.
P. Graves, *Welsh Poetry Old and New*, p. 112; tr. A. P. Graves, *A Celtic
Psaltery*, p. 105; tr. H. Idris Bell, *Poems from the Welsh*, pp. 17–18;
'**Cerdd yr Hen Chwarelwr**' (Welsh Portraits: The Old Quarryman), tr.
H. Idris Bell, *Poems from the Welsh*, p. 18; '**Cerdd yr Hen Longwr**'
(Welsh Portraits: The Old Sailor), tr. H. Idris Bell, *Poems from the
Welsh*, p. 19; '**Cerdd y Prydydd Ieuanc**' (Welsh Portraits: The Young
Poet), tr. H. Idris Bell, *Poems from the Welsh*, p. 20; '**Cofia**'
(Remember), tr. H. Idris Bell, *Welsh Poems of the Twentieth Century*,
p. 76; '**Er Cof am fy Chwaer**' (In Memoriam Sororis Meae), tr. H.
Idris Bell, *Poems from the Welsh*, p. 65; '**Er Cof am y Parch. Thomas
Rhys**' (In Memory of the Revd Thomas Rhys), tr. R. Gerallt Jones,
Poetry of Wales 1930–1970, p. 25; '**Dydd yn Ebrill**' (A Day in April),
tr. H. Idris Bell and C. C. Bell, *Welsh Poems of the Twentieth Century*,
p. 33; '**Gorffwys**' (Rest), tr. H. Idris Bell, *Poems from the Welsh*, p. 71;

---

[2] There is an additional translation of a poem by W. J. Gruffydd entitled (in
English) 'A Lullaby: New Style', tr. H. Idris Bell, *Welsh Poems of the
Twentieth Century*, p. 80. I have been unable to locate the source text from
collections of the poet's work or periodical research.

[3] Verses XXVII–XXXIV as published in *Caneuon a Cherddi* (Bangor:
Jarvis & Foster, 1906), pp. 17–19.

'**Gwerfyl Fychan**', tr. A. P. Graves, *Welsh Poetry Old and New*, p. 113; tr. H. Idris Bell and C. C. Bell, *Welsh Poems of the Twentieth Century*, p. 24; tr. H. Idris Bell, *A Celtic Anthology*, p. 276; '**Gwladys Rhys**', tr. D. M. Lloyd, *A Book of Wales* (1953), pp. 163–5; tr. Gwyn Williams, *To Look for a Word*, pp. 229–30; tr. D. M. Lloyd, *Oxford Book*, pp. 161–2; tr. D. M. Lloyd, *A Book of Wales* (1987), pp. 94–5; tr. Robert Minhinnick, *Bloodaxe Book*, pp. 54–5; '**In Memoriam**', tr. R. Gerallt Jones, *Poetry of Wales 1930–1970*, p. 23; tr. R. Gerallt Jones, *Oxford Book*, pp. 162–3; '**I'r Diwygiwr**' (The Reformer), tr. H. Idris Bell, *Welsh Poems of the Twentieth Century*, p. 79; '**Mae'r Pasiant Trosodd**' (The Pageant is Over), tr. R. Gerallt Jones, *Poetry of Wales 1930–1970*, p. 27; '**Merch y Mynydd**' (The Mountain Lass), tr. C. C. Bell, *Welsh Poems of the Twentieth Century*, p. 55; '**Tempora Mutantur**', tr. H. Idris Bell, *The Nationalist*, 1.12 (1908), 33; tr. H. Idris Bell, *Poems from the Welsh*, p. 43; '**Y Ddinas**' (The City), tr. C. C. Bell, *Poems from the Welsh*, p. 35; '**Y Farn Fawr**' (Judgement Day), tr. H. Idris Bell, *Welsh Poems of the Twentieth Century*, p. 72; '**Ymbil ar Hydref**' (Ode to Autumn), tr. H. Idris Bell, *Poems from the Welsh*, pp. 46–7; tr. H. Idris Bell, *Land of my Fathers*, p. 73; '**Yr Aderyn Cyfarwydd**' (The Bird), tr. C. C. Bell, *Welsh Poems of the Twentieth Century*, p. 58; '**Yr Arglwydd Rhys**', tr. H. Idris Bell, *A History of Welsh Literature*, pp. 393–4; '**Y Tlawd Hwn**' (This Poor Man), tr. Tony Conran, *The Penguin Book of Welsh Verse*, p. 239; tr. Joseph P. Clancy, *Twentieth Century Welsh Poems*, p. 38; tr. Gwyn Jones, *Oxford Book*, pp. 160–1; tr. Tony Conran, *Welsh Verse*, p. 268; tr. Tony Conran, *Bloodaxe Book*, p. 51; '**Yr Ieuanc wrth yr Hen**' (The Young to the Old), tr. H. Idris Bell and C. C. Bell, *Welsh Poems of the Twentieth Century*, pp. 15–16; tr. Robert Minhinnick, *Bloodaxe Book*, pp. 53–4; '**Yr Ysbryd**' (The Spirit), tr. H. Idris Bell, *Poems from the Welsh*, p. 45; '**Ywen Llanddeiniolen**' (The Yew of Llanddeiniolen), tr. H. Idris Bell and C. C. Bell, *Welsh Poems of the Twentieth Century*, p. 46; tr. Leonard Owen, *The London Welshman*, 19.7 (1964), 21; tr. Joseph P. Clancy, *Trivium*, 8 (1973), 111–12; tr. Joseph P. Clancy, *Twentieth Century Welsh Poems*, pp. 38–9; tr. Joseph P. Clancy, *Bloodaxe Book*, p. 52; '**Trystan ac Esyllt**' (Tristan and Iseult), tr. H. Idris Bell, *Poems from the Welsh*, pp. 61–2.

HARRI GWYNN (1913–85)

Individual Translations *Po.*
'**I Gyfarch yr Hwch**' (To Salute the Sow), tr. R. Gerallt Jones, *Poetry of Wales 1930–1970*, p. 261; '**Llundain, 1944**' (London, 1944), tr. R. Gerallt Jones, *Poetry of Wales 1930–1970*, p. 259; '**Pasg yr Hen Wyddonydd**' (The Old Scientist's Easter), tr. R. Gerallt Jones, *Poetry of Wales 1930–1970*, p. 263; '**Y Creadur**' (The Creature), tr. Colonel R. C. Ruck, *Dock Leaves*, 3.9 (1952), 20–9; tr. Robert Minhinnick, *Bloodaxe Book*, pp. 151–8; '**Y Ceiliog**' (The Cock), tr. A. G. Prys-Jones *The Anglo-Welsh Review*, 24.54 (1974), 87; tr. Joseph P. Clancy, *Twentieth Century Welsh Poems*, p. 164.

Individual Translations *Pr.*
'**Sut i Ddewis ac i Drin Gwraig**' (How to Choose and Treat a Wife), tr. Meic Stephens, *Illuminations*, pp. 77–82.

I. D. HOOSON (1880–1948)

Collections

Blodwen Edwards, *Poems*, Vol. I (Denbigh: Gee & Son, 1980).

Blodwen Edwards, *The Wine and Other Poems*, Vol. II (Denbigh: Gee & Son, 1980).

Individual Translations *Po.*
'**Daffodil**', tr. Joseph P. Clancy, *Twentieth Century Welsh Poems*, p. 37; '**Guto Benfelyn**' (Golden-Haired Guto), tr. R. Gerallt Jones, *Poetry of Wales 1930–1970*, p. 19; '**Tanau**' (Fires), tr. Joseph P. Clancy, *Twentieth Century Welsh Poems*, p. 36; '**Y Blodau Melyn**' (The Buttercups), tr. R. Gerallt Jones, *Poetry of Wales 1930–1970*, p. 17; '**Y Brain**' (The Crows), tr. R. Gerallt Jones, *Poetry of Wales 1930–1970*, p. 13; '**Y Dychwel**' (The Return), tr. R. Gerallt Jones, *Poetry of Wales 1930–1970*, p. 15; '**Y Cudyll Coch**' (The Red Kestrel), tr. Joseph P. Clancy, *Twentieth Century Welsh Poems*, pp. 36–7; '**Y Fflam**' (The Flame), tr. H. Idris Bell, *A History of Welsh Literature*, p. 422; tr. Tony Conran, *The Penguin Book of Welsh Verse*, p. 238; tr. Tony Conran, *Welsh Verse*, p. 267; tr. Tony Conran,

Bloodaxe Book, p. 47; '**Y Pabi Coch**' (The Red Poppy), tr. Gillian Clarke, *Bloodaxe Book*, p. 48.

B. T. HOPKINS (1897–1981)

Individual Translations *Po.*
'**Ein Tir**' (Our Land), tr. Gwyn Williams, *To Look for a Word*, p. 254; '**Rhos Helyg**', tr. Joseph P. Clancy, *Twentieth Century Welsh Poems*, pp. 59–60.

JOHN GRUFFYDD MOELWYN HUGHES (1866–1944)

Individual Translations *Po.*
'**Cwyno**' (Complaints), tr. H. Idris Bell and C. C. Bell, *Welsh Poems of the Twentieth Century*, p. 61.

T. ROWLAND HUGHES (1903–49)

Prose (Novels)
Chwalfa, *Out of their Night*, tr. Richard Ruck (Aberystwyth: Gwasg Aberystwyth, 1954).

O Law i Law, *From Hand to Hand*, tr. Richard Ruck (London: Methuen & Co. Ltd, 1950).

William Jones, *William Jones*, tr. Richard Ruck (Aberystwyth: Gwasg Aberystwyth, 1953).

Y Cychwyn, *The Beginning*, tr. Richard Ruck (Llandysul: Gwasg Gomer, 1969).

Yr Ogof, *Joseph of Arimathea*, tr. Richard Ruck (Aberystwyth: Gwasg Aberystwyth, 1961).

Individual Translations *Pr.*
from **Chwalfa** (Thrown into the River), tr. Richard Ruck, *A Book of Wales* (1987), pp. 102–5; tr. Richard Ruck, *The Heart of Wales: An*

Anthology, ed. James A. Davies (Bridgend: Seren, 1994), pp. 120–32; from *O Law i Law* (Cronies), tr. author, *The Welsh Review*, 5.1 (1946), 45–51; (Grinding Poverty), tr. Richard Ruck, *A Book of Wales* (1953), pp. 174–5; (An Old Quarryman), tr. Richard Ruck, *A Book of Wales* (1953), p. 219; tr. Richard Ruck, *The Heart of Wales: An Anthology*, ed. James A. Davies (Bridgend: Seren, 1994), pp. 69–76, 183–5, 200–3, 236–8; from *William Jones* (It's True People make the Place), tr. Richard Ruck, *A Rhondda Anthology* (Bridgend: Seren, 1993), pp. 116–22; from *Y Cychwyn* (A Preaching Debut), tr. Richard Ruck, *Wales: A Celebration*, ed. Dewi Roberts (Llanrwst: Gwasg Carreg Gwalch, 2000), pp. 166–7.

Individual Translations *Po.*
'**Crib Goch**', tr. R. Gerallt Jones, *Poetry of Wales 1930–1970*, p. 149; tr. Gwyn Williams, *To Look for a Word*, p. 237; tr. Catherine Fisher, *Bloodaxe Book*, p. 116; '**Coeden Afalau**' (Apple Tree), tr. Glyn Jones, *Glyn Jones: Collected Poems*, ed. Meic Stephens (Cardiff: University of Wales Press, 1996), p. 232; '**Emyn**' (Hymn), tr. Sally Roberts Jones, *Bloodaxe Book*, p. 115; '**Salem**', tr. Alan Llwyd, *Salem: y llun a'r llan/painting and chapel* (Swansea: Cyhoeddiadau Barddas, 1991), p. 51; tr. Sally Roberts Jones, *Bloodaxe Book*, pp. 116–17; '**Steil**' (Style), tr. Alan Llwyd, *Salem: y llun a'r llan/painting and chapel* (Swansea: Cyhoeddiadau Barddas, 1991), p. 57; '**Y Diwaith**' (The Unemployed), tr. R. Gerallt Jones, *Poetry of Wales 1930–1970*, p. 151.

E. MORGAN HUMPHREYS (1882–1955)

Individual Translations *Pr.*
'**Salem**', tr. Meic Stephens, *A Book of Wales* (1987), pp. 107–8; tr. Meic Stephens, *Illuminations*, pp. 61–3.

DAVID EMRYS JAMES (Dewi Emrys; 1881–1952)

Individual Translations *Po.*
from '**Pwllderi**', tr. Elin ap Hywel, *Bloodaxe Book*, pp. 48–50; '**Y Gorwel**' (The Horizon), tr. Tony Conran, *The Penguin Book of Welsh Verse*, p. 268; tr. Tony Conran, *Welsh Verse*, p. 305; '**Y Pysgotwr Bach**' (The Little Fisherman), tr. H. Idris Bell, *A History of Welsh Literature*, p. 428.

ELDRA JARMAN (1917–2000)

Individual Translations *Po.*
'Catacomb St. Emilion', tr. author, *Poetry Wales*, 9.3 (1973–4), 86–7;
'**Cyferbyniad**' (Contrast), tr. author, *Quaderno 2 di Lettera* (March,
1977), 55; '**Gwastraff**' (A Waste), tr. author, *Poetry Wales*, 10.2 (1974),
104–5; '**Haf Sych, Awst 1976**' (Summer Drought, August 1976), tr.
author, *Quaderno 2 di Lettera* (March, 1977), 59; '**Hydref**' (Autumn),
tr. author, *Poetry Wales*, 9.1 (1973), 58–60; '**O'r Awyren**' (From the
Plane), tr. author, *Poetry Wales*, 10.4 (1975), 76–7; '**Salamis**', tr.
author, *Poetry Wales*, 10.2 (1974), 105–6; '**Yr Hen Gartref**' (The Old
Home), tr. author, *Quaderno 2 di Lettera* (March, 1977), 57.

R. T. JENKINS (1881–1969)

Individual Translations *Pr.*
from **Edrych yn ôl** (A Merry and Delightful Place), tr. Meic
Stephens, *A Cardiff Anthology*, ed. Meic Stephens (Bridgend: Seren,
1987), pp. 31–2; '**Casglu Ffyrdd**' (On Collecting Roads), tr. Meic
Stephens, *Illuminations*, pp. 34–42.

ALUN JEREMIAH JONES (Alun Cilie; 1897–1975)

Individual Translations *Po.*
'**Curyll**' (Kestrel), tr. Joseph P. Clancy, *Twentieth Century Welsh
Poems*, p. 91; '**Yr Hen Gapel**' (The Old Chapel), tr. Joseph P. Clancy,
Twentieth Century Welsh Poems, pp. 91–3; tr. Joseph P. Clancy,
Bloodaxe Book, pp. 91–3.

DAFYDD JONES (Isfoel; 1881–1968)

Individual Translations *Po.*
'**Cywydd y Tractor**' (The Tractor), tr. Joseph P. Clancy, *Trivium*, 8
(1973), 113–14; tr. Joseph P. Clancy, *Twentieth Century Welsh
Poems*, pp. 41–2; tr. Joseph P. Clancy, *Bloodaxe Book*, p. 56;
'**Cywydd Diolch am Eog**' (The Salmon), tr. Joseph P. Clancy,
Twentieth Century Welsh Poems, pp. 42–3.

DAVID JAMES JONES (Gwenallt; 1899–1968)

Collections

Patrick Thomas, *Sensuous Glory: The Poetic Vision of D. Gwenallt Jones* (Norwich: Canterbury Press, 2000).
[*Sensuous Glory*]

Critical Editions

Dyfnallt Morgan, *D. Gwenallt Jones*, Writers of Wales (Cardiff: University of Wales Press, 1972).
[*D. Gwenallt Jones*]

Individual Translations Po.[4]
'**Adar Rhiannon**' (Birds of Rhiannon), tr. D. M. Lloyd, *A Book of Wales* (1953), pp. 254–5; '**Anllygredigaeth**' (Incorruption), tr. Keidrych Rhys, *Wales*, 4 (1944), 33; '**Beddargraff Amaethwr**' (On a Farmer), tr. H. Idris Bell, *The Welsh Review*, 5.2 (1946), 117; '**Ceiliog y Gwynt**' (The Weathercock), tr. Aneirin Talfan Davies, *Province*, 3.3 (1952), 81; '**Cip**' (A Glimpse), tr. Joseph P. Clancy, *Twentieth Century Welsh Poems*, p. 101; '**Colomennod**' (Pigeons), tr. B. S. Johnson and Ned Thomas, *Planet*, 29 (1975), 19; tr. Joseph P. Clancy, *Twentieth Century Welsh Poems*, p. 99; '**Cymru**' ['Er mor annheilwng ydwyt ti o'n serch'] (Wales), tr. H. Idris Bell, *Wales*, 5.7 (1945), 19; '**Cymru**' ['Gwlad grefyddol gysurus oedd hi'] (Wales), tr. Ceri Davies, *Welsh Literature and the Classical Tradition* (Cardiff: University of Wales Press, 1995), p. 143; '**Cymru**' ['Paham y rhoddaist inni'r tristwch hwn'] (Wales), tr. Joseph P. Clancy, *Twentieth Century Welsh Poems*, p. 95; tr. Joseph P. Clancy, *Bloodaxe Book*, pp. 94–5; *from* '**Cymru a'r Rhyfel**' (Wales and the War), tr. H. Idris Bell, *A History of Welsh Literature*, p. 417; '**Cymdogion**' (Neighbours), tr. B. S. Johnson and Ned Thomas, *Planet*, 29 (1975), 23; '**Dartmoor**',

---

[4] It would be wise to remind readers again that, with the exception of a small selection printed separately here, individual translations within collections of translations of Gwenallt's poems are not listed. It should therefore be borne in mind that there are several additional translations within the collections.

tr. Tony Conran, *The Penguin Book of Welsh Verse*, p. 251; tr. Emyr Humphreys, *Planet*, 43 (1978), 17–23; tr. Tony Conran, *Welsh Verse*, p. 280; tr. Emyr Humphreys, *Emyr Humphreys: Collected Poems* (Cardiff: University of Wales Press, 1999), p. 134; tr. Emyr Humphreys, *Bloodaxe Book*, p. 93; '**Dyn**' (Man), tr. H. Idris Bell, *Wales*, 6.22 (1946), 9; tr. H. Idris Bell, *Dock Leaves*, 4.10 (1953), 37; '**F. R. Könekamp**', tr. Tony Conran, *Planet*, 58 (1986), 27–9; tr. Tony Conran, *Welsh Verse*, pp. 284–5; '**Hen Ferch**' (An Old Woman), tr. H. Idris Bell, *The Welsh Review*, 5.2 (1946), 119; tr. H. Idris Bell, *Oxford Book*, p. 204; '**Iwdas Isgariot**' (Judas Iscariot), tr. R. Gerallt Jones, *Poetry of Wales 1930–1970*, p. 105; '**Morgannwg**' (Glamorgan), tr. B. S. Johnson and Ned Thomas, *Planet*, 29 (1975), 21; '**Oberammergau**', tr. Tony Conran, *Welsh Verse*, pp. 282–4; '**Pantycelyn**', tr. R. Gerallt Jones, *Poetry of Wales 1930–1970*, p. 111; tr. Joseph P. Clancy, *Twentieth Century Welsh Poems*, p. 95; '**Rhiannon**', tr. R. Gerallt Jones, *Poetry of Wales 1930–1970*, p. 95; '**Rygbi**' (Rugby), tr. B. S. Johnson and Ned Thomas, *Planet*, 29 (1975), 21; '**Testament yr Asyn**' (A Donkey's Last Will and Testament), tr. E. Glanffrwd James, *Wales*, 5.8/9 (1945), 61; *from* '**Trychineb Aber-fan**' (Aberfan), tr. Bryan Aspden, *The Anglo-Welsh Review*, 86 (1987), 68–9; '**Sir Gaerfyrddin**' (Carmarthenshire), tr. Joseph P. Clancy, *Twentieth Century Welsh Poems*, p. 96; '**Sir Forgannwg**' (Glamorgan), tr. B. S. Johnson and Ned Thomas, *Planet*, 29 (1975), 21; tr. Joseph P. Clancy, *Twentieth Century Welsh Poems*, p. 96; '**Sir Forgannwg a Sir Gaerfyrddin**' (Glamorgan and Carmarthenshire), tr. B. S. Johnson and Ned Thomas, *Planet*, 29 (1975), 22; tr. Ned Thomas and B. S. Johnson, *A Book of Wales* (1987), pp. 136–7; tr. Ned Thomas and B. S. Johnson, *Wales: A Celebration*, ed. Dewi Roberts (Llanrwst: Gwasg Carreg Gwalch, 2000), pp. 165–6; '**Swper yr Arglwydd**' (The Lord's Supper), tr. R. Gerallt Jones, *Poetry of Wales 1930–1970*, p. 113; '**Wal yr Wylofain**' (The Wailing Wall), tr. Grahame Davies, *The Chosen People: Wales & The Jews*, ed. Grahame Davies (Bridgend: Seren, 2002), pp. 74–5; '**Y Beddau**' (Graves), tr. B. S. Johnson and Ned Thomas, *Planet*, 29 (1975), 19–23; '**Y Ddaear**' (The Earth), tr. Dyfnallt Morgan, *Oxford Book*, pp. 200–1; '**Y Dirwasgiad**' (The Depression), tr. Tony Conran, *Poetry Wales*, 2.3 (1966), 14; tr. B. S. Johnson and Ned Thomas, *Planet*, 29 (1975), 22; tr. Tony Conran, *The Penguin Book of Welsh Verse*, p. 253; tr. Joseph P. Clancy, *Twentieth Century Welsh Poems*, pp. 98–9; tr. Tony Conran, *Welsh Verse*, pp. 281–2; tr. Tony Conran, *Bloodaxe Book*, 97–8; '**Y Draenog**'

(The Hedgehog), tr. Joseph P. Clancy, *Twentieth Century Welsh Poems*, p. 102; tr. Joseph P. Clancy, *Bloodaxe Book*, p. 97; 'Y Genedl' (The Nation), tr. Joseph P. Clancy, *Twentieth Century Welsh Poems*, p. 104; 'Y Sarff' (The Serpent), tr. Emyr Humphreys, *Emyr Humphreys: Collected Poems* (Cardiff: University of Wales Press, 1999), p. 22; 'Y Wal Wylofus' (The Wall of Wailing), tr. Grahame Davies, *The Chosen People: Wales & The Jews*, ed. Grahame Davies (Bridgend: Seren, 2002), p. 102; 'Yr Alarch' (The Swan), tr. Joseph P. Clancy, *Twentieth Century Welsh Poems*, pp. 102–3; 'Yr Eglwys' (The Church), tr. Joseph P. Clancy, *Twentieth Century Welsh Poems*, p. 94; 'Yr Eglwysi' (The Churches), tr. R. Gerallt Jones, *Poetry of Wales 1930–1970*, p. 103; 'Yr Esgob William Morgan' (Bishop William Morgan), tr. Joseph P. Clancy, *Twentieth Century Welsh Poems*, p. 103; 'Yr Hen Emynau' (The Old Hymns), tr. Bryan Martin Davies, *Poetry Wales*, 11.3 (1976), 80; tr. Joseph P. Clancy, *Twentieth Century Welsh Poems*, pp. 104–5.

Selection

Ar Gyfeiliorn (Adrift)
Aneirin Talfan Davies, *Cymry'r Groes*, 2.4 (1949), 120–1; Dyfnallt Morgan, *D. Gwenallt Jones*, pp. 14–15; R. Gerallt Jones, *Poetry of Wales 1930–1970*, p. 101; Joseph P. Clancy, *Twentieth Century Welsh Poems*, pp. 96–7; Patrick Thomas, *Sensuous Glory*, pp. 149–50; Joseph P. Clancy, *Bloodaxe Book*, p. 94.

Cymru ['Gorwedd llwch holl saint yr oesoedd'] (Wales)
R. O. F. Wynne, *Wales*, 6.3 (1946), 15; D. M. Lloyd, *A Book of Wales* (1953), pp. 269–70; William Cranfield [Waldo Williams], *Dock Leaves*, 6.17 (1955), 10–11; Sian Edwards, *Awen: Detholiad o Lenyddiaeth Fuddugol Eisteddfod Ryng-Golegol Prifysgol Cymru* (1970), pp. 20–1; Gwyn Jones, *Oxford Book*, pp. 201–2; Patrick Thomas, *Sensuous Glory*, pp. 98–9.

Pechod (Sin)
Dyfnallt Morgan, *D. Gwenallt Jones*, pp. 18–19; Gwyn Williams, *To Look for a Word*, p. 248; Joseph P. Clancy, *Twentieth Century Welsh Poems*, p. 94; R. Glyn Jones, *Barddas*, 192 (1993), 12; Patrick Thomas, *Sensuous Glory*, p. 147; Joseph P. Clancy, *Bloodaxe Book*, p. 95.

Rhydcymerau
Tony Conran, *Poetry Wales*, 1.2 (1965), 13; Tony Conran, *The Penguin Book of Welsh Verse*, pp. 254–5; R. Gerallt Jones, *Poetry of Wales 1930–1970*, pp. 107–9; Joseph P. Clancy, *Twentieth Century Welsh Poems*, pp. 100–1; Tony Conran, *Oxford Book*, pp. 199–200; Tony Conran, *Welsh Verse*, pp. 285–6; Tony Conran, *A Book of Wales* (1987), pp. 135–6; Leslie Norris, *Leslie Norris: Collected Poems* (Bridgend: Seren, 1996), pp. 116–17; Patrick Thomas, *Sensuous Glory*, pp. 114–15; Tony Conran, *Bloodaxe Book*, pp. 95–6.

Y Meirwon (The Dead)
Tony Conran, *Poetry Wales*, 1.2 (1965), 12; Tony Conran, *The Penguin Book of Welsh Verse*, pp. 251–2; Joseph P. Clancy, *Trivium*, 8 (1973), 112–13; R. Gerallt Jones, *Poetry of Wales 1930–1970*, pp. 97–9; Joseph P. Clancy, *Twentieth Century Welsh Poems*, pp. 97–8; B. S. Johnson and Ned Thomas, *Planet*, 29 (1975), 20; B. S. Johnson and Ned Thomas, *Profiles* (1980), pp. 74–5; Tony Conran, *Welsh Verse*, pp. 280–1; Joseph P. Clancy, *A Book of Wales* (1987), pp. 134–5; Leslie Norris, *Leslie Norris: Collected Poems* (Bridgend: Seren, 1996), p. 78; Patrick Thomas, *Sensuous Glory*, pp. 135–6; Tony Conran, *Bloodaxe Book*, pp. 98–9.

Individual Translations *Pr.*
Credaf (What I Believe), tr. André Morgan and Ned Thomas, *Planet*, 32 (1976), 1–10; tr. Meic Stephens, *Illuminations*, pp. 46–9; *from* **Plasau'r Brenin** (Mansions of the King), tr. Grahame Davies, *The Chosen People: Wales & The Jews*, ed. Grahame Davies (Bridgend: Seren, 2002), pp. 185–8.

GWILYM R. JONES (1903–93)

Individual Translations *Po.*
'**Ar Gofeb Rhyfel Ysgol Dyffryn Nantlle**' (On Dyffryn Nantlle School War Memorial), tr. R. Gerallt Jones, *Poetry of Wales 1930–1970*, p. 163; ''**Does Dim Rheswm**' (There is no Reason), tr. Gilbert Ruddock, *Quaderno 2 di Lettera* (March, 1977), 63; '**Offeren Berlioz**' (Mass by Berlioz), tr. Gilbert Ruddock, *Quaderno 2 di Lettera* (March, 1977), 61; '**Salm i'r Creaduriaid**' (Psalm to the Creatures), tr. Joseph P. Clancy, *Twentieth Century Welsh Poems*,

p. 120; tr. Joseph P. Clancy, *Oxford Book*, pp. 213–4; 'Y **Barcut**' (The Kite), tr. Gilbert Ruddock, *Quaderno 2 di Lettera* (March, 1977), 65; '**Y Ceiliog Gwynt**' (The Weathercock), tr. R. Gerallt Jones, *Poetry of Wales 1930–1970*, p. 161; *from* '**Y Ffatri Atomig**' (The Atomic Factory) ['**Cwm Tawelwch**' (The Quiet Valley)], tr. Catherine Fisher, *Bloodaxe Book*, pp. 117–19; '**Yr Hen Wynebau**' (The Old, Familiar Faces), tr. R. Gerallt Jones, *Poetry of Wales 1930–1970*, pp. 165–7.

Individual Translations *Pr.*
'**Wrth Dorri Barf**' (While Shaving), tr. Meic Stephens, *Illuminations*, pp. 138–41.

JENNIE JONES (b. 1903)

Prose
Tomos o Enlli, *Tomos of Bardsey by Jennie Jones*, tr. R. S. Thomas (MS in private collection).[5]

JOHN GWILYM JONES (1904–88)

Prose (Novel)
Y Goeden Eirin, *The Plum Tree*, tr. Meic Stephens (Bridgend: Seren Classics, 2004).

Individual Translations *Pr.*
'**Y Briodas**' (The Wedding), tr. Islwyn Ffowc Elis, *Twenty-Five Welsh Short Stories*, pp. 13–21; '**Y Goeden Eirin**' (The Plum Tree), tr. Elan Closs Stephens, *A Book of Wales* (1987), pp. 153–7.

---

[5] Reference in Jason Walford Davies, *Gororau'r Iaith: R. S. Thomas a'r Traddodiad Llenyddol Cymraeg* (Cardiff: University of Wales Press, 2003), p. 108. It is noted there also that a new translation by Gwen Robson, *Tomos o Enlli/Tomos the Islandman* has recently been published (Gwasg Carreg Gwalch: 1999). However, as this is not strictly literary prose it has only been recorded because of the interest in the earlier translator.

J. R. JONES (1911–70)

Individual Translations *Pr.*
'Gwaedd yng Nghymru' (Your Country Leaving You), tr. Meic
Stephens, *A Book of Wales* (1987), p. 157.

J. T. JONES (1894–1975)

Individual Translations *Po.*
'Clai' (Clay), tr. H. Idris Bell, *Welsh Poetry of the Twentieth Century
in English*, p. 50; 'Englyn', tr. Harri Webb, *Harri Webb: Collected
Poems* (Llandysul: Gomer, 1995), p. 334.

MOSES GLYN JONES (1913–94)

Individual Translations *Po.*
'Pry'r Gannwyll' (The Candle's Fly), tr. Mike Jenkins, *Bloodaxe
Book*, pp. 160–1; 'Mesurydd Tywod Amser' (Sand-time Measuring),
tr. Mike Jenkins, *Bloodaxe Book*, pp. 161–2; 'Y Ffynnon Fyw' (The
Living Spring), tr. Mike Jenkins, *Bloodaxe Book*, p. 160; 'Y Goleuni
Hen' (The Old Light), tr. Mike Jenkins, *Bloodaxe Book*, p. 159.

R. GERALLT JONES (1934–99)

Prose (Novel)
Triptych, tr. author (Llandysul: Gomer, 2001).

Individual Translations *Pr.*
'O Arfon i Loegr i Fôn' (Disenchantment), tr. Meic Stephens,
Illuminations, pp. 92–4; 'Y Llythyr' (The Letter), tr. author, *Twenty-
Five Welsh Short Stories*, pp. 55–61; tr. author, *Short Stories from
Wales*, selected and introduced by David Elias (Wheaton: 1978), pp.
14–19; tr. author, *A Book of Wales* (1987), pp. 162–6.

Individual Translations *Po.*[6]

'**Ar Fynydd Rhiw**' (On Rhiw Mountain), tr. author, *Poetry Wales*, 16.3 (1981), 26–7; '**Balŵn Las uwch y Sgwâr Coch**' (A Blue Balloon over Red Square), tr. author, *Modern Poetry in Translation*, pp. 67–8; '**Beirdd Canol Oed**' (Middle-aged Poets), tr. author, *Modern Poetry in Translation*, pp. 71–2; '**Bu Farw'r Llwynog**' (The Fox Died), tr. author, *Poetry of Wales 1930–1970*, p. 377; '**Cardotyn**' (The Beggar), tr. Joseph P. Clancy, *Transactions of the Honourable Society of Cymmrodorion*, 1 (1994), 114; tr. Joseph P. Clancy, *Other Words*, pp. 78–9; '**Cynhebrwng yn Llŷn**' (A Funeral in Llŷn), tr. author, *Poetry of Wales 1930–1970*, pp. 379–81; tr. Joseph P. Clancy, *Twentieth Century Welsh Poems*, pp. 210–11; tr. Joseph P. Clancy, *Writing the Wind: A Celtic Resurgence*, ed. Thomas Raine Crowe with Gwendal Denez and Tom Hubbard (United States: New Native Press, 1997), pp. 32–3; '**Gwyddau yng Ngregynog**' (Geese at Gregynog), tr. author, *Modern Poetry in Translation*, pp. 68–9; tr. Joseph P. Clancy, *Gwyddau yng Ngregynog: Geese at Gregynog* (Newtown: Gwasg Gregynog, 2000); tr. author, *Bloodaxe Book*, p. 241; '**I Derek Walcott, wrth Ddarllen ei Gerddi**' (To Derek Walcott), tr. author, *Bloodaxe Book*, p. 243; '**I Ewan MacLachlan**' (For Ewan McLachlan), tr. author, *Modern Poetry in Translation*, p. 70; tr. Joseph P. Clancy, *Writing the Wind*, pp. 33–4; tr. author, *Bloodaxe Book*, p. 240; '**Jarlshof, Shetland**' (Shetland), tr. author, *Writing the Wind: A Celtic Resurgence*, ed. Thomas Raine Crowe with Gwendal Denez and Tom Hubbard (United States: New Native Press, 1997), p. 35; '**Llwybr yr Afon**' (The Riverside Path), tr. author, *Modern Poetry in Translation*, pp. 69–70; '**Offeiriad Gwlad**' (Country Parson), tr. author, *Writing the Wind: A Celtic Resurgence*, ed. Thomas Raine Crowe with Gwendal Denez and Tom Hubbard (United States: New Native Press, 1997), p. 36; '**Yasnaya Polyana**', tr. Robert Minhinnick, *Bloodaxe Book*, pp. 242–3; '**Y Gwrandawr**' (The Listener), tr. author, *Poetry of Wales 1930–1970*, pp. 383–5; tr. Joseph P. Clancy, *Twentieth Century Welsh Poems*, pp. 209–10; '**Y Nyrs**' (The Nurse), tr. author, *Poetry of Wales 1930–1970*, p. 387; tr. Robert Minhinnick, *Bloodaxe Book*, p. 244.

---

[6] There are two additional translations of poems R. Gerallt Jones entitled (in English) 'Hillfort in Llŷn', tr. author, *Modern Poetry in Translation*, p. 71; and 'The Preacher', tr. author, *Writing the Wind*, p. 34. I have been unable to locate the source texts from collections of the poet's work or periodical research.

ROWLAND JONES (Rolant o Fôn; 1909–62)

Individual Translations *Po.*
'**Ewyn**' (Foam), tr. Tony Conran, *The Penguin Book of Welsh Verse*, p. 266; tr. Tony Conran, *Welsh Verse*, p. 303; tr. Tony Conran, *World Poetry: An Anthology of Verse from Antiquity to our Time*, ed. Katharine Washburn and John S. Major (New York; London: Norton, 1998), p. 1068.[7]

T. GWYNN JONES (1871–1949)

Individual Translations *Po.*[8]
'**Argoed**', tr. Tony Conran, *The Penguin Book of Welsh Verse*, pp. 230–6; tr. Joseph P. Clancy, *Twentieth Century Welsh Poems*, pp. 16–21; tr. Tony Conran, *Oxford Book*, pp. 146–52; tr. Tony Conran, *Welsh Verse*, pp. 260–6; tr. Tony Conran, *A Book of Wales* (1987), pp. 168–9; tr. Tony Conran, *Bloodaxe Book*, pp. 31–6; '**Atgof**' ['Wele nos welw yn nesu . . .'] (Memory), tr. H. Idris Bell, *Poems from the Welsh*, p. 33; '**Atgof: I W. J. G. Ar fwrdd llong adeg rhyfel**' (To W. J. Gruffydd Serving the Fleet in War-time), tr. H. Idris Bell, *Welsh Poems of the Twentieth Century*, p. 9; tr. H. Idris Bell, *A Celtic Anthology*, pp. 313–14; '**Awr Ferr**' (One Hour), tr. H. Idris Bell, *Poems from the Welsh*, p. 57; '**Broséliâwnd**', tr. Joseph P. Clancy, *Twentieth Century Welsh Poems*, pp. 13–15; '**Cân y Medd**' (Song of the Mead), tr. Gwyn Williams, *Planet*, 1 (1970), 42–25; tr. Gwyn Williams, *To Look for a Word*, p. 266; '**Cynddilig**', tr. Joseph P. Clancy, *Twentieth Century Welsh Poems*, pp. 21–33; '**Daear a Nef**' (Earth and Heaven), tr. H. Idris Bell, *Welsh Poems of the Twentieth Century*, p. 64; '**Dafydd ab Edmwnd**', tr. A. P. Graves, *The Nationalist*, 3.30 (1910), 9 and cont. 39; tr. H. Idris Bell, *Welsh Poems of the Twentieth Century*, p. 25; tr. A. P. Graves, *Welsh Poetry Old and New*, pp. 110–1; *from* '**Dynoliaeth**' (Humanity), tr. Gillian Clarke, *Bloodaxe Book*, pp. 40–4; '**Hwyr yn yr Hydref**' (An Autumn

---

[7] This is the only inclusion of modern Welsh poetry in this anthology.
[8] There is an additional translation of a poem by T. Gwynn Jones entitled (in English) 'A Summer Evening in War-Time', tr. H. Idris Bell, *Welsh Poems of the Twentieth Century*, p. 8. I have been unable to locate the source text from collections of the poet's work or periodical research.

Evening), tr. H. Idris Bell, *Welsh Poems of the Twentieth Century*, p. 40; '**Madog**', tr. Joseph P. Clancy, *Twentieth Century Welsh Poems*, pp. 3–12; '**Môr y Nos**' (Night on the Sea), tr. H. Idris Bell, *Poems from the Welsh*, p. 33; '**Nyth Gwag**' (The Empty Nest at Bro Gynin), tr. H. Idris Bell, *Welsh Poems of the Twentieth Century*, pp. 22–5; '**Penmon**', tr. Joseph P. Clancy, *Twentieth Century Welsh Poems*, pp. 1–3; tr. Joseph P. Clancy, *An Anglesey Anthology*, ed. Dewi Roberts (Gwasg Carreg Gwalch, 1999), pp. 40–2; *from* '**Pro Patria**', tr. Elin ap Hywel, *Bloodaxe Book*, pp. 36–9; '**Senghennydd**', tr. H. Idris Bell, *Welsh Poems of the Twentieth Century*, p. 42; tr. Gwyn Williams, *To Look for a Word*, p. 225; '**Telyn y Dydd**' (Remembrance), tr. Elined Prys, *The Welsh Outlook*, 2.2 (1924), 53; '**Y Bedd**' (The Grave), tr. H. Idris Bell, *The Welsh Outlook*, 1 (1914), 30; tr. H. Idris Bell, *Welsh Poems of the Twentieth Century*, p. 62; tr. Ernest Rhys, *A Celtic Anthology*, pp. 320–1; tr. H. Idris Bell, *A History of Welsh Literature*, p. 385; '**Y Fraint**' (The Privilege), tr. R. Gerallt Jones, *Poetry of Wales 1930–1970*, pp. 7–9; '**Y Gennad**' (The Messenger), tr. H. Idris Bell, *Welsh Poems of the Twentieth Century*, p. 38; tr. Abon, *The Welsh Outlook*, 12.8 (1925), 224; '**Y Saig**' (The Dish), tr. R. Gerallt Jones, *Poetry of Wales 1930–1970*, p. 5, tr. Tony Conran, *Bloodaxe Book*, pp. 39–40; *from* '**Ymadawiad Arthur**' (Arthur's Passing), tr. D. M. Lloyd, *A Book of Wales* (1953), pp. 265–6; tr. Tony Conran, *Welsh Verse*, pp. 257–60; '**Yr Haint**' (The Plague), tr. R. Gerallt Jones, *Poetry of Wales 1930–1970*, p. 3; '**Ystrad Fflur**' (Strata Florida), tr. Edwin Stanley James, *Wales*, 5.7 (1945), 19; tr. Alun Llywelyn-Williams, *Presenting Welsh Poetry*, p. 61; tr. Gwyn Williams, *To Look for a Word*, p. 227; tr. Joseph P. Clancy, *Twentieth Century Welsh Poems*, p. 13; tr. Joseph P. Clancy, *A Book of Wales* (1987), p. 169; tr. Rowan Williams, *After Silent Centuries* (Oxford: The Perpetua Press, 1994), p. 47; tr. Glyn Jones, *Glyn Jones: Collected Poems*, ed. Meic Stephens (Cardiff: University of Wales Press, 1996), p. 229.

Individual Translations *Pr.*
'**Gwas**' (Old Dent), tr. Meic Stephens, *Illuminations*, pp. 31–4.

T. HUGHES JONES (1895–1966)

Individual Translations *Pr.*
'Sgweier Hafila' (The Squire of Havilah), tr. T. Glynne Davies, *The Penguin Book of Welsh Short Stories*, pp. 186–216.

WILLIAM JONES (1896–1961)

Individual Translations *Po.*
'Y Llanc Ifanc o Lŷn (Young Fellow from Llŷn), tr. Harri Webb, *Triad: thirty three poems by Peter Griffith, Harri Webb, Meic Stephens* (Merthyr Tydfil: The Triskel Press, 1963), p. 51; tr. Harri Webb, *A Book of Wales* (1987), p. 171; tr. Harri Webb, *Harri Webb: Collected Poems* (Llandysul: Gomer, 1995), pp. 64–5; '**Adar Rhiannon**' (The Birds of Rhiannon), tr. Harri Webb, *Harri Webb: Collected Poems* (Llandysul: Gomer, 1995), pp. 302–8.

ALUN T. LEWIS (1905–89)

Individual Translations *Pr.*
'Perthnasau' (Relatives), tr. Hywel Teifi Edwards, *The New Penguin Book of Welsh Short Stories*, pp. 175–8.

SAUNDERS LEWIS (1893–1985)

Prose (Novel)
Monica, tr. Meic Stephens (Bridgend: Seren Books, 1997).

Collections

Plays
The Plays of Saunders Lewis Vol. I, tr. Joseph P. Clancy (Llandybie: Christopher Davies, 1985).
The Plays of Saunders Lewis Vol. II, tr. Joseph P. Clancy (Llandybie: Christopher Davies, 1985).

The Plays of Saunders Lewis Vol. III, tr. Joseph P. Clancy (Llandybie: Christopher Davies, 1985).
The Plays of Saunders Lewis Vol. IV, tr. Joseph P. Clancy (Llandybie: Christopher Davies, 1986).

Siwan, Plays of the Year, Vol. 21, tr. Emyr Humphreys (London: Elek Books, 1961), pp. 113–86.

Poetry
Joseph P. Clancy, *Selected Poems: Saunders Lewis* (Cardiff: University of Wales Press, 1993).
[*Selected Poems*]

Critical Editions[9]

Alun R. Jones and Gwyn Thomas (eds), *Presenting Saunders Lewis* (Cardiff: University of Wales Press, 1983).
[*Presenting Saunders Lewis*]

Harri Pritchard Jones, *Saunders Lewis: A Presentation of his Work* (Springfield, Illinois: Templegate Publishers, 1990).
[*Saunders Lewis: A Presentation*]

Individual Translations *Plays*
Amlyn ac Amig (Amis and Amile), tr. H. Idris Bell, *The Welsh Review*, 7.4 (1948), 232–55; tr. Tony Conran, *The Vow*, Radio 3 play (unpublished, 1988); *from* **Buchedd Garmon** (The Life of Garmon), tr. D. M. Lloyd, *A Book of Wales* (1953), pp. 37–8, 267–9; tr. D. M. Lloyd, *A Book of Wales* (1987), pp. 177–9; tr. D. M. Lloyd, *Wales: A Celebration*, ed. Dewi Roberts (Llanrwst: Gwasg Carreg Gwalch, 2000), pp. 135–6; tr. D. M. Lloyd, *Bloodaxe Book*, pp. 77–8; *from* **Esther**, tr. Grahame Davies, *The Chosen People: Wales & The Jews*, ed. Grahame Davies (Bridgend: Seren, 2002), pp. 32–4; *from* **Siwan**, tr. R. M. Jones, *Highlights in Welsh Literature: Talks with a Prince*

---

[9] These critical editions also include some seminal cultural, political and religious writings (and broadcasts) that shaped the intellectual climate of twentieth-century Wales.

(Llandybie: Christopher Davies, 1969), pp. 109–16; tr. R. Gerallt Jones, *Poetry of Wales 1930–1970*, pp. 89–91.

Individual Translations *Po.*
'**Awdl i'w Ras, Archesgob Caerdydd**' (Ode to his Grace the Archbishop of Cardiff), tr. Tony Conran, *Welsh Verse*, pp. 278–9; tr. Harri Pritchard Jones, *Materion Dwyieithog: Bilingual Matters*, 3 (1991), 7; tr. Harri Pritchard Jones, *Transactions of the Honourable Society of Cymmrodorion* (1993), 132; '**Emmäws**' (Emmaus), tr. R. Gerallt Jones, *Poetry of Wales 1930–1970*, p. 73; tr. Harri Pritchard Jones, *Transactions of the Honourable Society of Cymmrodorion* (1993), 131–2; '**Et Homo Factus Est. Crucifixus . . .**', tr. Joseph P. Clancy, *Twentieth Century Welsh Poems*, p. 88; tr. Joseph P. Clancy, *Bloodaxe Book*, pp. 84–5; '**Gweddi'r Terfyn**' (Prayer at the End), tr. Harri Pritchard Jones, *Transactions of the Honourable Society of Cymmrodorion* (1993), 137; tr. Joseph P. Clancy, *Bloodaxe Book*, p. 86; '**I'r Sagrafen Fendigaid**' (To the Blessed Sacrament), tr. Joseph P. Clancy, *Twentieth Century Welsh Poems*, pp. 81–2; tr. Harri Pritchard Jones, *Transactions of the Honourable Society of Cymmrodorion* (1993), 133; '**Mabon**', R. Gerallt Jones, *Poetry of Wales 1930–1970*, p. 81; '**Plentyn Siawns**' (Chance Child), tr. Joseph P. Clancy, *Planet*, 61 (1987), 92; tr. Joseph P. Clancy, *Bloodaxe Book*, pp. 85–6; '**Pregeth Olaf Dewi Sant**' (St David's Last Sermon), tr. Joseph P. Clancy, *Planet*, 97 (1993), 47–9; '**Y Dewis**' (The Choice), tr. Robert Wynne, *Wales*, 5, 8 & 9 (1945), 84; tr. Joseph P. Clancy, *Twentieth Century Welsh Poems*, p. 81; '**Y Saer**' (The Carpenter), tr. Harri Pritchard Jones, *Transactions of the Honourable Society of Cymmrodorion* (1993), 130–1.

Selection

Difiau Dyrchafael (Ascension Thursday)
Tony Conran, *The Penguin Book of Welsh Verse*, pp. 249–50; Gwyn Williams, *Planet*, 14 (1972), 34–46; R. Gerallt Jones, *Poetry of Wales 1930–1970*, p. 71; Gwyn Williams, *To Look for a Word*, p. 245; Joseph P. Clancy, *Twentieth Century Welsh Poems*, p. 87; Gwyn Thomas, *Oxford Book*, p. 188; Gwyn Thomas, *Presenting Saunders Lewis*, pp. 190–1; Tony Conran, *Welsh Verse*, p. 279; Joseph P. Clancy, *A Book of Wales* (1987), p. 179; Harri Pritchard Jones,

Saunders Lewis: A Presentation, p. 104; Greg Hill, *Materion Dwyieithog: Bilingual Matters*, 3 (1991), 8; Joseph P. Clancy, *Selected Poems*, p. 35; Gwyn Williams, *Bloodaxe Book*, p. 82.

Golygfa mewn Café (Café Scene)
Gwyn Williams, *Presenting Welsh Poetry*, pp. 64–5; Gwyn Williams, *To Look for a Word*, pp. 246–7; Joseph P. Clancy, *Twentieth Century Welsh Poems*, p. 79; Gwyn Thomas, *Presenting Saunders Lewis*, pp. 180–1; Joseph P. Clancy, *Selected Poems*, p. 4; Grahame Davies, *The Chosen People: Wales & The Jews*, ed. Grahame Davies (Bridgend: Seren, 2002), pp. 166–7; Joseph P. Clancy, *Bloodaxe Book*, pp. 78–9.

Haf Bach Mihangel 1941 (Saint Michael's Summer 1941)
Emyr Humphreys, *Planet*, 43 (1978), 17–23; Joseph P. Clancy, *Twentieth Century Welsh Poems*, pp. 80–1; Gwyn Thomas, *Presenting Saunders Lewis*, pp. 185–6; Joseph P. Clancy, *Selected Poems*, pp. 19–20; Emyr Humphreys, *Emyr Humphreys: Collected Poems* (Cardiff: University of Wales Press, 1999), pp. 132–33.

I'r Lleidr Da (To the Good Thief)
Robert Wynne, *Wales*, 5, 8/9 (1945), 83; Joseph P. Clancy, *Twentieth Century Welsh Poems*, p. 78; Gwyn Thomas, *Oxford Book*, pp. 187–8; Gwyn Thomas, *Presenting Saunders Lewis*, pp. 184–5; Harri Pritchard Jones, *Saunders Lewis: A Presentation*, pp. 94–5; Harri Pritchard Jones, *Transactions of the Honourable Society of Cymmrodorion* (1993), 129; Joseph P. Clancy, *Selected Poems*, p. 9.

Mair Fadlen (Mary Magdalene)
R. Gerallt Jones, *Poetry of Wales 1930–1970*, pp. 75–9; Joseph P. Clancy, *Twentieth Century Welsh Poems*, pp. 85–7; Gwyn Thomas, *Oxford Book*, pp. 185–7; Gwyn Thomas, *Presenting Saunders Lewis*, pp. 191–3; Harri Pritchard Jones, *Saunders Lewis: A Presentation*, pp. 95–7; Joseph P. Clancy, *Selected Poems*, pp. 23–5; Joseph P. Clancy, *Bloodaxe Book*, pp. 82–4.

Marwnad Syr John Edward Lloyd (Elegy for Sir John Edward Lloyd)
Leonard Owen, *Transactions of the Honourable Society of Cymmrodorion* (1962), 165–7; R. Gerallt Jones, *Poetry of Wales 1930–1970*, pp. 83–7; Gwyn Williams, *To Look for a Word*, pp.

242–4; Joseph P. Clancy, *Twentieth Century Welsh Poems*, pp. 83–5; Gwyn Thomas, *Presenting Saunders Lewis*, pp. 186–9; Joseph P. Clancy, *Selected Poems*, pp. 31–3.

Y Dilyw 1939 (The Deluge 1939)

Tony Conran, *Poetry Wales*, 2.1 (1966), 19; Tony Conran, *The Penguin Book of Welsh Verse*, pp. 246–9; Joseph P. Clancy, *Twentieth Century Welsh Poems*, pp. 75–7; Gwyn Thomas, *Oxford Book*, pp. 182–4; Tony Conran, *The Valleys*, ed. John Davies and Mike Jenkins (Poetry Wales Press, 1984), p. 42; Gwyn Thomas, *Presenting Saunders Lewis*, pp. 177–9; Tony Conran, *Welsh Verse*, pp. 274–7; Gwyn Thomas, *A Book of Wales* (1987), pp. 177–8; Joseph P. Clancy, *Selected Poems*, pp. 10–12; Emyr Humphreys, *Emyr Humphreys: Collected Poems* (Cardiff: University of Wales Press, 1999), p. 131; Tony Conran, *Bloodaxe Book*, pp. 79–81.

Y Pîn (The Pine)

Joseph P. Clancy, *Twentieth Century Welsh Poems*, p. 82; Gwyn Thomas, *Oxford Book*, p. 189; Gwyn Thomas, *Presenting Saunders Lewis*, p. 190; Greg Hill, *Materion Dwyieithog: Bilingual Matters*, 3 (1991), 10; Joseph P. Clancy, *Selected Poems*, p. 3.

Individual Translations *Pr.*
'**Weblai a St. Emilion**' (Weobley and St. Emilion), tr. Meic Stephens, *Illuminations*, pp. 25–8.

D. TECWYN LLOYD (E. H. Francis Thomas; 1914–92)

Individual Translations *Pr.*
'**Bore Da, Lloyd**' (Good Morning, Lloyd), tr. Meic Stephens, *Illuminations*, pp. 156–62.

ALUN LLYWELYN-WILLIAMS (1913–88)

Collections

Joseph P. Clancy, *The Light in the Gloom: Poems and Prose by Alun Llywelyn-Williams* (Denbigh: Gee & Son, 1998).

Individual Translations *Po.*
'**Acer o Dir**' (An Acre of Land), tr. Joseph P. Clancy, *Twentieth Century Welsh Poems*, p. 179; '**Ar Ymweliad**' (On a Visit), tr. R. Gerallt Jones, *Poetry of Wales 1930–1970*, pp. 273–7; tr. Joseph P. Clancy, *Twentieth Century Welsh Poems*, pp. 167–9; tr. R. S. Thomas, *Modern Poetry in Translation*, pp. 157–9; tr. Joseph P. Clancy, *Bloodaxe Book*, pp. 163–5; '**Bardd y Byd Sydd Ohoni**' (The Poet of the World as it is), tr. Joseph P. Clancy, *Twentieth Century Welsh Poems*, p. 172; '**Dadrith Doe neu Cofio'r Tridegau**' (Yesterday's Illusion *or* Remembering the Thirties), tr. R. Gerallt Jones, *Poetry of Wales 1930–1970*, p. 271; tr. R. Gerallt Jones, *Oxford Book*, p. 242; tr. R. Gerallt Jones, *A Book of Wales* (1987), pp. 188–9; tr. R. Gerallt Jones, *A Cardiff Anthology*, ed. Meic Stephens (Bridgend: Seren, 1987), p. 101; '**Ffarwel yr Orsef Lanio**' (Airport Goodbye), tr. Joseph P. Clancy, *Twentieth Century Welsh Poems*, p. 176; '**Gwyn fyd y Griafolen**' (The Mountain Ash), tr. Joseph P. Clancy, *Twentieth Century Welsh Poems*, p. 178; '**Pan oeddwn Fachgen**' (When I Was a Boy), tr. Gwyn Williams, *Presenting Welsh Poetry*, p. 67; tr. Joseph P. Clancy, *Trivium*, 8 (1973), 114–15; tr. R. Gerallt Jones, *Poetry of Wales 1930–1970*, p. 279; tr. Gwyn Williams, *To Look for a Word*, p. 255; tr. Joseph P. Clancy, *Twentieth Century Welsh Poems*, p. 165; tr. Gwyn Williams, *Oxford Book*, p. 240; tr. Gwyn Williams, *A Book of Wales* (1987), p. 188; tr. Gwyn Williams, *A Cardiff Anthology*, ed. Meic Stephens (Bridgend: Seren, 1987), p. 56; tr. Joseph P. Clancy, *Bloodaxe Book*, pp. 162–3; '**Pont y Caniedydd**', tr. Joseph P. Clancy, *Twentieth Century Welsh Poems*, pp. 172–6; tr. Joseph P. Clancy, *Oxford Book*, pp. 242–6; '**Rhyngom a Ffrainc**' (Between Us and France), tr. R. Gerallt Jones, *Poetry of Wales 1930–1970*, p. 267; '**Seren Bethlehem**' (Star of Bethlehem), tr. Tony Conran, *The Penguin Book of Welsh Verse*, pp. 262–3; tr. Joseph P. Clancy, *Twentieth Century Welsh Poems*, pp. 177–8; tr. Tony Conran, *Welsh Verse*, pp. 291–2; '**Taith i Lety'r Eos**' (A Trip to Llety'r Eos), tr. Joseph P. Clancy, *Twentieth Century Welsh Poems*, p. 177; tr. Joseph P. Clancy, *Wales: A Celebration*, ed. Dewi Roberts (Llanrwst: Gwasg Carreg Gwalch, 2000), pp. 138–9; '**Tynyfedw**', tr. Joseph P. Clancy, *Transactions of the Honourable Society of Cymmrodorion*, 1 (1994), 119–20; tr. Joseph P. Clancy, *Other Words*, p. 85; '**Ystrad Fellte**', tr. Joseph P. Clancy, *Twentieth Century Welsh Poems*, p. 166; '**Yma'n y Meysydd Tawel**' (Here in the Tranquil Fields), tr. H. Idris Bell, *A History of Welsh Literature*, pp. 431–2; '**Ym Merlin – Awst 1945: I.**

Lehrter Bahnof, II. Zehlendorf, III. Theater Des Westens' (In Berlin – August 1945 (i) Lehrter Bahnof (ii) Zehlendorf and (iii) Theater des Westens), tr. Frank Olding, *Poetry Wales*, 24.2 (1988), 53–6; tr. Joseph P. Clancy, *Oxford Book*, pp. 240–1; tr. Joseph P. Clancy, *Twentieth Century Welsh Poems*, pp. 169–72; tr. Joseph P. Clancy, *Bloodaxe Book*, pp. 165–7; **'Y Gwrth-Gyrch'** (The Counter-Attack), tr. Joseph P. Clancy, *Twentieth Century Welsh Poems*, p. 167; **'Y Lleuad a'r tu Hwnt'** (The Moon and Beyond), tr. Joseph P. Clancy, *Twentieth Century Welsh Poems*, p. 179; **'Yr Aethnen'** (The Aspen), tr. R. Gerallt Jones, *Poetry of Wales 1930–1970*, p. 269.

Individual Translations *Pr.*
from **Gwanwyn yn y Ddinas** (Springtime in the City), tr. Luned Meredith, *A Cardiff Anthology*, ed. Meic Stephens (Bridgend: Seren, 1987), pp. 70–9; tr. Meic Stephens, *Illuminations*, pp. 121–9.

DYFNALLT MORGAN (1917–94)

Individual Translations *Po.*
'Y Llen' (The Veil), tr. author, *Dock Leaves*, 4.12 (1953), 45–50; tr. Meic Stephens, *Bloodaxe Book*, 184–9.

Individual Translations *Pr.*
'Amser a Phellter' (Of Time and Distance), tr. Meic Stephens, *Illuminations*, pp. 141–5.

T. J. MORGAN (1907–86)

Individual Translations *Po.*
'Defaid yn y Rhondda' (Sheep in the Rhondda), tr. Meic Stephens, *A Rhondda Anthology* (Bridgend: Seren, 1993), pp. 141–4.

Individual Translations *Pr.*
'Mynd i'r Sercas' (A Trip to the Circus), tr. Meic Stephens, *Illuminations*, pp. 63–8.

T. E. NICHOLAS (Niclas y Glais; 1878–1971)

Collections

The Prison Sonnets, translations by Daniel Hughes, Dewi Emrys, Eris Davies and Wil Ifan (London: W. Griffiths & Co., 1948).

'Tros Ryddid Daear': *Cerddi Gwleidyddol: Political Verse*, Bilingual Edition (Mountain Ash: Niclas Books, 1981).

Individual Translations *Po.*[10]

'**Caernarfon 1969**', tr. Meic Stephens, *The London Welshman*, 25.8 (1970), 6; '**Hiraeth am Forgannwg**' (Hiraeth for Glamorgan), tr. Harri Webb, *Harri Webb: Collected Poems* (Llandysul: Gomer, 1995), p. 288; '**I Aderyn y To**' (To a Sparrow), tr. H. Idris Bell, in T. E. Nicholas, *Canu'r Carchar* (Llandysul: Gwasg Gomer, 1942), p. 53; tr. H. Idris Bell, *A History of Welsh Literature*, p. 424; tr. Joseph P. Clancy, *Twentieth Century Welsh Poems*, p. 35; tr. Joseph P. Clancy, *Bloodaxe Book*, p. 46; '**I Gofio Cymro**' (In Remembrance of a Son of Wales), tr. unsigned, *Wales*, I (1943), 71; '**Rwy'n Gweld o Bell**' (I see from afar), tr. Greg Hill, *Planet*, 49/50 (1980), 113; '**Syrcas Caernarfon 1969**' (Caernarfon 1969), tr. Robert Minhinnick, *Bloodaxe Book*, pp. 46–7; '**Y Llais**' (The Voice), tr. T. Islwyn Nicholas, *Wales*, 5.7 (1945), 20.

W. RHYS NICHOLAS (1914–96)

Individual Translations *Po.*

'**Adnabod**' (Knowing), tr. author, *Quaderno 2 di Lettera* (March, 1977), 71; '**Atgof**' (A Memory), tr. author, *Quaderno 2 di Lettera* (March, 1977), 73.

---

[10] There are two additional translations from poems by T. E. Nicholas entitled (in English) 'The Poet and the All', tr. H. Idris Bell, *Welsh Poems of the Twentieth Century*, pp. 70–1; and 'Saving a Cow (Pride Moreta of Thorn)', tr. Gwyn Williams, *To Look for a Word*, p. 231. I have been unable to locate the source texts from collections of the poet's work or periodical research.

J. DYFNALLT OWEN (Dyfnallt; 1873–1956)

Individual Translations *Po.*
'**Awr Arswyd**' (Hour of Fear), tr. Gillian Clarke, *Bloodaxe Book*, pp. 44–5.

GRUFFUDD PARRY (1916–2001)

Individual Translations *Pr.*
'**Adfyw**' (On Memory), tr. Meic Stephens, *Illuminations*, pp. 198–202.

R. WILLIAMS PARRY (1884–1956)

Miscellaneous

Y Mynydd/*The Mountain (An Impression of Nature)*, score for mixed voices, words translated by author, music by T. Osborne Roberts (London: Curwen, 1934).

Individual Translations *Po.*
'**A. E. Housman**', tr. Joseph P. Clancy, *Twentieth Century Welsh Poems*, pp. 53–4; tr. Joseph P. Clancy, *Bloodaxe Book*, p. 62; '**Angau**' (Death), tr. R. Gerallt Jones, *Poetry of Wales 1930–1970*, p. 33; '**Beddargraff Gwraig**' (A Wife's Epitaph), tr. David Bell, *Transactions of the Honourable Society of Cymmrodorion* (1941), 37; tr. unsigned, *Wales*, 5.7 (1945), 21; tr. Tony Conran, *The Penguin Book of Welsh Verse*, p. 267; tr. Tony Conran, *Welsh Verse*, p. 304; '**Cantre'r Gwaelod**', tr. H. Idris Bell, *Welsh Poems of the Twentieth Century*, p. 29; tr. H. Idris Bell, *A Celtic Anthology*, pp. 328–9; '**Chwilota**' (Sweet Research), tr. Emyr Humphreys, *Emyr Humphreys: Collected Poems* (Cardiff: University of Wales Press, 1999), pp. 128–9; '**Clychau'r Gog**' (Bluebells), tr. Harri Webb, *Welsh Nation* (1968), 6; tr. Joseph P. Clancy, *Twentieth Century Welsh Poems*, p. 48; tr. Joseph P. Clancy, *A Book of Wales* (1987), pp. 208–9; tr. Harri Webb, *Harri Webb: Collected Poems* (Llandysul: Gomer, 1995), pp. 103–4; '**Cymru 1937**' (Wales 1937), tr. R. Gerallt Jones, *Poetry of Wales 1930–1970*, p. 39; tr. Joseph P. Clancy, *Twentieth Century Welsh Poems*, p. 55; tr. Joseph P. Clancy, *Bloodaxe Book*, p. 64; '**Cysur Henaint**' (Age's Comfort), tr. Richard

Loomis, *Poetry Wales*, 15.4 (1980), 29; '**Diddanwch**' (Delight), tr. Joseph P. Clancy, *Twentieth Century Welsh Poems*, p. 44; tr. R. Gerallt Jones, *Planet*, 155 (2002), 55; '**Dinas Noddfa**' (City of Refuge), tr. R. Gerallt Jones, *Poetry of Wales 1930–1970*, p. 31; tr. Joseph P. Clancy, *Twentieth Century Welsh Poems*, p. 45; tr. R. Gerallt Jones, *Planet*, 155 (2002), 55; '**Drudwy Branwen**' (Branwen's Starling), tr. Emyr Humphreys, *Mabon*, 1.3 (1970), 10–13; tr. Gwynn Williams, *Mabon*, 1.3 (1970), 13–15; tr. Joseph P. Clancy, *Twentieth Century Welsh Poems*, pp. 49–53; tr. Gwyn Jones, *Oxford Book*, pp. 165–8; tr. Emyr Humphreys, *Emyr Humphreys: Collected Poems* (Cardiff: University of Wales Press, 1999), p. 123; ' "**Dwy Galon yn Ysgaru**" ' ("Two Hearts Divided"), tr. Joseph P. Clancy, *Twentieth Century Welsh Poems*, p. 58; tr. Joseph P. Clancy, *Oxford Book*, p. 165; '**Eifionydd**', tr. Harri Webb, *A Book of Wales* (1987), pp. 207–8; tr. Harri Webb, *Welsh Nation* (September 1963), 8; tr. Harri Webb, *Harri Webb: Collected Poems* (Llandysul: Gomer, 1995), pp. 66–7; '**Gadael Tir**' (Leaving Land), tr. H. Idris Bell, *Welsh Poems of the Twentieth Century*, p. 4; tr. Gwyn Williams, *To Look for a Word*, p. 233; '**Gofuned**' (A Wish), tr. unsigned, *The Welsh Outlook*, 13.2 (1926), 47; tr. unsigned, *A Celtic Anthology*, p. 331; tr. Tony Conran, *The Penguin Book of Welsh Verse*, pp. 240–1; tr. R. Gerallt Jones, *Poetry of Wales 1930–1970*, p. 43; tr. Joseph P. Clancy, *Twentieth Century Welsh Poems*, p. 58; tr. Tony Conran, *Welsh Verse*, p. 272; '"**Gorchestion Beirdd Cymru**" 1773',[11] tr. R. Gerallt Jones, *Poetry of Wales 1930–1970*, p. 37; '**Gwanwyn**' (Spring), tr. Joseph P. Clancy, *Twentieth Century Welsh Poems*, pp. 44–5; tr. Joseph P. Clancy, *Bloodaxe Book*, p. 59; '**Gwenci**' (Weasel), tr. Joseph P. Clancy, *Twentieth Century Welsh Poems*, p. 57; '**Gwyliadwriaeth y Nos**' (The Night Watch), tr. R. Gerallt Jones, *Planet*, 155 (2002), 57; '**Hedd Wyn**', tr. H. Idris Bell, *Welsh Poems of the Twentieth Century*, pp. 13–14; tr. H. Idris Bell, *A Book of Wales* (1953), pp. 223–4; tr. Joseph P. Clancy, *Trivium*, 8 (1973), 110–11; tr. Joseph P. Clancy, *Twentieth Century Welsh Poems*, pp. 46–7; tr. Joseph P. Clancy, *Bloodaxe Book*, pp. 60–1; '**Hen Gychwr Afon Angau**' (The Old Boatman of Death's River), tr. Tony Conran, *The Penguin Book of Welsh Verse*, pp. 242–3; tr. Gwyn Williams, *To Look for a Word*, p.

---

[11] *Gorchestion Beirdd Cymru*, literally translated 'The achievements or feats of the Welsh poets', was the first collection from the work of the Welsh court poets selected by Rhys Jones and published in 1773.

234; tr. Joseph P. Clancy, *Twentieth Century Welsh Poems*, p. 56; tr. Joseph P. Clancy, *Oxford Book*, p. 164; tr. Tony Conran, *Welsh Verse*, p. 271; tr. Tony Conran, *Bloodaxe Book*, p. 66; **'In Memoriam'** ['**Milwr**' (On a Soldier Killed in the Great War)], tr. H. Idris Bell, *The Welsh Review*, 5.2 (1946), 119; tr. H. Idris Bell, *Oxford Book*, p. 205; tr. H. Idris Bell, *Welsh Poems of the Twentieth Century*, pp. 11–12; tr. H. Idris Bell, *A Book of Wales* (1953), p. 225; ['**Morwr**' (A Sailor)], tr. Tony Conran, *The Penguin Book of Welsh Verse*, p. 272; tr. R. Gerallt Jones, *Poetry of Wales 1930–1970*, p. 45; tr. Tony Conran, *Welsh Verse*, p. 309; '**J.S.L**', tr. Joseph P. Clancy, *Twentieth Century Welsh Poems*, pp. 54–5; tr. Helen Heslop, *Planet*, 100 (1993), 39; tr. Greg Hill, *Planet*, 100 (1993), 38–9; tr. Emyr Humphreys, *Emyr Humphreys: Collected Poems* (Cardiff: University of Wales Press, 1999), p. 130; tr. Emyr Humphreys, *Bloodaxe Book*, pp. 63–4; '**Mae Hiraeth yn y Môr**' (Sonnet), tr. C. C. Bell, *Welsh Poems of the Twentieth Century*, p. 78; '**Marwoldeb**' (Mortality), tr. Martin Davis, *Bloodaxe Book*, pp. 65–6; '**Milwr o Feirion**' (Soldier from Merioneth), tr. H. Idris Bell, *Welsh Poems of the Twentieth Century*, pp. 11–12; tr. Keidrych Rhys, *Wales*, 4 (1944), 33; '**Pagan**', tr. Martin Davis, *Bloodaxe Book*, p. 63; '**Pantycelyn**', tr. C. C. Bell, *Welsh Poems of the Twentieth Century*, p. 26; tr. Joseph P. Clancy, *Twentieth Century Welsh Poems*, p. 45; '**Plygain**' (A Dawn: 1918), tr. C. C. Bell, *Welsh Poems of the Twentieth Century*, p. 6; tr. Joseph P. Clancy, *Twentieth Century Welsh Poems*, p. 46; tr. R. Gerallt Jones, *Planet*, 155 (2002), 57; '**Private Lewis Jones Williams, Pwllheli**' (Epitaph), tr. H. Idris Bell, *A Celtic Anthology*, p. 318; '**Propaganda'r Prydydd**' (The Propaganda of the Poet), tr. Tony Conran, *Poetry Wales*, 2.3 (1966), 13; tr. Tony Conran, *The Penguin Book of Welsh Verse*, p. 242; tr. Tony Conran, in R. M. Jones, *Highlights in Welsh Literature: Talks with a Prince* (Llandybie: Christopher Davies, 1969), p. 96; tr. R. Gerallt Jones, *Poetry of Wales 1930–1970*, p. 35; tr. Joseph P. Clancy, *Twentieth Century Welsh Poems*, p. 55; tr. Tony Conran, *Welsh Verse*, p. 271; tr. Tony Conran, *Bloodaxe Book*, p. 65; '**Rhyfeddodau'r Wawr**' (The Strangeness of Dawn), tr. David Bell, *The Welsh Review*, 1.3 (1939), 133; tr. Tony Conran, *The Penguin Book of Welsh Verse*, p. 241; tr. R. Gerallt Jones, *Poetry of Wales 1930–1970*, p. 41; tr. Joseph P. Clancy, *Twentieth Century Welsh Poems*, p. 56; tr. Joseph P. Clancy, *Oxford Book*, p. 164; tr. Tony Conran, *Welsh Verse*, p. 270; tr. Tony Conran, *Bloodaxe Book*, pp. 64–5; '**Tylluanod**' (The Owls), tr. David Bell,

Wales, 3 (1944), 11; tr. David Bell, *A Book of Wales* (1953), pp. 83–4; 'Y Ceiliog Ffesant' (The Cock Pheasant), tr. Gwyn Williams, *The Welsh Review*, 2.2 (1939), 77; tr. Keidrych Rhys, *Y Ddinas*, 16.7 (1961), 13; 'Y Ddrafft' (The Draft), tr. H. Idris Bell, *Welsh Poems of the Twentieth Century*, p. 5; 'Y Ffliwtydd' (The Flautist), tr. R. S. Thomas, *Modern Poetry in Translation*, p. 161; 'Y Gwynt' (The Wind), tr. H. Idris Bell, *Welsh Poems of the Twentieth Century*, p. 7; 'Y Gwyddau' (The Geese), tr. Joseph P. Clancy, *Twentieth Century Welsh Poems*, pp. 48–9; tr. Tony Conran, *Planet*, 41 (1978), 46; tr. Tony Conran, *Welsh Verse*, pp. 269–70; tr. Tony Conran, *Bloodaxe Book*, p. 61; 'Y Gylfinir' (The Curlew), tr. Gwyn Williams, *The Welsh Review*, 2.2 (1939), 77; tr. Keidrych Rhys, *Wales*, 5.7 (1945), 18; tr. Gwyn Williams, *To Look for a Word*, p. 232; 'Y Llwynog' (The Fox), tr. David Bell, *A History of Welsh Literature*, p. 400; tr. Gwyn Williams, *Presenting Welsh Poetry*, p. 63; tr. Tony Conran, in R. M. Jones, *Highlights in Welsh Literature: Talks with a Prince* (Llandybie: Christopher Davies, 1969), pp. 94–5; tr. Tony Conran, *The Penguin Book of Welsh Verse*, p. 240; tr. Tony Conran, *Poetry Wales*, 2.2 (1966), 13; tr. Gwyn Williams, *To Look for a Word*, p. 231; tr. Joseph P. Clancy, *Twentieth Century Welsh Poems*, p. 47; tr. Gwyn Williams, *Oxford Book*, p. 163; tr. Tony Conran, *Welsh Verse*, p. 269; tr. Gwyn Williams, *A Book of Wales* (1987), p. 208; tr. R. S. Thomas, *Modern Poetry in Translation*, pp. 160–1; tr. R. S. Thomas, in Jason Walford Davies, *Gororau'r Iaith: R. S. Thomas a'r Traddodiad Llenyddol Cymraeg* (Cardiff: University of Wales Press, 2003), p. 99; 'Y Mynydd a'r Allor' (Mountain and Altar), tr. H. Idris Bell, *Welsh Poems of the Twentieth Century*, pp. 44–5; 'Yn Angladd Silyn' (At Silyn's Burial), tr. Joseph P. Clancy, *Twentieth Century Welsh Poems*, p. 53; 'Y Peilon' (The Pylon), tr. Joseph P. Clancy, *Twentieth Century Welsh Poems*, p. 57; 'Yr Iberiad' (The Iberian), tr. H. Idris Bell, *Welsh Poems of the Twentieth Century*, p. 19.

Individual Translations *Pr.*
'Noson o Wynt' (A Windy Night), tr. Meic Stephens, *Illuminations*, pp. 9–12.

DAFYDD OWEN (1919–)

Individual Translations *Po.*
'**Er Cof am William Barclay**' (In Memory of William Barclay), tr. author, *Poetry Wales*, 14.1 (1978), 71–2.

THOMAS PARRY (1904–85)

Individual Translations *Po.*
'**Ansicrwydd**' (Uncertainty), tr. Gwyn Williams, *To Look for a Word*, p. 251.

T. H. PARRY-WILLIAMS (1887–1975)

Collections

Prose
Meic Stephens, *The White Stone* (Llandysul: Gwasg Gomer, 1987).

Poetry
Richard Poole, *That Fool July: Poems by T. H. Parry-Williams* (Nottingham: Shoestring Press, 2003).

Individual Translations *Po.*[12]
'**Anwadalwch**' (Fickleness), tr. R. Gerallt Jones, *Poetry of Wales 1930–1970*, p. 55; '**Argyhoeddiad**' (Conviction), tr. Joseph P. Clancy, *Poetry Wales*, 7.3 (1971), 60; tr. Joseph P. Clancy, *Twentieth Century Welsh Poems*, p. 61; tr. Richard Poole, *Bloodaxe Book*, p. 70; '**Bro**' (Locality), tr. R. Gerallt Jones, *Poetry of Wales 1930–1970*, p. 59; '**Byw**' (Life), tr. Richard Poole, *Bloodaxe Book*, pp. 74–5; '**Carol Nadolig**' (A Christmas Carol), tr. Joseph P. Clancy, *Poetry Wales*, 7.3 (1971), 63; tr. Joseph P. Clancy, *Twentieth Century Welsh Poems*, pp. 73–4; tr. Joseph P. Clancy, *Oxford Book*, pp. 171–2; tr. Joseph P.

---

[12] There is an additional translation from a poem by T. H. Parry Williams entitled 'Sonnet' and translated by C. C. Bell in *Welsh Poems of the Twentieth Century*, p. 77. I have been unable to locate the source text from collections of the poet's work or periodical research.

Clancy, *Bloodaxe Book*, pp. 75–6; '**Cesar**' (Caesar), tr. R. Gerallt Jones, *Poetry of Wales 1930–1970*, p. 67; '**Cyfaill**' (A Friend), tr. Joseph P. Clancy, *Twentieth Century Welsh Poems*, p. 71; '**Cynefin**' (Affinity), tr. D. M. Lloyd, *A Book of Wales* (1953), p. 271; '**Cyngor**' (Advice), tr. Wyn Hobson, *Barddas*, 224/225 (Dec/Jan 1995/1996), 35; '**Daear**' (Earth), tr. Joseph P. Clancy, *Poetry Wales*, 7.3 (1971), 58; tr. Joseph P. Clancy, *Twentieth Century Welsh Poems*, p. 68; '**Dafydd ap Gwilym**', tr. H. Idris Bell, *Transactions of the Honourable Society of Cymmrodorion* (1949–51), 40; '**Dwy Gerdd**' (Two Poems), tr. Richard Poole, *Bloodaxe Book*, pp. 71–2; '**Dychwelyd**' (The Return), tr. D. M. Lloyd, *A Book of Wales* (1953), p. 342; tr. H. Idris Bell, *A History of Welsh Literature*, p. 403; tr. Joseph P. Clancy, *Poetry Wales*, 7.3 (1971), 64; tr. H. Idris Bell, *Poetry Wales*, 10.1 (1974), 25–6; tr. R. Gerallt Jones, *Poetry of Wales 1930–1970*, p. 53; tr. Joseph P. Clancy, *Twentieth Century Welsh Poems*, p. 67; tr. Joseph P. Clancy, *Bloodaxe Book*, p. 76; *from* **Dyddlyfr Taith** (A Travel Diary) [2. '**Ar y Dec**' (On Deck)], tr. Tony Conran, *The Penguin Book of Welsh Verse*, p. 244; tr. Joseph P. Clancy, *Twentieth Century Welsh Poems*, p. 63; tr. Tony Conran, *Welsh Verse*, p. 273; tr. Tony Conran, *Bloodaxe Book*, p. 73; [6. '**Y Ferch ar y Cei yn Rio**' (The Girl on the Quay at Rio)], tr. Richard Poole, *Bloodaxe Book*, pp. 73–4; [10. '**Y Diwedd**' (Death in the Channel)], tr. Tony Conran, *The Penguin Book of Welsh Verse*, p. 245; tr. Tony Conran, *Poetry Wales*, 10.1 (1974), 25; tr. Tony Conran, *Welsh Verse*, p. 273; tr. Tony Conran, *Bloodaxe Book*, p. 73; '**Ffynnon**' (Well-Spring), tr. Joseph P. Clancy, *Twentieth Century Welsh Poems*, p. 70; '**Geiriau**' (Words), tr. Gwyn Williams, *Presenting Welsh Poetry*, p. 68; tr. Joseph P. Clancy, *Poetry Wales*, 7.3 (1971), 64; tr. Gwyn Williams, *To Look for a Word*, p. 241; tr. Joseph P. Clancy, *Twentieth Century Welsh Poems*, p. 68; '**Grand Canyon**', tr. Joseph P. Clancy, *Twentieth Century Welsh Poems*, pp. 69–70; tr. Joseph P. Clancy, *Transactions of the Honourable Society of Cymmrodorion*, 1 (1994), 108; tr. Joseph P. Clancy, *Other Words*, pp. 71–2; '**Gweddill**' (Remnant), tr. Joseph P. Clancy, *Poetry Wales*, 7.3 (1971), 58; tr. Joseph P. Clancy, *Twentieth Century Welsh Poems*, p. 65; '**Gwynt y Dwyrain**' (The East Wind), tr. Tony Conran, *The Penguin Book of Welsh Verse*, p. 244; tr. R. Gerallt Jones, *Poetry of Wales 1930–1970*, p. 65; tr. Joseph P. Clancy, *Twentieth Century Welsh Poems*, p. 68; tr. Tony Conran, *Welsh Verse*, pp. 272–3; '**Haul a Lloer**' (Sun and Moon), tr. Gwyn Williams, *To Look for a Word*, p. 241; '**Hon**' (This One), tr. D. R. Walden-

Jones, *Planet*, 49/50 (1980), 100; tr. John Simons, *Planet*, 49/50 (1980), 101; tr. Meic Stephens, *The London Welshman*, 21.7 (1966), 18; tr. Joseph P. Clancy, *Poetry Wales*, 7.3 (1971), 61; tr. R. Gerallt Jones, *Poetry of Wales 1930–1970*, p. 61; tr. Gwyn Williams, *To Look for a Word*, p. 240; tr. Joseph P. Clancy, *Twentieth Century Welsh Poems*, pp. 71–2; tr. Joseph P. Clancy, *A Book of Wales* (1987), p. 210; tr. Emyr Humphreys, *Emyr Humphreys: Collected Poems* (Cardiff: University of Wales Press, 1999), p. 136; tr. Joseph P. Clancy, *Wales: A Celebration*, ed. Dewi Roberts (Llanrwst: Gwasg Carreg Gwalch, 2000), pp. 146–7; tr. Emyr Humphreys, *Bloodaxe Book*, pp. 69–70; '**Jezebel**', tr. R. Gerallt Jones, *Poetry of Wales 1930–1970*, p. 57; '**John ac Ann**' (John and Ann), tr. Joseph P. Clancy, *Twentieth Century Welsh Poems*, p. 72; '**Moelni**' (Barrenness), tr. Joseph P. Clancy, *Trivium*, 8 (1973), 111; tr. Joseph P. Clancy, *Twentieth Century Welsh Poems*, p. 65; tr. Richard Poole, *Bloodaxe Book*, p. 68; '**Llyn y Gadair**', tr. Tony Conran, *Poetry Wales*, 2.2 (1966), 13; tr. Tony Conran, *The Penguin Book of Welsh Verse*, p. 245; tr. Tony Conran, in R. M. Jones, *Highlights in Welsh Literature: Talks with a Prince* (Llandybie: Christopher Davies, 1969), pp. 97–8; tr. Joseph P. Clancy, *Poetry Wales*, 7.3 (1971), 62; tr. Tony Conran, *Poetry Wales*, 10.1 (1974), 21–2; tr. R. Gerallt Jones, *Poetry of Wales 1930–1970*, p. 63; tr. Joseph P. Clancy, *Twentieth Century Welsh Poems*, p. 66; tr. Tony Conran, *Oxford Book*, p. 173; tr. Tony Conran, *Welsh Verse*, p. 274; tr. Joseph P. Clancy, *Wales: A Celebration*, ed. Dewi Roberts (Llanrwst: Gwasg Carreg Gwalch, 2000), p. 26; tr. Tony Conran, *Bloodaxe Book*, p. 69; '**Nef**' (Heaven), tr. H. Idris Bell, *The Welsh Review*, 1.3 (1939), 133; '**Oerddwr**', tr. Joseph P. Clancy, *Twentieth Century Welsh Poems*, p. 73; '**Ofn**' (Fear), tr. Joseph P. Clancy, *Twentieth Century Welsh Poems*, p. 62; '**Oedfa'r Hwyr**' (Evening Service), tr. Joseph P. Clancy, *Twentieth Century Welsh Poems*, p. 70; tr. Joseph P. Clancy, *Wales: A Celebration*, ed. Dewi Roberts (Llanrwst: Gwasg Carreg Gwalch, 2000), p. 151; '**Rhaid**' (My Tears), tr. H. Idris Bell, *Welsh Poems of the Twentieth Century*, p. 72; '**Rhieni**' (Parents), tr. Joseph P. Clancy, *Twentieth Century Welsh Poems*, pp. 64–5; '**Tylluan**' (Owl), tr. Joseph P. Clancy, *Poetry Wales*, 7.3 (1971), 58–9; tr. Joseph P. Clancy, *Twentieth Century Welsh Poems*, p. 61; '**Tŷ'r Ysgol**', tr. Joseph P. Clancy, *Poetry Wales*, 7.3 (1971), 62; tr. Joseph P. Clancy, *Twentieth Century Welsh Poems*, p. 67; tr. Joseph P. Clancy, *Bloodaxe Book*, pp. 68–9; '**Y Coed Mawr**' (The Giant Redwoods), tr. Joseph P. Clancy, *Twentieth Century Welsh Poems*, p. 69; *from* 'Y **Ddinas**' (The City), tr. Gwyn Williams, *To Look for a Word*, pp. 238–9; '**Y Diwedd**' (Finale), tr. Joseph P. Clancy, *Twentieth Century Welsh Poems*, p. 64; '**Ymwelydd**' (Visitor), tr. Joseph P. Clancy, *Twentieth Century Welsh Poems*, p. 66; '**Yr Esgyrn Hyn**' (These Bones), tr. H. Idris Bell, *The Welsh Review*, 1.3 (1939), 132; tr. H. Idris Bell, *A History of Welsh Literature*, pp. 402–3; tr. Joseph P. Clancy, *Poetry Wales*, 7.3 (1971), 59–60; tr. H. Idris Bell, *Poetry Wales*, 10.1 (1974), 22–3; tr. R. Gerallt Jones, *Poetry of Wales 1930–1970*, pp. 49–51; tr. Joseph P. Clancy, *Twentieth Century Welsh Poems*, pp. 62–3; tr. H. Idris Bell, *Oxford Book*, pp. 172–3; tr. H. Idris Bell, *A Book of Wales* (1987), pp. 209–10; tr. H. Idris Bell, *Love from Wales: An Anthology*, ed. Tony Curtis and Siân James (Bridgend: Seren Books, 1991), p. 139; '**Y Rheswm**' (The Reason), tr. Joseph P. Clancy, *Poetry Wales*, 7.3 (1971), 60; tr. Joseph P. Clancy, *Twentieth Century Welsh Poems*, p. 64.

Individual Translations *Pr.*
'**Boddi Cath**' (On Drowning a Cat), tr. Meic Stephens, *Planet*, 64 (1987), 30–3; tr. Meic Stephens, *Illuminations*, pp. 18–20; '**Hafod Lwyfog**', tr. Meic Stephens, *A Book of Wales* (1987), pp. 211–12; '**Dieithrwch**' (Strangeness), tr. Meic Stephens, *Planet*, 64 (1987), 28–30.

FFRANSIS G. PAYNE (1900–92)

Individual Translations *Pr.*
'**Chwaryddion Crwydrol**' (Strolling Players), tr. Meic Stephens, *Planet*, 100 (1993), 74–81; tr. Meic Stephens, *Illuminations*, pp. 50–7.

IORWERTH C. PEATE (1901–82)

Individual Translations *Po.*
'**Awyrblandy Sain Tathan**' (Airstrip St Athan), tr. Nigel Jenkins, *Bloodaxe Book*, pp. 103–4; '**Carol y Crefftwr**' (The Craftsman's Carol), tr. R. Gerallt Jones, *Poetry of Wales 1930–1970*, p. 129; '**Clegyr**' (To the River Clegyr), tr. H. Idris Bell, *A Book of Wales*

(1953), pp. 64–5; '**Men Ychen**', tr. H. Idris Bell, *A History of Welsh Literature*, p. 421; '**Nant yr Eira**', tr. Joseph P. Clancy, *Twentieth Century Welsh Poems*, p. 106; tr. Joseph P. Clancy, *A Book of Wales* (1987), pp. 212–13; tr. Joseph P. Clancy, *Bloodaxe Book*, pp. 101–2; '**Ronsyfál**' (Roncesvalles), tr. Nigel Jenkins, *Bloodaxe Book*, pp. 102–3; '**Y Deyrnas Goll**' (The Lost Kingdom), tr. R. Gerallt Jones, *Poetry of Wales 1930–1970*, p. 127; '**Y Gegin Gynt**' (Museum Piece), tr. Joseph P. Clancy, *Twentieth Century Welsh Poems*, p. 107; tr. Joseph P. Clancy, *Bloodaxe Book*, p. 103.

Individual Translations *Pr.*
'**Mynydd Epynt**' (Their Land they shall Lose), tr. Meic Stephens, *Illuminations*, pp. 42–5; *from* **Rhwng Dau Fyd** (The Garden Village), tr. Meic Stephens, *A Cardiff Anthology*, ed. Meic Stephens (Bridgend: Seren, 1987), pp. 83–6.

ELUNED PHILLIPS (1915?)

Individual Translations *Po.*
from '**Clymau**' (Ties), tr. Gillian Clarke, *Bloodaxe Book*, pp. 169–75.

CARADOG PRICHARD (1904–80)

Prose (Novel)
Un Nos Ola Leuad, *Full Moon*, tr. Menna Gallie (London: Hodder & Stoughton, 1973).
One Moonlit Night, tr. Philip Mitchell (Edinburgh: Canongate, 1995).
Un Nos Ola Leuad: One Moonlit Night, tr. Philip Mitchell (London: Penguin Books, 1999).

Individual Translations *Pr.*
from **Un Nos Ola Leuad**, tr. Menna Gallie, *A Book of Wales* (1987), pp. 215–18.

Individual Translations *Po.*
'**Acenion Diog-Ganu**' (Accents of Lazy-Singing), tr. R. Gerallt Jones, *Poetry of Wales 1930–1970*, p. 195; '**Sgwrs â'r Esgob**' (A Conversation with the Bishop), tr. R. Gerallt Jones, *Poetry of Wales*

1930–1970, p. 193; *from* '**Terfysgoedd Daear**' (Earthly Turmoil), tr. Martin Davis, *Bloodaxe Book*, pp. 120–3; '**Trwy Borth y Bedd**' (Through the Gate of the Grave), tr. Joseph P. Clancy, *Twentieth Century Welsh Poems*, pp. 124–5; '**Y Fargen**' (The Bargain), tr. Joseph P. Clancy, *Twentieth Century Welsh Poems*, pp. 125–6; tr. Joseph P. Clancy, *Bloodaxe Book*, pp. 123–5.

JOHN RODERICK REES (1920–)

Individual Translations *Po.*
'**Brenin Gwalia**', tr. author, *Bloodaxe Book*, pp. 194–5.

MARGARET BOWEN REES (1935–)

Individual Translations *Po.*
'**Y Bywyd Crwn**' (The Full Life), tr. Joseph P. Clancy, *Twentieth Century Welsh Poems*, p. 218.

E. PROSSER RHYS (1901–45)

Individual Translations *Po.*
from '**Atgof**' (Memory), tr. Martin Davis, *Bloodaxe Book*, pp. 100–1; '**Cymru**' (Wales), tr. D. M. Lloyd, *A Book of Wales* (1953), pp. 266–7; tr. R. Gerallt Jones, *Poetry of Wales 1930–1970*, pp. 117–19; tr. D. M. Lloyd, *A Book of Wales* (1987), pp. 221–2; '**Troi'r Gornel**' (Turning the Corner), tr. R. Gerallt Jones, *Poetry of Wales 1930–1970*, p. 123; '**Un ar Hugain**' (Twenty-One), tr. J. T. Jones, in J. T. Jones and E. Prosser Rhys, *Gwaed Ifanc* (Wrexham: Hughes & Son, 1923), p. 73; tr. C. C. Bell, *Welsh Poems of the Twentieth Century*, p. 60; tr. C. C. Bell, *A History of Welsh Literature*, p. 425; '**Yn Angladd 'Nhad**' (At my Father's Funeral), tr. R. Gerallt Jones, *Poetry of Wales 1930–1970*, p. 121; '**Y Pechadur**' (The Sinner), tr. Joseph P. Clancy, *Twentieth Century Welsh Poems*, p. 108.

THOMAS RICHARDS (1883–1958)

Individual Translations *Po.*
'**Y Ci Defaid**' (Sheepdog), tr. Tony Conran, *The Penguin Book of Welsh Verse*, p. 267; tr. Tony Conran, *Welsh Verse*, p. 304.

KATE ROBERTS (1891–1985)

Prose (Novels)
Traed Mewn Cyffion, *Feet in Chains*, tr. Idwal Walters and John Idris Jones (Cardiff: John Jones, 1977). Reprinted (London: Corgi, 1986); (Ruthin: John Jones, 1996); (Bridgend: Seren, 2002).

Y Byw sy'n Cysgu, *The Living Sleep*, tr. Wyn Griffith (Cardiff: John Jones Cardiff Ltd, 1976). Reprinted (London: Corgi, 1981).

Collections

A Summer Day and Other Stories, with a foreword by Storm Jameson (Cardiff: Penmark Press, 1946).[13]

Tea in the Heather, tr. Wyn Griffith (Ruthin: John Jones, 1968).

Two Old Men & Other Stories: Illustrated by Kyffin Williams, tr. Elan Closs Stephens and Wyn Griffith with an introduction by John Gwilym Jones (Gwasg Gregynog, 1981).

Sun and Storm and other Stories, tr. Carolyn Watcyn (Denbigh: Gee & Son, 2000).

Critical Editions

Joseph P. Clancy, *The World of Kate Roberts: Selected Stories 1925–1981* (Philadelphia: Temple University Press, 1991).

---

[13] With previously published translations by Wyn Griffith, Dafydd Jenkins and Walter Dowding.

Individual Translations *Pr.*
'**Buddugoliaeth Alaw Jim**' (The Victory of Alaw Jim), tr. Walter Dowding, *Life and Letters To-day*, 24 (1940), 280–7; '**Cathod Mewn Ocsiwn**' (Cats at an Auction), tr. Wyn Griffith, *Twenty-Five Welsh Short Stories*, pp. 23–30; *from* '**Chwiorydd**' (Sisters), tr. Walter Dowding, *A Book of Wales* (1953), pp. 226–7; '**Henaint**' (Old Age), tr. Wyn Griffith, *The Welsh Review*, 3.1 (1944), 21–5; tr. Wyn Griffith, *A Book of Wales* (1953), pp. 225–6; '**Nadolig y Cerdyn**' (Christmas Journey), tr. unsigned (but Wyn Griffith), *Short Stories from Wales*, selected and introduced by David Elias (Wheaton: 1978), pp. 1–6; '**Prynu Dol**' (Buying a Doll), tr. Joseph P. Clancy, *Planet*, 87 (1991), 32–5; *from* ***Traed Mewn Cyffion*** (The Chains around my Feet), tr. Ned Thomas, *Planet*, 2 (1970), 50–4; tr. Ned Thomas, *A Book of Wales* (1987), pp. 232–5; tr. Idwal Walters and John Idris Jones, *The Heart of Wales: An Anthology*, ed. James A. Davies (Bridgend: Seren, 1994), pp. 76–9, 118–20, 220–4, 244–6; tr. John Idris Jones and Idwal Walters, *Wales: A Celebration*, ed. Dewi Roberts (Llanrwst: Gwasg Carreg Gwalch, 2000), pp. 61–3; *from* ***Y Byw sy'n Cysgu*** (The Living Sleep), tr. Wyn Griffith, *The Anglo-Welsh Review*, 25.55 (1975), 49–52; '**Y Condemniedig**' (The Condemned), tr. Dafydd Jenkins, *The Welsh Review*, 1.2 (1939), 72–8; tr. Dafydd Jenkins, *A Book of Wales* (1987), pp. 230–2; tr. Joseph P. Clancy, *The New Penguin Book of Welsh Short Stories*, pp. 10–18; '**Y Golled**' (The Loss), tr. Walter Dowding, *The Penguin Book of Welsh Short Stories*, pp. 94–101.

General
'The Craft of the Short Story: Interview with Kate Roberts', tr. *Planet*, 51 (1985), 39–48;
'Kate Roberts in Person', tr. unsigned, *Planet*, 42 (1978), 27–30.[14]

DAFYDD ROWLANDS (1931–2001)

Individual Translations *Po.*
'**Archipelago**', tr. Meic Stephens, *Bloodaxe Book*, p. 228; '**Awst y Chweched**' (The Sixth of August), tr. Bryan Martin Davies, *Poetry*

---

[14] Translated text of broadcast interview with Kate Roberts about her life and work.

Wales, 10.2 (1974), 25; '**Criced**' (Cricket), tr. Meic Stephens, *Bloodaxe Book*, p. 227; *from* '**Dadeni**' (Renaissance), tr. Bryan Martin Davies, *Poetry Wales*, 10.2 (1974), 23–4; '**Dangosaf iti Lendid**' (I Will Show you Beauty), tr. R. Gerallt Jones, *Poetry of Wales 1930–1970*, p. 365; '**I'r Gymru sydd ohoni**' (To Wales Today), tr. Bryan Martin Davies, *Poetry Wales*, 10.2 (1974), 22–3; from '**Meini**' ('There was an eisteddfod on the Baran years ago . . .'), tr. Bryan Martin Davies, *Poetry Wales*, 10.2 (1974), 21–2; *from* '**Llaw'r Bwystfil**' (The Hand of the Beast) [I '**Yng ngwawr y bwystfil**' (In the dawn of the beast)], tr. Bryan Martin Davies, *Poetry Wales*, 10.2 (1974), 24; [IX '**Awst y Chweched**' (The Sixth of August)], tr. Bryan Martin Davies, *Poetry Wales*, 10.2 (1974), 25; '**Llifio'i Wraig yn Ddwy**' (Sawing His Wife in Half), tr. Meic Stephens, *Bloodaxe Book*, pp. 228–9; '**Nant Gwrtheyrn**', tr. author, *Poetry Wales*, 12.1 (1976), 35–7; '**Roedd yr Haf yn Haf Bryd Hynny**' ('The summer was summer then'), tr. Bryan Martin Davies, *Poetry Wales*, 10.2 (1974), 20; '**Schutzstaffeln – 45326**', tr. Meic Stephens, *Bloodaxe Book*, pp. 224–5; '**Theatr y Fflam**' (The Theatre of the Flame), tr. Bryan Martin Davies, *Poetry Wales*, 10.2 (1974), 21; '**Wrth Fynd o nyth ein Dwylo**' (As you Leave the Nest of our Hands), tr. R. Gerallt Jones, *Poetry of Wales 1930–1970*, p. 363; '**Y Pentref Hwn**' (The Village), tr. Meic Stephens, *Bloodaxe Book*, 25–6; '**Y Sgidie Bach**' (The Little Boots), tr. Meic Stephens, *Bloodaxe Book*, pp. 222–4.

Individual Translations *Pr.*
'**Sgidie Bach Llandeilo**' (The Little Llandeilo Boots), tr. Meic Stephens, *Illuminations*, pp. 105–7; tr. author, *A Book of Wales* (1987), pp. 238–40; *from* '**1939**' (A Child's War), tr. author, *A Book of Wales* (1987), pp. 239–40; *from* '**Joseff**' (Joseph the Milk), tr. author, *A Book of Wales* (1987), pp. 238–9.

GILBERT RUDDOCK (1938–98)

Individual Translations *Po.*
'**Bws Deulawr**' (Double Decker), tr. author, *Poetry Wales*, 11.3 (1976), 72; tr. author, *Bloodaxe Book*, p. 262; '**Ffôn**' ('Phone), tr. author, *Poetry Wales*, 10.4 (1975), 79–81; '**Machlud a Môr**' (Sunset and Sea), tr. author, *Poetry Wales*, 9.1 (1973), 60–1; '**Priodas**' (Wedding), tr. author, *A Cardiff Anthology*, ed. Meic Stephens

(Bridgend: Seren, 1987), pp. 158–9; 'Sianel Arall' (Another Channel), tr. author, *Quaderno 2 di Lettera* (March, 1977), 77; 'Un Sianel' (One Channel), tr. author, *Quaderno 2 di Lettera* (March, 1977), 75; 'Wrth Fam Ddall' (To a Blind Mother), tr. Mike Jenkins, *Bloodaxe Book*, pp. 261–2.

R. S. THOMAS (1913–2000)

Prose

R. S. Thomas, *Autobiographies: Former Paths, The Creative Writer's Suicide, No-one, A Year in Llŷn*, translated with an introduction and notes by Jason Walford Davies (London: J. M. Dent, 1997).

Individual Translations *Pr.*
'Abercuawg', tr. John Phillips, *R. S. Thomas: Selected Prose*, ed. Sandra Anstey (Bridgend: Poetry Wales Press, 1983), pp. 155–66 (1995: 122–32); 'Dau Gapel' (Two Chapels), tr. Catherine Thomas, *R. S. Thomas: Selected Prose*, ed. Sandra Anstey (Bridgend: Poetry Wales Press, 1983), pp. 43–7 (1995: 36–40); 'Hunanladdiad y Llenor' (The Creative Writer's Suicide), tr. Gwyn Davies, *R. S. Thomas: Selected Prose*, ed. Sandra Anstey (Bridgend: Poetry Press Wales, 1983), pp. 169–74 (1995: 134–9); 'Llenyddiaeth Eingl-Gymreig' (Anglo-Welsh Literature), tr. Ned Thomas, *R. S. Thomas: Selected Prose*, ed. Sandra Anstey (Bridgend: Poetry Wales Press, 1983), pp. 51–3 (1995: 41–3); *from Neb* (An Exile), tr. Meic Stephens, *Illuminations: An Anthology of Welsh Short Prose* (Welsh Academic Press, 1998), pp. 180–3; 'Pe Medrwn yr Iaith . . .' (If I had the language . . .), tr. Meic Stephens, *R. S. Thomas: Selected Prose* Third Edition, ed. Sandra Anstey (Bridgend: Seren, 1995), pp. 140–4; [Review of *Bury my Heart at Wounded Knee* by Dee Brown], tr. John Phillips, *Planet*, 49/50 (1980), 111; tr. John Phillips, *R. S. Thomas: Selected Prose*, ed. Sandra Anstey (Bridgend: Poetry Wales Press, 1983), pp. 177–81 (1995: 114–17); 'Undod' (Unity), tr. Katie Gramich, *R. S. Thomas: Selected Prose* Third Edition, ed. Sandra Anstey (Bridgend: Seren, 1995), pp. 143–58; 'Y Llwybrau Gynt 2' (The Paths Gone By), tr. John Phillips, *R. S. Thomas: Selected Prose*, ed. Sandra Anstey (Bridgend: Poetry Wales Press, 1983), pp. 131–45 (1995: 100–13).

THOMAS JACOB THOMAS (Sarnicol; 1873–1945)

Individual Translations *Po.*
'Bòs y Pwll' (The Pit Boss), tr. H. Idris Bell, *They Look at Wales: An Anthology of Prose and Verse* (Cardiff: University of Wales Press, 1941), p. 55; tr. H. Idris Bell, *A History of Welsh Literature*, p. 407; '**Dic Siôn Dafydd**', tr. H. Idris Bell, *They Look at Wales: An Anthology of Prose and Verse* (Cardiff: University of Wales Press, 1941), p. 55; tr. H. Idris Bell, *Oxford Book*, p. 157; tr. H. Idris Bell, *A Book of Wales* (1987), p. 265; '**Gŵyl Ddewi**' (St David's Day), tr. H. Idris Bell, *Poems from the Welsh*, pp. 71–2; '**Pregethwr, Byddar, a Blaenor**' (The Preacher and the Deaf Man), tr. H. Idris Bell, *A History of Welsh Literature*, p. 407; '**Y Sant**' (The Saint), tr. H. Idris Bell, *They Look at Wales: An Anthology of Prose and Verse* (Cardiff: University of Wales Press, 1941), p. 55; '**Y Torrwr Cerryg**' (The Stonebreaker), tr. unsigned, *The Welsh Outlook*, 5 (1918), 188.

GWILYM R. TILSLEY (1911–97)

Individual Translations *Po.*
'Awdl Foliant i'r Glowr' (An Ode in Praise of the Coalminer), tr. Joseph P. Clancy, *Bloodaxe Book*, p. 149.

D. J. WILLIAMS (1885–1970)

Prose
Hen Dŷ Ffarm, *The Old Farmhouse*, tr. Waldo Williams (London: Harrap, 1961). Reprinted (Carmarthen: Golden Grove, 1987); (Llandysul: Gomer, 2001).

Individual Translations *Pr.*
'Blwyddyn Lwyddiannus' (A Good Year), tr. Wyn Griffith, *Welsh Short Stories* (1937), pp. 373–80; tr. Wyn Griffith, *Twenty-Five Welsh Short Stories*, pp. 225–9; tr. Glyn Jones, *Planet*, 5/6 (1971), 69–75; tr. Glyn Jones, *The Penguin Book of Welsh Short Stories*, pp. 122–30; tr. Wyn Griffith, *A Book of Wales* (1987), pp. 293–7; '**Colbo Jones yn Ymuno â'r Fyddin**' (Clouter Jones Joins the Army), tr. Katie Gramich, *Planet*, 67 (1988), 85–94; *from **Hen Wynebau**: '**Bob,**

yr hen gel glas' (Bob, the old grey nag), tr. Wil Ifan, *Dock Leaves*, 3.8 (1952), 14–16; **'Meca'r Genedl'** (The Mecca of the Nation), tr. R. Gerallt Jones, *The New Penguin Book of Welsh Short Stories*, pp. 189–205; **'Myfyrion Dydd Coroni (1953)'** (Thoughts on Coronation Day, 1953), tr. Meic Stephens, *Illuminations*, pp. 68–72; **'Pwll-yr-Onnen'**, tr. Dafydd Jenkins, *Welsh Short Stories*, ed. Gwyn Jones, (Oxford: Oxford University Press, 1936), pp. 313–21; **'Y Cwpwrdd Tridarn'** (The Court Cupboard), tr. Dafydd Jenkins, *Wales*, 5, 8 & 9 (1945), 74–81; tr. Dafydd Jenkins, *A Book of Wales* (1953), pp. 177–9; tr. Dafydd Jenkins, *Welsh Short Stories* (1959), pp. 232–41; from **Yr Hen Dŷ Ffarm** (The Old Farmhouse), tr. Waldo Williams, *A Book of Wales* (1987), pp. 291–3; tr. Waldo Williams, *Wales: A Celebration*, ed. Dewi Roberts (Llanrwst: Gwasg Carreg Gwalch, 2000), pp. 64–6.

GWYN WILLIAMS (1904–90)

Individual Translations *Po.*
'Dwy gerdd i Gymru' (Two poems for Wales), tr. author, *Poetry Wales*, 11.1 (1976), 68–9; **'Rhagflas Gaeafol'** (Winter Foretaste), tr. author, *Poetry Wales*, 17.2 (1981), 39.

G. J. WILLIAMS (1892–1963)

Individual Translations *Po.*
'Gwladus Ddu', tr. A. G. Prys-Jones, *The Anglo-Welsh Review*, 24.54 (1974), 88; tr. R. S. Thomas, *Modern Poetry in Translation*, pp. 159–60; **'Yr Henwyr'** (The Old Men), tr. Gwyn Williams, *Wales*, 6.23 (1946), 14; tr. Gwyn Williams, *To Look for a Word*, p. 235.

IFOR WILLIAMS (1881–1965)

Individual Translations *Pr.*
'I'r Mynydd' (To the Mountain), tr. Meic Stephens, *Illuminations*, pp. 83–7.

ISLWYN WILLIAMS (1903–57)

Individual Translations *Pr.*
'**Cap Wil Thomas**' (Will Thomas's Cap), tr. author, *Short Stories from Wales*, selected and introduced by David Elias (Wheaton: 1978), pp. 26–31; tr. author, *A Book of Wales* (1987), pp. 300–4; '**Y Feirniadaeth**' (Adjudication), tr. author, *Twenty-Five Welsh Short Stories*, pp. 79–84.

R. BRYN WILLIAMS (1902–81)

Individual Translations *Po.*
from '**Patagonia**', tr. Joseph P. Clancy, *Bloodaxe Book*, pp. 111–13.

RICHARD HUGHES WILLIAMS (Dic Tryfan; 1878?–1919)

Individual Translations *Pr.*
'**Siôn William**', tr. Wyn Griffith, *Welsh Short Stories* (1937), pp. 409–15; tr. unsigned (but Wyn Griffith), *Short Stories from Wales*, selected and introduced by David Elias (Wheaton: 1978), pp. 69–72; '**Yr Hogyn Drwg**' (Good-for-Nothing), tr. Dafydd Rowlands, *The New Penguin Book of Welsh Short Stories*, pp. 159–66.

RHYDWEN WILLIAMS (1916–97)

Collections

Rhydwen Williams, *Rhondda Poems* (Swansea: Christopher Davies, 1987).

Individual Translations *Po.*
'**Alcestis**', tr. R. Gerallt Jones, *Poetry of Wales 1930–1970*, pp. 285–7; '**Cerdd**' (Poem), tr. author, *Poetry Wales*, 28.2 (1992), 42–3; '**Côt-Fawr 'Nhad**' (My Father's Overcoat), tr. author, *Poetry Wales*, 28.2 (1992), 40; '**Cŵn**' (Dogs), tr. Nigel Jenkins, *Bloodaxe Book*, pp. 175–6; '**Gwleidyddiaeth**' (Politics), tr. J. Gwyn Griffiths, *Welsh Nation* (February/March 1965), 4; '**John Mathews**', tr. Joseph P.

Clancy, *Twentieth Century Welsh Poems*, pp. 180–2; '**Mesach**', tr. R. Gerallt Jones, *Poetry of Wales 1930–1970*, p. 289; '**Y Babŵn**' (The Baboon), tr. R. Gerallt Jones, *Poetry of Wales 1930–1970*, p. 283; tr. Joseph P. Clancy, *Twentieth Century Welsh Poems*, pp. 182–3; tr. R. Gerallt Jones, *Oxford Book*, pp. 262–3; *from* '**Y Ffynhonnau**' (Mountain Streams), tr. author, *A Rhondda Anthology*, ed. Meic Stephens (Bridgend: Seren Books, 1993), pp. 181–9; tr. Meic Stephens, *Bloodaxe Book*, pp. 177–83.

Individual Translations *Pr.*
'**Nadolig yn y Cwm**' (Christmas in the Valley), tr. Meic Stephens, *Illuminations*, pp. 166–9.

WALDO WILLIAMS (1904–71)

Collections

Tony Conran, *The Peacemakers: Selected Poems* (Llandysul: Gomer, 1997).

Individual Translations *Po.*
'**Adnabod**' (Acknowledge), tr. Tony Conran, *Materion Dwyieithog: Bilingual Matters*, 3 (1991), 18; '**Ar Weun Cas' Mael**' (On Puncheston Moor), tr. R. Gerallt Jones, *Poetry of Wales 1930–1970*, pp. 207–9; tr. Joseph P. Clancy, *Twentieth Century Welsh Poems*, pp. 127–8; tr. Joseph P. Clancy, *Wales: A Celebration*, ed. Dewi Roberts (Llanrwst: Gwasg Carreg Gwalch, 2000), p. 47; '**Cân Bom**' (Song for a Bomb), tr. Rowan Williams, *After Silent Centuries: Poems by Rowan Williams* (Oxford: The Perpetua Press, 1994), p. 48; '**Cofio**' (Remembrance), tr. D. M. Lloyd, *A Book of Wales* (1953), pp. 345–6; tr. R. Gerallt Jones, *Poetry of Wales 1930–1970*, p. 201; tr. Gwyn Williams, *To Look for a Word*, p. 250; tr. D. M. Lloyd, *A Book of Wales* (1987), p. 315; '**Cwmwl Haf**' (A Summer Cloud), tr. Joseph P. Clancy, *Twentieth Century Welsh Poems*, pp. 130–1; tr. Joseph P. Clancy, *Oxford Book*, pp. 217–18; tr. Tony Conran, *Modern Poetry in Translation*, pp. 199–200; tr. Tony Conran, *Bloodaxe Book*, pp. 126–7; '**Cymru a Chymraeg**' (Welsh Land, Welsh Language), tr. Joseph P. Clancy, *Trivium*, 8 (1973), 115; tr. Joseph P. Clancy, *Twentieth Century Welsh Poems*, p. 130; tr. Joseph P. Clancy,

Transactions of the Honourable Society of Cymmrodorion, 1 (1994), 109; tr. Joseph P. Clancy, *Other Words*, p. 73; tr. Tony Conran, *Bloodaxe Book*, pp. 127–8; '**Cymru'n Un**' (Wales One), tr. Tony Conran, *Swansea Review*, 14 (1995), 11; '**Cywydd Diolch am Fotffon**' (The Thumbstick), tr. Joseph P. Clancy, *Twentieth Century Welsh Poems*, pp. 136–7; '**Daffodil**', tr. R. Gerallt Jones, *Poetry of Wales 1930–1970*, p. 223; tr. Gwyn Jones, *Oxford Book*, pp. 220–1; '**Daw'r Wennol yn ôl i'w Nyth**' (The Swallow will find her Nest), tr. Tony Conran, *Modern Poetry in Translation*, pp. 200–1; '**Die Bibelforscher**' (For the Protestant martyrs of the Third Reich), tr. Rowan Williams, *After Silent Centuries: Poems by Rowan Williams* (Oxford: The Perpetua Press, 1994), p. 52; tr. Rowan Williams, *Bloodaxe Book*, pp. 133–4; '**Eirlysiau**' (Snowdrops), tr. R. Gerallt Jones, *Poetry of Wales 1930–1970*, p. 199; tr. Joseph P. Clancy, *Other Words*, pp. 6–7; '**Geneth Ifanc**' (A Young Girl), tr. Gwenith Davies, *Poetry Wales*, 6.1 (1970), 20–1; tr. A. G. Prys-Jones, *The Anglo-Welsh Review*, 21.47 (1972), 191; tr. Joseph P. Clancy, *Twentieth Century Welsh Poems*, p. 134; tr. Greg Hill, *Bastard Englyns* (Bow Street: Nant Publications, 2000), p. 26; tr. Tony Conran, *Bloodaxe Book*, p. 131; '**Gwenallt**', tr. Tony Conran, *Swansea Review*, 14 (1995), 13; '**Gŵyl Ddewi**' (St David's Day), tr. Joseph P. Clancy, *Twentieth Century Welsh Poems*, pp. 128–9; tr. Joseph P. Clancy, *Wales: A Celebration*, ed. Dewi Roberts (Llanrwst: Gwasg Carreg Gwalch, 2000), pp. 151–2; '**Linda**' (In Memoriam), tr. Siân James, *Love from Wales*, ed. Tony Curtis and Siân James (Bridgend: Seren, 1991), p. 140; '**Llandysilio-yn-Nyfed**', tr. Tony Conran, *Swansea Review*, 14 (1995), 14; '**Llwyd**', tr. R. Gerallt Jones, *Poetry of Wales 1930–1970*, pp. 203–5; '**Mewn Dau Gae**' (In Two Fields), tr. Tony Conran, *Poetry Wales*, 2.3 (1966), 12–13; tr. Tony Conran, *The Penguin Book of Welsh Verse*, pp. 258–60; tr. R. M. Jones on Tony Conran, *Highlights in Welsh Literature: Talks with a Prince* (Llandybie: Christopher Davies, 1969), pp. 119–21; tr. R. Gerallt Jones, *Poetry of Wales 1930–1970*, pp. 219–21; tr. Joseph P. Clancy, *Twentieth Century Welsh Poems*, pp. 135–6; tr. Gwyn Jones, *Oxford Book*, pp. 219–20; tr. Tony Conran, *Welsh Verse*, pp. 289–90; tr. Tony Conran, *A Book of Wales* (1987), pp. 313–14; tr. R. S. Thomas, *Modern Poetry in Translation*, pp. 156–7; tr. Tony Conran, *Bloodaxe Book*, pp. 130–1; '**Nid oes yng ngwreiddyn bod . . .**', tr. Tony Conran, *Materion Dwyieithog: Bilingual Matters*, 3 (1991), 17–18; '**Pa Beth yw Dyn?**' (What is Man?), tr. Emyr Humphreys, *Planet*, 43 (1978),

17–23; tr. Emyr Humphreys, *A Book of Wales* (1987), p. 312; tr. Emyr Humphreys, *Emyr Humphreys: Collected Poems* (Cardiff: University of Wales Press, 1999), p. 135; tr. Emyr Humphreys, *Bloodaxe Book*, p. 129; '**Preseli**', tr. Joseph P. Clancy, *Twentieth Century Welsh Poems*, p. 129; tr. Joseph P. Clancy, *A Book of Wales* (1987), p. 314; tr. Tony Conran, *Bloodaxe Book*, pp. 125–6; '**Tri Bardd o Sais a Lloegr**' (Three English Poets and England), tr. Tony Conran, *Bloodaxe Book*, pp. 132–3; '**Wedi'r Canrifoedd Mudan**' (After the Mute Centuries), tr. Tony Conran, *Poetry Wales*, 2.1 (1966), 20; tr. Tony Conran, *The Penguin Book of Welsh Verse*, pp. 260–1; tr. R. Gerallt Jones, *Poetry of Wales 1930–1970*, pp. 215–6; tr. Joseph P. Clancy, *Twentieth Century Welsh Poems*, p. 133; tr. Tony Conran, *Welsh Verse*, pp. 290–1; tr. Rowan Williams, *After Silent Centuries: Poems by Rowan Williams* (Oxford: The Perpetua Press, 1994), p. 50; tr. Rowan Williams, *Bloodaxe Book*, pp. 128–9; '**Y Ci Coch**' (The Red Dog), tr. Dafydd Wyn Jones, *Barddas*, 224/225 (Dec/Jan 1995/1996), 35; '**Y Dderwen Gam**' (The Crooked Oak), tr. Joseph P. Clancy, *Twentieth Century Welsh Poems*, p. 138; '**Y Geni**' (The Birth), tr. Joseph P. Clancy, *Twentieth Century Welsh Poems*, p. 132; tr. Tony Conran, *Swansea Review*, 14 (1995), 10; '**Yn Nyddiau'r Cesar**' (In the Days of Caesar), tr. Rowan Williams, *After Silent Centuries: Poems by Rowan Williams* (Oxford: The Perpetua Press, 1994), p. 49; tr. Tony Conran, *Swansea Review*, 14 (1995), 12; '**Yr Eiliad**' (The Moment), tr. Tony Conran, *The Penguin Book of Welsh Verse*, p. 258; tr. Joseph P. Clancy, *Twentieth Century Welsh Poems*, p. 136; tr. Tony Conran, *Welsh Verse*, p. 288; tr. Greg Hill, *Bastard Englyns* (Bow Street: Nant Publications, 2000), p. 28; '**Yr Heniaith**' (The Old Language), tr. R. Gerallt Jones, *Poetry of Wales 1930–1970*, p. 211; tr. Joseph P. Clancy, *Twentieth Century Welsh Poems*, pp. 132–3; tr. Tony Conran, *Modern Poetry in Translation*, p. 198; '**Y Tangnefeddwyr**' (The Peacemakers), tr. R. Gerallt Jones, *Poetry of Wales 1930–1970*, p. 213; tr. Tony Conran, *A Swansea Anthology*, ed. James A. Davies (Bridgend: Seren, 1996), p. 104; ['**Ni saif a llunio arfaeth orffenedig**'] (God), tr. Greg Hill, *Bastard Englyns* (Bow Street: Nant Publications, 2000), p. 27.[15]

---

[15] *Englyn* published in 'Paham yr wyf yn Grynwr' (1956), reprinted in *Waldo Williams: Rhyddiaith*, ed. Damian Walford Davies (Cardiff: University of Wales Press, 2001), pp. 319–23 [p. 322].

T. ARFON WILLIAMS (1935–98)

Individual Translations *Po.*
'**Eira Undydd**' (One-day Snow), tr. Emyr Lewis, *Bloodaxe Book*, pp. 250–1; '**Ewyn**' ['Pan chwery chwa . . .'] (Foam), tr. Emyr Lewis, *Bloodaxe Book*, p. 249; '**Gwas y Neidr**' (The Dragonfly), tr. author, *Modern Poetry in Translation*, p. 172; '**Mai**' ['Oesoedd bu'n bwrw'i phrentisiaeth'] (May), tr. author, *Quaderno 2 di Lettera* (March, 1977), 75; '**Mam yw'r Ddaear**' (Mother Earth), tr. author, *Quaderno 2 di Lettera* (March, 1977), 85; '**Mis Mai**' ['Cilio'n ôl wna marwolaeth . . .'] (May), tr. Emyr Lewis, *Bloodaxe Book*, p. 250; '**Non**', tr. author, *Modern Poetry in Translation*, p. 174; '**R S Thomas**', tr. author, *Modern Poetry in Translation*, p. 174; '**Y Delyn**' (The Harp), tr. author, *Quaderno 2 di Lettera* (March, 1977), 85; '**Y Gwanwyn**' (The Spring), tr. author, *Quaderno 2 di Lettera* (March, 1977), 83; '**Y Llechfaen**' ['Agorais gyfrol garreg . . .'] (Quarry), tr. Emyr Lewis, *Bloodaxe Book*, p. 249; '**Y Nos**' (The Night), tr. author, *Quaderno 2 di Lettera* (March, 1977), 85; '**Yr Afon**' (The River), tr. author, *Quaderno 2 di Lettera* (March, 1977), 83; '**Y Traeth**' (The Beach), tr. author, *Modern Poetry in Translation*, p. 173.

WILLIAM WILLIAMS (Crwys; 1875–1968)

Individual Translations *Po.*
'**Dysgub y Dail**' (Gathering Leaves), tr. Tony Conran, *The Penguin Book of Welsh Verse*, p. 237; tr. Tony Conran, *Welsh Verse*, p. 267; '**Gwynfyd**' (Paradise), tr. H. Idris Bell, *Welsh Poems of the Twentieth Century*, p. 69; '**Melin Trefin**' (The Mill at Trefin), tr. H. Idris Bell, *A History of Welsh Literature*, p. 406; tr. Joseph P. Clancy, *Twentieth Century Welsh Poems*, p. 34.

LLENYDDIAETH GYFOES: CONTEMPORARY WRITING

Anthologies

Poetry

R. Gerallt Jones, *Poetry of Wales 1930–1970* (Llandysul: Gwasg Gomer, 1974).
[*Poetry of Wales 1930–1970*]

Joseph P. Clancy, *Twentieth Century Welsh Poems* (Llandysul: Gomer, 1982).
[*Twentieth Century Welsh Poems*]

Modern Poetry in Translation (with Dafydd Johnston as guest editor), 7 (1995).
[*Modern Poetry in Translation*]

Grahame Davies and Amy Wack (eds), *Oxygen* (Bridgend: Seren, 2000).
[*Oxygen*]

The Literary Review: Re-Imagining Wales, 44.2 (2001).
[*The Literary Review*]

Thomas Rain Crowe (ed. with Gwendal Denez and Tom Hubbard), *Writing the Wind: A Celtic Resurgence* (United States: New Native Press, 1997).
[*Writing the Wind*]

E. S. Shaffer (ed.), *Comparative Criticism: Literary devolution: writing in Scotland, Ireland, Wales and England*, Volume 19 (Cambridge: Cambridge University Press, 1997).
[*Comparative Criticism*]

Robert Minhinnick, *The Adulterer's Tongue* (Manchester: Carcanet Press, 2003).
[*The Adulterer's Tongue*]

Menna Elfyn and John Rowlands (eds), *The Bloodaxe Book of Modern Welsh Poetry: 20th century Welsh language poetry in translation* (Newcastle Upon Tyne: Bloodaxe Books, 2003).
[*Bloodaxe Book*]

Prose

Gwyn Jones and Islwyn Ffowc Elis (eds), *Twenty-Five Welsh Short Stories* (London: Oxford University Press, 1971). Reprinted as *Classic Welsh Short Stories* (Oxford: Oxford University Press, 1992).
[*Twenty-Five Welsh Short Stories*][1]

Alun Richards (ed.), *The Penguin Book of Welsh Short Stories* (Middlesex: Penguin Books, 1976).
[*The Penguin Book of Welsh Short Stories*]

Alun Richards (ed.), *The New Penguin Book of Welsh Short Stories* (Harmondsworth: Penguin Books, 1994).
[*The New Penguin Book of Welsh Short Stories*]

Meic Stephens, *Illuminations: an Anthology of Welsh Short Prose* (Welsh Academic Press, 1998).
[*Illuminations*]

Meic Stephens, *A White Afternoon & Other Stories* (Cardiff: Parthian Books, 1998).
[*A White Afternoon*]

---

[1] Page numbers remain the same.

SIÔN ALED (1957–)

Individual Translations *Po.*
'**Cledrau Hiraeth**' (Tracks of Longing), tr. Grahame Davies, *Bloodaxe Book*, pp. 343–4; '**Machlud dros Lŷn** (Sunset over Llŷn), tr. Grahame Davies, *Bloodaxe Book*, p. 344; '**Rhagolygon y Tywydd**' (Weather Forecast), tr. Grahame Davies, *Bloodaxe Book*, pp. 342–3.

NICI BEECH (1969–)

Individual Translations *Po.*
'**Camau Cyntaf**' (First Steps), tr. Elin ap Hywel, *Oxygen*, p. 161; '**Dal Breuddwyd yn y Bore**' (Holding a Dream), tr. Elin ap Hywel, *Oxygen*, p. 163.

BRYAN MARTIN DAVIES (1933–)

Individual Translations *Po.*
'**Berne**', tr. Elin ap Hywel, *Bloodaxe Book*, pp. 232–3; '**Cloddio**' (Mining), tr. author, *Poetry Wales*, 11.3 (1976), 75; '**Eco'r Haiku**' (The Echo of the Haiku), tr. author, *Poetry Wales*, 11.3 (1976), 76; '**Eira yn Wrecsam**' (Snow in Wrexham), tr. Elin ap Hywel, *Bloodaxe Book*, pp. 231–2; '**Er Cof**' (In Memoriam), tr. author, *Poetry Wales*, 12.1 (1976), 32–3; '**Erthylu**' (Abortion), tr. author, *Poetry Wales*, 10.4 (1975), 77–9; '**Fioled**' (Violet), tr. R. Gerallt Jones, *Poetry of Wales 1930–1970*, pp. 371–3; tr. R. Gerallt Jones, *Love from Wales: An Anthology*, ed. Tony Curtis and Siân James (Bridgend: Seren Books, 1991), pp. 81–2; '**Gêm Bêl-droed**' (A Football Game), tr. Grahame Davies, *Wales: A Celebration*, ed. Dewi Roberts (Llanrwst: Gwasg Carreg Gwalch, 2000), pp. 69–70; '**Glas**' (Blue), tr. Elin ap Hywel, *Bloodaxe Book*, pp. 229–30; '**Glaw yn Auvers**' (Rain in Auvers), tr. Huw Jones, *The Anglo-Welsh Review*, 25.56 (1976), 128; '**Gweddw**' (Widow), tr. Elin ap Hywel, *Bloodaxe Book*, pp. 230–1; '**Hen Bethel**' (Old Bethel), tr. Joseph P. Clancy, *Twentieth Century Welsh Poems*, pp. 212–13; '**Lleu**', tr. R. Gerallt Jones, *Poetry of Wales 1930–1970*, p. 369; '**Tairgwaith**', tr. author, *Poetry Wales*, 15.4 (1980), 14–16; tr. author, *The Valleys*, ed. John Davies and Mike Jenkins (Poetry Wales Press, 1984), p. 84; '**Una Paloma Blanca**', tr. author,

Quaderno 2 di Lettera (March 1977), 19; '**Wylaf Wers**' (I Weep Awhile), tr. author, *Quaderno 2 di Lettera* (March 1977), 17; '**Y Berllan**' (The Orchard), tr. Huw Jones, *The Anglo-Welsh Review*, 25.56 (1976), 129; '**Y Croeso**' (The Welcome), tr. author, *Poetry Wales*, 13.3 (1977), 68–70; '**Y Niwl, y Nos, a'r Ynys**' (The Mist, the Night, and the Island), tr. author, *Poetry Wales*, 9.3 (1973–4), 84–6; '**Y Parthenon**' (The Parthenon), tr. Joseph P. Clancy, *Twentieth Century Welsh Poems*, pp. 213–4; '**Ystyriaeth (ar Noson o Chwefror '86)**' (Consideration [on a February night, 1986]), tr. Elin ap Hywel, *Bloodaxe Book*, pp. 233–4.

Individual Translations *Pr.*
'**Y Llwynog dan y Gwydr**' (The Fox under Glass), tr. Meic Stephens, *Illuminations*, pp. 183–6.

GRAHAME DAVIES (1964–)

Collections

Elin ap Hywel and Grahame Davies, *Ffiniau: Borders* (Llandysul: Gomer Press, 2002).

Individual Translations *Po.*
'**Ar y Rhandir**' (On the Allotment), tr. author, *Wales: A Celebration*, ed. Dewi Roberts (Llanrwst: Gwasg Carreg Gwalch, 2000), p. 137; '**Coch**' (Red), tr. author, *Oxygen*, p. 145; tr. author, *The Literary Review*, p. 226; tr. author, *Bloodaxe Book*, p. 397; '**Cyfannu**' (Making Whole), tr. author, *Beyond the Difference: Welsh Literature in Comparative Contexts*, ed. Alyce von Rothkirch and Daniel Williams (Cardiff: University of Wales Press, 2004), p. 205; '**DIY**', tr. author, *Bloodaxe Book*, pp. 393–4; '**Gwastraff**' (Waste), tr. author, *Bloodaxe Book*, pp. 394–5; '**Lerpwl**' (Liverpool), tr. author, *Bloodaxe Book*, p. 396; '**Mynwent Iddewon Merthyr**' (Merthyr Jewish Cemetery), tr. author, *The Chosen People: Wales & The Jews*, ed. Grahame Davies (Bridgend: Seren, 2002), pp. 42–3; '**Rough Guide**', tr. author, *Oxygen*, p. 149; tr. author, *Poetry London*, 36 (2000), 3; tr. author, *The Literary Review*, p. 227; tr. author, *Bloodaxe Book*, pp. 396–7; '**Villanelle y Cymoedd**' (Valley Villanelle), tr. author, *Oxygen*, p. 147.

MARTIN DAVIS (1957–)

Individual Translations *Pr.*
'Rhith Rheolaeth' (Water), tr. Meic Stephens, *A White Afternoon*, pp. 51–9.

MERERID PUW DAVIES (1970–)

Individual Translations *Po.*
'Bardd ar "Feirdd ar Feirdd", a cherddi eraill' (A Poet on 'Poets on Poets': And other poems), tr. author, *Bloodaxe Book*, pp. 422–3; 'Dros Apéritif' (Over an Apéritif), tr. Elin ap Hywel, *Oxygen*, p. 165; tr. author, *Bloodaxe Book*, pp. 420–1; 'Mae'r Cyfrifiadur Hefyd yn Fardd' (Computers are Poets too), tr. Elin ap Hywel, *Oxygen*, p. 167; tr. author, *Bloodaxe Book*, pp. 421–2.

MARION EAMES (1921–)

Prose (Novels)
Y Stafell Ddirgel, *The Secret Room*, tr. Margaret Phillips (Swansea: Christopher Davies, 1975). Reprinted (London: Corgi, 1987).

Y Rhandir Mwyn, *Fair Wilderness*, tr. Elin Garlick in conjunction with author (Swansea: Christopher Davies, 1976). Reprinted (London: Corgi, 1987).

I Hela Cnau, *The Golden Road*, tr. author (Llandysul: Gomer, 1990).

DYFED EDWARDS (1966–)

Individual Translations *Pr.*
'Y Llyfrgellydd' (The Librarian), tr. Meic Stephens, *A White Afternoon*, pp. 60–4.

HUW MEIRION EDWARDS (1965–)

Individual Translations *Po.*
'**Glaw**' (Rain), tr. Elin ap Hywel, *Oxygen*, p. 153; '**Hwiangerdd**' (Lullaby), tr. Grahame Davies, *Oxygen*, p. 151.

JANE EDWARDS (1938–)

Individual Translations *Pr.*
'**Ar Golli Cymar**' (Now Alone), tr. Elin Williams, *Planet*, 100 (1993), 53–60; '**Blind Dêt**' (Blind Date), tr. Derec Llwyd Morgan, *A Book of Wales* (1987), pp. 50–4; tr. Derec Llwyd Morgan, *The Penguin Book of Welsh Short Stories*, pp. 234–40; tr. Derec Llwyd Morgan, *Love from Wales: An Anthology*, ed. Tony Curtis and Siân James (Bridgend: Seren Books, 1991), pp. 39–40 (extract); tr. Derec Llwyd Morgan, *An Anglesey Anthology*, ed. Dewi Roberts (Gwasg Carreg Gwalch, 1999), pp. 160–5; '**Disgwyl i'r Glaw Dorri**' (Waiting for the Rain to Break), tr. Elin Williams, *The New Penguin Book of Welsh Short Stories*, pp. 332–9.

SONIA EDWARDS (1961–)

Prose (Novel)
Rhwng Noson Wen a Phlygain, *A White Veil for Tomorrow*, tr. author (Cardiff: Parthian Books, 2001).

Individual Translations *Pr.*
'**Prynhawn Gwyn**' (A White Afternoon), tr. Meic Stephens, *A White Afternoon & other stories*, pp. 7–12.

Individual Translations *Po.*
'**Lle Gwag**' (An Empty Place), tr. Sally Roberts Jones, *Bloodaxe Book*, p. 375; '**Rhwng Dau**' (Between Two Lovers), tr. Sally Roberts Jones, *Bloodaxe Book*, p. 376.

SIÔN EIRIAN (1954–)

Individual Translations *Po.*
'**Brain**' (Crows), tr. author, *Quaderno 2 di Lettera* (March 1977), 81; '**Fy Newis i**' (My Choice), tr. author, *Quaderno 2 di Lettera* (March 1977), 79; ''**Nhad versus Ginsberg**' (My Dad versus Ginsberg), tr. Robert Minhinnick, *Bloodaxe Book*, pp. 324–5; *from* '**Profiadau Llencyndod**' (Adolescent Experiences) ['**Dysgu**' (Learning), '**Concwest**' (Conquest), '**Saesnes**' (An Englishwoman) '**Diweddgan**' (Endsong)], tr. Robert Minhinnick, *Bloodaxe Book*, pp. 325–8; '**Y Boen**' (The Pain), tr. Robert Minhinnick, *Bloodaxe Book*, p. 324.

MENNA ELFYN (1951–)

Collections

Eucalyptus (Llandysul: Gomer, 1995).

Cell Angel (Newcastle Upon Tyne: Bloodaxe Books, 1996).

Cusan Dyn Dall: Blind Man's Kiss (Northumberland: Bloodaxe Books, 2001).

Individual Translations *Po.*
'**Ambyr (i Tony)**' (Amber (for Tony)), tr. Gillian Clarke, in *Thirteen Ways of Looking at Tony Conran*, ed. Nigel Jenkins (Welsh Union of Writers, 1995), p. 12; '**Blodau Gwylltion**' (Wild Flowers), tr. Elin ap Hywel, *Writing the Wind*, pp. 57–8; '**Bore Da yn Broadway**' (Broadway Morning), tr. Gillian Clarke, *Bloodaxe Book*, pp. 322–3; '**Cân y di-lais i British Telecom**' (Song of a Voiceless Person to British Telecom), tr. R. S. Thomas, *Poetry Wales*, 29.4 (1994), 13–14; tr. R. S. Thomas, *Comparative Criticism*, pp. 103–4; tr. R. S. Thomas, *Metamorphoses*, 12 (Spring/Fall 2004), 120–1; '**Cell Angel**', tr. Gillian Clarke, *Comparative Criticism*, pp. 112–13; tr. Gillian Clarke, *Writing the Wind*, pp. 56–7; tr. Gillian Clarke, *Bloodaxe Book*, pp. 315–17; '**Chwarae Plant**' (Kid's Play), tr. Tony Conran, *Modern Poetry in Translation*, pp. 35–7; tr. Nigel Jenkins, *Ambush* (Llandysul: Gomer Press, 1998), pp. 49–50; '**Clorian Cariad**' (Love's Scales), tr. Nigel Jenkins, *Ambush* (Llandysul: Gomer Press, 1998), p. 52; '**Cwfaint**'

(Nunnery), tr. Gillian Clarke, *Writing the Wind*, pp. 54–5; '**Coch yr Oeron**' (Cranberries), tr. Tony Conran, *Comparative Criticism*, pp. 110–11; '**Cot Law yn Asheville**' (Raincoat in Asheville), tr. Nigel Jenkins, *Ambush* (Llandysul: Gomer Press, 1998), pp. 53–4; *from Cyfrinachau* (Secrets) [I. '**Diwinyddiaeth Gwallt**' (The Theology of Hair)], tr. Elin ap Hywel, *Bloodaxe Book*, pp. 318–19; [IV '**Mamiaith**' (The Mother Tongue)], tr. Elin ap Hywel, *Comparative Criticism*, pp. 114–15; '**Cyplau**' (Couplings), tr. Joseph P. Clancy, *Poetry Wales*, 33.1 (1997), 31–2; tr. Joseph P. Clancy, *The Literary Review*, p. 230; tr. Joseph P. Clancy, *Bloodaxe Book*, p. 319; '**Dau Gyfnod**' (Different Periods), tr. Elin ap Hywel, *Comparative Criticism*, pp. 108–9; '**Dim ond Camedd**' (Nothing but Curves), tr. Elin ap Hywel, *Bloodaxe Book*, pp. 319–21; '**Esgidiau**' (Shoes), tr. Nigel Jenkins, *Ambush* (Llandysul: Gomer Press, 1998), p. 51; '**Eucalyptus**', tr. Tony Conran, *Modern Poetry in Translation*, pp. 34–5; tr. Tony Conran, *Writing the Wind*, pp. 59–60; '**Ffôn Adre**' (Phoning Home), tr. Gillian Clarke, *Poetry Wales*, 29.4 (1994), 12–13; '**Gyrru i Ben**' (Driver), tr. Tony Conran, *Bloodaxe Book*, pp. 317–18; '**Gwely Dwbwl**' (Double Bed) tr. author and Gillian Clarke, *Writing the Wind*, p. 55; '**Llusernau Tseina**' (Chinese Lanterns), tr. Tony Conran, *Writing the Wind*, p. 60; '**Mae pethau wedi newid, Mr Frost**' (Things have changed Mr Frost), tr. author, *Planet*, 64 (1987), 20–2; '**Misglwyf-Mis-y-clwyf**' (Bleedings), tr. Tony Conran, *Modern Poetry in Translation*, p. 30; '**Mynd yn Dywyll**' (Going Dim), tr. Joseph P. Clancy, *The Literary Review*, p. 232; '**Neges**' (Message), tr. R. S. Thomas, *Writing the Wind*, p. 61; '**Pabwyr Nos**' (Night Light), tr. Tony Conran, *Modern Poetry in Translation*, pp. 31–2; '**Papurau Reis**' (Rice Papers), tr. Nigel Jenkins, *Bloodaxe Book*, pp. 321–2; '**Perl̈io Geiriau**' (The Worth of Words), tr. Joseph P. Clancy, *Beyond the Difference: Welsh Literature in Comparative Contexts*, ed. Alyce von Rothkirch and Daniel Williams (Cardiff: University of Wales Press, 2004), p. 99; '**Pysgotwr**' (Fisherman), tr. Elin ap Hywel, *Modern Poetry in Translation*, pp. 37–8; '**'rwy'n caru mhlant yn fwy na neb**' (i love my children more than anyone), tr. author, *Poetry Wales*, 22.3 (1987), 30–1; '**Saffir**' (Sapphire), tr. Gillian Clarke, *The Literary Review*, p. 233; '**Sefyll**' (Standing by *[in a doctor's surgery]*), tr. Joseph P. Clancy, *The Literary Review*, p. 231; '**Siapau o Gymru**' (Wales – The Shapes She Makes), tr. Elin ap Hywel, *Metamorphoses*, 12 (Spring/Fall 2004), 116–17; '**Tocyn Colled**' (Ticket of Loss), tr. Tony Conran, *Modern Poetry in Translation*, pp. 33–4; '**Toriad Trydan**' (Power Cut), tr. Tony

Conran, *Modern Poetry in Translation*, pp. 32–3. 'Troedlath Serch' (Love's Treadle), tr. Nigel Jenkins, *Poetry Wales*, 33.3 (1998), 16–17; tr. Nigel Jenkins, *The Literary Review*, p. 229; 'Wedi'r Achos' (After the Court Case), tr. Elin ap Hywel, *Writing the Wind*, p. 58; tr. author and Elin ap Hywel, *Comparative Criticism*, pp. 107–8; 'Y Dydd ar ôl Dydd Ffolant' (February 15th), tr. Elin ap Hywel, *Poetry Wales*, 33.3 (1998), 18–20; 'Y Genhadaeth' (Missionary Collection), tr. Nest Lloyd, *Poetry Wales*, 25.2 (1989), 31; 'Y Gneuen Wag' (The Empty Shell), tr. Tony Conran, *Modern Poetry in Translation*, p. 34.

ELIN AP HYWEL (1962–)

Collections

Elin ap Hywel and Grahame Davies, *Ffiniau: Borders* (Llandysul: Gomer Press, 2002).

Individual Translations *Po.*
'Adroddiad' (Owl Report), tr. author, *Writing the Wind*, pp. 77–8; 'Aur' (Gold), tr. author, *Writing the Wind*, pp. 74–5; tr. Robert Minhinnick, *The Adulterer's Tongue*, pp. 103–5; 'Cawl' (Soup), tr. author, *Oxygen*, pp. 131–3; tr. Robert Minhinnick, *The Adulterer's Tongue*, p. 113; 'Deall Goleuni' (Understanding the Light), tr. author, *Oxygen*, p. 129, tr. Robert Minhinnick, *The Adulterer's Tongue*, tr. author, p. 115; *Bloodaxe Book*, pp. 381–2; tr. author, http://www.brindin.com/pohywdea.htm; 'Defnyddiol' (Really Useful), tr. author, *Oxygen*, pp. 133–5; tr. Robert Minhinnick, *The Adulterer's Tongue*, p. 117; 'Distawrwydd' (Silence), tr. author, *Writing the Wind*, p. 78; 'Diosg' (Disarmed), tr. Robert Minhinnick, *The Adulterer's Tongue*, p. 99; 'Duwiesau' (Goddesses), tr. author, *Oxygen*, pp. 129–31; tr. Robert Minhinnick, *The Adulterer's Tongue*, p. 119; tr. author, *Bloodaxe Book*, pp. 384–5; 'Galvanic' (Thing), tr. author, *Bloodaxe Book*, pp. 380–1; 'Glas' (Blue), tr. author, *Writing the Wind*, p. 79; tr. Robert Minhinnick, *The Adulterer's Tongue*, p. 107; tr. author, *Bloodaxe Book*, pp. 383–4; 'Gwener y Groglith' (Good Friday), tr. author, *Materion Dwyieithog: Bilingual Matters*, 2 (1990), 6; 'Pwytho' (Stitching), tr. Robert Minhinnick, *The Adulterer's Tongue*, p. 101; 'Unwaith' (History), tr. Robert Minhinnick, *The Adulterer's Tongue*, p. 121; 'Yn Nhŷ fy Mam' (In My

Mother's House), tr. author, *Writing the Wind*, pp. 75–6; tr. Robert Minhinnick, *The Adulterer's Tongue*, pp. 109–11; tr. author, *Bloodaxe Book*, pp. 382–3.

MEG ELIS (1950–)

Individual Translations *Pr.*
'**Mynd i Mewn**' (Going In), tr. Meic Stephens, *A White Afternoon*, pp. 165–70.

JOHN EMYR (1950–)

Individual Translations *Pr.*
'**Wrth Afonydd Babilon**' (By the Waters of Babylon), tr. Meic Stephens, *A White Afternoon*, pp. 131–8.

ALED LEWIS EVANS (1961–)

Collections

Wavelengths (Connah's Quay, Clwyd: I D Books, 1995).
Mixing the Colours (Connah's Quay, Clwyd: I D Books, 2000).

Individual Translations *Po.*
from '**Unigedd**' (Alone), tr. Peter Finch, *Bloodaxe Book*, pp. 377–9.

Individual Translations *Pr.*
'**Dean a Debs**' (Dean and Debs), tr. Meic Stephens, *A White Afternoon*, pp. 36–42.

BETHAN EVANS (1962–)

Individual Translations *Pr.*
'**Un Letusen ni Wna Salad**' (One Lettuce Does not a Salad Make), tr. Meic Stephens, *A White Afternoon*, pp. 111–26.

DONALD EVANS (1940–)

Individual Translations *Po.*
'**Chwil-rasio**' (Joy-riding), tr. author, *Modern Poetry in Translation*, pp. 44–5; '**Cread Crist**' (Creation), tr. Gillian Clarke, *Bloodaxe Book*, p. 267; '**Cymru '99**' (Wales '99), tr. Gillian Clarke, *Bloodaxe Book*, p. 263; '**Diwrnod Lladd Mochyn**' (Pig Killing Day), tr. Gillian Clarke, *Bloodaxe Book*, pp. 264–5; '**Gig Bont**' (Gig at Bont), tr. author, *Modern Poetry in Translation*, pp. 40–1; '**Gwerin**' (The People), tr. Gillian Clarke, *Bloodaxe Book*, pp. 265–6; '**Iddewes**' ['Roedd yn byw ar fferm yn ardal Llanrhystud yr adeg yma'] (A Jewess), tr. Grahame Davies, *The Chosen People: Wales & The Jews*, ed. Grahame Davies (Bridgend: Seren, 2002), pp. 207–8; '**Iddewes**' ['Yma, ar dir y môr dwys . . .'] (A Jewess), tr. Grahame Davies, *The Chosen People: Wales & The Jews*, ed. Grahame Davies (Bridgend: Seren, 2002), pp. 207–8; '**I Gethin Moelifor**' (To Gethin Moelifor), tr. author, *Modern Poetry in Translation*, pp. 41–2; '**Nentydd Iaith**' (Language Streams), tr. author, *Modern Poetry in Translation*, pp. 42–3; '**Y Draffordd**' (Motorway), tr. author, *Modern Poetry in Translation*, pp. 39–40; '**Y Parchedig Ffred Jenkins**' (The Reverend Fred Jenkins), tr. author, *Poetry Wales*, 16.3 (1981), 15–16; '**Y Teithwyr Newydd**' (Travellers), tr. author, *Modern Poetry in Translation*, pp. 43–4; '**Y Tip Sbwriel**' (The Rubbish Tip), tr. Gillian Clarke, *Bloodaxe Book*, p. 264.

LOWRI ANGHARAD EVANS (1966–)

Individual Translations *Pr.*
'**Y Gôt**' (The Coat), tr. Meic Stephens, *A White Afternoon*, pp. 139–48.

JOHN FITZGERALD (1927–)

Individual Translations *Po.*
'**Aber-fan**', tr. Joseph P. Clancy, *Twentieth Century Welsh Poems*, p. 189; '**Bodolyn**' (Being (Human)), tr. Joseph P. Clancy, *Bloodaxe Book*, p. 210; '**Cawr Mawr Bychan**' (Great Little One), tr. Joseph P. Clancy, *Bloodaxe Book*, pp. 209–10; '**Duw Cudd, Duw Ffydd**' (God in Hiding, God of Faith), tr. Joseph P. Clancy, *Bloodaxe Book*, pp. 208–9; '**Gwahanglwyf**' (Leprosy), tr. Joseph P. Clancy, *Trivium*, 8

(1973), 120; tr. Joseph P. Clancy, *Twentieth Century Welsh Poems*, p. 189; '**Nid oes Iawn Gyfaill ond Un**' (There Is But One True Friend), tr. Joseph P. Clancy, *Bloodaxe Book*, p. 209; '**Y Tŷ Hwnt**' (The House Beyond), tr. Joseph P. Clancy, *Bloodaxe Book*, pp. 207–8.

CARMEL GAHAN (1954–)

Individual Translations *Po.*
'**Gofyn amdani**' (asking for it), tr. Robert Minhinnick, *Bloodaxe Book*, pp. 329–30.

EIRWYN GEORGE (1936–)

Individual Translations *Po.*
'**Perthnasau**' (Family), tr. Peter Finch, *Bloodaxe Book*, pp. 251–2.

GWYNN AP GWILYM (1950–)

Individual Translations *Po.*
'**Penyberth**', tr. Joseph P. Clancy, *Bloodaxe Book*, p. 306; '**Y Mochyn Daear**' (The Badger), tr. Grahame Davies, *Bloodaxe Book*, pp. 307–8.

MERERID HOPWOOD (1964–)

Individual Translations *Po.*
'**Dadeni**' (Rebirth), tr. Elin ap Hywel, *Bloodaxe Book*, pp. 402–5; tr. Elin ap Hywel, www.unesco.it/poesia/babele/poesia/autori/autori.htm.

VAUGHAN HUGHES (1947–)

Individual Translations *Po.*
'**Artist**', tr. author, *Quaderno 2 di Lettera* (March 1977), 39.

EMYR HUMPHREYS (1919–)

Individual Translations *Po.*
'**Ar y Guincho**' (On the Guincho), tr. Elin ap Hywel, *Bloodaxe Book*, pp. 192–3; '**Poughkeepsie**', tr. Elin ap Hywel, *Bloodaxe Book*, pp. 193–4.

GWILYM REES HUGHES (1930–)

Individual Translations *Po.*
'**Madarch**' (Mushroom), tr. R. Gerallt Jones, *Poetry of Wales 1930–1970*, p. 357; '**Penhwyad**' (Pike), tr. R. Gerallt Jones, *Poetry of Wales 1930–1970*, p. 359; tr. Joseph P. Clancy, *Twentieth Century Welsh Poems*, p. 208.

DAFYDD HUWS (Goronwy Jones; 1949–)

Individual Translations *Pr.*
from '**Dyddiadur Dyn Dwad**' (Down and Out), tr. Meic Stephens, *A White Afternoon*, pp. 102–10.

MEIRION MACINTYRE HUWS (1963–)

Individual Translations *Po.*
'**Côt**' (Coat), tr. Grahame Davies, *Oxygen*, p. 137; tr. Grahame Davies, *Bloodaxe Book*, p. 388; '**Cydwybod**' (Conscience), tr. Geraint Løvgreen, *Bloodaxe Book*, pp. 386–7; '**Dinas**' (The City), tr. Geraint Løvgreen, *Bloodaxe Book*, pp. 387–8; '**Ffenest**' (Window), tr. Geraint Løvgreen, *Bloodaxe Book*, pp. 385–6; '**Lle mae Cychod y Tlodion**' (The Boats of the Poor), tr. Grahame Davies, *Oxygen*, pp. 137–9.

SIÂN PRYDDERCH HUWS (1970–)

Individual Translations *Pr.*
'**Mr a Mrs Tiresias**' (Mr and Mrs Tiresias), tr. Meic Stephens, *A White Afternoon*, pp. 212–19.

DAFYDD IFANS (1949–)

Individual Translations *Po.*
'**Deffro**' (The Awakening), tr. author, *Quaderno 2 di Lettera* (March 1977), 43; '**Ha' Bach Mihangel**' (Michaelmas Day), tr. author, *Quaderno 2 di Lettera* (March 1977), 41.

IFOR AP GLYN (1961–)

Individual Translations *Po.*
'**Ciwcymbars Wolverhampton**' (The Cucumbers of Wolverhampton), tr. Nigel Jenkins, *Bloodaxe Book*, pp. 370–1; '**Croesi'r Bont**' (Crossing Over), tr. author, *Oxygen*, p. 123; '**Englynion**' (Englyns), tr. Nigel Jenkins, *Bloodaxe Book*, pp. 372–3; *from* '**Golau yn y Gwyll: Clirio'r tŷ mewn cwmwl tystion**' (Light in the Darkness: Cleaning the house in a cloud of witnesses), tr. author, *Oxygen*, pp. 119–21; '**I've always wished I could speak Welsh**', tr. author, *Oxygen*, p. 121; '**Tri Darlleniad Trychinebus Ynys Prydain: Rhif 1 – Caerdydd 1989**' (The Three Disastrous Poetry Readings of the Island of Britain: No. 1 – Cardiff 1989), tr. author, *Oxygen*, pp. 117–19; '**Y Fi yw'r Boi hefo'r Bol**' (I'm the Guy with the Gut), tr. unsigned [but author], *Poetry Wales*, 35.1 (1999), 16–18; tr. author, *Bloodaxe Book*, pp. 373–4.

DYLAN IORWERTH (1957–)

Individual Translations *Po.*
from '**Tywod**' (Sand), tr. author, *Bloodaxe Book*, pp. 345–9.

ALED ISLWYN (1953–)

Individual Translations *Po.*
'**Cotiau**' (Coats), tr. author, *Quaderno 2 di Lettera* (March 1977), 11;
'**Diwrnod Arall**' (Another Day), tr. author, *Quaderno 2 di Lettera*
(March 1977), 7–9; '**Gwragedd Priod**' (Married Women), tr. author,
Quaderno 2 di Lettera (March 1977), 13; '**Perthyn**' (Related), tr.
author, *Quaderno 2 di Lettera* (March 1977), 15.

Individual Translations *Pr.*
'**Stori Linda**' (Linda's Story), tr. Meic Stephens, *A White Afternoon*,
pp. 13–23.

DAFYDD IWAN (1943–)

Individual Translations *Po.*
'**Pam fod Eira'n Wyn?**' (Why Snow is White), tr. Geraint Løvgreen,
Bloodaxe Book, p. 274.

MELERI WYN JAMES (1970–)

Individual Translations *Pr.*
'**Stripio**' (Striptease), tr. Meic Stephens, *A White Afternoon*, pp. 171–4.

GERAINT JARMAN (1950–)

Individual Translations *Po.*
'**Cân Ionawr I**' (January Song), tr. Meic Stephens, *A Cardiff
Anthology*, ed. Meic Stephens (Bridgend: Seren, 1987), pp. 147–8;
'**Dad a Minne**' (Dad and Me), tr. Peter Finch, *Bloodaxe Book*, pp.
308–9; '**Y Coed**' (The Wood), tr. Peter Finch, *Bloodaxe Book*, p. 309.

ANGHARAD JONES (1962–)

Individual Translations *Pr.*
'**Annwyl Mr Atlas**' (Dear Mr Atlas), tr. Meic Stephens, *A White Afternoon*, pp. 29–35.

ALUN FFRED JONES (1949–)

Individual Translations *Pr.*
'**Y Reff**' (The Referee), tr. Meic Stephens, *A White Afternoon*, pp. 90–101.

BOBI JONES (R. M. Jones; 1929–)

Collections

Joseph P. Clancy, *Selected Poems* (Swansea: Christopher Davies, 1987).

Individual Translations *Po.*
'**Aber-porth**', tr. Joseph P. Clancy, *Twentieth Century Welsh Poems*, pp. 201–2; '**Aberystwyth**', tr. Joseph P. Clancy, *Poetry Wales*, 21.1 (1985), 71; '**Afon Sain Lawren**' (St Lawrence River), tr. Joseph P. Clancy, *Twentieth Century Welsh Poems*, p. 202; '**Amwythig**' (Shrewsbury), tr. Joseph P. Clancy, *Twentieth Century Welsh Poems*, p. 196; '**Atgyfodiad yr Adar**' (The Resurrection of the Birds), tr. Joseph P. Clancy, *Twentieth Century Welsh Poems*, pp. 203–4; '**Bwyta'n Te**' (Having our Tea), tr. Joseph P. Clancy, *Twentieth Century Welsh Poems*, pp. 198–9; tr. Joseph P. Clancy, *A Book of Wales* (1987), pp. 128–9; tr. Joseph P. Clancy, *Bloodaxe Book*, pp. 212–13; '**Cacynen**' (Wasp), tr. Joseph P. Clancy, *The Literary Review*, pp. 272–3; tr. Robert Minhinnick, *The Adulterer's Tongue*, pp. 9–11; '**Byddar a Byddar**' (The Conversation of the Deaf), tr. Joseph P. Clancy, *The Literary Review*, pp. 271–2; tr. Joseph P. Clancy, *Bloodaxe Book*, p. 216; '**Caerdydd**' (Cardiff), tr. Joseph P. Clancy, *A Cardiff Anthology*, ed. Meic Stephens (Bridgend: Seren, 1987), pp. 114–15; '**Cân Ionawr**' (January Song), tr. Joseph P. Clancy, *Twentieth Century Welsh Poems*, p. 192; '**Cân Wrthsemitaidd**' (Antisemitic Song), tr. Grahame Davies, *The Chosen People: Wales & The Jews*, ed.

Grahame Davies (Bridgend: Seren, 2002), pp. 204–5; '**Capel Celyn**', tr. Joseph P. Clancy, *Twentieth Century Welsh Poems*, p. 206; '**Castanwydden yn Penderfynu Hedfan ym Mai**' (The Chestnut Tree Deciding to Fly in May), tr. Joseph P. Clancy, *Bloodaxe Book*, pp. 218–21; '**Castell y Bere**', tr. Joseph P. Clancy, *Twentieth Century Welsh Poems*, p. 207; '**Cerdd Foliant**' (A Poem of Praise), tr. Joseph P. Clancy, *Writing the Wind*, pp. 23–4; '**Cloch Diwrnod Newydd**' (A New Day's Bell), tr. Joseph P. Clancy, *Twentieth Century Welsh Poems*, p. 204; '**C'lommennod Rasio**' (Racing Pigeons), tr. Joseph P. Clancy, *Transactions of the Honourable Society of Cymmrodorion*, 1 (1994), 120–1; tr. Joseph P. Clancy, *Modern Poetry in Translation*, pp. 177–9; tr. Joseph P. Clancy, *Writing the Wind*, pp. 25–6; tr. Joseph P. Clancy, *Other Words*, pp. 86–7; '**Clustiau Beethoven**' (Beethoven's Ears), tr. Robert Minhinnick, *The Adulterer's Tongue*, pp. 17–19; '**Corfflosgi Mam-gu**' (Grandmother's Cremation), tr. Joseph P. Clancy, *Twentieth Century Welsh Poems*, pp. 199–200; '**Cymro Di-Gymraeg**' (A Welshless Welshman), tr. Joseph P. Clancy, *Twentieth Century Welsh Poems*, p. 201; tr. Joseph P. Clancy, *Writing the Wind*, p. 23; '**Cysgod**' (Shadow), tr. Joseph P. Clancy, *Twentieth Century Welsh Poems*, p. 200; '**Da bo i'r Caracoa**' (Goodbye to the Caracoa), tr. Joseph P. Clancy, *Modern Poetry in Translation*, pp. 56–7; '**Dau**' (Two), tr. Joseph P. Clancy, *Modern Poetry in Translation*, pp. 53–4; '**Dryw ym Mynwent Aberystwyth**' (A Wren in Aberystwyth Cemetery), tr. Joseph P. Clancy, *Materion Dwyieithog: Bilingual Matters*, 4 (1992), 17; tr. Joseph P. Clancy, *Modern Poetry in Translation*, p. 55; '**Gwanwyn Nant Dywelan**' (Spring at Nant Dywelan), tr. Joseph P. Clancy, *Trivium*, 8 (1973), 116–17; tr. Joseph P. Clancy, *Twentieth Century Welsh Poems*, pp. 193–4; tr. Joseph P. Clancy, *Oxford Book*, pp. 279–80; '**Gweddill Fam o Ethiopia**' (What's Left of a Mother in Ethiopia), tr. Joseph P. Clancy, *The Literary Review*, p. 270; '**Gwennol y Bondo**' (House Martin), tr. Joseph P. Clancy, *Modern Poetry in Translation*, pp. 51–2; *from* '**Gwlad Llun**' (Land of Form), tr. Joseph P. Clancy, *Writing the Wind*, pp. 27–31; '**Heno**' (Tonight), tr. Joseph P. Clancy, *Twentieth Century Welsh Poems*, p. 207; '**I Gymdeithasau'r Beirdd yng Nghymru**' (To the Poetry Societies in Wales), tr. R. Gerallt Jones, *Poetry of Wales 1930–1970*, p. 343; tr. Tony Conran, *Welsh Verse*, p. 293; '**I'm Cariad**' (To My Love), tr. Joseph P. Clancy, *Twentieth Century Welsh Poems*, p. 197; '**Llansteffan**', tr. Joseph P. Clancy, *Wales: A Celebration*, ed. Dewi Roberts (Llanrwst: Gwasg Carreg Gwalch, 2000), p. 34;

'**Llwybr y Mynydd**' (The Mountain Path), tr. Joseph P. Clancy, *Poetry Wales*, 29.4 (1994), 35; '**Merch Fach**' (A Small Girl), tr. Joseph P. Clancy, *Twentieth Century Welsh Poems*, p. 198; tr. Joseph P. Clancy, *Other Words*, p. 10; '**Mynwent Bilbao**' (Bilbao Cemetery), tr. Joseph P. Clancy, *Modern Poetry in Translation*, p. 47; tr. Robert Minhinnick, *The Adulterer's Tongue*, p. 7; '**Neb**' (Nobody), tr. Joseph P. Clancy, *Modern Poetry in Translation*, pp. 49–51; '**Paent Vermeer**' (Vermeer's Paint), tr. Robert Minhinnick, *The Adulterer's Tongue*, p. 5; '**Penrhyn Ynys Lochtyn**' (Ynys Lochtyn's Headland), tr. Joseph P. Clancy, *The Literary Review*, pp. 268–9; '**Pibydd Ysbyty Bron-glais**' (The Piper of Bronglais Hospital and the Listener), tr. Joseph P. Clancy, *Modern Poetry in Translation*, p. 49; '**Pistyll Cain**', tr. R. Gerallt Jones, *Poetry of Wales 1930–1970*, p. 349; '**Portread o Fenyw Feichiog**' (Portrait of a Pregnant Woman), tr. Joseph P. Clancy, *Twentieth Century Welsh Poems*, p. 197; tr. Joseph P. Clancy, *Oxford Book*, p. 281; tr. Joseph P. Clancy, *A Book of Wales* (1987), p. 128; tr. Joseph P. Clancy, *Love from Wales: An Anthology*, ed. Tony Curtis and Siân James (Bridgend: Seren Books, 1991), p. 103; tr. Joseph P. Clancy, *Bloodaxe Book*, p. 213; '**Portread o Fenyw Orboblogedig**' (Portrait of an Overpopulated Woman), tr. Joseph P. Clancy, *Bloodaxe Book*, pp. 217–18; '**Portread o Grwtyn Dall**' (Portrait of a Blind Boy), tr. Joseph P. Clancy, *Poetry Wales*, 29.4 (1994), 33–4; '**Portread o Leian**' (Portrait of a Nun), tr. Joseph P. Clancy, *Twentieth Century Welsh Poems*, p. 195; tr. Joseph P. Clancy, *Oxford Book*, pp. 280–1; '**Portread o Yrrwr Trên**' (Portrait of an Engine Driver), tr. Joseph P. Clancy, *Twentieth Century Welsh Poems*, pp. 192–3; tr. Joseph P. Clancy, *Oxford Book*, pp. 278–9; tr. Robert Minhinnick, *The Adulterer's Tongue*, p. 3; '**Portread o Fardd**' (Portrait of a Poet), tr. R. Gerallt Jones, *Poetry of Wales 1930–1970*, p. 353; '**Portread o gynorthwyydd mewn siop ddillad**' (Portrait of an Assistant in a Clothes Shop), tr. Joseph P. Clancy, *Modern Poetry in Translation*, p. 54; '**Portread o "Hunanbortread" 1661**' (Portrait of a 'Self Portrait' 1661), tr. Joseph P. Clancy, *Poetry Wales*, 35.1 (1999), 59–60; '**Tirlun heb Het**' (Landscape without a Hat), tr. Robert Minhinnick, *The Adulterer's Tongue*, p. 15; '**Traeth y De (Aberystwyth)**' (The South Shore [Aberystwyth]), tr. Tony Conran, *Welsh Verse*, p. 294; tr. Tony Conran, *Bloodaxe Book*, p. 214; '**Ŵyn Mawrth**' (March Lambs), tr. Robert Minhinnick, *The Adulterer's Tongue*, p. 13; '**Y Bychan Newydd-eni**' (The Newborn), tr. R. Gerallt Jones, *Poetry of Wales 1930–1970*, p. 351; '**Y Byd a Beti**' (The World and Beti), tr. R. Gerallt Jones, *Poetry of Wales 1930–1970*, p. 345; tr. unsigned, *Love from Wales: An Anthology*, ed. Tony Curtis and Siân James (Bridgend: Seren Books, 1991), pp. 70–1; '**Y Fuwch o Iseldir yr Andes**' (The Cow from the Andes Lowlands), tr. Joseph P. Clancy, *Modern Poetry in Translation*, pp. 47–8; '**Y Gwragedd ar ben y Pwll**' (The Women at the Pit-head), tr. Joseph P. Clancy, *Modern Poetry in Translation*, pp. 52–3; tr. Joseph P. Clancy, *Bloodaxe Book*, p. 215; '**Yn Isel yn y Goedwig**' (Low in the Forest), tr. Joseph P. Clancy, *Twentieth Century Welsh Poems*, pp. 205–6; '**Yn yr Hwyr**' (In the Evening), tr. R. Gerallt Jones, *Poetry of Wales 1930–1970*, p. 347; tr. Joseph P. Clancy, *Twentieth Century Welsh Poems*, p. 195; '**Y Rhondda**' (The Rhondda), tr. Joseph P. Clancy, *A Rhondda Anthology*, ed. Meic Stephens (Bridgend: Seren, 1993), p. 180; '**Y Siaradwyr Iddeweg**' (The Speakers of Yiddish), tr. Grahame Davies, *The Chosen People: Wales & The Jews*, ed. Grahame Davies (Bridgend: Seren, 2002), pp. 203–4.

Individual Translations *Pr.*
'**Y Ffos Olaf**' (The Last Ditch), tr. Elizabeth Edwards, *Twenty-Five Welsh Short Stories*, pp. 135–42.

CERI WYN JONES (1967–)

Individual Translations *Po.*
'**Anrhydedd**' (Honour), tr. Robert Minhinnick, *Bloodaxe Book*, pp. 413–14; '**Dylanwad**' (Influence), tr. Elin ap Hywel, *Oxygen*, p. 159; tr. Elin ap Hywel, *Bloodaxe Book*, p. 414; *from* '**Gwaddol**' (Legacy), tr. Dafydd Wyn Jones, *Bloodaxe Book*, pp. 414–17; '**Y Gymrâg**' (The Welsh Language), tr. Grahame Davies, *Oxygen*, p. 159.

DAFYDD ARTHUR JONES (1957–)

Individual Translations *Pr.*
'**Myfyrdod ar Fin y Pwll**' (Reflections by a Pool), tr. Meic Stephens, *A White Afternoon*, pp. 43–50.

DEWI STEPHEN JONES (1940–)

Individual Translations *Po.*
'**Diptych: 1. Tai yn y Nos, 2. Tymheredd y Graig**' (Diptych: 1. Houses at Night, 2. The Temperature of the Rock), tr. Joseph P. Clancy, *Bloodaxe Book*, pp. 267–9; '**Fel Mewn Gwendid**' (In Weakness . . .), tr. author, *The Poetry Book Society Anthology* 2, ed. Ann Stevenson (London: Hutchinson, 1991), p. 24; tr. author, *Writing the Wind*, p. 38; '**Ffenest Olaf**' (Last Window), tr. author, *Modern Poetry in Translation*, p. 62; tr. author, *Writing the Wind*, p. 38; tr. author, *Bloodaxe Book*, p. 271; '**Llwybr**' (The Path), tr. author, *Modern Poetry in Translation*, pp. 61–2; '**Tew Oleuni**' (A Density of Light), tr. author, *Modern Poetry in Translation*, p. 61; tr. author, *Writing the Wind*, p. 38; '**Y Glorian**' (The Balance), tr. author, *The Poetry Book Society Anthology* 2, ed. Ann Stevenson (London: Hutchinson, 1991), p. 24; tr. author, *Writing the Wind*, p. 39; '**Y Gôt**' (The Coat), tr. author, *Modern Poetry in Translation*, p. 59; tr. author, *Writing the Wind*, p. 40; tr. author, *Bloodaxe Book*, p. 269; '**Y Mynydd: Dinlle Gwrygon**' (The Wrekin), an Interpretation by Ann Stevenson, *Planet*, 140 (2000), 61; '**Y Noson o Risial**' (The Night of Crystal), tr. Grahame Davies, *The Chosen People: Wales & The Jews*, ed. Grahame Davies (Bridgend: Seren, 2002), pp. 199–200; '**Yn y Gwydr Hardd**' (In the Beautiful Glass), tr. Joseph P. Clancy, *Bloodaxe Book*, pp. 271–2; '**Y Perl**' (The Pearl), tr. author, *Modern Poetry in Translation*, p. 58; '**Yr Ysgawen**' (The Elder Tree), tr. author, *Writing the Wind*, p. 39; '**Y Tŷ**' (The House), tr. author, *Modern Poetry in Translation*, pp. 59–60; tr. author, *Bloodaxe Book*, pp. 270–1.

EINIR JONES (1950–)

Individual Translations *Po.*
'**Cocos**' (Cockles), tr. Joseph P. Clancy, *Bloodaxe Book*, p. 314; '**Cysgodion Coed ar y Lawnt, Ionawr**' (Shadows of Trees on the Lawn, January), tr. Joseph P. Clancy, *Bloodaxe Book*, pp. 310–11; '**Eryri wedi Chernobyl**' (Snowdonia after Chernobyl), tr. Joseph P. Clancy, *Bloodaxe Book*, p. 312; '**Ffynnon Grandis**', tr. Joseph P. Clancy, *Bloodaxe Book*, p. 311; '**Llwyd**' (Grey), tr. Joseph P. Clancy, *Bloodaxe Book*, pp. 314–15; '**Y Llun**' (The Picture), tr. Joseph P. Clancy, *Bloodaxe Book*, p. 313.

D. CYRIL JONES (1947–)

Individual Translations *Po.*
from '**Cyfannu: Llythyron at Gyfaill o Kenya**' (Letters to a Kenyan Friend) ['**Julius**', '**Dychmyga**' (Imagine)], tr. Peter Finch, *Bloodaxe Book*, pp. 292–5.

HARRI PRITCHARD JONES (1933–)

Collections

Harri Pritchard Jones [with translations by Harri Webb], *Corner People* (Llandysul: Gwasg Gomer, 1991).

Individual Translations *Pr.*
'**Menter Morfydd**' (Morfydd's Celebration), tr. Harri Webb, *The Penguin Book of Welsh Short Stories*, pp. 241–7; '**Paradwys Ffŵl**' (Fool's Paradise), tr. author, *The New Penguin Book of Welsh Short Stories*, pp. 313–20; '**Yr Estron**' (The Stranger), tr. author, *The Literary Review*, pp. 274–83; *from* '**Y Gwylnos**' (The Vigil), tr. author, *A Cardiff Anthology*, ed. Meic Stephens (Bridgend: Seren, 1987), pp. 124–9; '**Y Wyrth**' (The Miracle), tr. author, *Twenty-Five Welsh Short Stories*, pp. 85–91.

HUW JONES (1955–)

Collections

Ceiliogod Otse: The Cockerels of Otse (Llanrwst: Gwasg Carreg Gwalch, 1996).[2]

Individual Translations *Po.*
'**Cefn Digoll**' (Long Mountain), tr. author, *Poetry Wales*, 32.4 (1997), 17–18; '**Cofio**' (Two Poems), tr. author, *Poetry Wales*, 13.2 (1977), 82–4;

---

[2] This is not a collection of translations *per se* but a bilingual publication that includes parallel text poems in English and Welsh recording the poet's experiences as a teacher in Botswana.

'**Din Llugwy**', tr. author, *Modern Poetry in Translation*, p. 65; '**Disgwyl Glaw, Botswana**' (Waiting for Rain, Botswana), tr. author, *Modern Poetry in Translation*, pp. 65–6; '**Eira**' (Two Poems), tr. author, *Poetry Wales*, 13.2 (1977), 82–4; '**Llais y Mynydd**' (View from Snowdon), tr. author, *Poetry Wales*, 29.4 (1994), 15–16; '**Mannyelanong**', tr. author, *Modern Poetry in Translation*, p. 66; tr. author, *Bloodaxe Book*, pp. 330–1; '**Merch fach ar Draeth**' (Girl on Beach), tr. author, *Modern Poetry in Translation*, p. 64; '**Morgrug Gwynion**' (Termites), tr. author, *Poetry Wales*, 32.4 (1997), 19–20; '**Nant Gwrtheyrn**', tr. author, *Modern Poetry in Translation*, p. 64; '**Pry Cop, Gwybed a Sgorpionau**' (Tarantulas, Flies and Scorpions), tr. author, *Poetry Wales*, 32.4 (1997), 18–19; '**Storm ym Mhenmon**' (Storm at Penmon), tr. author, *Materion Dwyieithog: Bilingual Matters*, 2 (1990), 9; '**Tachwedd**' (November), tr. author, *Poetry Wales*, 29.4 (1994), 16; '**Ystrad Marchell**', tr. author, *Modern Poetry in Translation*, p. 63.

RICHARD LEWIS JONES (Dic Jones; 1934–)

Individual Translations *Po.*
from '**Cynhaeaf**' and '**Gwanwyn**' (Harvest and Spring: extracts from two poems), tr. author, *Bloodaxe Book*, pp. 238–9; '**Galarnad**' (Lamentation), tr. Tony Conran, *Bloodaxe Book*, pp. 236–7; '**Gofyn am Godiad Cyflog**' (Petition for a pay-rise), tr. Joseph P. Clancy, *Twentieth Century Welsh Poems*, pp. 214–15; '**Medi**' (Reaping), tr. Joseph P. Clancy, *Twentieth Century Welsh Poems*, pp. 216–17; tr. Joseph P. Clancy, *Bloodaxe Book*, p. 235–6; '**Wrth Weld Oen Marw**' (On Seeing a Dead Lamb), tr. Gillian Clarke, *Bloodaxe Book*, p. 237.

NESTA WYN JONES (1946–)

Individual Translations *Po.*
'**Cae o Wenith**' (A Field of Wheat), tr. R. Gerallt Jones, *Poetry of Wales 1930–1970*, p. 427; tr. Joseph P. Clancy, *Twentieth Century Welsh Poems*, p. 237; tr. Joseph P. Clancy, *Writing the Wind*, p. 46; '**Cysgodion**' (Shadows), tr. R. Gerallt Jones, *Poetry of Wales 1930–1970*, pp. 423–5; tr. Tony Conran, *Writing the Wind*, pp. 44–5; tr. Tony Conran, *Bloodaxe Book*, pp. 288–9; '**Lleisiau**'

(Voices), tr. Joseph P. Clancy, *Twentieth Century Welsh Poems*, p. 236; tr. Tony Conran, *Welsh Verse*, p. 300; tr. Joseph P. Clancy, *Writing the Wind*, pp. 42–3; tr. Tony Conran, *Bloodaxe Book*, pp. 286–7; '**Sgrech!**' (Scream), tr. Robert Minhinnick, *Bloodaxe Book*, pp. 289–90; '**Traethau**' (Beaches), tr. Catherine Fisher, *Bloodaxe Book*, pp. 290–2; '**Y Pabi Coch**' (Poppies), tr. Tony Conran, *Welsh Verse*, p. 301; tr. Tony Conran [misprinted as Joseph P. Clancy], *Writing the Wind*, pp. 43–4; tr. Tony Conran, *Bloodaxe Book*, pp. 287–8.

T. JAMES JONES (1934–)

Individual Translations *Po.*
'**Dylan**', tr. Jon Dressel, *Bloodaxe Book*, p. 245; '**Dyfed a Siomwyd?**' (Dyfed Devastated?), tr. Jon Dressel, *Bloodaxe Book*, pp. 246–7; *from* '**Cerddi Ianws**' (Janus Poems) ['**Iau**' (Thursday)], tr. Jon Dressel, *Bloodaxe Book*, p. 247;[3] *from* '**Wyneb yn Wyneb**' (Face to Face), tr. Jon Dressel, *Bloodaxe Book*, p. 248.

TUDUR DYLAN JONES (1965–)

Individual Translations *Po.*
'**Garddio**' (Gardening), tr. Elin ap Hywel, *Bloodaxe Book*, pp. 406–8; '**Tŷ Gwydr Llanarthne**' (The Great Glasshouse at the National Botanic Garden of Wales), tr. Elin ap Hywel, *Bloodaxe Book*, p. 406.

T. LLEW JONES (1915–)

Prose (Novels)
Lleuad yn Olau, *One Moonlit Night*, tr. Gillian Clarke (Llandysul: Pont Books, 1991).

Tân ar y Comin, *Gipsy Fires*, tr. Carol Byrne Jones and T. Llew Jones (Llandysul: Pont Books, 1994).

---

[3] Poems from *Cerddi Ianws* are in fact adaptations/co-authored poems by/with Dressel (the 'translator' here).

EMYR LEWIS (1957–)

Individual Translations *Po.*
from **Gwawr** (Dawn) ['**Gwynt Gwyllt fel Magnet o'i go**' (Mad Magnet of a Wild Wind)], tr. author, *Modern Poetry in Translation*, pp. 75–6; tr. author, *Bloodaxe Book*, p. 361; ['**Hen boer yw trên y Bore**' (Stale Spit is the Morning Train)], tr. author, *Modern Poetry in Translation*, pp. 75–6; tr. author, *Bloodaxe Book*, pp. 361–2; ['**Hwn yw fy Llyfr**' (This is My Book)], tr. author, *Bloodaxe Book*, p. 362; '**Malu**' (Drivel), tr. author, *Modern Poetry in Translation*, pp. 77–9; tr. author, *Bloodaxe Book*, pp. 356–9; '**Mewn Eglwys**' (In a Church), tr. Elin ap Hywel, *Oxygen*, p. 105; *from* **Rhyddid** (Freedom), tr. Grahame Davies, *Oxygen*, pp. 103–5; tr. Grahame Davies, *Bloodaxe Book*, pp. 360–1; '**A Once-in-a-lifetime, Never-to-be-repeated Cywydd in English following a chance meeting with the late Allen Ginsberg**', *Bloodaxe Book*, p. 359.[4]

GWYNETH LEWIS (1959–)

Collections

Gwyneth Lewis, *Keeping Mum* (Newcastle upon Tyne: Bloodaxe Books, 2003).[5]

Individual Translations *Po.*
'**Adroddiad y Patholegydd**' (Pathology Report), tr. Richard Poole, *Oxygen*, p. 115; '**Cân y Gwneuthurwr Mapiau**' (The Mapmaker's Song), tr. Richard Poole and author, *Bloodaxe Book*, p. 364; '**Ceffyl Gwyn**' (White Horse), tr. Richard Poole and author, *Bloodaxe Book*, pp. 363–4; **Cyfannu** (Wholeness), tr. author, *Modern Poetry in*

---

[4] Bloodaxe note: 'The American Beat Poet Allen Ginsberg visited Wales in the mid-90s and was overawed by the large congregation of Welsh-language poets who attended a *Cerdd Dafod* conference at Aberystwyth. He is reported to have exclaimed: "Are all these people poets?" This poem by Emyr Lewis is not strictly a translation, but he writes almost exclusively in Welsh, and this *cywydd* could be regarded metaphorically as a translation.'

[5] Translations by the author and Richard Poole from *Y Llofrudd Iaith* (The Language Murderer), pp. 13–23.

Translation, pp. 83–90; *from* **Cyfannu** ['**Bedydd yn Llanbadarn 1843**' (Llanbadarn Baptism 1843)], tr. author, *Bloodaxe Book*, pp. 367–8; ['**Hanner**' (Half)], tr. author, *Writing the Wind*, p. 68; tr. author, *Bloodaxe Book*, p. 368; ['**Dameg y Ferch Chwithig**' (Parable of the Awkward Woman)], tr. author, *New England Review and Bread Loaf Quarterly*, 10.4 (1988), 405–7; *from* **Dolenni** (Links), tr. Richard Poole, *Writing the Wind*, pp. 68–73; *from* **Llofrudd Iaith** (The Language Murderer) ['**Bardd yn Pysgota**' (The Poet Fishing)], tr. Robert Minhinnick, *The Adulterer's Tongue*, p. 83; ['**Cyfweliad â'r Bardd**' (Interview with the Poet)], tr. author, *Poetry Wales*, 38.1 (2002), 11; tr. Robert Minhinnick, *The Adulterer's Tongue*, p. 79; tr. author, *Bloodaxe Book*, pp. 364–5; ['**Dechrau'r Anghofio**' (Beginning to Forget)], tr. Robert Minhinnick, *The Adulterer's Tongue*, p. 81; tr. Geraint Løvgreen, *Bloodaxe Book*, pp. 365–6; ['**Defod**' (Ritual)], tr. Robert Minhinnick, *The Adulterer's Tongue*, p. 85; ['**Ewyllys yr Iaith**' (The Language's Will and Testament)], tr. Robert Minhinnick, *The Adulterer's Tongue*, p. 87; ['**Llawysgrif y Ffarmwr**' (The Farmer's Evidence)], tr. Robert Minhinnick, *The Adulterer's Tongue*, p. 91; ['**Y Munudau Olaf**' (The Last Minutes)], tr. Robert Minhinnick, *The Adulterer's Tongue*, p. 93; tr. Richard Poole and author, *Bloodaxe Book*, pp. 366–7; ['**Yn yr Awyr Agored**' (In the Open Air)], tr. Robert Minhinnick, *The Adulterer's Tongue*, p. 89; '**Melodïau**' (Melodies), tr. Richard Poole, *Poetry Wales*, 32.2 (1997), 6–11; '**Rhodd**' (Gift), tr. Richard Poole, *Oxygen*, p. 113; tr. Robert Minhinnick, *The Adulterer's Tongue*, p. 95; '**Rhyfel a Heddwch**' (War and Peace), tr. Joseph P. Clancy, *Poetry Wales*, 29.4 (1994), 10; '**Strip-tease**', tr. author, *Poetry Wales*, 29.4 (1994), 9–10; tr. Joseph P. Clancy, *Bloodaxe Book*, p. 369.

MARED LEWIS (1964–)

Individual Translations *Pr.*
'**Los Angeles Drws Nesa i Afallon**' (Next Door to Avalon), tr. Meic Stephens, *A White Afternoon*, pp. 155–64.

ALAN LLWYD (1948–)

Individual Translations *Po.*

'**AIDS**', tr. author, *Modern Poetry in Translation*, p. 105; '**Bysedd y Cŵn** ['Â'i holl wisg fel pe'n llosgi . . .'] (Foxglove), tr. author, *Modern Poetry in Translation*, p. 105; '**Cain**', tr. author, *Modern Poetry in Translation*, pp. 97–8; '**Cerddorion Auschwitz**' (The Musicians of Auschwitz), tr. author, *Modern Poetry in Translation*, p. 103; '**Chaplin ac Eraill**' (Chaplin and Others), tr. Joseph P. Clancy, *Bloodaxe Book*, pp. 303–5; '**Cloch Llangyfelach ar Fore o Fawrth**' (Llangyfelach's bell on a March morning), tr. Joseph P. Clancy, *Celtic Visions: Visions International*, 56 (1998), 42; '**Criafolen ym Mai**' (The Mountain Ash in May), tr. author, *International Poetry Review* (Celtic Issue), 5 (Spring 1979), 44; '**Dant y Llew ym Mai**' (Dandelion in May), tr. author, *Modern Poetry in Translation*, p. 105; '**Dyhead**' (A Wish), tr. author, *Modern Poetry in Translation*, p. 98; tr. author, *Cultural Connections: Celebrating Poetry* (London: Department for Culture, Media and Sport, 1998), p. 14; '**Ein Dyddiau DiDduw**' (Our Godless Days), tr. Joseph P. Clancy, *Bloodaxe Book*, pp. 300–1; '**Eirlysiau yn Ionawr**' (Snowdrops in January), tr. author, *Modern Poetry in Translation*, p. 105; '**Francis Ledwidge a Hedd Wyn**' (Francis Ledwidge and Hedd Wyn), tr. author, *Modern Poetry in Translation*, pp. 101–2; '**Gwiber**' (Viper), tr. Joseph P. Clancy, *Celtic Visions: Visions International*, 56 (1998), 40–1; '**Gwyddau**' (Geese), tr. author, *Poetry Wales*, 16.3 (1981), 31–2; tr. author, *Poetry Wales: 25 Years*, ed. Cary Archard (Bridgend: Seren, 1990), pp. 166–8; tr. author, *The Streets and the Stars*, ed. John Davies and Melvyn Jones (Bridgend: Seren, 1992), pp. 108–9; tr. author, *Modern Poetry in Translation*, pp. 95–6; '**Gyrrwr Ambiwlans**' (Ambulance Driver), tr. author, *Modern Poetry in Translation*, pp. 94–5; '**Ivor Gurney**', tr. author, *Modern Poetry in Translation*, p. 101; '**James Bulger**', tr. author, *Modern Poetry in Translation*, p. 105; '**Lleuadau Llŷn**' (The Moons of Llŷn), tr. Joseph P. Clancy, *Bloodaxe Book*, pp. 302–3; '**Llŷn**' ['Erbyn hyn, lle yn y meddwl . . .'] (Llŷn Peninsula), tr. author, *Asheville Review*, 2 (Fall/ Winter 1995), 38–9; tr. author, *Writing the Wind*, pp. 49–50; '**Tarw Bryncelyn**' (The Bull of Bryncelyn), tr. Joseph P. Clancy, *Bloodaxe Book*, pp. 298–9; '**Y Cof**' (Memory), tr. author, *Modern Poetry in Translation*, p. 102; tr. author, *Writing the Wind*, p. 49; '**Y Gwyliwr**' (The Horizon-gazer), tr. author, *Modern Poetry in Translation*, pp. 96–7; tr. author,

Asheville Review, 2 (Fall/Winter 1995), 40–1; tr. author, *Writing the Wind*, pp. 50–1; 'Y Gymraeg' (The Welsh Language), tr. author, *A Book of Wales* (1987), p. 184; tr. author, *Modern Poetry in Translation*, pp. 93–4; tr. author, *Writing the Wind*, p. 52; tr. Joseph P. Clancy, *Bloodaxe Book*, p. 301; 'Y Lle' (The Place), tr. author, *Writing the Wind*, p. 48; 'Y Meirch' (The Horses), tr. author, *Modern Poetry in Translation*, p. 100; 'Yr Hebog uwch Felindre' (The Hawk above Felindre), tr. author, *Modern Poetry in Translation*, p. 99; tr. Joseph P. Clancy, *Bloodaxe Book*, pp. 297–8; 'Y Sgrech' (The Scream), tr. author, *Modern Poetry in Translation*, pp. 102–3; tr. Joseph P. Clancy, *Bloodaxe Book*, p. 300.

IWAN LLWYD (Iwan Llwyd Williams; 1957–)

Individual Translations *Po.*
'Aneirin', tr. Twm Morys, *Poetry Wales*, 31.2 (1995), 21–2; tr. author and version by Thomas Rain Crowe, *Writing the Wind*, p. 65; tr. unsigned, *Comparative Criticism*, p. 96; 'Angylion' (Angels), tr. Twm Morys, *Poetry Wales*, 31.2 (1995), 23; 'Awyr Denau' (Thin Air), tr. author, *The Literary Review*, pp. 294–5; 'Beddau, Bodelwyddan' (Graves, Bodelwyddan), tr. author, *The Literary Review*, p. 292; 'Blŵs Bananas' (Dust Truck Blues), tr. Geraint Løvgreen, *Bloodaxe Book*, p. 355; 'Ceir' (Automobiles), tr. Robert Minhinnick, *The Adulterer's Tongue*, p. 61; 'Corryn' (Spider), tr. Robert Minhinnick, *The Adulterer's Tongue*, p. 75; 'Dan Ddylanwad' (Under the Influence), tr. Grahame Davies, *Oxygen*, pp. 109–11; 'Englynion', tr. author, *Poetry Wales*, 29.4 (1994), 23; 'Far Rockaway', tr. author, *The Literary Review*, p. 291; tr. Robert Minhinnick, *The Adulterer's Tongue*, p. 63; 'Gadael Tir' (Leaving Land), tr. author, *Modern Poetry in Translation*, p. 109; tr. author and version by Thomas Rain Crowe, *Writing the Wind*, p. 64; *from* 'Gwreichion' ['*Golygfa 3*: Mai 1981 Hen Ffotograff' (An Old Photograph)], tr. Richard Poole, *Bloodaxe Book*, pp. 355–6; 'Harley Davidson', tr. Robert Minhinnick, *The Adulterer's Tongue*, pp. 69–71; 'Iawn, gei di ofyn cwestiwn personol' (Sure, you can ask me a personal question), tr. Grahame Davies, *Oxygen*, pp. 107–9; tr. Grahame Davies, *Bloodaxe Book*, pp. 349–50; 'Jemez', tr. author, *Modern Poetry in Translation*, p. 110; '*Meet me at the St Francis*', tr. Robert Minhinnick, *The Adulterer's Tongue*, p. 73; 'Olion Bysedd' (Fingerprints), tr. Geraint

Løvgreen, *Bloodaxe Book*, pp. 353–4; '**Rhyfel a Heddwch**' (War and Peace), tr. author, *Modern Poetry in Translation*, pp. 111–12; '**Teithio**' (Travelling), tr. author, *The Literary Review*, pp. 293–4; '**Tina Turner**', tr. author, *Poetry Wales*, 29.4 (1994), 23; '**Tra Byddwn . . .**' (As Long . . .) tr. author, *Writing the Wind*, p. 66; '**Tir neb**' (No Man's Land), tr. author, *Bloodaxe Book*, pp. 350–1; '**Tywydd**' (Weather), tr. author, *Modern Poetry in Translation*, p. 107; tr. author, *Writing the Wind*, pp. 65–6; *from* '**Woodstock**', tr. Robert Minhinnick, *The Adulterer's Tongue*, pp. 65–7; '**Y Diflanedig**' (The Disappeared), tr. Grahame Davies, *Poetry Wales*, 37.1 (2001), 53–5; tr. Grahame Davies, *Bloodaxe Book*, pp. 351–3; '**Y Gwylwyr**' (The Watch), tr. author, *Modern Poetry in Translation*, pp. 107–8; '**Yn Llanfair ym Muallt – Mehefin 1998**' (In Builth Wells – June 1998), tr. author, *Poetry Wales*, 35.3 (2000), 43; tr. author, *Wales: A Celebration*, ed. Dewi Roberts (Llanrwst: Gwasg Carreg Gwalch, 2000), p. 84; '**Yr Ŵyl Gerddi**' (The Garden Festival), tr. author, *Modern Poetry in Translation*, p. 106.

ROBIN LLYWELYN (1958–)

Prose (Novel)
O'r Harbwr Gwag i'r Cefnfor Gwyn, *From Empty Harbour to White Ocean*, tr. author (Cardiff: Parthian Books, 1996).

Individual Translations *Pr.*
'**Amser y Gwcw yw Ebrill a Mai**' (The Cuckoo's Time is April and May), tr. Meic Stephens, *A White Afternoon*, pp. 206–11; *from* **O'r Harbwr Gwag i'r Cefnfor Gwyn**, tr. author, *The Literary Review*, pp. 296–306; tr. author, http://www.llywelyn.com/; *from* **Seren Wen ar Gefndir Gwyn** (White Star Bright Sky), tr. author, http://www. llywelyn.com/; *from* **Y Dŵr Mawr Llwyd: Llawn iawn yw'r môr** (The Sea is Full), (Reptiles Welcome), tr. author, http://www.llywelyn. com/.

GERAINT LØVGREEN (1955–)

Individual Translations *Po.*
'**Dyfi Junctions Bywyd**' (Life's Dovey Junctions), tr. author, *Bloodaxe Book*, pp. 332–3; '**Y Diwrnod Cyntaf**' (The First Day), tr. author, *Bloodaxe Book*, pp. 331–2.

OWEN MEREDITH (1969–)

Individual Translations *Pr.*
'**Y Dyn Pizza**' (The Pizza Man), tr. Meic Stephens, *A White Afternoon*, pp. 187–97.

GARETH MILES (1938–)

Individual Translations *Pr.*
[Broadcast BBC Cymru, 23 July 1982] (A Scene from Military Life), tr. Meic Stephens, *Illuminations*, pp. 178–80.

DEREC LLWYD MORGAN (1943–)

Individual Translations *Po.*
'**Bwa a Saeth**' (Bow and Arrow), tr. Joseph P. Clancy, *Twentieth Century Welsh Poems*, pp. 231–2; tr. Joseph P. Clancy, *Bloodaxe Book*, pp. 275–6; '**Dolur**' (Ulcer), tr. author, *Poetry of Wales 1930–1970*, p. 419; '**Eclips**' (Eclipse), tr. author, *Poetry of Wales 1930–1970*, p. 411; '**Helynt Cofrestru'r Fechan**' (Trouble Registering the Little One), tr. author, *Poetry of Wales 1930–1970*, pp. 413–17; tr. author, *A Book of Wales* (1987), pp. 192–3; tr. Catherine Fisher, *Bloodaxe Book*, pp. 276–8; '**Yr Angau Gwyn**' (The White Death), tr. Joseph P. Clancy, *Twentieth Century Welsh Poems*, pp. 232–3.

ELIN LLWYD MORGAN (1966–)

Individual Translations *Po.*

'**Cyn y Cwymp**' (Before the Fall), tr. author, *Modern Poetry in Translation*, pp. 114–15; '**Estrysaidd dy Anian**' (Your Ostrich Nature), tr. author, *Poetry Wales*, 29.4 (1994), 24–5; tr. author and Richard Poole, *Bloodaxe Book*, pp. 411–13; '**Holiadur Ofer**' (Futile Questionnaire), tr. author, *Oxygen*, p. 157; '**Paid gofyn Pam**' (Why is the Silliest Question), tr. author, *Modern Poetry in Translation*, p. 113; '**Rapwnsel**' (Rapunzel), tr. author, *Modern Poetry in Translation*, pp. 113–14; '**Sgitso Picasso**' (Schizo de Picasso), tr. author, *Oxygen*, p. 155; tr. author, *Bloodaxe Book*, pp. 410–11; '**Trengholiad Chwarelwr**' (Inquest of a Quarryman), tr. author, *Modern Poetry in Translation*, pp. 115–16; '**Y Jesebel Gyfoes**' (The Contemporary Jezebel), tr. Richard Poole and author, *Bloodaxe Book*, pp. 409–10.

Individual Translations *Pr.*

'**Ffarwél Frank**' (Farewell, Frank), tr. Meic Stephens, *A White Afternoon*, pp. 69–78.

MIHANGEL MORGAN (1955–)

Individual Translations *Po.*

'**Anfon Hedbeth Annabyddedig yn Llatai**' (Unidentified Flying Object on an Errand of Love), tr. Martin Davis, *Bloodaxe Book*, pp. 333–4; '**Bod yn Ffan i Elizabeth Taylor**' (I'm a Fan of Elizabeth Taylor), tr. Simon Brooks, *Modern Poetry in Translation*, p. 120; '**Chwedl y Bobyddes a'i Merch**' (The Legend of the Baker and her Daughter), tr. Martin Davis, *Bloodaxe Book*, p. 337; '**Diflaniad Fy Fi**' (Disappearance of My Me), tr. Simon Brooks, *Modern Poetry in Translation*, p. 119; '**Esgidiau Sodlau-uchel Coch**' (Red High-heeled Shoes), tr. Martin Davis, *Bloodaxe Book*, pp. 335–6; '**Franz Kafka, Gustav Janouch a'r Ci Bach**' (Franz Kafka, Gustaf Janouch and the Small Dog), tr. Simon Brooks, *Poetry Wales*, 29.4 (1994), 10–11; '**Fy Nghyfeillion**' (My Friends), tr. Simon Brooks, *Modern Poetry in Translation*, p. 121; '**Mimi, Mae Dy Long wedi Mynd**' (Mimi, Your Ship has Gone), tr. Simon Brooks, *Modern Poetry in Translation*, p. 122; [**Pennill**] (Verse), tr. Simon Brooks, *Modern Poetry in Translation*, pp. 123–5; '**Ymddiddan**' (Conversation), tr. Martin Davis, *Bloodaxe*

Book, p. 335; '**Yr Iddew Crwydr**' (The Wandering Jew), tr. Grahame Davies, *Chosen People: Wales & The Jews*, ed. Grahame Davies (Bridgend: Seren, 2002), pp. 300–1.

Individual Translations *Pr.*
*from **Melog***, tr. George Jones, *The Literary Review*, pp. 326–37; '**Te Gyda'r Frenhines**' (Tea with the Queen), tr. Meic Stephens, *A White Afternoon*, pp. 178–86.

TWM MORYS (1961–)

Individual Translations *Po.*
'**Mi gan 'nhw Ddisgwyl**' (They'll have to Wait), tr. author, *Oxygen*, p. 127; '**Sefyll 'Rown**' (Welsh Airs), tr. author, *Oxygen*, p. 125; '**Y Teithiwr**' (The Traveller), tr. author, *Oxygen*, pp. 125–6.

ELERI LLEWELYN MORRIS (1950–)

Individual Translations *Pr.*
'**Mae'n ddrwg gen i, Joe Rees**' (I'm Sorry, Joe Rees), tr. Meic Stephens, *A White Afternoon*, pp. 65–8.

MYRDDIN AP DAFYDD (1956–)

Individual Translations *Po.*
'**Dim ond Geiriau ydy Iaith**' (A Language is only Words), tr. Tony Conran, *Poetry Wales*, 29.4 (1994), 17; tr. Tony Conran, *Wales: A Celebration*, ed. Dewi Roberts (Llanrwst: Gwasg Carreg Gwalch, 2000), pp. 145–6; tr. Tony Conran, *Bloodaxe Book*, p. 338; '**Er cof am Roberts, Dylasau**' (In Memoriam John Roberts, Dylasau), tr. Tony Conran, *Poetry Wales*, 29.4 (1994), 17; '**Gwenllian**', tr. Tony Conran, *Poetry Wales*, 29.4 (1994), 17; tr. Tony Conran, *Bloodaxe Book*, pp. 340–1; '**Y risg wrth yswirio beirdd**' (The Poet's Insurance Risk), tr. Gillian Clarke, *Bloodaxe Book*, pp. 339–40.

JAMES NICHOLAS (1928–)

Individual Translations *Po.*
'**Wrth Wylio Geneth Ifanc yn Addoli mewn Eglwys Babyddol**' (On Watching a Young Girl Worshipping in a Roman Catholic Church), tr. R. Gerallt Jones, *Poetry of Wales 1930–1970*, p. 339; '**Y Berth**' (The Bush), tr. R. Gerallt Jones, *Poetry of Wales 1930–1970*, pp. 335–7; tr. Joseph P. Clancy, *Twentieth Century Welsh Poems*, pp. 190–1; tr. Joseph P. Clancy, *Bloodaxe Book*, pp. 211–12.

EURYN OGWEN (1942–)

Individual Translations *Po.*
'**Bryn Celli Ddu**', tr. author, *Quaderno 2 di Lettera* (March 1977), 31; '**Eira ar y Pasg**' (Snow at Easter), tr. author, *Quaderno 2 di Lettera* (March 1977), 33; '**Pe . . . nillion Telyn**' (Stanzas for the harp), tr. author, *Quaderno 2 di Lettera* (March 1977), 37; '**Salm y Gwladgarwr**' (A Patriot's Psalm), tr. author, *Quaderno 2 di Lettera* (March 1977), 35.

FRANK OLDING (1963–)

Individual Translations *Po.*
'**Crog Cwmiau**' (The Cwmyoy Road), tr. author, *Poetry Wales*, 29.4 (1994), 38; '**Capel y Ffin**', tr. author, *Poetry Wales*, 29.4 (1994), 38.

GERALLT LLOYD OWEN (1944–)

Individual Translations *Po.*
'**Cilmeri**' (the ode), tr. Dafydd Johnston, *Modern Poetry in Translation*, pp. 127–45; '**Cilmeri**' (the poem), tr. Joseph P. Clancy, *Twentieth Century Welsh Poems*, p. 234; tr. Greg Hill, *Bastard Englyns* (Bow Street: Nant Publications, 2000), p. 32; tr. Joseph P. Clancy, *Bloodaxe Book*, pp. 283–4; '**Cywilydd Llan-faes**' (The Shame of Llanfaes), tr. R. S. Thomas, *Modern Poetry in Translation*, p. 160; tr. R. S. Thomas, *Bloodaxe Book*, p. 283; '**Etifeddiaeth**' (Inheritance), tr. Greg Hill, *Bastard Englyns* (Bow Street: Nant

Publications, 2000), p. 33; tr. Gillian Clarke, *Bloodaxe Book*, p. 285; **'Gardd Goffa Dulyn'** (Dublin Remembrance Garden), tr. Greg Hill, *Bastard Englyns* (Bow Street: Nant Publications, 2000), p. 31; **'Gwawr'**, tr. Greg Hill, *Bastard Englyns* (Bow Street: Nant Publications, 2000), p. 30; **'Hen Genedl'** (An Ancient Nation), tr. Greg Hill, *Bastard Englyns* (Bow Street: Nant Publications, 2000), p. 31; **'Hil-laddiad y Cymry'** (Genocide of the Welsh), tr. Greg Hill, *Poetry Wales*, 28.4 (1993), 59; tr. Greg Hill, *Bastard Englyns* (Bow Street: Nant Publications, 2000), p. 29; **'I'r Farwolaeth'** (To the Death), tr. Gillian Clarke, *Bloodaxe Book*, pp. 285–6; **'Murddun'** (Ruin), tr. Greg Hill, *Bastard Englyns* (Bow Street: Nant Publications, 2000), p. 30; **'Tŷ Haf'** (Holiday Home), tr. Greg Hill, *Poetry Wales*, 28.4 (1993), 59; tr. Greg Hill, *Bastard Englyns* (Bow Street: Nant Publications, 2000), p. 29; **'Y Fro Gymraeg'**, tr. Greg Hill, *Poetry Wales*, 28.4 (1993), 59; tr. Greg Hill, *Bastard Englyns* (Bow Street: Nant Publications, 2000), p. 29; **'Y Gŵr sydd ar y Gorwel'** (The Man on the Horizon), tr. Joseph P. Clancy, *Twentieth Century Welsh Poems*, pp. 234–5; tr. Joseph P. Clancy, *Bloodaxe Book*, p. 284; **'Yr Isymwybod'** (The Unconscious), tr. Greg Hill, *Bastard Englyns* (Bow Street: Nant Publications, 2000), p. 30.

MEIRION PENNAR (1944–)

Individual Translations *Po.*
'Ceinciau Mabinogi' (Branches of a Mabinogi), tr. Martin Davis, *Bloodaxe Book*, pp. 281–2; **'Ecce Homo'**, tr. Martin Davis, *Bloodaxe Book*, pp. 279–80; **'Serchogion'** (Lovers), tr. Martin Davis, *Bloodaxe Book*, pp. 280–1; **'Wrth Ddarllen Croce'** (Reading Croce), tr. Martin Davis, *Bloodaxe Book*, p. 279; **'I'**, tr. author, *Quaderno 2 di Lettera* (March 1977), 67; **'II'**, tr. author, *Quaderno 2 di Lettera* (March 1977), 69.

NORMAN CLOSS PARRY (1940–)

Individual Translations *Po.*
'Cadwyn Bwyd' (Food Chain), tr. Frank Olding, *Poetry Wales*, 29.4 (1994), 29; **'Innsbruck'**, tr. Richard Poole, *Poetry Wales*, 29.4 (1994), 31.

ROBAT POWELL (1948–)

Individual Translations *Po.*
'Heysel', tr. author, *Bloodaxe Book*, pp. 296–7; '**I Jurij Koch**' (For Jurij Koch), tr. author, *Bloodaxe Book*, pp. 295–6.

ANGHARAD PRICE (1972–)

Individual Translations *Pr.*
'**O Fan Hyn**' (The Woman Next Door), tr. Meic Stephens, *A White Afternoon*, pp. 198–205.

ELINOR WYN REYNOLDS (1970–)

Individual Translations *Po.*
'**Blodau'r Haul**' (The Sun's Flowers), tr. author and version by Thomas Rain Crowe, *Writing the Wind*, p. 81; '**Ces syniad really dda am gerdd yng Nghynwyl Elfed**' (I had a Really Good Idea for a Poem in Cynwil Elfed), tr. Grahame Davies, *Poetry Wales*, 36.1 (2000), 47; tr. Grahame Davies, *Bloodaxe Book*, p. 418; '**Cwpwloleg**' (Coupleology), tr. author, *Writing the Wind*, p. 81; '**Dŵr**' (Water), tr. author, *Writing the Wind*, p. 82; '**Mae 'na ddynion yn gorwedd mewn caeau ym mhob man drwy Gymru**' (There are men lying in fields throughout Wales), tr. author, *Poetry Wales*, 33.2 (1997) 50–1; tr. author, *Oxygen*, p. 171; '**Y Gynddaredd**' (Rabid), tr. author, *Poetry Wales*, 33.2 (1997), 49–50; tr. author, *Oxygen*, p. 169; '**Y Noson yr Enillais i'r Goron yn Eisteddfod Genedlaethol fy Mreuddwydion**' (The Night I won the Crown in the National Eisteddfod of My Dreams), tr. author, *Bloodaxe Book*, pp. 419–20.

MANON RHYS (1948–)

Individual Translations *Pr.*
'**Cwtsho**' (Cuddling), tr. Meic Stephens, *A White Afternoon*, pp. 149–54.

EIGRA LEWIS ROBERTS (1939–)

Individual Translations *Pr.*
'**Cytiau Bach**' (The Little Huts), tr. Meic Stephens, *Illuminations*, pp. 189–91; '**Y Golled**' (Deprivation), tr. Enid R. Morgan, *Twenty-Five Welsh Short Stories*, pp. 205–12; tr. Enid R. Morgan, *A Book of Wales* (1987), pp. 224–9; '**Gormod o Haul**' (An Overdose of Sun), tr. author, *The Penguin Book of Welsh Short Stories*, pp. 217–20.

EMRYS ROBERTS (1929–)

Individual Translations *Po.*
'**Primo Levi**', tr. Richard Poole, *Bloodaxe Book*, pp. 221–2.

ESYLLT NEST ROBERTS (1972–)

Individual Translations *Pr.*
'**Calon Dafydd Bach**' (The Heart of Dafydd Bach), tr. Meic Stephens, *A White Afternoon*, pp. 79–85.

GWENAN M. ROBERTS (1974–)

Individual Translations *Pr.*
'**Llithro**' (Falling), tr. Meic Stephens, *A White Afternoon*, pp. 127–30.

MELERI ROBERTS (1967–)

Individual Translations *Pr.*
'**Gwyn y Gwêl**' (Mothers), tr. Meic Stephens, *A White Afternoon*, pp. 24–8.

WILLIAM OWEN ROBERTS (1960–)

Prose (Novel)
Y Pla, *Pestilence*, tr. Elisabeth Roberts (London: Hamish
Hamilton, 1991); Second edition (Bridgend: Seren, 1997).

Individual Translations *Pr.*
'**Rhosyn Coch**' (Foreign Investments), tr. Meic Stephens, *A White
Afternoon*, pp. 226–31; *from* **Y Pla**, tr. Elisabeth Roberts, *The
Literary Review*, pp. 343–51.

JOHN ROWLANDS (1938–)

Prose (Novel)
Ienctid yw 'Mhechod, *A Taste of Apples*, tr. Richard Ruck
(London: Library 33 Ltd, 1966).

SIONED PUW ROWLANDS (1972–)

Individual Translations *Pr.*
'**Ffantasi Deyrnged i Feddyg Esgyrn**' (A Fantasy in Memory of the
Anglesey Bone Doctors), tr. Meic Stephens, *A White Afternoon*,
pp. 220–5; tr. Meic Stephens, *The Literary Review*, pp. 352–6.

MEIC STEVENS (1942–)

Individual Translations *Po.*
'**Sylvia**', tr. author, *Bloodaxe Book*, pp. 272–3.

GWYN THOMAS (1936–)

Collections

Joseph P. Clancy and Gwyn Thomas, *Living a Life: Selected Poems
1962–82* (The Netherlands: Bridges Books, 1982).

Individual Translations *Po.*
'**Ac Oblegid Eich Plant**' (And for Your Children), tr. Tony Conran,
Welsh Verse, pp. 297–8; '**Adar**' (Birds), tr. author, *Poetry of Wales
1930–1970*, p. 397; '**Adeiladwaith**' (Construct), tr. Joseph P. Clancy,
Twentieth Century Welsh Poems, pp. 221–2; '**Angau Bach**' (Little
Death), tr. Joseph P. Clancy, *Trivium*, 8 (1973), 117–18; tr. Joseph P.
Clancy, *Twentieth Century Welsh Poems*, p. 221; '**Austin**', tr. author,
Modern Poetry in Translation, pp. 152–3; '**Bryn Celli Ddu**', tr. R.
Gerallt Jones, *Poetry of Wales 1930–1970*, p. 401; tr. Joseph P.
Clancy, *Twentieth Century Welsh Poems*, p. 224; tr. Joseph P. Clancy,
Wales: A Celebration, ed. Dewi Roberts (Llanrwst: Gwasg Carreg
Gwalch, 2000), p. 85; '**Ceffylau**' (Horses), tr. Joseph P. Clancy,
Twentieth Century Welsh Poems, p. 227; tr. Joseph P. Clancy, *A Book
of Wales* (1987), pp. 259–60; tr. Joseph P. Clancy, *The Streets and the
Stars*, ed. John Davies and Melvyn Jones (Bridgend: Seren, 1992), p.
111; tr. Joseph P. Clancy, *Bloodaxe Book*, p. 254; '**Ci Lladd Defaid**'
(Killer Dog), tr. Joseph P. Clancy, *Twentieth Century Welsh Poems*,
pp. 225–6; tr. Joseph P. Clancy, *Bloodaxe Book*, pp. 252–3; '**Croesi
Traeth**' (Crossing a Shore), tr. Tony Conran, *Welsh Verse*, pp. 298–9;
'**Cwestiwn**' (Question), tr. author, *Poetry of Wales 1930–1970*, p. 391;
'**Cwmorthin**', tr. Joseph P. Clancy, *Twentieth Century Welsh Poems*,
p. 222; '**Cyfarchion**' (Greetings), tr. author, *Modern Poetry in
Translation*, p. 149; tr. author, *Bloodaxe Book*, pp. 257–8; '**Deilen**'
(Leaf), tr. Tony Conran, *The Penguin Book of Welsh Verse*, p. 264; tr.
Tony Conran, *Welsh Verse*, p. 295; '**Dim llawer o Jôc**' (Not Much of
Joke), tr. author, *Modern Poetry in Translation*, p. 147; '**Din Lligwy**',
tr. author, *Poetry of Wales 1930–1970*, p. 395; '**Drama'r Nadolig**'
(The Nativity Play), tr. author, *Bloodaxe Book*, pp. 254–5; '**Dros**'
(For), tr. author, *Modern Poetry in Translation*, p. 148; tr. author,
Bloodaxe Book, p. 257; '**Dros y Gaeaf**' (Winter Resident), tr. author,
Poetry Wales, 12.1 (1976), 37–40; '**Ffoadur**' (A Refugee), tr.
Grahame Davies, *The Chosen People: Wales & The Jews*, ed.
Grahame Davies (Bridgend: Seren, 2002), pp. 294–5; '**Geiriau**'
(Words), tr. author, *Modern Poetry in Translation*, p. 146; '**Gogi**'
(Goggy), tr. Tony Conran, *Welsh Verse*, pp. 295–6; '**Gwylanod**'
(Seagulls), tr. Joseph P. Clancy, *Twentieth Century Welsh Poems*, p.
228; '**Haf Cynnar**' (Early Summer), tr. Joseph P. Clancy, *Twentieth
Century Welsh Poems*, p. 223; '**Hen Beth**' (An Old Thing), tr. Joseph
P. Clancy, *Twentieth Century Welsh Poems*, pp. 223–4; tr. Joseph P.
Clancy, *A Book of Wales* (1987), p. 260; '**Hen Fam**' (Old Mother), tr.

author, *The Literary Review*, p. 371; '**Hitleriaeth etc.**' (Hitler and Co.), tr. Bryan Aspden, *Poetry Wales*, 24.1 (1988), 16–17; '**Letus Leidr**' (Lettuce Thief), tr. author, *The Literary Review*, pp. 370–1; '**Llysywen**' (Catching an Eel), tr. Bryan Aspden, *Poetry Wales*, 24.1 (1988), 17; '**Lusard**' (Lizard), tr. author, *Modern Poetry in Translation*, pp. 148–9; '**Meicroscôp**' (Microscope), tr. Joseph P. Clancy, *Twentieth Century Welsh Poems*, pp. 226–7; tr. Joseph P. Clancy, *Bloodaxe Book*, pp. 253–4; '**Môr**' (Sea), tr. R. Gerallt Jones, *Poetry of Wales 1930–1970*, p. 399; '**Nos Mewn Tref**' (Night in Town), tr. Joseph P. Clancy, *Twentieth Century Welsh Poems*, p. 219; '**Parrot**', tr. author, *The Literary Review*, p. 370; '**Roger Casement**', tr. author, *Poetry Wales*, 2.2 (1966), 23; '**Sgwrs Bach wrth y Tân**' (A Little Chat by the Fire), tr. author, *Modern Poetry in Translation*, pp. 150–1; '**Unigrwydd**' (Loneliness), tr. Joseph P. Clancy, *Twentieth Century Welsh Poems*, pp. 220–1; '**Wil Draenog**', tr. Joseph P. Clancy, *Transactions of the Honourable Society of Cymmrodorion*, 1 (1994), 115–16; tr. Joseph P. Clancy, *Other Words*, pp. 80–1; '**Y Cymry Cymraeg**' (The Welsh-speaking Welsh), tr. author, *Bloodaxe Book*, p. 256; '**Y Ddraenen Ddu**' (The Blackthorn), tr. Joseph P. Clancy, *Twentieth Century Welsh Poems*, p. 219; '**Y Ffordd o Gamelot**' (The Way Out of Camelot), tr. author, *Modern Poetry in Translation*, pp. 149–50; '**Yn yr Hwyr**' (In the Evening), tr. author, *Poetry of Wales 1930–1970*, p. 393; '**Y Pethau Diwethaf**' (The Last Things), tr. author, *Bloodaxe Book*, pp. 256–7; '**Y Pysgotwr**' (The Fisherman), tr. Joseph P. Clancy, *Twentieth Century Welsh Poems*, pp. 229–30. '**Yr Awr Hon**' (Now), tr. author, *Modern Poetry in Translation*, pp. 153–4; '**Y Rhyfel Mawr**' (The Great War), tr. Joseph P. Clancy, *Twentieth Century Welsh Poems*, p. 225.

ANGHARAD TOMOS (1958–)

Prose (Novel)
Si Hei Lwli, tr. Elin ap Hywel (Llandysul: Gwasg Gomer, 2004).

GERWYN WILIAMS (1963–)

Individual Translations *Po.*
'**Adduned**' (Pledge), tr. Richard Poole and author, *Oxygen*, p. 143; tr. Richard Poole and author, *Bloodaxe Book*, pp. 392–3; '**Cynnydd**' (Forward March), tr. Richard Poole and author, *Bloodaxe Book*, p 391; '**Diwedd y Gân**' (Final Curtain), tr. Richard Poole and author, *Bloodaxe Book*, p. 390; *from* ***Dolenni*** (Bonds) ['**Baghdad**'], tr. author, *Modern Poetry in Translation*, p. 167; ['**Harlem**'], tr. author, *Modern Poetry in Translation*, p. 166; ['**Lockerbie**'], tr. author, *Modern Poetry in Translation*, pp. 164–5; ['**Pentref**' (Village)], tr. author, *Modern Poetry in Translation*, pp. 163–4; ['**Rhywle**' (Somewhere)], tr. author, *Modern Poetry in Translation*, p. 165; ['**Washington**'], tr. author, *Modern Poetry in Translation*, pp. 167–9; tr. Richard Poole and author, *Bloodaxe Book*, pp. 391–2; '**Fy Nghymru i?**' (My Wales?), tr. author, *Comparative Criticism*, p. 95; tr. Richard Poole and author, *Bloodaxe Book*, p. 389; '**Hunllef Awdur**' (Author's Nightmare), tr. author, *Comparative Criticism*, p. 94; '**Molawd Pry Genwair**' (In Praise of an Earthworm), tr. Richard Poole and author, *Oxygen*, p. 141.

GWYNNE WILLIAMS (1937–)

Individual Translations *Po.*
'**Bara'r Burren**' (The Burren Bread), tr. Frank Olding, *Poetry Wales*, 28.1 (1992), 56; '**Curyll y Gwynt**' (The Wind Hawk), tr. R. Gerallt Jones, *Poetry of Wales 1930–1970*, p. 407; '**Derwen**' (Oak Tree), tr. Christopher Meredith, *Bloodaxe Book*, pp. 258–9; '**Eogiaid**' (Salmon), tr. Frank Olding, *Poetry Wales*, 28.1 (1992), 57; '**Gwneud Gwin**' (Winemaking), tr. Christopher Meredith, *Bloodaxe Book*, pp. 259–60; '**Lleu**', tr. R. Gerallt Jones, *Poetry of Wales 1930–1970*, p. 405; '**Llygoden y Gerdd**' (Poem Mouse), tr. Frank Olding, *Poetry Wales*, 28.1 (1992), 58; '**Pysgodyn**' (Fish), tr. Frank Olding, *Poetry Wales*, 28.1 (1992), 58; '**Wedi'r Arholiad**' (After the Exam), tr. Christopher Meredith, *Bloodaxe Book*, p. 260; '**Y Pysgotwr**' (The Fisherman), tr. Joseph P. Clancy, *Trivium*, 8 (1973), 119–20; tr. Joseph P. Clancy, *Twentieth Century Welsh Poems*, pp. 229–30.

LLION WILLIAMS (Twm Miall; 1956–)

Individual Translations *Pr.*
'**Gerald**', tr. Meic Stephens, *A White Afternoon*, pp. 175–7.

EIRUG WYN (1950–2004)

Individual Translations *Pr.*
'**Y Trwsiwr Ffenestri**' (The Window Mender), tr. Meic Stephens, *A White Afternoon*, pp. 86–9.

/